A Prophet's Voice

MESSAGES FROM

THOMAS S. MONSON

A Prophet's Voice

MESSAGES FROM

THOMAS S.
MONSON

DESERET
BOOK

Library of Congress Cataloging-in-Publication Data
Monson, Thomas S., 1927–   author.
  A prophet's voice : messages from President Thomas S. Monson / Thomas S. Monson.
      pages cm
  Includes bibliographical references and index.
  ISBN 978-1-60907-218-6 (hardbound : alk. paper)
1. The Church of Jesus Christ of Latter-day Saints—Doctrines.   2. Christian life—Mormon authors.   3. Mormon Church—Doctrines.   I. Title.
  BX8637.M63 2012
  230'.93—dc23   2012026809

Printed in the United States of America

10 9 8 7 6 5 4 3 2 1

CONTENTS

CONTENTS

SECTION TWO
OTHER CLASSIC MESSAGES

The Blessings of Service

The Worth of Souls

CONTENTS

The Hope of the Rising Generation

The Power of Self-Mastery

The Path of a Disciple

PREFACE

PRESIDENT THOMAS S. MONSON's vivid and memorable speeches have touched Church members around the world for many years. Filled with his warmth, personal experiences, and wonderful illustrations taken from real life, his addresses give us insight into the character and personality of a great leader. This compilation was created to offer a wide selection of those messages for easy reference and ongoing inspiration.

The messages in this book have been divided into two major sections. Section One contains, in chronological order, the major general conference addresses President Monson has delivered since becoming President of the Church. These addresses are presented just as they were given, providing a valuable historic record of the first several years of his presidency.

Section Two contains dozens of additional messages that were selected to give a well-rounded, comprehensive view of Thomas S. Monson's five-decade ministry as a prophet, seer, and revelator. The addresses in this section have been grouped thematically and edited to remove occasion-specific references and eliminate repetition. In some cases, similar messages have been combined, so no attempt has been made to identify the original setting of these talks.

It is our hope that readers will find this book to be a meaningful collection, a handy resource for teaching families and friends, and a source of counsel and guidance for the turbulent times in which we live.

SECTION ONE

THE PRESIDENT'S GENERAL CONFERENCE MESSAGES

1

EXAMPLES OF RIGHTEOUSNESS

General Conference Priesthood Session
April 5, 2008

TONIGHT I AM AWARE THAT YOU, my brethren, both here in the Conference Center and in thousands of other locations, represent the largest gathering of the priesthood ever to assemble. We are a part of the greatest brotherhood in all the world. How fortunate and blessed we are to be holders of the priesthood of God.

We have been instructed and uplifted as we have listened to inspired messages. I pray that I might have an interest in your faith and prayers as I share with you those thoughts and feelings that have been in my mind lately as I have prepared to address you.

As bearers of the priesthood, we have been placed on earth in troubled times. We live in a complex world with currents of conflict everywhere to be found. Political machinations ruin the stability of nations, despots grasp for power, and segments of society seem forever downtrodden, deprived of opportunity, and left with a feeling of failure.

We who have been ordained to the priesthood of God can make a difference. When we qualify for the help of the Lord, we can build boys, we can mend men, we can accomplish miracles in His holy service. Our opportunities are without limit.

Ours is the task to be fitting examples. We are strengthened by the truth that the greatest force in this world today is the power of God as it works through man. If we are on the Lord's errand, we are entitled to the Lord's help. Never forget that truth. That divine help, of course, is predicated upon our worthiness. Each must ask: Are my hands clean? Is my heart pure? Am I a worthy servant of the Lord?

We are surrounded by so much that is designed to divert our attention from those things which are virtuous and good and to tempt us with that which would cause us to be unworthy to exercise the priesthood we bear. I speak not just to the young men of the Aaronic Priesthood but to those of all ages. Temptations come in various forms throughout our lives.

Brethren, are we qualified at all times to perform the sacred duties associated with the priesthood we bear? Young men—you who are priests—are you clean in body and spirit as you sit at the sacrament table on Sunday and bless the emblems of the sacrament? Young men who are teachers, are you worthy to prepare the sacrament? Deacons, as you pass the sacrament to the members of the Church, do you do so knowing that you are spiritually qualified to do so? Does each of you fully understand the importance of *all* the sacred duties you perform?

My young friends, be strong. The philosophies of men surround us. The face of sin today often wears the mask of tolerance. Do not be deceived; behind that facade is heartache, unhappiness, and pain. You know what is right and what is wrong, and no disguise, however appealing, can change that. The character of transgression remains the same. If your so-called friends urge you to do anything you know to be wrong, *you* be the one to make a stand for right, even if you stand alone. Have the moral courage to be a light for others to follow. There is no friendship more valuable than your own clear conscience, your own moral cleanliness—and what a glorious feeling it is to know that you stand in your appointed place clean and with the confidence that you are worthy to do so.

Brethren of the Melchizedek Priesthood, do you strive diligently each day to live as you should? Are you kind and loving to your wife and your children? Are you honest in your dealings with those around you—at all times and in all circumstances?

If any of you has slipped along the way, there are those who will help you to become clean and worthy once again. Your bishop or branch president is anxious and willing to help, and will, with understanding and compassion, do all within his power to assist you in the repentance process, that you may once again stand in righteousness before the Lord.

Many of you will remember President N. Eldon Tanner, who served as a counselor to four Presidents of the Church. He provided an undeviating example of righteousness throughout a career in industry, during service in the government in Canada, and consistently in his private life. He gave us this inspired counsel:

"Nothing will bring greater joy and success than to live according to the teachings of the gospel. Be an example; be an influence for good. . . .

"Every one of us has been foreordained for some work as [God's] chosen servant on whom he has seen fit to confer the priesthood and power to act in his name. Always remember that people are looking to you for leadership and you are influencing the lives of individuals either for good or for bad, which influence will be felt for generations to come."[1]

My brethren, I reiterate that, as holders of the priesthood of God, it is our duty to live our lives in such a way that we may be examples of righteousness for others to follow. As I have pondered how we might best provide such examples, I have thought of an experience I had some years ago while attending a stake conference. During the general session, I observed a young boy sitting with his family on the front row of the stake center. I was seated on the stand. As the meeting progressed, I began to notice that if I crossed one leg over the other, the young boy would do the same thing. If I reversed the motion and crossed the other leg, he would follow suit. I would put my hands in my lap, and he would do the same. I rested my chin in my hand, and he also did so. Whatever I did, he would imitate my actions. This continued until the time approached for me to address the congregation. I decided to put him to the test. I looked squarely at him, certain I had his attention, and then I wiggled my ears. He made a vain attempt to do the same, but I had him! He just couldn't quite get his ears to wiggle. He turned to his father, who was sitting next to him, and whispered something to him. He pointed to his ears and then to me. As his father looked in my direction, obviously to see my ears wiggle, I sat solemnly with my arms folded, not moving a muscle. The father glanced back skeptically at his son, who looked slightly defeated. He finally gave me a sheepish grin and shrugged his shoulders.

I have thought about that experience over the years as I've contemplated how, particularly when we're young, we tend to imitate the example of our parents, our leaders, our peers. The prophet Brigham Young said: "We should never permit ourselves to do anything that we are not willing to see our children do. We should set them an example that we wish them to imitate."[2]

To you who are fathers of boys or who are leaders of boys, I say, strive to be the kind of example the boys need. The father, of course, should be the prime example, and the boy who is blessed with a worthy father is fortunate indeed. Even an exemplary family, however, with diligent and faithful father and mother, can use all the supportive help they can get from good men who genuinely care. There is also the boy who has no father, or whose father is not currently providing the type of example needed. For that boy, the Lord has provided a network of helpers within the Church—bishops, advisers, teachers, Scoutmasters, home teachers. When the Lord's program is in effect and properly working, no young man in the Church should be without the influence of good men in his life.

The effectiveness of an inspired bishop, adviser, or teacher has very little to do with the outward trappings of power or an abundance of this world's goods. The leaders who have the most influence are usually those who set hearts afire with devotion to the truth, who make obedience to duty seem the essence of manhood, who transform some ordinary routine occurrence so that it becomes a vista where we see the person we aspire to be.

Not to be overlooked—and in fact, our primary example— is our Savior, Jesus Christ. His birth was foretold by prophets; angels heralded the announcement of His earthly ministry. He "grew, and waxed strong in spirit, filled with wisdom: and the grace of God was upon him."[3]

Baptized of John in the river known as Jordan, He commenced His official ministry to men. To the sophistry of Satan, Jesus turned his back. To the duty designated by His Father, He turned His face, pledged His heart, and gave His life. And what a sinless, selfless, noble, and divine life it was. Jesus labored. Jesus loved. Jesus served. Jesus testified. What finer example could we strive to emulate? Let us begin now, this very night, to do so. Cast off forever will be the old self and with it defeat, despair, doubt, and disbelief. To a newness of life we come—a life of faith, hope, courage, and joy. No task looms too large; no responsibility weighs too heavily; no duty is a burden. All things become possible.

Many years ago I spoke of one who took his example from the Savior, one who stood firm and true, strong and worthy through the storms of life. He courageously magnified his priesthood callings. He provides an example to each of us. His name was Thomas Michael Wilson, the son of Willie and Julia Wilson of Lafayette, Alabama.

When he was but a teenager and he and his family were not yet members of the Church, he was stricken with cancer, followed by painful radiation therapy, and then blessed remission. This illness caused his family to realize that not only is life precious but it can also be short. They began to look to religion to help them through this time of tribulation. Subsequently, they were introduced to the Church, and eventually all but the father were baptized. After accepting the gospel, young Brother Wilson yearned for the opportunity of being a missionary, even though he was older than most young men when they began their missionary service. At the age of 23, a mission call came for him to serve in the Utah Salt Lake City Mission.

Elder Wilson's missionary companions described his faith as unquestioning, undeviating, and unyielding. He was an example to all. However, after 11 months of missionary service, illness returned. Bone cancer now required the amputation of his arm and shoulder. Yet he persisted in his missionary labors.

Elder Wilson's courage and consuming desire to remain on his mission so touched his nonmember father that he investigated the teachings of the Church and also became a member.

I learned that an investigator whom Elder Wilson had taught was baptized but then wanted to be confirmed by Elder Wilson, whom she respected so much. She, with a few others, journeyed to Elder Wilson's bedside in the hospital. There, with his remaining hand resting upon her head, Elder Wilson confirmed her a member of The Church of Jesus Christ of Latter-day Saints.

Elder Wilson continued month after month his precious but painful service as a missionary. Blessings were given; prayers were offered. Because of his example of dedication, his fellow missionaries lived closer to God.

Elder Wilson's physical condition deteriorated. The end

drew near, and he was to return home. He asked to serve but one additional month, and his request was granted. He put his faith in God, and He whom Thomas Michael Wilson silently trusted opened the windows of heaven and abundantly blessed him. His parents, Willie and Julia Wilson, and his brother Tony came to Salt Lake City to help their son and brother home to Alabama. However, there was yet a prayed-for, a yearned-for blessing to be bestowed. The family invited me to come with them to the Jordan River Temple, where those sacred ordinances which bind families for eternity, as well as for time, were performed.

I said good-bye to the Wilson family. I can see Elder Wilson yet as he thanked me for being with him and his loved ones. He said, "It doesn't matter what happens to us in this life as long as we have the gospel of Jesus Christ and live it. It doesn't matter whether I teach the gospel on this or the other side of the veil, so long as I can teach it." What courage. What confidence. What love. The Wilson family made the long trek home to Lafayette, where Elder Thomas Michael Wilson slipped from here to eternity. He was buried there with his missionary tag in place.

My brethren, as we now leave this general priesthood meeting, let us all determine to prepare for our time of opportunity and to honor the priesthood we bear through the service we render, the lives we bless, and the souls we are privileged to help save. You "are a chosen generation, a royal priesthood, an holy nation,"[4] and you can make a difference. To these truths I testify in the name of Jesus Christ, our Savior, amen.

NOTES

1. "For They Loved the Praise of Men More Than the Praise of God," *Ensign*, November 1975, 74.
2. *Deseret News*, June 21, 1871, 235; see also *Journal of Discourses*, 26 vols. (1854–1886), 14:192.
3. Luke 2:40.
4. 1 Peter 2:9.

2

LOOKING BACK AND MOVING FORWARD

General Conference Sunday Morning Session
April 6, 2008

I THINK THIS HAS BEEN A remarkable session. The messages have been inspiring; the music has been beautiful, the testimonies sincere. I think anyone who has attended this session will never forget it—for the Spirit we've felt.

My beloved brothers and sisters, over 44 years ago, in October of 1963, I stood at the pulpit in the Tabernacle, having just been sustained as a member of the Quorum of the Twelve Apostles. On that occasion I mentioned a small sign I had seen on another pulpit. The words on the sign were these: "Who stands at this pulpit, let him be humble." I assure you that I was humbled by my call to the Twelve at that time. However, as I stand at *this* pulpit today, I address you from the absolute depths of humility. I feel very keenly my dependence upon the Lord. I humbly seek the guidance of the Spirit as I share with you the feelings of my heart.

Just two months ago we said farewell to our dear friend and leader Gordon B. Hinckley, the fifteenth President of The Church of Jesus Christ of Latter-day Saints, an outstanding ambassador of truth to the entire world and beloved of all. We miss him. More than 53,000 men, women, and children journeyed to the beautiful Hall of the Prophets in this very building to pay their last respects to this giant of the Lord, who now belongs to the ages.

With the passing of President Hinckley, the First Presidency was dissolved. President Eyring and I, who served as counselors to President Hinckley, returned to our places in the Quorum of the Twelve Apostles, and that quorum became the presiding authority of the Church.

On Saturday, February 2, 2008, funeral services for President Hinckley were held in this magnificent Conference Center—a building which will ever stand as a monument to his foresight and vision. During the funeral, beautiful and loving tributes were paid to this man of God.

The following day, all 14 ordained Apostles living on the earth assembled in an upper room of the Salt Lake Temple. We met in a spirit of fasting and prayer. During that solemn and sacred gathering, the Presidency of the Church was reorganized in accordance with well-established precedent, after the pattern which the Lord Himself put in place.

Members of the Church around the world convened yesterday in a solemn assembly. You raised your hands in a sustaining vote to approve the action which was taken in that meeting in the temple to which I have just referred. As your hands were raised toward heaven, my heart was touched. I felt your love and support, as well as your commitment to the Lord.

I know without question, my brothers and sisters, that God lives. I testify to you that this is His work. I testify as well that our Savior Jesus Christ is at the head of this Church which bears His name. I know that the sweetest experience in all this life is to feel His promptings as He directs us in the furtherance of His work. I felt those promptings as a young bishop, guided to the homes where there was spiritual—or perhaps temporal—want. I felt them again as a mission president in Toronto,

11

Canada, working with wonderful missionaries who were a living witness and testimony to the world that this work is divine and that we are led by a prophet. I have felt them throughout my service in the Twelve and in the First Presidency and now as President of the Church. I testify that each one of us can feel the Lord's inspiration as we live worthily and strive to serve Him.

I am keenly aware of the 15 men who preceded me as President of the Church. Many of them I have known personally. I have had the blessing and privilege of serving as a counselor to three of them. I am grateful for the abiding legacy left by each one of those 15 men. I have the sure knowledge, as I am confident they had, that God directs His prophet. My earnest prayer is that I might continue to be a worthy instrument in His hands to carry on this great work and to fulfill the tremendous responsibilities which come with the office of President.

I thank the Lord for wonderful counselors. President Henry B. Eyring and President Dieter F. Uchtdorf are men of great ability and sound understanding. They are counselors in the true sense of the word. I value their judgment. I believe they have been prepared by the Lord for the positions they now occupy.

I love the members of the Quorum of the Twelve Apostles and treasure my association with them. They too are dedicated to the work of the Lord and are spending their lives in His service. I look forward to serving with Elder [D. Todd] Christofferson, who has now been called to that quorum and who has received your sustaining vote. He, too, has been prepared for the position to which he has been called. It has also been a joy to serve with the members of the Quorums of the Seventy and with the Presiding Bishopric. New members of the Seventy have been called and were sustained yesterday, and I look forward to associating with them in the work of the Master.

A sweet spirit of unity exists among the General Authorities. The Lord has declared, "If ye are not one ye are not mine."[1] We will continue to be united in one purpose—namely, the furtherance of the work of the Lord.

I feel to express thanks to my Heavenly Father for His countless blessings to me. I can say, as did Nephi of old, that I was born of goodly parents, whose own parents and grandparents were gathered out of the lands of Sweden and Scotland and England by dedicated missionaries. As those missionaries bore humble testimonies, they touched the hearts and the spirits of my forebears. After joining the Church, these noble men, women, and children made their way to the valley of the Great Salt Lake. Many were the trials and heartaches they encountered along the way.

In the spring of 1848, my great-great-grandparents Charles Stewart Miller and Mary McGowan Miller, who had joined the Church in their native Scotland, left their home in Rutherglen, Scotland, and journeyed to St. Louis, Missouri, with a group of Saints, arriving there in 1849. One of their 11 children, Margaret, would become my great-grandmother.

While the family was in St. Louis working to earn enough money to complete their journey to the Salt Lake Valley, a plague of cholera swept through the area, leaving death and heartache in its wake. The Miller family was hard hit. In the space of two weeks, four of the family members succumbed. The first, on June 22, 1849, was 18-year-old William. Five days later Mary McGowan Miller, my great-great-grandmother, and the mother of the family, died. Two days afterward, 15-year-old Archibald passed away, and five days after his death, my great-great-grandfather, Charles Stewart Miller, father of the family, succumbed. The children who survived were left orphans, including my great-grandmother Margaret, who was 13 years old at the time.

Because of so many deaths in the area, there were no

caskets available, at any price, in which to bury the deceased family members. The older surviving boys dismantled the family's oxen pens in order to make caskets for the family members who had passed away.

Little is recorded of the heartache and struggles of the nine remaining Miller children as they continued to work and save for that journey their parents and brothers would never make. We know that they left St. Louis in the spring of 1850 with four oxen and one wagon, arriving finally in the Salt Lake Valley that same year.

Others of my ancestors faced similar hardships. Through it all, however, their testimonies remained steadfast and firm. From all of them I received a legacy of total dedication to the gospel of Jesus Christ. Because of these faithful souls, I stand before you today.

I thank my Father in Heaven for my sweet companion, Frances. This October she and I will celebrate 60 wonderful years of marriage. Although my Church service began at an early age, she has never once complained when I've left home to attend meetings or to fulfill an assignment. For many years my assignments as a member of the Twelve took me away from Salt Lake City often—sometimes for five weeks at a time—leaving her alone to care for our small children and our home. Beginning when I was called as a bishop at the age of 22, we have seldom had the luxury of sitting together during a Church service. I could not have asked for a more loyal, loving, and understanding companion.

I express gratitude to my Heavenly Father for our three children and their companions, for eight wonderful grandchildren, and for four beautiful great-grandchildren.

It's difficult for me to find the words to convey to you, my brothers and sisters, my heartfelt appreciation for the lives you live, for the good you do, for the testimonies you bear. You serve one another willingly. You are dedicated to the gospel of Jesus Christ.

During more than 44 years as a General Authority, I have had the opportunity to travel the world over. One of my greatest joys has been to meet with you, the members, wherever you may be—to feel of your spirit and your love. I look forward to many more such opportunities.

Throughout the journey along the pathway of life, there are casualties. Some depart from the road markers which point toward life eternal, only to discover the detour chosen ultimately leads to a dead end. Indifference, carelessness, selfishness, and sin all take their costly toll in human lives.

Change for the better can come to all. Over the years we have issued appeals to the less active, the offended, the critical, the transgressor—to come back. "Come back and feast at the table of the Lord, and taste again the sweet and satisfying fruits of fellowship with the Saints."[2]

In the private sanctuary of one's own conscience lies that spirit, that determination to cast off the old person and to measure up to the stature of true potential. In this spirit, we again issue that heartfelt invitation: Come back. We reach out to you in the pure love of Christ and express our desire to assist you and to welcome you into full fellowship. To those who are wounded in spirit or who are struggling and fearful, we say, Let us lift you and cheer you and calm your fears. Take literally the Lord's invitation, "Come unto me, all ye that labour and are heavy laden, and I will give you rest. Take my yoke upon you, and learn of me; for I am meek and lowly in heart: and ye shall find rest unto your souls. For my yoke is easy, and my burden is light."[3]

It was said of the Savior that he "went about doing good . . . for God was with him."[4] May we follow that perfect example. In this sometimes precarious journey through mortality, may we also follow that advice from the Apostle Paul which will help to keep us safe and on course: "Whatsoever things are true, whatsoever things are honest, whatsoever things are just, whatsoever things are pure, whatsoever things are lovely, whatsoever things are of good report; if there be any virtue, and if there be any praise, think on these things."[5]

I would encourage members of the Church wherever they may be to show kindness and respect for all people everywhere. The world in which we live is filled with diversity. We can and should demonstrate respect toward those whose beliefs differ from ours.

May we also demonstrate kindness and love within our own families. Our homes are to be more than sanctuaries; they should also be places where God's Spirit can dwell, where the storm stops at the door, where love reigns and peace dwells.

The world can at times be a frightening place in which to live. The moral fabric of society seems to be unraveling at an alarming speed. None—whether young or old or in-between—is exempt from exposure to those things which have the potential to drag us down and destroy us. Our youth, our precious youth, in particular, face temptations we can scarcely comprehend. The adversary and his hosts seem to be working nonstop to cause our downfall.

We are waging a war with sin, my brothers and sisters, but we need not despair. It is a war we can and will win. Our Father in Heaven has given us the tools we need in order to do so. He is at the helm. We have nothing to fear. He is the God of light. He is the God of hope. I testify that He loves us—each one.

Mortality is a period of testing, a time to prove ourselves worthy to return to the presence of our Heavenly Father. In order to be tested, we must sometimes face challenges and difficulties. At times there appears to be no light at the tunnel's end—no dawn to break the night's darkness. We feel surrounded by the pain of broken hearts, the disappointment of shattered dreams, and the despair of vanished hopes. We join in uttering the biblical plea "Is there no balm in Gilead"?[6] We are inclined to view our own personal misfortunes through the distorted prism of pessimism. We feel abandoned, heartbroken, alone. If you find yourself in such a situation, I plead with you to turn to our Heavenly Father in faith. He will lift you and guide you. He will not always take your afflictions from you, but He will comfort and lead you with love through whatever storm you face.

With all my heart and the fervency of my soul, I lift my voice in testimony today as a special witness and declare that God does live. Jesus is His Son, the Only Begotten of the Father in the flesh. He is our Redeemer; He is our Mediator with the Father. He loves us with a love we cannot fully comprehend, and because He loves us, He gave His life for us. My gratitude to Him is beyond expression.

I invoke His blessings upon you, my beloved brothers and sisters, in your homes, in your work, in your service to one another and to the Lord Himself. Together we shall move forward doing His work.

I pledge my life, my strength—all that I have to offer—in serving Him and in directing the affairs of His Church in accordance with His will and by His inspiration, and I do so in His holy name—even the Lord Jesus Christ—amen.

NOTES

1. Doctrine and Covenants 38:27.
2. First Presidency statement, in *Ensign*, March 1986, 88.
3. Matthew 11:28–30.
4. Acts 10:38.
5. Philippians 4:8.
6. Jeremiah 8:22.

3

Abundantly Blessed

General Conference Sunday Afternoon Session
April 6, 2008

I'VE BEEN ATTENDING CONFERENCE for a long time, but I think I've never felt quite as richly blessed as during this session. We've had rapid-fire messages from a lot of speakers, but every one touched on a very important subject. We've had a smorgasbord today of faith, of love, and of counsel. Let's incorporate these things in our lives.

Brother Ballard, several years ago my dear wife went to the hospital. She left a note behind for the children: "Dear children, do not let Daddy touch the microwave"—followed by a comma, "or the stove, or the dishwasher, or the dryer." I'm embarrassed to add any more to that list.

I think it was President Uchtdorf who said, "You told the audience today about your heritage on your mother's side. What about your father's side?" So I conclude with just a word or two about my father's side.

My father's father came from Sweden, and his wife from England. They met on the ship coming over. He waited for her to grow up, and then he proposed marriage. They were married in the Salt Lake Temple, and he wrote in his journal,

"Today is the happiest day of my life. My sweetheart and I were married for time and eternity in the holy temple."

Three days later, on April 23, 1898, he wrote, "Took the train at the Rio Grande Western Depot enroute eventually to Scandinavia, where I have been called as a missionary." Off he went to Sweden, leaving his bride of three days.

His journal, written in pencil, came to me from an uncle who somehow chose me to receive his father's journal. The most frequent entry in the journal was, "My feet are wet." But the most beautiful entry said: "Today we went to the Jansson home. We met Sister Jansson. She had a lovely dinner for us. She is a good cook." And then he said, "The children all sang or played a harmonica or did a little dance, and then she paid her tithing. Five krona for the Lord and one for my companion, Elder Ipson, and one for me." And then there were listed the names of the children.

When I read that in the journal, there was my wife's father's name, Franz Jansson, as one who was in that household, one who probably sang a song, one who became the father of only one daughter, the girl I married.

The first day I saw Frances, I knew I'd found the right one. The Lord brought us together later, and I asked her to go out with me. I went to her home to call on her. She introduced me, and her father said, "'Monson'—that's a Swedish name, isn't it?"

I said, "Yes."

He said, "Good."

Then he went into another room and brought out a picture of two missionaries with their top hats and their copies of the Book of Mormon.

"Are you related to this Monson," he said, "Elias Monson?"

I said, "Yes, he's my grandfather's brother. He too was a missionary in Sweden."

Her father wept. He wept easily. He said, "He and his

companion were among the missionaries who visited our home frequently when my family embraced the gospel." He kissed me on the cheek. And then her mother cried, and she kissed me on the other cheek. And then I looked around for Frances. She said, "I'll go get my coat."

My sweet Frances had a terrible fall a few years ago. She went to the hospital. She lay in a coma for about 18 days. I sat by her side. She never moved a muscle. The children cried, the grandchildren cried, and I wept. Not a movement.

And then one day, she opened her eyes. I set a speed record in getting to her side. I gave her a kiss and a hug, and I said, "You're back. I love you." And she said, "I love you, too, Tom, but we're in serious trouble." I thought, *What do you know about trouble, Frances?* She said, "I forgot to mail in our fourth-quarter income tax payment."

I said to her, "Frances, if you had said that before you extended a kiss to me and told me you love me, I might have left you here."

Brethren, let's treat our wives with dignity and with respect. They're our eternal companions. Sisters, honor your husbands. They need to hear a good word. They need a friendly smile. They need a warm expression of true love.

Leaving my own family now, may I say that this has been a wonderful conference. We have been edified by wise and inspired messages. Our testimonies have been strengthened. I believe we are all the more determined to live the principles of the gospel of Jesus Christ.

Not only have we been blessed by the fine talks which have been given; we have also been uplifted by the beautiful music which has been provided. We are abundantly blessed in the Church by those who share their musical talents with us. Every choir and chorus has performed so well during the past two days.

I express my great love for all those who have participated

and to all of you who have listened. I have felt your prayers in my behalf and have been sustained and blessed during the two months since our beloved President Hinckley left us. Once again, I appreciate your sustaining vote.

I cannot adequately express my gratitude for the Restoration of the gospel in these latter days and for what that has meant in my life. Each of us has been influenced and shaped as we have followed the Savior and have adhered to the principles of His gospel.

To you who are parents, I say, show love to your children. You know you love them, but make certain they know it as well. They are so precious. Let them know. Call upon our Heavenly Father for help as you care for their needs each day and as you deal with the challenges which inevitably come with parenthood. You need more than your own wisdom in rearing them.

We commend our wonderful young people who stand up to the iniquity in the world and who live the commandments to the best of their ability.

To you who are able to attend the temple, I would counsel you to go often. Doing so will help to strengthen marriages and families.

Let us be kind to one another, be aware of each other's needs, and try to help in that regard.

My dear brothers and sisters, I love you, and I pray for you. Please pray for me. And together we will reap the blessings our Heavenly Father has in store for each one of us. This is my prayer, my plea as I add my testimony. This work is true. In the name of Jesus Christ, amen.

4

TO LEARN, TO DO, TO BE

General Conference Priesthood Session
October 4, 2008

Y OU'VE SEEN A WITNESS TONIGHT of the strength of the two counselors in this First Presidency. I stand before you and declare this First Presidency is united as one under the direction of the Lord Jesus Christ.

I want to especially thank this missionary choir. I had an experience I think they may be interested in, and you may find it interesting also. Many years ago I had a desperate call from the head of the missionary training center. He said, "President Monson, I have a missionary who is going home. Nothing can prevent him from quitting."

I replied, "Well, that's not singular. It's happened before. What's his problem?"

He said, "He's been called to a Spanish-speaking mission, and he's absolutely certain he cannot learn Spanish."

I said, "I have a suggestion for you. Tomorrow morning have him attend a class learning Japanese. And then have him report to you at 12:00 noon."

The next morning he phoned at 10:00! He said, "The

22

young man is here with me now, and he wants me to know he's absolutely certain he can learn Spanish."

Where there's a will, there's a way.

Now, as I speak to you tonight, truly you are a royal priesthood, assembled in many places but in unity. In all likelihood this is the largest assemblage of priesthood holders ever to come together. Your devotion to your sacred callings is inspiring. Your desire to learn your duty is evident. The purity of your souls brings heaven closer to you and your families.

Many areas of the world have experienced difficult economic times. Businesses have failed, jobs have been lost, and investments have been jeopardized. We must make certain that those for whom we share responsibility do not go hungry or unclothed or unsheltered. When the priesthood of this church works together as one in meeting these vexing conditions, near miracles take place.

We urge all Latter-day Saints to be prudent in their planning, to be conservative in their living, and to avoid excessive or unnecessary debt. The financial affairs of the Church are being managed in this manner, for we are aware that your tithing and other contributions have not come without sacrifice and are sacred funds.

Let us make of our homes sanctuaries of righteousness, places of prayer, and abodes of love, that we might merit the blessings that can come only from our Heavenly Father. We need His guidance in our daily lives.

In this vast throng are priesthood power and the capacity to reach out and share the glorious gospel with others. We have the hands to lift others from complacency and inactivity. We have the hearts to serve faithfully in our priesthood callings and thereby inspire others to walk on higher ground and to avoid the swamps of sin which threaten to engulf so many. The worth of souls is indeed great in the sight of God. Ours is the precious privilege, armed with this knowledge, to make a difference in the lives of others. The words found in Ezekiel could well pertain to all of us who follow the Savior in this sacred work:

"A new heart . . . will I give you, and a new spirit will I put within you. . . .

"And I will put my spirit within you, and cause you to walk in my statutes, and ye shall keep my judgments, and do them.

"And ye shall dwell in the land that I gave to your fathers; and ye shall be my people, and I will be your God."[1]

How might we merit this promise? What will qualify us to receive this blessing? Is there a guide to follow?

May I suggest three imperatives for our consideration. They apply to the deacon as well as the high priest. They are within our reach. A kind Heavenly Father will help us in our quest.

First, learn what we should learn.

Second, do what we should do.

Third, be what we should be.

Let us discuss these objectives, that we might be profitable servants in the sight of our Lord.

First, *learn what we should learn.* The Apostle Paul placed an urgency on our efforts to learn. He said to the Philippians: "One thing I do, forgetting those things which are behind, and reaching forth unto those things which are before, I press toward the mark for the prize of the high calling of God in Christ Jesus."[2] And to the Hebrews he urged: "Lay aside . . . sin[;] . . . let us run with patience the race . . . set before us, looking [for an example] unto Jesus the author and finisher of our faith."[3]

President Stephen L Richards, who served for many years in the Quorum of the Twelve Apostles and then in the First Presidency, spoke often to holders of the priesthood and emphasized his philosophy pertaining to it. He declared: "The Priesthood is usually simply defined as 'the power of God delegated to man.' This definition, I think, is accurate."

He continued: "But for practical purposes I like to define the Priesthood in terms of service and I frequently call it 'the perfect plan of service.' I do so because it seems to me that it is only through the utilization of the divine power conferred on men that they may ever hope to realize the full import and vitality of this endowment. It is an instrument of service . . . and the man who fails to use it is apt to lose it, for we are plainly told by revelation that he who neglects it 'shall not be counted worthy to stand.'"[4]

President Harold B. Lee, eleventh President of the Church and one of the great teachers in the Church, put his counsel in easy-to-understand terms. Said he: "When one becomes a holder of the priesthood, he becomes an agent of the Lord. He should think of his calling as though he were on the Lord's errand."[5]

Now, some of you may be shy by nature or consider yourselves inadequate to respond affirmatively to a calling. Remember that this work is not yours and mine alone. It is the Lord's work, and when we are on the Lord's errand, we are entitled to the Lord's help. Remember that the Lord will shape the back to bear the burden placed upon it.

While the formal classroom may be intimidating at times, some of the most effective teaching takes place other than in the chapel or the classroom. Well do I remember that some years ago, members holding the Aaronic Priesthood would eagerly look forward to an annual outing commemorating the restoration of the Aaronic Priesthood. By the busload the young men of our stake journeyed 90 miles (145 km) north to the Clarkston Cemetery, where we viewed the grave of Martin Harris, one of the Three Witnesses of the Book of Mormon. While surrounding the beautiful granite shaft which marks his grave, a high councilor would present background concerning the life of Martin Harris, read from the Book of Mormon his testimony, and then bear his own witness to the truth. The young men listened with rapt attention, touched the granite marker, and pondered the words they had heard and the feelings they had felt.

At a park in Logan, lunch was enjoyed. The group of young men would then lie down on the lawn at the Logan Temple and gaze upward at its lofty spires. Often beautiful white clouds would hurry past the spires, moved along by a gentle breeze. The purpose of temples was taught. Covenants and promises became much more than words. The desire to be worthy to enter those temple doors entered those youthful hearts. Heaven was very close. Learning what we should learn was assured.

Number two, *do what we should do.* In a revelation on priesthood, given through Joseph Smith the Prophet, recorded as the 107th section of the Doctrine and Covenants, "learning" moves to "doing" as we read, "Wherefore, now let every man learn his duty, and to act in the office in which he is appointed, in all diligence."[6]

Each priesthood holder attending this session tonight has a calling to serve, to put forth his best efforts in the work assigned to him. No assignment is menial in the work of the Lord, for each has eternal consequences. President John Taylor warned us: "If you do not magnify your calling, God will hold you responsible for those whom you might have saved had you done your duty."[7] And who of us can afford to be responsible for the delay of eternal life of a human soul? If great joy is the reward of saving one soul, then how terrible must be the remorse of those whose timid efforts have allowed a child of God to go unwarned or unaided so that he has to wait until a dependable servant of God comes along.

The old adage is ever true: "Do your duty, that is best; leave unto the Lord the rest."

Most service given by priesthood holders is accomplished quietly, without fanfare. A friendly smile, a warm handclasp, a sincere testimony of truth can literally lift lives, change human nature, and save precious souls.

An example of such service was the missionary experience of Juliusz and Dorothy Fussek, who were called to fill a two-year mission in Poland. Brother Fussek was born in Poland. He spoke the language. He loved the people. Sister Fussek was English and knew little of Poland and its people.

Trusting in the Lord, they embarked on their assignment. The living conditions were primitive, the work lonely, their task immense. A mission had not at that time been established in Poland. The assignment given the Fusseks was to prepare the way, that a mission could be established so that other missionaries could be called to serve, people could be taught, converts could be baptized, branches could be established, and chapels could be erected.

Did Elder and Sister Fussek despair because of the enormity of their assignment? Not for a moment. They knew their calling was from God. They prayed for His divine help, and they devoted themselves wholeheartedly to their work. They remained in Poland not two years but five years. All of the foregoing objectives were realized.

Elders Russell M. Nelson, Hans B. Ringger, and I, accompanied by Elder Fussek, met with Minister Adam Wopatka of the Polish government, and we heard him say, "Your church is welcome here. You may build your buildings; you may send your missionaries. You are welcome in Poland. This man," pointing to Juliusz Fussek, "has served your church well. You can be grateful for his example and his work."

Like the Fusseks, let us do what we should do in the work of the Lord. Then we can, with Juliusz and Dorothy Fussek, echo the Psalm: "My help cometh from the Lord, which made heaven and earth . . . : he that keepeth thee will not slumber. Behold, he that keepeth Israel shall neither slumber nor sleep."[8]

Third, *be what we should be.* Paul counseled his beloved friend and associate Timothy, "Be thou an example of the believers, in word, in conversation, in charity, in spirit, in faith, in purity."[9]

I would urge all of us to pray concerning our assignments

27

and to seek divine help, that we might be successful in accomplishing that which we are called to do. Someone has said that "the recognition of power higher than man himself does not in any sense debase him."[10] He must seek, believe in, pray, and hope that he will find. No such sincere, prayerful effort will go unanswered: that is the very constitution of the philosophy of faith. Divine favor will attend those who humbly seek it.

From the Book of Mormon comes counsel that says it all. The Lord speaks: "Therefore, what manner of men ought ye to be? Verily I say unto you, even as I am."[11]

And what manner of man was He? What example did He set in His service? From John chapter 10 we learn:

"I am the good shepherd: the good shepherd giveth his life for the sheep.

"But he that is an hireling, and not the shepherd, whose own the sheep are not, seeth the wolf coming, and leaveth the sheep, and fleeth: and the wolf catcheth them, and scattereth the sheep.

"The hireling fleeth, because he is an hireling, and careth not for the sheep."

Said the Lord: "I am the good shepherd, and know my sheep, and am known of mine.

"As the Father knoweth me, even so know I the Father: and I lay down my life for the sheep."[12]

Brethren, may we *learn what we should learn, do what we should do, and be what we should be.* By so doing, the blessings of heaven will attend. We will know that we are not alone. He who notes the sparrow's fall will, in His own way, acknowledge us.

Several years ago I received a letter from a longtime friend. He bore his testimony in that letter. I would like to share part of it with you tonight, since it illustrates the strength of the priesthood in one who learned what he should learn, who did what he should do, and who always tried to be what he should be.

I shall read excerpts of that letter from my friend Theron W. Borup, who passed away three years ago at the age of 90:

"At the age of eight, when I was baptized and received the Holy Ghost, I was much impressed about being good and able to have the Holy Ghost to be a help throughout my life. I was told that the Holy Ghost associated only in good company and that when evil entered our lives, he would leave. Not knowing when I would need his promptings and guidance, I tried to so live that I would not lose this gift. On one occasion it saved my life.

"During World War II, I was an engineer-gunner in a B-24 bomber fighting in the South Pacific. One day there was an announcement that the longest bombing flight ever made would be attempted to knock out an oil refinery. The promptings of the Spirit told me I would be assigned on this flight but that I would not lose my life. At the time I was the president of the LDS group.

"The combat was ferocious as we flew over Borneo. Our plane was hit by attacking planes and soon burst into flames, and the pilot told us to prepare to jump. I went out last. We were shot at by enemy pilots as we floated down. I had trouble inflating my life raft. Bobbing up and down in the water, I began to drown and passed out. I came to momentarily and cried, 'God save me!' . . . Again I tried inflating the life raft and this time was successful. With just enough air in it to keep me afloat, I rolled over on top of it, too exhausted to move.

"For three days we floated about in enemy territory with ships all about us and planes overhead. Why they couldn't see a yellow group of rafts on blue water is a mystery," he wrote. "A storm came up, and waves thirty feet high almost tore our rafts apart. Three days went by with no food or water. The others asked me if I prayed. I answered that I did pray and that we would indeed be rescued. That evening we saw our submarine that was there to rescue us, but it passed by. The next morning it did [the same. We knew] this was the last day [it would] be in the area. Then came the promptings of the Holy Ghost. 'You have the Priesthood. Command the sub to pick you up.' Silently I prayed, 'In the name of Jesus Christ, and by the power of the priesthood, turn about and pick us up.' In a few minutes, they were alongside of us. When on deck, the captain . . . said, 'I don't know how we ever found you, for we were not even looking for you.' *I* knew."[13]

I leave with you my testimony that this work in which we are engaged is true. The Lord is at the helm. That we may ever follow Him is my sincere prayer, and I ask it in the name of Jesus Christ, amen.

NOTES

1. Ezekiel 36:26–28.
2. Philippians 3:13–14.
3. Hebrews 12:1–2.
4. Stephen L Richards, in Conference Report, April 1937, 46.
5. Harold B. Lee, *Stand Ye in Holy Places* (1974), 255.
6. Doctrine and Covenants 107:99.
7. John Taylor, "Discourse," *Deseret News*, August 7, 1878, 2.
8. Psalm 121:2–4.
9. 1 Timothy 4:12.
10. Stephen L Richards, in Conference Report, October 1937, 34.
11. 3 Nephi 27:27.
12. John 10:11–15.
13. Personal correspondence; emphasis added.

5

<center>~~~~~</center>

Finding Joy in the Journey

General Conference Sunday Morning Session
October 5, 2008

MY DEAR BROTHERS AND SISTERS, I am humbled as I stand before you this morning. I ask for your faith and prayers in my behalf as I speak about those things which have been on my mind and which I have felt impressed to share with you.

I begin by mentioning one of the most inevitable aspects of our lives here upon the earth, and that is *change*. At one time or another we've all heard some form of the familiar adage: "Nothing is as constant as change."

Throughout our lives, we must deal with change. Some changes are welcome, some are not. There are changes in our lives which are sudden, such as the unexpected passing of a loved one, an unforeseen illness, the loss of a possession we treasure. But most of the changes take place subtly and slowly.

This conference marks 45 years since I was called to the Quorum of the Twelve Apostles. As the junior member of the Twelve then, I looked up to 14 exceptional men, all of whom were senior to me in the Twelve and the First Presidency. One by one, each of these men has returned home. When President

Hinckley passed away eight months ago, I realized that I had become the senior Apostle. The changes over a period of 45 years that were incremental now seem monumental.

This coming week Sister Monson and I will celebrate our 60th wedding anniversary. As I look back to our beginnings, I realize just how much our lives have changed since then. Our beloved parents, who stood beside us as we commenced our journey together, have passed on. Our three children, who filled our lives so completely for many years, are grown and have families of their own. Most of our grandchildren are grown, and we now have four great-grandchildren.

Day by day, minute by minute, second by second we went from where we were to where we are now. The lives of all of us, of course, go through similar alterations and changes. The difference between the changes in my life and the changes in yours is only in the details. Time never stands still; it must steadily march on, and with the marching come the changes.

This is our one and only chance at mortal life—here and now. The longer we live, the greater is our realization that it is brief. Opportunities come, and then they are gone. I believe that among the greatest lessons we are to learn in this short sojourn upon the earth are lessons that help us distinguish between what is important and what is not. I plead with you not to let those most important things pass you by as you plan for that illusive and nonexistent future when you will have time to do all that you want to do. Instead, find joy in the journey—now.

I am what my wife Frances calls a "show-a-holic." I thoroughly enjoy many musicals, and one of my favorites was written by the American composer Meredith Willson and is entitled *The Music Man.* Professor Harold Hill, one of the principal characters in the show, voices a caution that I share with you. Says he: "You pile up enough tomorrows, and you'll find you've collected a lot of empty yesterdays."[1]

My brothers and sisters, there is no tomorrow to remember if we don't do something today.

I've shared with you previously an example of this philosophy. I believe it bears repeating. Many years ago, Arthur Gordon wrote in a national magazine:

"When I was around thirteen and my brother ten, Father had promised to take us to the circus. But at lunchtime there was a phone call; some urgent business required his attention downtown. We braced ourselves for disappointment. Then we heard him say [into the phone], 'No, I won't be down. It'll have to wait.'

"When he came back to the table, Mother smiled. 'The circus keeps coming back, you know,' [she said].

"'I know,' said Father, 'but childhood doesn't.'"[2]

If you have children who are grown and gone, in all likelihood you have occasionally felt pangs of loss and the recognition that you didn't appreciate that time of life as much as you should have. Of course, there is no going back, but only forward. Rather than dwelling on the past, we should make the most of today, of the here and now, doing all we can to provide pleasant memories for the future.

If you are still in the process of raising children, be aware that the tiny fingerprints that show up on almost every newly cleaned surface, the toys scattered about the house, the piles and piles of laundry to be tackled, will disappear all too soon and that you will—to your surprise—miss them profoundly.

Stresses in our lives come regardless of our circumstances. We must deal with them the best we can. But we should not let them get in the way of what is most important—and what is most important almost always involves the people around us. Often we assume that they *must* know how much we love them. But we should never assume; we should let them know. Wrote William Shakespeare, "They do not love that do not show their love."[3] We will never regret the kind words spoken or the affection shown. Rather, our regrets will come if such things are omitted from our relationships with those who mean the most to us.

Send that note to the friend you've been neglecting; give your child a hug; give your *parents* a hug; say "I love you" more; always express your thanks. Never let a problem to be solved become more important than a person to be loved. Friends move away, children grow up, loved ones pass on. It's so easy to take others for granted, until that day when they're gone from our lives and we are left with feelings of "what if" and "if only." Said author Harriet Beecher Stowe, "The bitterest tears shed over graves are for words left unsaid and deeds left undone."[4]

In the 1960s, during the Vietnam War, Church member Jay Hess, an airman, was shot down over North Vietnam. For two years his family had no idea whether he was dead or alive. His captors in Hanoi eventually allowed him to write home, but limited his message to less than 25 words. What would you and I say to our families if we were in the same situation—not having seen them for over two years and not knowing if we would ever see them again? Wanting to provide something his family could recognize as having come from him and also wanting to give them valuable counsel, Brother Hess wrote: "These things are important: temple marriage, mission, college. Press on, set goals, write history, take pictures twice a year."[5]

Let us relish life as we live it, find joy in the journey, and share our love with friends and family. One day each of us will run out of tomorrows.

In the book of John in the New Testament, chapter 13, verse 34, the Savior admonishes us: "As I have loved you, . . . love one another."

Some of you may be familiar with Thornton Wilder's classic drama *Our Town*. If you are, you will remember the town of Grover's Corners, where the story takes place. In the play Emily Webb dies in childbirth, and we read of the lonely grief of her young husband, George, left with their four-year-old son. Emily does not wish to rest in peace; she wants to experience again the joys of her life. She is granted the privilege of returning to earth and reliving her 12th birthday. At first it is exciting to be young again, but the excitement wears off quickly. The day holds no joy, now that Emily knows what is in store for the future. It is unbearably painful to realize how unaware she had been of the meaning and wonder of life while she was alive. Before returning to her resting place, Emily laments, "Do . . . human beings ever realize life while they live it—every, every minute?"

Our realization of what is most important in life goes hand in hand with gratitude for our blessings.

Said one well-known author, "Both abundance and lack [of abundance] exist simultaneously in our lives, as parallel realities. It is always our conscious choice which secret garden we will tend . . . when we choose not to focus on what is missing from our lives but are grateful for the abundance that's present—love, health, family, friends, work, the joys of nature, and personal pursuits that bring us [happiness]—the wasteland of illusion falls away and we experience heaven on earth."[6]

In the Doctrine and Covenants, section 88, verse 33, we are told: "For what doth it profit a man if a gift is bestowed upon him, and he receive not the gift? Behold, he rejoices not in that which is given unto him, neither rejoices in him who is the giver of the gift."

The ancient Roman philosopher Horace admonished, "Whatever hour God has blessed you with, take it with grateful hand, nor postpone your joys from year to year, so that in whatever place you have been, you may say that you have lived happily."

Many years ago I was touched by the story of Borghild Dahl. She was born in Minnesota in 1890 of Norwegian parents and

35

from her early years suffered severely impaired vision. She had a tremendous desire to participate in everyday life despite her handicap and, through sheer determination, succeeded in nearly everything she undertook. Against the advice of educators, who felt her handicap was too great, she attended college, receiving her bachelor of arts degree from the University of Minnesota. She later studied at Columbia University and the University of Oslo. She eventually became the principal of eight schools in western Minnesota and North Dakota.

She wrote the following in one of the 17 books she authored: "I had only one eye, and it was so covered with dense scars that I had to do all my seeing through one small opening in the left of the eye. I could see a book only by holding it up close to my face and by straining my one eye as hard as I could to the left."[7]

Miraculously, in 1943—when she was over 50 years old—a revolutionary procedure was developed which finally restored to her much of the sight she had been without for so long. A new and exciting world opened up before her. She took great pleasure in the small things most of us take for granted, such as watching a bird in flight, noticing the light reflected in the bubbles of her dishwater, or observing the phases of the moon each night. She closed one of her books with these words: "Dear . . . Father in heaven, I thank Thee. I thank Thee."[8]

Borghild Dahl, both before and after her sight was restored, was filled with gratitude for her blessings.

In 1982, two years before she died, at the age of 92 her last book was published. Its title: *Happy All My Life*. Her attitude of thankfulness enabled her to appreciate her blessings and to live a full and rich life despite her challenges.

In 1 Thessalonians in the New Testament, chapter 5, verse 18, we are told by the Apostle Paul, "In every thing give thanks: for this is the will of God."

Recall with me the account of the 10 lepers: "And as [Jesus] entered into a certain village, there met him ten men that were lepers, which stood afar off:

"And they lifted up their voices, and said, Jesus, Master, have mercy on us.

"And when he saw them, he said unto them, Go shew yourselves unto the priests. And it came to pass, that, as they went, they were cleansed.

"And one of them, when he saw that he was healed, turned back, and with a loud voice glorified God,

"And fell down on his face at his feet, giving him thanks: and he was a Samaritan.

"And Jesus answering said, Were there not ten cleansed? but where are the nine?

"There are not found that returned to give glory to God, save this stranger."[9]

Said the Lord in a revelation given through the Prophet Joseph Smith, "In nothing doth man offend God, or against none is his wrath kindled, save those who confess not his hand in all things."[10] May we be found among those who give our thanks to our Heavenly Father. If ingratitude be numbered among the serious sins, then gratitude takes its place among the noblest of virtues.

Despite the changes which come into our lives, and with gratitude in our hearts, may we fill our days—as much as we can—with those things which matter most. May we cherish those we hold dear and express our love to them in word and in deed.

In closing, I pray that all of us will reflect gratitude for our Lord and Savior, Jesus Christ. His glorious gospel provides answers to life's greatest questions: Where did we come from? Why are we here? Where does my spirit go when I die?

He taught us how to pray. He taught us how to serve. He taught us how to live. His life is a legacy of love. The sick He healed; the downtrodden He lifted; the sinner He saved.

The time came when He stood alone. Some Apostles doubted; one betrayed Him. The Roman soldiers pierced His side. The angry mob took His life. There yet rings from Golgotha's hill His compassionate words, "Father, forgive them; for they know not what they do."[11]

Earlier, perhaps perceiving the culmination of His earthly mission, He spoke the lament, "Foxes have holes, and the birds of the air have nests; but the Son of man hath not where to lay his head."[12] "No room in the inn"[13] was not a singular expression of rejection—just the first. Yet He invites you and me to receive Him. "Behold, I stand at the door, and knock: if any man hear my voice, and open the door, I will come in to him, and will sup with him, and he with me."[14]

Who was this Man of sorrows, acquainted with grief? Who is the King of glory, this Lord of hosts? He is our Master. He is our Savior. He is the Son of God. He is the Author of our salvation. He beckons, "Follow me."[15] He instructs, "Go, and do thou likewise."[16] He pleads, "Keep my commandments."[17]

Let us follow Him. Let us emulate His example. Let us obey His word. By so doing, we give to Him the divine gift of gratitude.

Brothers and sisters, my sincere prayer is that we may adapt to the changes in our lives, that we may realize what is most important, that we may express our gratitude always and thus find joy in the journey. In the name of Jesus Christ, amen.

NOTES

1. Meredith Willson and Franklin Lacey, *The Music Man* (1957).
2. Arthur Gordon, "A Touch of Wonder" (1974), 77–78.
3. William Shakespeare, *Two Gentlemen of Verona*, act 1, scene 2, line 31.
4. Harriet Beecher Stowe, in Gorton Carruth and Eugene Erlich, comp., *The Harper Book of American Quotations* (1988), 173.
5. Personal correspondence.
6. Sarah Ban Breathnach, in John Cook, comp., *The Book of Positive Quotations*, 2nd ed. (2007), 342.
7. Borghild Dahl, *I Wanted to See* (1944), 1.
8. Dahl, *I Wanted to See*, 210.

9. Luke 17:12–18.
10. Doctrine and Covenants 59:21.
11. Luke 23:34.
12. Matthew 8:20.
13. See Luke 2:7.
14. Revelation 3:20.
15. Mark 2:14.
16. Luke 10:37.
17. Doctrine and Covenants 11:6.

6

BE YOUR BEST SELF

General Conference Priesthood Session
April 4, 2009

MY BELOVED BRETHREN of the priesthood assembled here in this full Conference Center and in locations throughout the world, I am humbled by the responsibility which is mine to address you. I endorse those messages which have already been presented and express to each of you my sincere love, as well as my appreciation for your faith and your devotion.

Brethren, our responsibilities as bearers of the priesthood are most significant, as outlined in the Doctrine and Covenants: "The power and authority of the higher, or Melchizedek Priesthood, is to hold the keys of all the spiritual blessings of the church."[1] And further, "The power and authority of the lesser, or Aaronic Priesthood, is to hold the keys of the ministering of angels, and to administer in outward ordinances, the letter of the gospel, the baptism of repentance for the remission of sins, agreeable to the covenants and commandments."[2]

In 1958 Elder Harold B. Lee, who later served as the eleventh President of the Church, described the priesthood as "the Lord's . . . troops against the forces of evil."[3]

40

President John Taylor stated that "the power manifested by the priesthood is simply the power of God."[4]

These stirring declarations from prophets of God help us to understand that each man and each boy who holds the priesthood of God must be worthy of that great privilege and responsibility. Each must strive to learn his duty and then to do it to the best of his ability. As we do so, we provide the means by which our Heavenly Father and His Son, Jesus Christ, can accomplish Their work here upon the earth. It is we who are Their representatives here.

In the world today we face difficulties and challenges, some of which can seem truly daunting. However, with God on our side we cannot fail. As we bear His holy priesthood worthily, we will be victorious.

To you who hold the Aaronic Priesthood, may I say that I sincerely hope each of you is aware of the significance of your priesthood ordination. Yours is a vital role in the life of every member of your ward as you participate in the administration and passing of the sacrament each Sunday.

I had the privilege to serve as the secretary of my deacons quorum. I recall the many assignments we members of that quorum had the opportunity to fill. Passing the sacred sacrament, collecting the monthly fast offerings, and looking after one another come readily to mind. The most frightening one, however, happened at the leadership session of our ward conference. The member of our stake presidency who was presiding called on a number of the ward officers to speak. They did so. Then, without the slightest warning, he stood and said, "We will now call on one of our younger ward officers, Thomas S. Monson, secretary of the deacons quorum, to give us an accounting of his service and to bear his testimony." I don't remember a single thing I said, but I have never forgotten the experience or the lesson that it taught me. It was the Apostle Peter who said, "Be ready always to give an answer to every man that asketh you a reason of the hope that is in you."[5]

In an earlier generation, the Lord gave this promise to holders of the priesthood: "I will go before your face. I will be on your right hand and on your left, and my Spirit shall be in your hearts, and mine angels round about you, to bear you up."[6]

This is not a time for fear, brethren, but rather a time for faith—a time for each of us who holds the priesthood to be his best self.

Although our journey through mortality will at times place us in harm's way, may I offer to you tonight three suggestions which, when observed and followed, will lead us to safety. They are:

1. Study diligently.
2. Pray fervently.
3. Live righteously.

These suggestions are not new; they have been taught and repeated again and again. If we incorporate them into our lives, however, we will have the strength to withstand the adversary. Should we ignore them, we will be opening the door for Satan to have influence and power over us.

First, **study diligently**. Every holder of the priesthood should participate in daily scripture study. Crash courses are not nearly so effective as the day-to-day reading and application of the scriptures in our lives. Become acquainted with the lessons the scriptures teach. Learn the background and setting of the Master's parables and the prophets' admonitions. Study them as though they were speaking to you, for such is the truth.

The prophet Lehi and his son Nephi were each shown in vision the importance of obtaining and then holding fast to the word of God. Concerning the rod of iron shown him, Nephi said this to his disbelieving brothers, Laman and Lemuel:

"And I said unto them that [the rod] was the word of God; and whoso would hearken unto the word of God, and would hold fast unto it, they would never perish; neither could the temptations and the fiery darts of the adversary overpower them unto blindness, to lead them away to destruction.

"Wherefore, I, Nephi, did exhort them to give heed unto the word of the Lord; yea, I did exhort them with all the energies of my soul, and with all the faculty which I possessed, that they would give heed to the word of God and remember to keep his commandments always in all things."[7]

I promise you, whether you hold the Aaronic or the Melchizedek Priesthood, that if you will study the scriptures diligently, your power to avoid temptation and to receive direction of the Holy Ghost in all you do will be increased.

Second, **pray fervently**. With God, all things are possible. Men of the Aaronic Priesthood, men of the Melchizedek Priesthood, remember the prayer of the Prophet Joseph, offered in that grove called sacred. Look around you and see the result of that answered prayer.

Adam prayed; Jesus prayed. We know the outcome of their prayers. He who notes the fall of a sparrow surely hears the pleadings of our hearts. Remember the promise: "If any of you lack wisdom, let him ask of God, that giveth to all men liberally, and upbraideth not; and it shall be given him."[8]

To those within the sound of my voice who are struggling with challenges and difficulties large and small, prayer is the provider of spiritual strength; it is the passport to peace. Prayer is the means by which we approach our Father in Heaven, who loves us. Speak to Him in prayer and then listen for the answer. Miracles are wrought through prayer.

Sister Daisy Ogando lives in New York City, home to more than eight million people. Some years ago Sister Ogando met with the missionaries and was taught the gospel. Gradually, she and the missionaries lost contact. Time passed. Then, in 2007, the principles of the gospel she had been taught by the missionaries stirred within her heart.

One day while getting into a taxi, Daisy saw the missionaries at a distance, but she was unable to make contact with them before they disappeared from view. She prayed fervently to our Heavenly Father and promised Him that if He would somehow direct the missionaries to her once again, she would open her door to them. She returned home that day with faith in her heart that God would hear and answer her prayer.

In the meantime, two young missionaries who had been sincerely praying and working to find people to teach were one day examining the tracting records of missionaries who had previously served in their area. As they did so, they came across the name of Daisy Ogando. When they approached her apartment the very afternoon that Sister Ogando offered that simple but fervent prayer, she opened the door and said those words that are music to every missionary who has ever heard them: "Elders, come in. I've been waiting for you!"

Two fervent prayers were answered, contact was reestablished, missionary lessons were taught, and arrangements were made for Daisy and her son Eddy to be baptized.

Remember to pray fervently.

My final suggestion, my brethren: **live righteously**. Isaiah, that great prophet of the Old Testament, gave this stirring charge to holders of the priesthood: "Touch no unclean thing; . . . be ye clean, that bear the vessels of the Lord."[9] That's about as straight as it could be.

Holders of the priesthood may not necessarily be eloquent in their speech. They may not hold advanced degrees in difficult fields of study. They may very well be men of humble means. But God is no respecter of persons, and He will sustain His servants in righteousness as they avoid the evils of our day and live lives of virtue and purity. May I illustrate.

Some 900 miles (1,400 km) north of Salt Lake City is the

beautiful city of Calgary, Alberta, Canada, home of the famous Calgary Stampede, one of Canada's largest annual events and the world's largest outdoor rodeo. The ten-day event features a rodeo competition, exhibits, agricultural competitions, and chuck wagon races. The Stampede Parade, which occurs on opening day, is one of the festival's oldest and largest traditions. The parade follows a nearly three-mile (five-km) route in downtown Calgary, with attendance reaching 350,000 spectators, many dressed in western attire.

Several years ago, a marching band from a large high school in Utah had auditioned for and had received one of the coveted entries to march in the Calgary Stampede Parade. Months of fund-raising, early-morning practices up and down the streets, and other preparations were undertaken in order for the band to travel to Calgary and participate in the parade, where one band would be selected to receive the first-place honor.

Finally the day for departure arrived, with the eager students and their leaders boarding the buses and heading north for the long journey to Calgary.

While en route, the caravan stopped in Cardston, Alberta, Canada, where the group remained for an overnight stay. The local Relief Society sisters there prepared sack lunches for the band members to enjoy before departing again. Brad, one of the band members, who was a priest in the Aaronic Priesthood, was not hungry and decided to keep his lunch until later.

Brad liked to sit in the back of the bus. As he took his usual seat there in preparation for the remainder of the journey to Calgary, he tossed his sack lunch on the shelf behind the last row of seats. There the lunch sat by the rear window as the July afternoon sun shone through. Unfortunately, the sack lunch contained an egg salad sandwich. For those of you who don't understand the significance of this, may I just say that egg salad must be refrigerated. If it is not, and if it is subjected to high heat such as that which would be produced by the sun beating through a bus window on a sunny day, it becomes a rather efficient incubator for various strains of bacteria that can result in what may commonly be referred to as food poisoning.

Sometime before arriving in Calgary, Brad grew hungry. Remembering the sack lunch, he gulped down the egg salad sandwich. As the buses arrived in Calgary and drove around the city, the members of the band grew excited—all except for Brad. Unfortunately, all that grew within him were severe stomach pains and other discomforts associated with food poisoning. You know what they are.

Upon arriving at their destination, the band members exited the bus. Brad, however, did not. Although he knew his fellow band members were counting on him to play his drum in the parade the following morning, Brad was doubled over in pain and was too sick to leave the bus. Providentially for him, two of his friends, Steve and Mike, who had recently graduated from high school and who had also recently been ordained to the office of elder in the Melchizedek Priesthood, found that Brad was missing and decided to look for him.

Finding Brad in the rear of the bus and learning what the problem was, Steve and Mike felt helpless. Finally it occurred to them that they were elders and held the power of the Melchizedek Priesthood to bless the sick. Despite their total lack of experience in giving a priesthood blessing, these two new elders had faith in the power they held. They laid their hands on Brad's head and, invoking the authority of the Melchizedek Priesthood, in the name of Jesus Christ uttered the simple words to bless Brad to be made well.

From that moment, Brad's symptoms were completely gone. The next morning he took his place with the rest of the band members and proudly marched down the streets of Calgary. The band received first-place honors and the coveted blue ribbon. Far more important, however, was that two young, inexperienced but worthy priesthood holders had answered the call to represent the Lord in serving their fellowman. When it was necessary for them to exercise their priesthood in behalf of one who was desperately in need of their help, they were able to respond because they lived their lives righteously.

Brethren, are we prepared for our journey through life? The pathway can at times be difficult. Chart your course, be cautious, and determine to **study diligently, pray fervently,** and **live righteously**.

Let us never despair, for the work in which we are engaged is the work of the Lord. It has been said, "The Lord shapes the back to bear the burden placed upon it."

The strength which we earnestly seek in order to meet the challenges of a complex and changing world can be ours when, with fortitude and resolute courage, we stand and declare with Joshua, "As for me and my house, we will serve the Lord."[10] To this divine truth I testify and do so in the name of Jesus Christ, our Lord, amen.

NOTES

1. Doctrine and Covenants 107:18.
2. Doctrine and Covenants 107:20.
3. Harold B. Lee, "Priesthood" (address to seminary and institute personnel, Brigham Young University, July 17, 1958), 1.
4. John Taylor, *The Gospel Kingdom,* sel. G. Homer Durham (1941), 129.
5. 1 Peter 3:15.
6. Doctrine and Covenants 84:88.
7. 1 Nephi 15:24–25.
8. James 1:5.
9. Isaiah 52:11.
10. Joshua 24:15.

7

Be of Good Cheer

General Conference Sunday Morning Session
April 5, 2009

M y dear brothers and sisters, I express my love to you. I am humbled by the responsibility to address you, and yet I am grateful for the opportunity to do so.

Since last we met together in a general conference six months ago, there have been continuing signs that circumstances in the world aren't necessarily as we would wish. The global economy, which six months ago appeared to be sagging, seems to have taken a nosedive, and for many weeks now the financial outlook has been somewhat grim. In addition, the moral footings of society continue to slip, while those who attempt to safeguard those footings are often ridiculed and, at times, picketed and persecuted. Wars, natural disasters, and personal misfortunes continue to occur.

It would be easy to become discouraged and cynical about the future—or even fearful of what might come—if we allowed ourselves to dwell only on that which is wrong in the world and in our lives. Today, however, I'd like us to turn our thoughts and our attitudes away from the troubles around us and to focus instead on our blessings as members of the Church. The

Apostle Paul declared, "God hath not given us the spirit of fear; but of power, and of love, and of a sound mind."[1]

None of us makes it through this life without problems and challenges—and sometimes tragedies and misfortunes. After all, in large part we are here to learn and grow from such events in our lives. We know that there are times when we will suffer, when we will grieve, and when we will be saddened. However, we are told, "Adam fell that men might be; and men are, that they might have joy."[2]

How might we have joy in our lives, despite all that we may face? Again from the scriptures: "Wherefore, be of good cheer, and do not fear, for I the Lord am with you, and will stand by you."[3]

The history of the Church in this, the dispensation of the fulness of times, is replete with the experiences of those who have struggled and yet who have remained steadfast and of good cheer as they have made the gospel of Jesus Christ the center of their lives. This attitude is what will pull us through whatever comes our way. It will not remove our troubles from us but rather will enable us to face our challenges, to meet them head-on, and to emerge victorious.

Too numerous to mention are the examples of all the individuals who have faced difficult circumstances and yet who have persevered and prevailed because their faith in the gospel and in the Savior has given them the strength they have needed. This morning, however, I'd like to share with you three such examples.

First, from my own family, I mention a touching experience that has always been an inspiration to me.

My maternal great-grandparents Gibson and Cecelia Sharp Condie lived in Clackmannan, Scotland. Their families were engaged in coal mining. They were at peace with the world, surrounded by relatives and friends, and were housed in fairly comfortable quarters in a land they loved. Then they listened to the message of the missionaries from The Church of Jesus Christ of Latter-day Saints and, to the depths of their very souls, were converted. They heard the call to gather to Zion and knew they must answer that call.

Sometime around 1848, they sold their possessions and prepared for the hazardous voyage across the mighty Atlantic Ocean. With five small children, they boarded a sailing vessel, all their worldly possessions in one tiny trunk. They traveled 3,000 miles (4,800 km) across the waters—eight long, weary weeks on a treacherous sea, watching and waiting, with poor food, poor water, and no help beyond the length and breadth of that small ship.

In the midst of this soul-trying situation, one of their young sons became ill. There were no doctors, no stores at which they might purchase medicine to ease his suffering. They watched, they prayed, they waited, and they wept as day by day his condition deteriorated. When his eyes were at last closed in death, their hearts were torn asunder. To add to their grief, the laws of the sea must be obeyed. Wrapped in a canvas weighed down with iron, the little body was consigned to a watery grave. As they sailed away, only those parents knew the crushing blow dealt to wounded hearts.[4] However, with a faith born of their deep conviction of the truth and their love of the Lord, Gibson and Cecelia held on. They were comforted by the words of the Lord: "In the world ye shall have tribulation: but be of good cheer; I have overcome the world."[5]

How grateful I am for ancestors who had the faith to leave hearth and home and to journey to Zion, who made sacrifices I can scarcely imagine. I thank my Heavenly Father for the examples of faith, of courage, and of determination Gibson and Cecelia Sharp Condie provide for me and for all their posterity.

I introduce next a gentle, faith-filled man who epitomized the peace and joy which the gospel of Jesus Christ can bring into one's life.

Late one evening on a Pacific isle, a small boat slipped silently to its berth at the crude pier. Two Polynesian women helped Meli Mulipola from the boat and guided him to the well-worn pathway leading to the village road. The women marveled at the bright stars, which twinkled in the midnight sky. The moonlight guided them along their way. However, Meli Mulipola could not appreciate these delights of nature—the moon, the stars, the sky—for he was blind.

Brother Mulipola's vision had been normal until a fateful day when, while working on a pineapple plantation, light turned suddenly to darkness and day became perpetual night. He was depressed and despondent until he learned the good news of the gospel of Jesus Christ. His life was brought into compliance with the teachings of the Church, and he once again felt hope and joy.

Brother Mulipola and his loved ones had made a long voyage, having learned that one who held the priesthood of God was visiting among the islands of the Pacific. He sought a blessing, and it was my privilege, along with another who held the Melchizedek Priesthood, to provide that blessing to him. As we finished, I noted that tears were streaming from his sightless eyes, coursing down his brown cheeks and tumbling finally upon his native dress. He dropped to his knees and prayed: "O God, thou knowest I am blind. Thy servants have blessed me that my sight might return. Whether in Thy wisdom I see light or whether I see darkness all the days of my life, I will be eternally grateful for the truth of Thy gospel, which I now see and which provides the light of my life."

He rose to his feet and, smiling, thanked us for providing the blessing. He then disappeared into the still of the night. Silently he came; silently he departed. But his presence I shall never forget. I reflected upon the message of the Master: "I am the light of the world: he that followeth me shall not walk in darkness, but shall have the light of life."[6]

My brothers and sisters, each of us has that light in his or her life. We are not left to walk alone, no matter how dark our pathway.

I love the words penned by M. Louise Haskins:

And I said to the man who stood at the gate of the year:
"Give me a light, that I may tread safely into the
unknown!"
And he replied:
"Go out into the darkness and put your hand into the
Hand of God.
That shall be to you better than [a] light and safer than a
known way."[7]

The setting for my final example of one who persevered and ultimately prevailed, despite overwhelmingly difficult circumstances, begins in East Prussia following World War II.

In about March 1946, less than a year after the end of the war, Ezra Taft Benson, then a member of the Quorum of the Twelve, accompanied by Frederick W. Babbel, was assigned a special postwar tour of Europe for the express purpose of meeting with the Saints, assessing their needs, and providing assistance to them. Elder Benson and Brother Babbel later recounted, from a testimony they heard, the experience of a Church member who found herself in an area no longer controlled by the government under which she had resided.

She and her husband had lived an idyllic life in East Prussia. Then had come the second great world war within their lifetimes. Her beloved young husband was killed during the final days of the frightful battles in their homeland, leaving her alone to care for their four children.

The occupying forces determined that the Germans in East Prussia must go to Western Germany to seek a new home. The woman was German, and so it was necessary for her to go. The journey was over a thousand miles (1,600 km), and she had no way to accomplish it but on foot. She was allowed to take only such bare necessities as she could load into her small wooden-wheeled wagon. Besides her children and these meager possessions, she took with her a strong faith in God and in the gospel as revealed to the latter-day prophet Joseph Smith.

She and the children began the journey in late summer. Having neither food nor money among her few possessions, she was forced to gather a daily subsistence from the fields and forests along the way. She was constantly faced with dangers from panic-stricken refugees and plundering troops.

As the days turned into weeks and the weeks to months, the temperatures dropped below freezing. Each day, she stumbled over the frozen ground, her smallest child—a baby—in her arms. Her three other children struggled along behind her, with the oldest—seven years old—pulling the tiny wooden wagon containing their belongings. Ragged and torn burlap was wrapped around their feet, providing the only protection for them, since their shoes had long since disintegrated. Their thin, tattered jackets covered their thin, tattered clothing, providing their only protection against the cold.

Soon the snows came, and the days and nights became a nightmare. In the evenings she and the children would try to find some kind of shelter—a barn or a shed—and would huddle together for warmth, with a few thin blankets from the wagon on top of them.

She constantly struggled to force from her mind overwhelming fears that they would perish before reaching their destination.

And then one morning the unthinkable happened. As she awakened, she felt a chill in her heart. The tiny form of her three-year-old daughter was cold and still, and she realized that death had claimed the child. Though overwhelmed with grief, she knew that she must take the other children and travel on. First, however, she used the only implement she had—a tablespoon—to dig a grave in the frozen ground for her tiny, precious child.

Death, however, was to be her companion again and again on the journey. Her seven-year-old son died, either from starvation or from freezing or both. Again her only shovel was the tablespoon, and again she dug hour after hour to lay his mortal remains gently into the earth. Next, her five-year-old son died, and again she used her tablespoon as a shovel.

Her despair was all consuming. She had only her tiny baby daughter left, and the poor thing was failing. Finally, as she was reaching the end of her journey, the baby died in her arms. The spoon was gone now, so hour after hour she dug a grave in the frozen earth with her bare fingers. Her grief became unbearable. How could she possibly be kneeling in the snow at the graveside of her last child? She had lost her husband and all her children. She had given up her earthly goods, her home, and even her homeland.

In this moment of overwhelming sorrow and complete bewilderment, she felt her heart would literally break. In despair she contemplated how she might end her own life, as so many of her fellow countrymen were doing. How easy it would be to jump off a nearby bridge, she thought, or to throw herself in front of an oncoming train.

And then, as these thoughts assailed her, something within her said, "Get down on your knees and pray." She ignored the prompting until she could resist it no longer. She knelt and prayed more fervently than she had in her entire life:

"Dear Heavenly Father, I do not know how I can go on. I have nothing left—except my faith in Thee. I feel, Father, amidst the desolation of my soul, an overwhelming gratitude for the atoning sacrifice of Thy Son, Jesus Christ. I cannot express adequately my love for Him. I know that because He suffered and died, I shall live again with my family; that because He broke the chains of death, I shall see my children again and will have the joy of raising them. Though I do not at this moment wish to live, I will do so, that we may be reunited as a family and return—together—to Thee."

When she finally reached her destination of Karlsruhe, Germany, she was emaciated. Brother Babbel said that her face was a purple-gray, her eyes red and swollen, her joints protruding. She was literally in the advanced stages of starvation. In a Church meeting shortly thereafter, she bore a glorious testimony, stating that of all the ailing people in her saddened land, she was one of the happiest because she knew that God lived, that Jesus is the Christ, and that He died and was resurrected so that we might live again. She testified that she knew if she continued faithful and true to the end, she would be reunited with those she had lost and would be saved in the celestial kingdom of God.[8]

From the holy scriptures we read, "Behold, the righteous, the saints of the Holy One of Israel, they who have believed in [Him], they who have endured the crosses of the world, . . . they shall inherit the kingdom of God, . . . and their joy shall be full forever."[9]

I testify to you that our promised blessings are beyond measure. Though the storm clouds may gather, though the rains may pour down upon us, our knowledge of the gospel and our love of our Heavenly Father and of our Savior will comfort and sustain us and bring joy to our hearts as we walk uprightly and keep the commandments. There will be nothing in this world that can defeat us.

My beloved brothers and sisters, fear not. Be of good cheer. The future is as bright as your faith.

I declare that God lives and that He hears and answers our prayers. His Son, Jesus Christ, is our Savior and our Redeemer. Heaven's blessings await us. In the name of Jesus Christ, amen.

NOTES

1. 2 Timothy 1:7.
2. 2 Nephi 2:25.
3. Doctrine and Covenants 68:6.
4. Adapted from Thomas A Condie, "History of Gibson and Cecelia Sharp Condie" (1937); unpublished.
5. John 16:33.
6. John 8:12.
7. From "The Gate of the Year," in James Dalton Morrison, ed., *Masterpieces of Religious Verse* (1948), 92.
8. From personal conversations and from Frederick W. Babbel, *On Wings of Faith* (1972), 40–42.
9. 2 Nephi 9:18.

8

SCHOOL THY FEELINGS, O MY BROTHER

General Conference Priesthood Session
October 3, 2009

BRETHREN, WE ARE ASSEMBLED as a mighty body of the priesthood, both here in the Conference Center and in locations throughout the world. We have heard inspired messages this evening, and I express my appreciation to those Brethren who have addressed us. I am honored, yet humbled, by the privilege to speak to you, and I pray that the inspiration of the Lord may attend me.

Recently as I watched the news on television, I realized that many of the lead stories were similar in nature, in that the tragedies reported all basically traced back to one emotion: *anger.* The father of an infant had been arrested for physical abuse of the baby. It was alleged that the baby's crying had so infuriated him that he had broken one of the child's limbs and several ribs. Alarming was the report of growing gang violence, with the number of gang-related killings having risen sharply. Another story that night involved the shooting of a woman by her estranged husband, who was reportedly in a jealous rage after finding her with another man. Then, of course, there was the usual coverage of wars and conflicts throughout the world.

I thought of the words of the Psalmist: "Cease from anger, and forsake wrath."[1]

Many years ago, a young couple called my office and asked if they could come in for counseling. They indicated they had suffered a tragedy in their lives and that their marriage was in serious jeopardy. An appointment was arranged.

The tension between this husband and wife was apparent as they entered my office. Their story unfolded slowly at first as the husband spoke haltingly and the wife cried quietly and participated very little in the conversation.

The young man had returned from serving a mission and was accepted to a prestigious university in the eastern part of the United States. It was there, in a university ward, that he had met his future wife. She was also a student at the university. After a year of dating, they journeyed to Utah and were married in the Salt Lake Temple, returning east shortly afterward to finish their schooling.

By the time they graduated and returned to their home state, they were expecting their first child and the husband had employment in his chosen field. The wife gave birth to a baby boy. Life was good.

When their son was about 18 months old, they decided to take a short vacation to visit family members who lived a few hundred miles away. This was at a time when car seats for children and seat belts for adults were scarcely heard of, let alone used. The three members of the family all rode in the front seat with the toddler in the middle.

Sometime during the trip, the husband and wife had a disagreement. After all these years, I cannot recall what caused it. But I do remember that their argument escalated and became so heated that they were eventually yelling at one another. Understandably, this caused their young son to begin crying, which the husband said only added to his anger. Losing total control of his temper, he picked up a toy the child had dropped on the seat and flung it in the direction of his wife.

He missed hitting his wife. Instead, the toy struck their son, with the result that he was brain damaged and would be handicapped for the rest of his life.

This was one of the most tragic situations I had ever encountered. I counseled and encouraged them. We talked of commitment and responsibility, of acceptance and forgiveness. We spoke of the affection and respect which needed to return to their family. We read words of comfort from the scriptures. We prayed together. Though I have not heard from them since that day so long ago, they were smiling through their tears as they left my office. All these years I've hoped they made the decision to remain together, comforted and blessed by the gospel of Jesus Christ.

I think of them whenever I read the words, "Anger doesn't solve anything. It builds nothing, but it can destroy everything."[2]

We've all felt anger. It can come when things don't turn out the way we want. It might be a reaction to something which is said of us or to us. We may experience it when people don't behave the way we want them to behave. Perhaps it comes when we have to wait for something longer than we expected. We might feel angry when others can't see things from our perspective. There seem to be countless possible reasons for anger.

There are times when we can become upset at imagined hurts or perceived injustices. President Heber J. Grant, seventh President of the Church, told of a time as a young adult when he did some work for a man who then sent him a check for $500 with a letter apologizing for not being able to pay him more. Then President Grant did some work for another man—work which he said was ten times more difficult, involving ten times more labor and a great deal more time. This second man sent him a check for $150. Young Heber felt he had been treated most unfairly. He was at first insulted and then incensed.

He recounted the experience to an older friend, who asked, "Did that man intend to insult you?"

President Grant replied, "No. He told my friends he had rewarded me handsomely."

To this the older friend replied, "A man's a fool who takes an insult that isn't intended."[3]

The Apostle Paul asks, in Ephesians, chapter four, verse 26 of the Joseph Smith Translation: "Can ye be angry, and not sin? let not the sun go down upon your wrath." I ask, is it possible to feel the Spirit of our Heavenly Father when we are angry? I know of no instance where such would be the case.

From 3 Nephi in the Book of Mormon, we read: "There shall be no disputations among you. . . .

"For verily, verily I say unto you, he that hath the spirit of contention is not of me, but is of the devil, who is the father of contention, and he stirreth up the hearts of men to contend with anger, one with another.

"Behold, this is not my doctrine, to stir up the hearts of men with anger, one against another; but this is my doctrine, that such things should be done away."[4]

To be angry is to yield to the influence of Satan. No one can *make* us angry. It is our choice. If we desire to have a proper spirit with us at all times, we must choose to refrain from becoming angry. I testify that such is possible.

Anger, Satan's tool, is destructive in so many ways.

I believe most of us are familiar with the sad account of Thomas B. Marsh and his wife, Elizabeth. Brother Marsh was one of the first modern-day Apostles called after the Church was restored to the earth. He eventually became President of the Quorum of the Twelve Apostles.

While the Saints were in Far West, Missouri, Elizabeth Marsh, Thomas's wife, and her friend Sister Harris decided they would exchange milk in order to make more cheese than they otherwise could. To be certain all was done fairly, they agreed that they should not save what were called the strippings, but that the milk and strippings should all go together. Strippings came at the end of the milking and were richer in cream.

Sister Harris was faithful to the agreement, but Sister Marsh, desiring to make some especially delicious cheese, saved a pint of strippings from each cow and sent Sister Harris the milk without the strippings. This caused the two women to quarrel. When they could not settle their differences, the matter was referred to the home teachers to settle. They found Elizabeth Marsh guilty of failure to keep her agreement. She and her husband were upset with the decision, and the matter was then referred to the bishop for a Church trial. The bishop's court decided that the strippings were wrongfully saved and that Sister Marsh had violated her covenant with Sister Harris.

Thomas Marsh appealed to the high council, and the men comprising this council confirmed the bishop's decision. He then appealed to the First Presidency of the Church. Joseph Smith and his counselors considered the case and upheld the decision of the high council.

Elder Thomas B. Marsh, who sided with his wife through all of this, became angrier with each successive decision—so angry, in fact, that he went before a magistrate and swore that the Mormons were hostile toward the state of Missouri. His affidavit led to—or at least was a factor in—Governor Lilburn Boggs's cruel extermination order, which resulted in over 15,000 Saints being driven from their homes, with all the terrible suffering and consequent death that followed. All of this occurred because of a disagreement over the exchange of milk and cream.[5]

After 19 years of rancor and loss, Thomas B. Marsh made his way to the Salt Lake Valley and asked President Brigham Young for forgiveness. Brother Marsh also wrote to Heber C. Kimball, First Counselor in the First Presidency, of the lesson he had learned. Said Brother Marsh: "The Lord could get along very well without me and He . . . lost nothing by my falling out of the ranks; But O what have I lost?! Riches, greater riches than all this world or many planets like this could afford."[6]

Apropos are the words of the poet John Greenleaf Whittier: "Of all sad words of tongue or pen, the saddest are these: 'It might have been!'"[7]

My brethren, we are all susceptible to those feelings which, if left unchecked, can lead to anger. We experience displeasure or irritation or antagonism, and if we so choose, we lose our temper and become angry with others. Ironically, those others are often members of our own families—the people we really love the most.

Many years ago I read the following Associated Press dispatch which appeared in the newspaper: An elderly man disclosed at the funeral of his brother, with whom he had shared, from early manhood, a small, one-room cabin near Canisteo, New York, that following a quarrel, they had divided the room in half with a chalk line and neither had crossed the line or spoken a word to the other since that day—62 years before. Just think of the consequence of that anger. What a tragedy!

May we make a conscious decision, each time such a decision must be made, to refrain from anger and to leave unsaid the harsh and hurtful things we may be tempted to say.

I love the words of the hymn written by Elder Charles W. Penrose, who served in the Quorum of the Twelve and in the First Presidency during the early years of the 20th century:

> *School thy feelings, O my brother;*
> *Train thy warm, impulsive soul.*
> *Do not its emotions smother,*
> *But let wisdom's voice control.*
> *School thy feelings; there is power*
> *In the cool, collected mind.*

Passion shatters reason's tower,
Makes the clearest vision blind.[8]

Each of us is a holder of the priesthood of God. The oath and covenant of the priesthood pertains to all of us. To those who hold the Melchizedek Priesthood, it is a declaration of our requirement to be faithful and obedient to the laws of God and to magnify the callings which come to us. To those who hold the Aaronic Priesthood, it is a pronouncement concerning future duty and responsibility, that you may prepare yourselves here and now.

This oath and covenant is set forth by the Lord in these words:

"For whoso is faithful unto the obtaining these two priesthoods of which I have spoken, and the magnifying their calling, are sanctified by the Spirit unto the renewing of their bodies.

"They become the sons of Moses and of Aaron and the seed of Abraham, and the church and kingdom, and the elect of God.

"And also all they who receive this priesthood receive me, saith the Lord;

"For he that receiveth my servants receiveth me;

"And he that receiveth me receiveth my Father;

"And he that receiveth my Father receiveth my Father's kingdom; therefore all that my Father hath shall be given unto him."[9]

Brethren, great promises await us if we are true and faithful to the oath and covenant of this precious priesthood which we hold. May we be worthy sons of our Heavenly Father. May we ever be exemplary in our homes and faithful in keeping all of the commandments, that we may harbor no animosity toward any man but rather be peacemakers, ever remembering the Savior's admonition, "By this shall all men know that ye are my disciples, if ye have love one to another."[10] This is my plea tonight at the conclusion of this great priesthood meeting, and it's also my humble and sincere prayer, for I love you, brethren, with all my heart and soul. And I pray our Heavenly Father's blessing to attend each of you in your life, in your home, in your heart, in your soul, in the name of Jesus Christ, amen.

NOTES

1. Psalm 37:8.
2. Lawrence Douglas Wilder, quoted in "Early Hardships Shaped Candidates," *Deseret News,* December 7, 1991, A2.
3. See Heber J. Grant, *Gospel Standards,* comp. G. Homer Durham (1969), 288–89.
4. 3 Nephi 11:28–30.
5. See George A. Smith, "Discourse," *Deseret News,* April 16, 1856, 44.
6. Thomas B. Marsh to Heber C. Kimball, May 5, 1857, Brigham Young Collection, Church History Library.
7. "Maud Muller," *The Complete Poetical Works of John Greenleaf Whittier* (1876), 206.
8. "School Thy Feelings," *Hymns,* no. 336.
9. Doctrine and Covenants 84:33–38.
10. John 13:35.

9

WHAT HAVE I DONE FOR SOMEONE TODAY?

General Conference Sunday Morning Session
October 4, 2009

MY BELOVED BROTHERS AND SISTERS, I greet you on this beautiful morning with love in my heart for the gospel of Jesus Christ and for each of you. I am grateful for the privilege to stand before you, and I pray that I might effectively communicate to you that which I have felt prompted to say.

A few years ago I read an article written by Jack McConnell, MD. He grew up in the hills of southwest Virginia in the United States as one of seven children of a Methodist minister and a stay-at-home mother. Their circumstances were very humble. He recounted that during his childhood, every day as the family sat around the dinner table, his father would ask each one in turn, "And what did you do for someone today?"[1] The children were determined to do a good turn every day so they could report to their father that they had helped someone. Dr. McConnell calls this exercise his father's most valuable legacy, for *that* expectation and *those* words inspired him and his siblings to help others throughout their lives. As they grew and matured, their motivation for providing service changed to an inner desire to help others.

Besides Dr. McConnell's distinguished medical career—where he directed the development of the tuberculosis tine test, participated in the early development of the polio vaccine, supervised the development of Tylenol, and was instrumental in developing the magnetic resonance imaging procedure, or MRI—he created an organization he calls Volunteers in Medicine, which gives retired medical personnel a chance to volunteer at free clinics serving the working uninsured. Dr. McConnell said his leisure time since he retired has "evaporated into 60-hour weeks of unpaid work, but [his] energy level has increased and there is a satisfaction in [his] life that wasn't there before." He made this statement: "In one of those paradoxes of life, I have benefited more from Volunteers in Medicine than my patients have."[2] There are now over 70 such clinics across the United States.

Of course, we can't all be Dr. McConnells, establishing medical clinics to help the poor; however, the needs of others are ever present, and each of us can do something to help someone.

The Apostle Paul admonished, "By love serve one another."[3] Recall with me the familiar words of King Benjamin in the Book of Mormon: "When ye are in the service of your fellow beings ye are only in the service of your God."[4]

The Savior taught His disciples, "For whosoever will save his life shall lose it: but whosoever will lose his life for my sake, the same shall save it."[5]

I believe the Savior is telling us that unless we lose ourselves in service to others, there is little purpose to our own lives. Those who live only for themselves eventually shrivel up and figuratively lose their lives, while those who lose themselves in service to others grow and flourish—and in effect save their lives.

In the October 1963 general conference—the conference at which I was sustained as a member of the Quorum of the

Twelve Apostles—President David O. McKay made this statement: "Man's greatest happiness comes from losing himself for
the good of others."[6]

Often we live side by side but do not communicate heart
to heart. There are those within the sphere of our own influence who, with outstretched hands, cry out, "Is there no balm
in Gilead"?[7]

I am confident it is the *intention* of each member of the
Church to serve and to help those in need. At baptism we
covenanted to "bear one another's burdens, that they may be
light."[8] How many times has your heart been touched as you
have witnessed the need of another? How often have you *intended* to be the one to help? And yet how often has day-to-day
living interfered and you've left it for others to help, feeling
that "oh, surely someone will take care of that need."

We become so caught up in the busyness of our lives. Were
we to step back, however, and take a good look at what we're
doing, we may find that we have immersed ourselves in the
"thick of thin things." In other words, too often we spend most
of our time taking care of the things which do not really matter much at all in the grand scheme of things, neglecting those
more important causes.

Many years ago I heard a poem which has stayed with me,
by which I have tried to guide my life. It's one of my favorites:

> *I have wept in the night*
> *For the shortness of sight*
> *That to somebody's need made me blind;*
> *But I never have yet*
> *Felt a tinge of regret*
> *For being a little too kind.*[9]

My brothers and sisters, we are surrounded by those in
need of our attention, our encouragement, our support, our
comfort, our kindness—be they family members, friends,

acquaintances, or strangers. We are the Lord's hands here upon the earth, with the mandate to serve and to lift His children. He is dependent upon each of us.

You may lament: I can barely make it through each day, doing all that I need to do. How can I provide service for others? What can I possibly do?

Just over a year ago, I was interviewed by the *Church News* prior to my birthday. At the conclusion of the interview, the reporter asked what I would consider the ideal gift that members worldwide could give to me. I replied, "Find someone who is having a hard time or is ill or lonely, and do something for him or her."[10]

I was overwhelmed when this year for my birthday I received hundreds of cards and letters from members of the Church around the world telling me how they had fulfilled that birthday wish. The acts of service ranged from assembling humanitarian kits to doing yard work.

Dozens and dozens of Primaries challenged the children to provide service, and then those acts of service were recorded and sent to me. I must say that the methods for recording them were creative. Many came in the form of pages put together into various shapes and sizes of books. Some contained cards or pictures drawn or colored by the children. One very creative Primary sent a large jar containing hundreds of what they called "warm fuzzies," each one representing an act of service performed during the year by one of the children in the Primary. I can only imagine the happiness these children experienced as they told of their service and then placed a "warm fuzzy" in the jar.

I share with you just a few of the countless notes contained in the many gifts I received. One small child wrote, "My grandpa had a stroke, and I held his hand." From an eight-year-old girl: "My sister and I served my mom and family by organizing and cleaning the toy closet. It took us a few hours and we had fun. The best part was that we surprised my mom and made her happy because she didn't even ask us to do it." An eleven-year-old girl wrote: "There was a family in my ward that did not have a lot of money. They have three little girls. The mom and dad had to go somewhere, so I offered to watch the three girls. The dad was just about to hand me a $5 bill. I said, 'I can't take [it].' My service was that I watched the girls for free." A Primary child in Mongolia wrote that he had brought in water from the well so his mother wouldn't have to do so. From a four-year-old boy, no doubt written by a Primary teacher: "My dad is gone for army training for a few weeks. My special job is to give my mom hugs and kisses." Wrote a nine-year-old girl: "I picked strawberries for my great-grandma. I felt good inside!" And another: "I played with a lonely kid."

From an eleven-year-old boy: "I went to a lady's house and asked her questions and sang her a song. It felt good to visit her. She was happy because she never gets visitors." Reading this particular note reminded me of words penned long years ago by Elder Richard L. Evans of the Quorum of the Twelve. Said he: "It is difficult for those who are young to understand the loneliness that comes when life changes from a time of preparation and performance to a time of putting things away. . . . To be so long the center of a home, so much sought after, and then, almost suddenly, to be on the sidelines watching the procession pass by—this is living into loneliness. . . . We have to live a long time to learn how empty a room can be that is filled only with furniture. It takes someone . . . beyond mere hired service, beyond institutional care or professional duty, to thaw out the memories of the past and keep them warmly living in the present. . . . We cannot bring them back the morning hours of youth. But we can help them live in the warm glow of a sunset made more beautiful by our thoughtfulness . . . and unfeigned love."[11]

My birthday cards and notes came also from teenagers in

Young Men and Young Women classes who made blankets for hospitals, served in food pantries, were baptized for the dead, and performed numerous other acts of service.

Relief Societies, where help can always be found, provided service above and beyond that which they would normally have given. Priesthood groups did the same.

My brothers and sisters, my heart has seldom been as touched and grateful as it was when Sister Monson and I literally spent hours reading of these gifts. My heart is full now as I speak of the experience and contemplate the lives which have been blessed as a result, for both the giver and the receiver.

The words from the 25th chapter of Matthew come to mind:

"Come, ye blessed of my Father, inherit the kingdom prepared for you from the foundation of the world:

"For I was an hungred, and ye gave me meat: I was thirsty, and ye gave me drink: I was a stranger, and ye took me in:

"Naked, and ye clothed me: I was sick, and ye visited me: I was in prison, and ye came unto me.

"Then shall the righteous answer him, saying, Lord, when saw we thee an hungred, and fed thee? or thirsty, and gave thee drink?

"When saw we thee a stranger, and took thee in? or naked, and clothed thee?

"Or when saw we thee sick, or in prison, and came unto thee?

"And the King shall answer and say unto them, Verily I say unto you, Inasmuch as ye have done it unto one of the least of these my brethren, ye have done it unto me."[12]

My brothers and sisters, may we ask ourselves the question which greeted Dr. Jack McConnell and his brothers and sisters each evening at dinnertime: "What have I done for someone today?" May the words of a familiar hymn penetrate our very souls and find lodgment in our hearts:

> *Have I done any good in the world today?*
> *Have I helped anyone in need?*
> *Have I cheered up the sad and made someone feel glad?*
> *If not, I have failed indeed.*
> *Has anyone's burden been lighter today*
> *Because I was willing to share?*
> *Have the sick and the weary been helped on their way?*
> *When they needed my help was I there?*[13]

That service to which all of us have been called is the service of the Lord Jesus Christ.

As He enlists us to His cause, He invites us to draw close to Him. He speaks to you and to me:

"Come unto me, all ye that labour and are heavy laden, and I will give you rest.

"Take my yoke upon you, and learn of me; for I am meek and lowly in heart: and ye shall find rest unto your souls.

"For my yoke is easy, and my burden is light."[14]

If we truly listen, we may hear that voice from far away say to us, as it spoke to another, "Well done, thou good and faithful servant."[15] That each may qualify for this blessing from our Lord is my prayer, and I offer it in His name, even Jesus Christ, our Savior, amen.

NOTES

1. Jack McConnell, "And What Did You Do for Someone Today?" *Newsweek*, June 18, 2001, 13.
2. McConnell, "And What Did You Do for Someone Today?" 13.
3. Galatians 5:13.
4. Mosiah 2:17.
5. Luke 9:24.
6. David O. McKay, in Conference Report, October 1963, 8.
7. Jeremiah 8:22.
8. Mosiah 18:8.

9. Author unknown; quoted in Richard L. Evans, "The Quality of Kindness," *Improvement Era,* May 1960, 340.
10. See Gerry Avant, "Prophet's Birthday," *Church News,* August 23, 2008, 4.
11. Richard L. Evans, "Living into Loneliness," *Improvement Era,* July 1948, 445.
12. Matthew 25:34–40.
13. "Have I Done Any Good?" *Hymns,* no. 223.
14. Matthew 11:28–30.
15. Matthew 25:21.

10

PREPARATION BRINGS BLESSINGS

General Conference Priesthood Session
April 3, 2010

Brethren, you who are here in the Conference Center in Salt Lake City are an inspiring sight to behold. It is amazing to realize that in thousands of chapels throughout the world, others of you—fellow holders of the priesthood of God—are receiving this broadcast by way of satellite transmission. Your nationalities vary, and your languages are many, but a common thread binds us together. We have been entrusted to bear the priesthood and to act in the name of God. We are the recipients of a sacred trust. Much is expected of us.

One of my most vivid memories is attending priesthood meeting as a newly ordained deacon and singing the opening hymn, "Come, All Ye Sons of God." Tonight I echo the spirit of that special hymn and say to you, "Come, all ye sons of God who have received the priesthood."[1] Let us consider our callings, let us reflect on our responsibilities, and let us follow Jesus Christ, our Lord.

Twenty years ago I attended a sacrament meeting where the children responded to the theme, "I Belong to The Church of Jesus Christ of Latter-day Saints." These boys and girls demonstrated they were in training for service to the Lord and to others. The music was beautiful, the recitations skillfully rendered, and the spirit heaven-sent. One of my grandsons, who was 11 years old at the time, had spoken of the First Vision as he presented his part on the program. Afterward, as he came to his parents and grandparents, I said to him, "Tommy, I think you are almost ready to be a missionary."

He replied, "Not yet. I still have a lot to learn."

Through the years that followed, Tommy did learn, thanks to his parents and to teachers and advisers at church, who were dedicated and conscientious. When he was old enough, he was called to serve a mission. He did so in a most honorable fashion.

Young men, I admonish you to prepare for service as a missionary. There are many tools to help you learn the lessons which will be beneficial to you as well as helping you to live the life you will need to have lived to be worthy. One such tool is the booklet entitled *For the Strength of Youth,* published under the direction of the First Presidency and Quorum of the Twelve Apostles. It features standards from the writings and teachings of Church leaders and from scripture, adherence to which will bring the blessings of our Heavenly Father and the guidance of His Son to each of us. In addition, there are lesson manuals, carefully prepared after prayerful consideration. Families have family home evenings, where gospel principles are taught. Almost all of you have the opportunity to attend seminary classes, taught by dedicated teachers who have much to share.

Begin to prepare for a temple marriage as well as for a mission. Proper dating is a part of that preparation. In cultures where dating is appropriate, do not date until you are 16 years old. "Not all teenagers need to date or even want to. . . . When you begin dating, go in groups or on double dates. . . . Make sure your parents meet [and become acquainted with] those you date." Because dating is a preparation for marriage, "date only those who have high standards."[2]

Be careful to go to places where there is a good environment, where you won't be faced with temptation.

A wise father said to his son, "If you ever find yourself in a place where you shouldn't ought to be, get out!" Good advice for all of us.

Servants of the Lord have always counseled us to dress appropriately to show respect for our Heavenly Father and for ourselves. The way you dress sends messages about yourself to others and often influences the way you and others act. Dress in such a way as to bring out the best in yourself and those around you. Avoid extremes in clothing and appearance, including tattoos and piercings.

Everyone needs good friends. Your circle of friends will greatly influence your thinking and behavior, just as you will theirs. When you share common values with your friends, you can strengthen and encourage each other. Treat everyone with kindness and dignity. Many nonmembers have come into the Church through friends who have involved them in Church activities.

The oft-repeated adage is ever true: "Honesty is the best policy."[3] A Latter-day Saint young man lives as he teaches and as he believes. He is honest with others. He is honest with himself. He is honest with God. He is honest by habit and as a matter of course. When a difficult decision must be made, he never asks himself, "What will others think?" but rather, "What will I think of myself?"

For some, there will come the temptation to dishonor a personal standard of honesty. In a business law class at the university I attended, I remember that one particular classmate never prepared for the class discussions. I thought to myself, "How is he going to pass the final examination?"

I discovered the answer when he came to the classroom for

the final exam on a winter's day wearing on his bare feet only a pair of sandals. I was surprised and watched him as the class began. All of his books had been placed upon the floor, as per the instruction. He slipped the sandals from his feet; and then, with toes that he had trained and had prepared with glycerin, he skillfully turned the pages of one of the books which he had placed on the floor, thereby viewing the answers to the examination questions.

He received one of the highest grades in that course on business law. But the day of reckoning came. Later, as he prepared to take his comprehensive exam, for the first time the dean of his particular discipline said, "This year I will depart from tradition and will conduct an oral, rather than a written, test." Our favorite, trained-toe expert found that he had his foot in his mouth on that occasion and failed the exam.

How you speak and the words you use tell much about the image you choose to portray. Use language to build and uplift those around you. Profane, vulgar, or crude language and inappropriate or off-color jokes are offensive to the Lord. Never misuse the name of God or Jesus Christ. The Lord said, "Thou shalt not take the name of the Lord thy God in vain."[4]

Our Heavenly Father has counseled us to seek after "anything virtuous, lovely, or of good report or praiseworthy."[5] Whatever you read, listen to, or watch makes an impression on you.

Pornography is especially dangerous and addictive. Curious exploration of pornography can become a controlling habit, leading to coarser material and to sexual transgression. Avoid pornography at all costs.

Don't be afraid to walk out of a movie, turn off a television set, or change a radio station if what's being presented does not meet your Heavenly Father's standards. In short, if you have any question about whether a particular movie, book, or other form of entertainment is appropriate, don't see it, don't read it, don't participate.

The Apostle Paul declared: "Know ye not that ye are the temple of God, and that the Spirit of God dwelleth in you? . . . The temple of God is holy, which temple ye are."[6] Brethren, it is our responsibility to keep our temples clean and pure.

Hard drugs, wrongful use of prescription drugs, alcohol, coffee, tea, and tobacco products destroy your physical, mental, and spiritual well-being. Any form of alcohol is harmful to your spirit and your body. Tobacco can enslave you, weaken your lungs, and shorten your life.

Music can help you draw closer to your Heavenly Father. It can be used to educate, edify, inspire, and unite. However, music can, by its tempo, beat, intensity, and lyrics, dull your spiritual sensitivity. You cannot afford to fill your minds with unworthy music.

Because sexual intimacy is so sacred, the Lord requires self-control and purity before marriage, as well as full fidelity after marriage. In dating, treat your date with respect and expect your date to show that same respect for you. Tears inevitably follow transgression.

President David O. McKay, ninth president of the Church, advised, "I implore you to think clean thoughts." He then made this significant declaration of truth: "Every action is preceded by a thought. If we want to control our actions, we must control our thinking." Brethren, fill your minds with good thoughts, and your actions will be proper. May each of you be able to echo in truth the line from Tennyson spoken by Sir Galahad: "My strength is as the strength of ten, because my heart is pure."[7]

Not long ago the author of a paper on teenage sexuality summed up his research by saying that society sends teens a mixed message: advertisements and the mass media convey "very heavy messages that sexual activity is acceptable and expected," inducements that sometimes drown out the warnings of experts and the pleas of parents. The Lord cuts through all the media messages with clear and precise language when He declares to us, "Be ye clean."[8]

Whenever temptation comes, remember the wise counsel of the Apostle Paul, who declared: "There hath no temptation taken you but such as is common to man: but God is faithful, who will not suffer you to be tempted above that ye are able; but will with the temptation also make a way to escape, that ye may be able to bear it."[9]

When you were confirmed a member of the Church, you received the right to the companionship of the Holy Ghost. He can help you make good choices. When challenged or tempted, you do not need to feel alone. Remember that prayer is the passport to spiritual power.

If any has stumbled in his journey, there is a way back. The process is called repentance. Our Savior died to provide you and me that blessed gift. Though the path is difficult, the promise is real: "Though your sins be as scarlet, they shall be as white as snow."[10]

Don't put your eternal life at risk. Keep the commandments of God. If you have sinned, the sooner you begin to make your way back, the sooner you will find the sweet peace and joy that come with the miracle of forgiveness. Happiness comes from living the way the Lord wants you to live and from service to God and others.

Spiritual strength frequently comes through selfless service. Some years ago I visited what was then called the California Mission, where I interviewed a young missionary from Georgia. I recall saying to him, "Do you send a letter home to your parents every week?"

He replied, "Yes, Brother Monson."

Then I asked, "Do you enjoy receiving letters from home?"

He didn't answer. At length, I inquired, "When was the last time you had a letter from home?"

With a quavering voice, he responded, "I've never had a letter from home. Father's just a deacon, and Mother's not a member of the Church. They pleaded with me not to come. They said that if I left on a mission, they would not be writing to me. What shall I do, Brother Monson?"

I offered a silent prayer to my Heavenly Father: "What should I tell this young servant of Thine, who has sacrificed everything to serve Thee?" And the inspiration came. I said, "Elder, you send a letter home to your mother and father every week of your mission. Tell them what you are doing. Tell them how much you love them and then bear your testimony to them."

He asked, "Will they then write to me?"

I responded, "Then they will write to you."

We parted, and I went on my way. Months later I was attending a stake conference in Southern California when a young missionary came up to me and said, "Brother Monson, do you remember me? I'm the missionary who had not received a letter from my mother or my father during my first nine months in the mission field. You told me, 'Send a letter home every week, Elder, and your parents will write to you.'"

Then he asked, "Do you remember that promise, Elder Monson?"

I remembered. I inquired, "Have you heard from your parents?"

He reached into his pocket and took out a sheaf of letters with an elastic band around them, took a letter from the top of the stack, and said, "Have I heard from my parents! Listen to this letter from my mother: 'Son, we so much enjoy your letters. We're proud of you, our missionary. Guess what? Dad has been ordained a priest. He's preparing to baptize me. I'm meeting with the missionaries; and one year from now we want to come to California as you complete your mission, for we, with you, would like to become a forever family by entering the temple of the Lord.'"

This young missionary asked, "Brother Monson, does

Heavenly Father always answer prayers and fulfill an Apostle's promises?"

I replied, "When one has faith as you have demonstrated, our Heavenly Father hears such prayers and answers in His own way."

Clean hands, a pure heart, and a willing mind had touched heaven. A blessing, heaven-sent, had answered the fervent prayer of a missionary's humble heart.

Brethren, it is my prayer that we may so live that we too may touch heaven and be similarly blessed, each and every one, in the name of the Giver of all blessings, even Jesus Christ, amen.

NOTES

1. "Come, All Ye Sons of God," *Hymns,* no. 322.
2. *For the Strength of Youth* (booklet, 2001), 24, 25.
3. Miguel de Cervantes, in John Bartlett, comp., *Familiar Quotations,* 14th ed. (1968), 197.
4. Exodus 20:7.
5. Articles of Faith 1:13.
6. 1 Corinthians 3:16–17.
7. Alfred Lord Tennyson, in *Familiar Quotations,* 647.
8. Doctrine and Covenants 38:42.
9. 1 Corinthians 10:13.
10. Isaiah 1:18.

11

He Is Risen!

General Conference Sunday Morning Session
April 4, 2010

T HIS HAS BEEN A REMARKABLE session. In behalf of all who participated thus far in word or music, as the President of the Church, I have chosen simply to say to you at this moment just two words, known as the two most important words in the English language. To Sister Cheryl Lant and her counselors, the choir, the musicians, the speakers, those words are "Thank you."

Many years ago, while in London, England, I visited the famed Tate art gallery. Works by Gainsborough, Rembrandt, Constable, and other renowned artists were displayed in room after room. I admired their beauty and recognized the skill which had been required to create these masterpieces. Tucked away in a quiet corner of the third floor, however, was a painting which not only caught my attention but also captured my heart. The artist, Frank Bramley, had painted a humble cottage facing a windswept sea. Two women, the mother and the wife of an absent fisherman, had watched and waited the night through for his return. Now the night had passed, and the realization had set in that he had been lost at sea and would not return.

Kneeling at the side of her mother-in-law, her head buried in the lap of the older woman, the young wife wept in despair. The spent candle on the window ledge told of the fruitless vigil.

I sensed the young woman's heartache; I felt her grief. The hauntingly vivid inscription which the artist gave to his work told the tragic story. It read, *A Hopeless Dawn*.

Oh, how the young woman longed for the comfort, even the reality, of Robert Louis Stevenson's "Requiem":

> *Home is the sailor, home from the sea,*
> *And the hunter home from the hill.*[1]

Among all the facts of mortality, none is so certain as its end. Death comes to all; it is our "universal heritage. It may claim its victim[s] in infancy or youth, [it may visit] in the period of life's prime, or its summons may be deferred until the snows of age have gathered upon the . . . head; it may befall as the result of accident or disease, . . . or . . . through natural causes; but come it must."[2] It inevitably represents a painful loss of association and, particularly in the young, a crushing blow to dreams unrealized, ambitions unfulfilled, and hopes vanquished.

What mortal being, faced with the loss of a loved one or, indeed, standing himself or herself on the threshold of infinity, has not pondered what lies beyond the veil which separates the seen from the unseen?

Centuries ago, the man Job—so long blessed with every material gift, only to find himself sorely afflicted by all that can befall a human being—sat with his companions and uttered the timeless, ageless question, "If a man die, shall he live again?"[3] Job spoke what every other living man or woman has pondered.

This glorious Easter morning I'd like to consider Job's question—"If a man die, shall he live again?"—and provide the answer which comes not only from thoughtful consideration but also from the revealed word of God. I begin with the essentials.

If there is a design in this world in which we live, there must be a Designer. Who can behold the many wonders of the universe without believing that there is a design for all mankind? Who can doubt that there is a Designer?

In the book of Genesis we learn that the Grand Designer created the heaven and the earth: "And the earth was without form, and void; and darkness was upon the face of the deep."

"Let there be light," said the Grand Designer, "and there was light." He created a firmament. He separated the land from the waters and said, "Let the earth bring forth grass, . . . the fruit tree yielding fruit after his kind, whose seed is in itself."

Two lights He created—the sun and the moon. Came the stars by His design. He called for living creatures in the water and fowls to fly above the earth. And it was so. He made cattle, beasts, and creeping things. The design was nearly complete.

Last of all, He created man in His own image—male and female—with dominion over all other living things.[4]

Man alone received intelligence—a brain, a mind, and a soul. Man alone, with these attributes, had the capacity for faith and hope, for inspiration and ambition.

Who could persuasively argue that man—the noblest work of the Great Designer, with dominion over all living things, with a brain and a will, with a mind and a soul, with intelligence and divinity—should come to an end when the spirit forsakes its earthly temple?

To understand the meaning of death, we must appreciate the purpose of life. The dim light of belief must yield to the noonday sun of revelation, by which we know that we lived before our birth into mortality. In our premortal state, we were doubtless among the sons and daughters of God who shouted for joy because of the opportunity to come to this challenging yet necessary mortal existence.[5] We knew that our purpose was to gain a physical body, to overcome trials, and to prove that we would keep the commandments of God. Our Father knew that because of the nature of mortality, we would be tempted, would sin, and would fall short. So that we might have every chance of success, He provided a Savior who would suffer and die for us. Not only would He atone for our sins, but as a part of that Atonement, He would also overcome the physical death to which we would be subject because of the Fall of Adam.

Thus, more than 2,000 years ago, Christ, our Savior, was born to mortal life in a stable in Bethlehem. The long foretold Messiah had come.

There was very little written of the boyhood of Jesus. I love the passage from Luke: "And Jesus increased in wisdom and stature, and in favour with God and man."[6] And from the book of Acts, there is a short phrase concerning the Savior which has a world of meaning: "[He] went about doing good."[7]

He was baptized by John in the river Jordan. He called the Twelve Apostles. He blessed the sick. He caused the lame to walk, the blind to see, the deaf to hear. He even raised the dead to life. He taught, He testified, and He provided a perfect example for us to follow.

And then the mortal mission of the Savior of the world drew to its close. A last supper with His Apostles took place in an upper room. Ahead lay Gethsemane and Calvary's cross.

No mere mortal can conceive the full import of what Christ did for us in Gethsemane. He, himself, later described the experience: "[The] suffering caused myself, even God, the greatest of all, to tremble because of pain, and to bleed at every pore, and to suffer both body and spirit."[8]

Following the agony of Gethsemane, now drained of strength, He was seized by rough, crude hands and taken before Annas, Caiaphas, Pilate, and Herod. He was accused and cursed. Vicious blows further weakened His pain-wracked body. Blood ran down His face as a cruel crown fashioned of sharp thorns was forced onto his head, piercing His brow. And then once again He was taken to Pilate, who gave in to the cries of the angry mob: "Crucify him, crucify him."[9]

He was scourged with a whip into whose multiple leather strands sharp metals and bones were woven. Rising from the cruelty of the scourge, with stumbling steps He carried His own cross until He could go no farther and another shouldered the burden for Him.

Finally, on a hill called Calvary, while helpless followers looked on, His wounded body was nailed to a cross. Mercilessly He was mocked and cursed and derided. And yet He cried out, "Father, forgive them; for they know not what they do."[10]

The agonizing hours passed as His life ebbed. From his parched lips came the words, "Father, into thy hands I commend my spirit: and having said thus, he gave up the ghost."[11]

As the serenity and solace of a merciful death freed Him from the sorrows of mortality, He returned to the presence of His Father.

At the last moment, the Master could have turned back. But he did not. He passed beneath all things that He might save all things. His lifeless body was hurriedly but gently placed in a borrowed tomb.

No words in Christendom mean more to me than those spoken by the angel to the weeping Mary Magdalene and the other Mary when, on the first day of the week, they approached the tomb to care for the body of their Lord. Spoke the angel:

"Why seek ye the living among the dead?

"He is not here, but is risen."[12]

Our Savior lived again. The most glorious, comforting, and reassuring of all events of human history had taken place—the victory over death. The pain and agony of Gethsemane and Calvary had been wiped away. The salvation of mankind had been secured. The Fall of Adam had been reclaimed.

The empty tomb that first Easter morning was the answer to Job's question, "If a man die, shall he live again?" To all within the sound of my voice, I declare, If a man die, he *shall* live again. We know, for we have the light of revealed truth.

"For since by man came death, by man came also the resurrection of the dead.

"For as in Adam all die, even so in Christ shall all be made alive."[13]

I have read—and I believe—the testimonies of those who experienced the grief of Christ's Crucifixion and the joy of His Resurrection. I have read—and I believe—the testimonies of those in the New World who were visited by the same risen Lord.

I believe the testimony of one who, in this dispensation, spoke with the Father and the Son in a grove now called Sacred and who gave his life, sealing that testimony with his blood. Declared he:

"And now, after the many testimonies which have been given of him, this is the testimony, last of all, which we give of him: That he lives!

"For we saw him, even on the right hand of God; and we heard the voice bearing record that he is the Only Begotten of the Father."[14]

The darkness of death can always be dispelled by the light of revealed truth. "I am the resurrection, and the life," spoke the Master.[15] "Peace I leave with you, my peace I give unto you."[16]

Over the years I have heard and read testimonies too numerous to count, shared with me by individuals who testify of the reality of the Resurrection and who have received, in their hours of greatest need, the peace and comfort promised by the Savior.

I will mention just part of one such account. Two weeks ago I received a touching letter from a father of seven who wrote about his family and, in particular, his son Jason, who had become ill when 11 years of age. Over the next few years, Jason's illness recurred several times. This father told of Jason's positive attitude and sunny disposition, despite his health challenges. Jason received the Aaronic Priesthood at age 12 and "always willingly magnified his responsibilities with excellence, whether he felt well or not." He received his Eagle Scout award when he was 14 years old.

Last summer, not long after Jason's 15th birthday, he was once again admitted to the hospital. On one of his visits to see Jason, his father found him with his eyes closed. Not knowing whether Jason was asleep or awake, he began talking softly to him. "Jason," he said, "I know you have been through a lot in your short life and that your current condition is difficult. Even though you have a giant battle ahead, I don't ever want you to lose your faith in Jesus Christ." He said he was startled as Jason immediately opened his eyes and said "Never!" in a clear, resolute voice. Jason then closed his eyes and said no more.

His father wrote: "In this simple declaration, Jason expressed one of the most powerful, pure testimonies of Jesus Christ that I have ever heard. . . . As his declaration of 'Never!' became imprinted on my soul that day, my heart filled with joy that my Heavenly Father had blessed me to be the father of such a tremendous and noble boy. . . . [It] was the last time I heard him declare his testimony of Christ."

Although his family was expecting this to be just another routine hospitalization, Jason passed away less than two weeks later. An older brother and sister were serving missions at the time. Another brother, Kyle, had just received his mission call. In fact, the call had come earlier than expected, and on August 5, just a week before Jason's passing, the family gathered in his hospital room so that Kyle's mission call could be opened there and shared with the entire family.

In his letter to me, this father included a photograph of Jason in his hospital bed, with his big brother Kyle standing beside the bed, holding his mission call. This caption was written beneath the photograph: "Called to serve their missions together—on both sides of the veil."

Jason's brother and sister already serving missions sent beautiful, comforting letters home to be shared at Jason's funeral. His sister, serving in the Argentina Buenos Aires West Mission, as part of her letter, wrote: "I know that Jesus Christ lives, and because He lives, all of us, including our beloved Jason, will live again too. . . . We can take comfort in the sure knowledge we have that we have been sealed together as an eternal family. . . . If we do our very best to obey and do better in this life, we will see [him again]." She continued, "[A] scripture that I have long loved now takes on new significance and importance at this time. . . . [From] Revelation chapter 21, verse 4: 'And God shall wipe away all tears from their eyes; and there shall be no more death, neither sorrow, nor crying, neither shall there be any more pain: for the former things are passed away.'"

My beloved brothers and sisters, in our hour of deepest sorrow, we can receive profound peace from the words of the angel that first Easter morning: "He is not here: for he is risen."[17]

> *He is risen! He is risen!*
> *Tell it out with joyful voice.*
> *He has burst his three days' prison;*
> *Let the whole wide earth rejoice.*
> *Death is conquered; man is free.*
> *Christ has won the victory.*[18]

As one of His special witnesses on earth today, this glorious Easter Sunday, I declare that this is true, in His sacred name—even the name of Jesus Christ, our Savior—amen.

NOTES

1. Robert Louis Stevenson, "Requiem," from *An Anthology of Modern Verse*, ed. A. Methuen (1921), 208.

2. James E. Talmage, *Jesus the Christ*, 3rd ed. (1916), 20.

3. Job 14:14.
4. See Genesis 1:1–27.
5. Job 38:7.
6. Luke 2:52.
7. Acts 10:38.
8. Doctrine and Covenants 19:18.
9. Luke 23:21.
10. Luke 23:34.
11. Luke 23:46.
12. Luke 24:5–6.
13. 1 Corinthians 15:21–22.
14. Doctrine and Covenants 76:22–23.
15. John 11:25.
16. John 14:27.
17. Matthew 28:6.
18. "He Is Risen!" *Hymns,* no. 199.

12

THE THREE RS OF CHOICE

General Conference Priesthood Session
October 2, 2010

Mʏ ʙᴇʟᴏᴠᴇᴅ ʙʀᴇᴛʜʀᴇɴ ᴏғ ᴛʜᴇ priesthood, my earnest prayer tonight is that I might enjoy the help of our Heavenly Father in giving utterance to those things which I feel impressed to share with you.

I have been thinking recently about choices and their consequences. Scarcely an hour of the day goes by but what we are called upon to make choices of one sort or another. Some are trivial, some more far-reaching. Some will make no difference in the eternal scheme of things, and others will make *all* the difference.

As I've contemplated the various aspects of choice, I've put them into three categories: First, the *right* of choice; second, the *responsibility* of choice; and third, the *results* of choice. I call these the three Rs of choice.

I mention first the *right* of choice. I am so grateful to a loving Heavenly Father for His gift of agency, or the right to choose. President David O. McKay, ninth President of the Church, said, "Next to the bestowal of life itself, the right to direct that life is God's greatest gift to man."[1]

90

We know that we had our agency before this world was and that Lucifer attempted to take it from us. He had no confidence in the principle of agency or in us and argued for imposed salvation. He insisted that with his plan none would be lost, but he seemed not to recognize—or perhaps not to care—that in addition, none would be any wiser, any stronger, any more compassionate, or any more grateful if his plan were followed.

We who chose the Savior's plan knew that we would be embarking on a precarious, difficult journey, for we walk the ways of the world and sin and stumble, cutting us off from our Father. But the Firstborn in the Spirit offered Himself as a sacrifice to atone for the sins of all. Through unspeakable suffering He became the Great Redeemer, the Savior of all mankind, thus making possible our successful return to our Father.

The prophet Lehi tells us, "Wherefore, men are free according to the flesh; and all things are given them which are expedient unto man. And they are free to choose liberty and eternal life, through the great Mediator of all men, or to choose captivity and death, according to the captivity and power of the devil; for he seeketh that all men might be miserable like unto himself."[2]

Brethren, within the confines of whatever circumstances we find ourselves, we will always have the *right* to choose.

Next, with the *right* of choice comes the *responsibility* to choose. We cannot be neutral; there is no middle ground. The Lord knows this; Lucifer knows this. As long as we live upon this earth, Lucifer and his hosts will never abandon the hope of claiming our souls.

Our Heavenly Father did not launch us on our eternal journey without providing the means whereby we could receive from Him God-given guidance to assist in our safe return at the end of mortal life. I speak of prayer. I speak, too, of the whisperings from that still, small voice within each of us, and

I do not overlook the holy scriptures, written by mariners who successfully sailed the seas we too must cross.

Each of us has come to this earth with all the tools necessary to make correct choices. The prophet Mormon tells us, "The Spirit of Christ is given to every man, that he may know good from evil."[3]

We are surrounded—even at times bombarded—by the messages of the adversary. Listen to some of them; they are no doubt familiar to you: "Just this once won't matter." "Don't worry; no one will know." "You can stop smoking or drinking or taking drugs any time you want." "Everybody's doing it, so it can't be that bad." The lies are endless.

Although in our journey we will encounter forks and turnings in the road, we simply cannot afford the luxury of a detour from which we may never return. Lucifer, that clever pied piper, plays his lilting melody and attracts the unsuspecting away from the safety of their chosen pathway, away from the counsel of loving parents, away from the security of God's teachings. He seeks not just the so-called refuse of humanity; he seeks all of us, including the very elect of God. King David listened, wavered, and then followed and fell. So did Cain in an earlier era and Judas Iscariot in a later one. Lucifer's methods are cunning, his victims numerous.

We read of him in Second Nephi: "Others will he pacify, and lull them away into carnal security."[4] "Others he flattereth away, and telleth them there is no hell . . . until he grasps them with his awful chains."[5] "And thus the devil cheateth their souls, and leadeth them away carefully down to hell."[6]

When faced with significant choices, how do we decide? Do we succumb to the promise of momentary pleasure? To our urges and passions? To the pressure of our peers?

Let us not find ourselves as indecisive as is Alice in Lewis Carroll's classic *Alice's Adventures in Wonderland.* You will remember that she comes to a crossroads with two paths before her, each stretching onward but in opposite directions. She is confronted by the Cheshire cat, of whom Alice asks, "Which path shall I follow?"

The cat answers, "That depends where you want to go. If you do not know where you want to go, it doesn't matter which path you take."[7]

Unlike Alice, we all know where we want to go, and it *does* matter which way we go, for by choosing our path, we choose our destination.

Decisions are constantly before us. To make them wisely, courage is needed—the courage to say no, the courage to say yes. Decisions *do* determine destiny.

I plead with you to make a determination right here, right now, not to deviate from the path which will lead to our goal: eternal life with our Father in Heaven. Along that straight and true path there are other goals: missionary service, temple marriage, Church activity, scripture study, prayer, temple work. There are countless worthy goals to reach as we travel through life. Needed is our commitment to reach them.

Finally, brethren, I speak of the *results* of choice. All of our choices have consequences, some of which have little or nothing to do with our eternal salvation and others of which have *everything* to do with it.

Whether you wear a green T-shirt or a blue one makes no difference in the long run. However, whether you decide to push a key on your computer which will take you to pornography can make *all* the difference in your life. You will have just taken a step off the straight, safe path. If a friend pressures you to drink alcohol or to try drugs and you succumb to the pressure, you are taking a detour from which you may not return. Brethren, whether we are 12-year-old deacons or mature high priests, we are susceptible. May we keep our eyes, our hearts, and our determination focused on that goal which is eternal and worth any price we will have to pay, regardless of the sacrifice we must make to reach it.

No temptation, no pressure, no enticing can overcome us unless we allow such. If we make the wrong choice, we have no one to blame but ourselves. President Brigham Young once expressed this truth by relating it to himself. Said he, "If Brother Brigham should take a wrong track, and be shut out of the Kingdom of heaven, no person will be to blame but Brother Brigham. I am the only being in heaven, earth, or hell, that can be blamed." He continued, "This will equally apply to every Latter-day Saint. Salvation is an individual operation."[8]

The Apostle Paul has assured us, "There hath no temptation taken you but such as is common to man: but God is faithful, who will not suffer you to be tempted above that ye are able; but will with the temptation also make a way to escape, that ye may be able to bear it."[9]

We have all made incorrect choices. If we have not already corrected such choices, I assure you that there is a way to do so. The process is called repentance. I plead with you to correct your mistakes. Our Savior died to provide you and me that blessed gift. Although the path is not easy, the promise is real: "Though your sins be as scarlet, they shall be as white as snow."[10] "And I, the Lord, remember them no more."[11] Don't put your eternal life at risk. If you have sinned, the sooner you begin to make your way back, the sooner you will find the sweet peace and joy that come with the miracle of forgiveness.

Brethren, you are of a noble birthright. Eternal life in the kingdom of our Father is your goal. Such a goal is not achieved in one glorious attempt, but rather is the result of a lifetime of righteousness, an accumulation of wise choices, even a constancy of purpose. As with anything really worthwhile, the reward of eternal life requires effort.

The scriptures are clear:

"Ye shall observe to do . . . as the Lord your God hath

commanded you: ye shall not turn aside to the right hand or to the left.

"Ye shall walk in all the ways which the Lord your God hath commanded you."[12]

In closing may I share with you an example of one who determined early in life what his goals would be. I speak of Brother Clayton M. Christensen, a member of the Church who is a professor of business administration in the business school at Harvard University.

When he was 16 years old, Brother Christensen decided, among other things, that he would not play sports on Sunday. Years later, when he attended Oxford University in England, he played center on the basketball team. That year they had an undefeated season and went through to the British equivalent of what in the United States would be the NCAA basketball tournament.

They won their games fairly easily in the tournament, making it to the final four. It was then that Brother Christensen looked at the schedule and, to his absolute horror, saw that the final basketball game was scheduled to be played on a Sunday. He and the team had worked so hard to get where they were, and he was the starting center. He went to his coach with his dilemma. His coach was unsympathetic and told Brother Christensen he expected him to play in the game.

Prior to the final game, however, there was a semifinal game. Unfortunately, the backup center dislocated his shoulder, which increased the pressure on Brother Christensen to play in the final game. He went to his hotel room. He knelt down. He asked his Heavenly Father if it would be all right, just this once, if he played that game on Sunday. He said that before he had finished praying, he received the answer: "Clayton, what are you even asking me for? You know the answer."

He went to his coach, telling him how sorry he was that he wouldn't be playing in the final game. Then he went to the

Sunday meetings in the local ward while his team played without him. He prayed mightily for their success. They did win.

That fateful, difficult decision was made more than 30 years ago. Brother Christensen has said that as time has passed he considers it one of the most important decisions he ever made. It would have been very easy to have said, "You know, in general, keeping the Sabbath day holy is the right commandment, but in my particular extenuating circumstance, it's okay, just this once, if I don't do it." However, he says his entire life has turned out to be an unending stream of extenuating circumstances, and had he crossed the line just that once, then the next time something came up that was so demanding and critical, it would have been so much easier to cross the line again. The lesson he learned is that it is easier to keep the commandments 100 percent of the time than it is 98 percent of the time.[13]

My beloved brethren, may we be filled with gratitude for the *right* of choice, accept the *responsibility* of choice, and ever be conscious of the *results* of choice. As bearers of the priesthood, all of us united as one can qualify for the guiding influence of our Heavenly Father as we choose carefully and correctly. We are engaged in the work of the Lord Jesus Christ. We, like those of olden times, have answered His call. We are on His errand. We shall succeed in the solemn charge: "Be ye clean, that bear the vessels of the Lord."[14] That this may be so is my solemn and humble prayer. In the name of Jesus Christ, our Master, amen.

NOTES

1. *Teachings of Presidents of the Church: David O. McKay* (2003), 208.
2. 2 Nephi 2:27.
3. Moroni 7:16.
4. 2 Nephi 28:21.
5. 2 Nephi 28:22.
6. 2 Nephi 28:21.
7. Adapted from Lewis Carroll, *Alice's Adventures in Wonderland* (1898), 89.
8. *Teachings of Presidents of the Church: Brigham Young* (1997), 294.
9. 1 Corinthians 10:13.

10. Isaiah 1:18.
11. Doctrine and Covenants 58:42.
12. Deuteronomy 5:32–33.
13. See Clayton M. Christensen, "Decisions for Which I've Been Grateful" (Brigham Young University–Idaho devotional, June 8, 2004), www.byui .edu/presentations.
14. Isaiah 52:11.

13

THE DIVINE GIFT OF GRATITUDE

General Conference Sunday Morning Session
October 3, 2010

THIS HAS BEEN A marvelous session.

When I was appointed President of the Church, I said, "I'll take one assignment for myself. I'll be the adviser for the Tabernacle Choir." I'm very proud of my choir!

My mother once said of me, "Tommy, I'm very proud of all that you've done. But I have one comment to make to you. You should have stayed with the piano."

So I went to the piano and played a number for her: "Here we go, [here we go] to a birthday party."[1] Then I gave her a kiss on the forehead, and she embraced me.

I think of her. I think of my father. I think of all those General Authorities who've influenced me, and others, including the widows whom I visited—84 of them—with a chicken for the oven, sometimes a little money for their pocket.

I visited one late one night. It was midnight, and I went to the nursing home, and the receptionist said, "I'm sure she's asleep, but she told me to be sure to awaken her, for she said, 'I know he'll come.'"

I held her hand; she called my name. She was wide awake.

She pressed my hand to her lips and said, "I knew you'd come." How could I not have come?

Beautiful music touches me that way.

My beloved brothers and sisters, we have heard inspired messages of truth, of hope, and of love. Our thoughts have turned to Him who atoned for our sins, who showed us the way to live and how to pray, and who demonstrated by His own actions the blessings of service—even our Lord and Savior, Jesus Christ.

In the book of Luke, chapter 17, we read of Him:

"And it came to pass, as he went to Jerusalem, that he passed through the midst of Samaria and Galilee.

"And as he entered into a certain village, there [he met] ten men that were lepers, which stood afar off:

"And they lifted up their voices, and said, Jesus, Master, have mercy on us.

"And when he saw them, he said unto them, Go shew yourselves unto the priests. And it came to pass, that, as they went, they were cleansed.

"And one of them, when he saw that he was healed, turned back, and with a loud voice glorified God,

"And fell down on his face at his feet, giving him thanks: and he was a Samaritan.

"And Jesus answering said, Were there not ten cleansed? but where are the nine?

"There are not found that returned to give glory to God, save this stranger.

"And he said unto him, Arise, go thy way: thy faith hath made thee whole."[2]

Through divine intervention, those who were lepers were spared from a cruel, lingering death and given a new lease on life. The expressed gratitude by one merited the Master's blessing, the ingratitude shown by the nine His disappointment.

My brothers and sisters, do we remember to give thanks

for the blessings we receive? Sincerely giving thanks not only helps us recognize our blessings, but it also unlocks the doors of heaven and helps us feel God's love.

My beloved friend President Gordon B. Hinckley said, "When you walk with gratitude, you do not walk with arrogance and conceit and egotism, you walk with a spirit of thanksgiving that is becoming to you and will bless your lives."[3]

In the book of Matthew in the Bible, we have another account of gratitude, this time as an expression from the Savior. As He traveled in the wilderness for three days, more than 4,000 people followed and traveled with Him. He took compassion on them, for they may not have eaten during the entire three days. His disciples, however, questioned, "Whence should we have so much bread in the wilderness, as to fill so great a multitude?" Like many of us, the disciples saw only what was lacking.

"And Jesus saith unto them, How many loaves have ye? And [the disciples] said, Seven, and a few little fishes.

"And [Jesus] commanded the multitude to sit down on the ground.

"And he took the seven loaves and the fishes, and *gave thanks,* and brake them, and gave to his disciples, and the disciples to the multitude."

Notice that the Savior gave thanks for what they had—and a miracle followed: "And they did all eat, and were filled: and they took up of the broken meat that was left seven baskets full."[4]

We have all experienced times when our focus is on what we lack, rather than on our blessings. Said the Greek philosopher Epictetus, "He is a wise man who does not grieve for the things which he has not, but rejoices for those which he has."[5]

Gratitude is a divine principle. The Lord declared through a revelation given to the Prophet Joseph Smith:

"Thou shalt thank the Lord thy God in all things. . . .

"And in nothing doth man offend God, or against none is his wrath kindled, save those who confess not his hand in all things."[6]

In the Book of Mormon we are told to "live in thanksgiving daily, for the many mercies and blessings which [God] doth bestow upon you."[7]

Regardless of our circumstances, each of us has much for which to be grateful if we will but pause and contemplate our blessings.

This is a wonderful time to be on earth. While there is much that is wrong in the world today, there are many things that are right and good. There are marriages that make it, parents who love their children and sacrifice for them, friends who care about us and help us, teachers who teach. Our lives are blessed in countless ways.

We can lift ourselves and others as well when we refuse to remain in the realm of negative thought and cultivate within our hearts an attitude of gratitude. If ingratitude be numbered among the serious sins, then gratitude takes its place among the noblest of virtues. Someone has said that "gratitude is not only the greatest of virtues, but the parent of all others."[8]

How can we cultivate within our hearts an attitude of gratitude? President Joseph F. Smith, sixth President of the Church, provided an answer. Said he, "The grateful man sees so much in the world to be thankful for, and with him the good outweighs the evil. Love overpowers jealousy, and light drives darkness out of his life." He continued, "Pride destroys our gratitude and sets up selfishness in its place. How much happier we are in the presence of a grateful and loving soul, and how careful we should be to cultivate, through the medium of a prayerful life, a thankful attitude toward God and man!"[9]

President Smith is telling us that a prayerful life is the key to possessing gratitude.

Do material possessions make us happy and grateful? Perhaps momentarily. However, those things which provide deep and lasting happiness and gratitude are the things which money cannot buy: our families, the gospel, good friends, our health, our abilities, the love we receive from those around us. Unfortunately, these are some of the things we allow ourselves to take for granted.

The English author Aldous Huxley wrote, "Most human beings have an almost infinite capacity for taking things for granted."[10]

We often take for granted the very people who most deserve our gratitude. Let us not wait until it is too late for us to express that gratitude. Speaking of loved ones he had lost, one man declared his regret this way: "I remember those happy days, and often wish I could speak into the ears of the dead the gratitude which was due them in life, and so ill returned."[11]

The loss of loved ones almost inevitably brings some regrets to our hearts. Let's minimize such feelings as much as humanly possible by frequently expressing our love and gratitude to them. We never know how soon it will be too late.

A grateful heart, then, comes through expressing gratitude to our Heavenly Father for His blessings and to those around us for all that they bring into our lives. This requires conscious effort—at least until we have truly learned and cultivated an attitude of gratitude. Often we feel grateful and *intend* to express our thanks but forget to do so or just don't get around to it. Someone has said that "feeling gratitude and not expressing it is like wrapping a present and not giving it."[12]

When we encounter challenges and problems in our lives, it is often difficult for us to focus on our blessings. However, if we reach deep enough and look hard enough, we will be able to feel and recognize just how much we have been given.

I share with you an account of one family which was able to find blessings in the midst of serious challenges. This is an

account I read many years ago and have kept because of the
message it conveys. It was written by Gordon Green and appeared in an American magazine over 50 years ago.

Gordon tells how he grew up on a farm in Canada, where
he and his siblings had to hurry home from school while the
other children played ball and went swimming. Their father,
however, had the capacity to help them understand that their
work amounted to something. This was especially true after
harvest time, when the family celebrated Thanksgiving, for on
that day their father gave them a great gift. He took an inventory of everything they had.

On Thanksgiving morning he would take them to the cellar with its barrels of apples, bins of beets, carrots packed in
sand, and mountains of sacked potatoes as well as peas, corn,
string beans, jellies, strawberries, and other preserves which
filled their shelves. He had the children count everything carefully. Then they went out to the barn and figured how many
tons of hay there were and how many bushels of grain in the
granary. They counted the cows, pigs, chickens, turkeys, and
geese. Their father said he wanted to see how they stood, but
they knew he really wanted them to realize on that feast day
how richly God had blessed them and had smiled upon all their
hours of work. Finally, when they sat down to the feast their
mother had prepared, the blessings were something they felt.

Gordon indicated, however, that the Thanksgiving he remembered most thankfully was the year they seemed to have
nothing for which to be grateful.

The year started off well: they had leftover hay, lots of seed,
four litters of pigs, and their father had a little money set aside
so that someday he could afford to buy a hay loader—a wonderful machine most farmers just dreamed of owning. It was also
the year that electricity came to their town—although not to
them because they couldn't afford it.

One night when Gordon's mother was doing her big wash,

his father stepped in and took his turn over the washboard and asked his wife to rest and do her knitting. He said, "You spend more time doing the wash than sleeping. Do you think we should break down and get electricity?" Although elated at the prospect, she shed a tear or two as she thought of the hay loader that wouldn't be bought.

So the electrical line went up their lane that year. Although it was nothing fancy, they acquired a washing machine that worked all day by itself and brilliant lightbulbs that dangled from each ceiling. There were no more lamps to fill with oil, no more wicks to cut, no more sooty chimneys to wash. The lamps went quietly off to the attic.

The coming of electricity to their farm was almost the last good thing that happened to them that year. Just as their crops were starting to come through the ground, the rains started. When the water finally receded, there wasn't a plant left anywhere. They planted again, but more rains beat the crops into the earth. Their potatoes rotted in the mud. They sold a couple of cows and all the pigs and other livestock they had intended to keep, getting very low prices for them because everybody else had to do the same thing. All they harvested that year was a patch of turnips which had somehow weathered the storms.

Then it was Thanksgiving again. Their mother said, "Maybe we'd better forget it this year. We haven't even got a goose left."

On Thanksgiving morning, however, Gordon's father showed up with a jackrabbit and asked his wife to cook it. Grudgingly she started the job, indicating it would take a long time to cook that tough old thing. When it was finally on the table with some of the turnips that had survived, the children refused to eat. Gordon's mother cried, and then his father did a strange thing. He went up to the attic, got an oil lamp, took it back to the table, and lighted it. He told the children to turn out the electric lights. When there was only the lamp again, they could hardly believe that it had been that dark before.

They wondered how they had ever seen anything without the bright lights made possible by electricity.

The food was blessed, and everyone ate. When dinner was over, they all sat quietly. Wrote Gordon:

"In the humble dimness of the old lamp we were beginning to see clearly again. . . .

"It [was] a lovely meal. The jack rabbit tasted like turkey and the turnips were the mildest we could recall. . . .

" . . . [Our] home, for all its want, was so rich [to] us."[13]

My brothers and sisters, to express gratitude is gracious and honorable, to enact gratitude is generous and noble, but to live with gratitude ever in our hearts is to touch heaven.

As I close this morning, it is my prayer that in addition to all else for which we are grateful, we may ever reflect our gratitude for our Lord and Savior, Jesus Christ. His glorious gospel provides answers to life's greatest questions: Where did we come from? Why are we here? Where do our spirits go when we die? That gospel brings to those who live in darkness the light of divine truth.

He taught us how to pray. He taught us how to live. He taught us how to die. His life is a legacy of love. The sick He healed; the downtrodden He lifted; the sinner He saved.

Ultimately, He stood alone. Some Apostles doubted; one betrayed Him. The Roman soldiers pierced His side. The angry mob took His life. There yet rings from Golgotha's hill His compassionate words, "Father, forgive them; for they know not what they do."[14]

Who is this "man of sorrows, . . . acquainted with grief"?[15] "Who is this King of glory,"[16] this Lord of lords? He is our Master. He is our Savior. He is the Son of God. He is the Author of Our Salvation. He beckons, "Follow me."[17] He instructs, "Go, and do thou likewise."[18] He pleads, "Keep my commandments."[19]

Let us follow Him. Let us emulate His example. Let us

obey His words. By so doing, we give to Him the divine gift of gratitude.

My sincere, heartfelt prayer is that we may, in our individual lives, reflect that marvelous virtue of gratitude. May it permeate our very souls, now and evermore. In the sacred name of Jesus Christ, our Savior, amen.

NOTES

1. John Thompson, "Birthday Party," *Teaching Little Fingers to Play* (1936), 8.
2. Luke 17:11–19.
3. *Teachings of Gordon B. Hinckley* (1997), 250.
4. Matthew 15:33–37; emphasis added.
5. *The Discourses of Epictetus; with the Encheiridion and Fragments,* trans. George Long (1888), 429.
6. Doctrine and Covenants 59:7, 21.
7. Alma 34:38.
8. Cicero, in *A New Dictionary of Quotations on Historical Principles,* sel. H. L. Mencken (1942), 491; from "Pro Plancio," 54 B.C.
9. Joseph F. Smith, *Gospel Doctrine,* 5th ed. (1939), 263.
10. Aldous Huxley, *Themes and Variations* (1954), 66.
11. William H. Davies, *The Autobiography of a Super-Tramp* (1908), 4.
12. William Arthur Ward, in Allen Klein, comp., *Change Your Life!* (2010), 15.
13. Adapted from H. Gordon Green, "The Thanksgiving I Don't Forget," *Reader's Digest,* November 1956, 69–71.
14. Luke 23:34.
15. Isaiah 53:3.
16. Psalm 24:8.
17. Matthew 4:19.
18. Luke 10:37.
19. John 14:15.

14

PRIESTHOOD POWER

General Conference Priesthood Session
April 2, 2011

Brethren, IT HAS BEEN GOOD for us to be together this evening. We've heard wonderful and timely messages concerning the priesthood of God. I, with you, have been uplifted and inspired.

Tonight I wish to address matters which have been much on my mind of late and which I have felt impressed to share with you. In one way or another, they all relate to the personal worthiness required to receive and exercise the sacred power of the priesthood which we hold.

May I begin by reading to you from section 121 of the Doctrine and Covenants:

"The rights of the priesthood are inseparably connected with the powers of heaven, and . . . the powers of heaven cannot be controlled nor handled only upon the principles of righteousness.

"That they may be conferred upon us, it is true; but when we undertake to cover our sins, or to gratify our pride, our vain ambition, or to exercise control or dominion or compulsion upon the souls of the children of men, in any degree of unrighteousness, behold, the heavens withdraw themselves; the Spirit of the Lord is grieved; and when it is withdrawn, Amen to the priesthood or the authority of that man."[1]

Brethren, that is the definitive word of the Lord concerning His divine authority. We cannot be in doubt as to the obligation this places upon each of us who bears the priesthood of God.

We have come to the earth in troubled times. The moral compass of the masses has gradually shifted to an "almost anything goes" position.

I've lived long enough to have witnessed much of the metamorphosis of society's morals. Where once the standards of the Church and the standards of society were mostly compatible, now there is a wide chasm between us, and it's growing ever wider.

Many movies and television shows portray behavior which is in direct opposition to the laws of God. Do not subject yourself to the innuendo and outright filth which are so often found there. The lyrics in much of today's music fall in the same category. The profanity so prevalent around us today would never have been tolerated in the not-too-distant past. The Lord's name is taken in vain over and over again. Recall with me the commandment—one of the ten—which the Lord revealed to Moses on Mt. Sinai: "Thou shalt not take the name of the Lord thy God in vain; for the Lord will not hold him guiltless that taketh his name in vain."[2] I am sorry that any of us is subjected to profane language, and I plead with you not to use it. I implore you not to say or to do anything of which you cannot be proud.

Stay completely away from pornography. Do not allow yourself to view it, ever. It has proven to be an addiction which is more than difficult to overcome. Avoid alcohol and tobacco or any other drugs, also addictions which you would be hard pressed to conquer.

What will protect you from the sin and evil around you? I maintain that a strong testimony of our Savior and of His gospel will help see you through to safety. If you have not read the Book of Mormon, read it. If you do so prayerfully and with a sincere desire to know the truth, the Holy Ghost will manifest its truth to you. If it is true—and it *is*—then Joseph Smith was a prophet who saw God the Father and His Son Jesus Christ. The Church is true. If you do not already have a testimony of these things, do that which is necessary to obtain one. It is essential for you to have your own testimony, for the testimonies of others will carry you only so far. Once obtained, a testimony needs to be kept vital and alive through obedience to the commandments of God and through regular prayer and scripture study. Attend church. You young men, attend seminary or institute if such is available to you.

Should there be anything amiss in your life, there is open to you a way out. Cease any unrighteousness. Talk with your bishop. Whatever the problem, it can be worked out through proper repentance. You can become clean once again. Said the Lord, speaking of those who repent, "Though your sins be as scarlet, they shall be as white as snow,"[3] "and I, the Lord, remember them no more."[4]

The Savior of mankind described himself as being in the world but not of the world.[5] We, also, can be in the world but not of the world as we reject false concepts and false teachings and remain true to that which God has commanded.

Now, I have thought a lot lately about you young men who are of an age to marry but who have not yet felt to do so. I see lovely young ladies who desire to be married and to raise families, and yet their opportunities are limited because so many young men are postponing marriage.

This is not a new situation. Much has been said concerning this matter by past presidents of the Church. I share with you just one or two examples of their counsel.

Said President Harold B. Lee, "We are not doing our duty as holders of the priesthood when we go beyond the marriageable age and withhold ourselves from an honorable marriage to these lovely women."[6]

President Gordon B. Hinckley said this: "My heart reaches out to . . . our single sisters, who long for marriage and cannot seem to find it. . . . I have far less sympathy for the young men, who under the customs of our society have the prerogative to take the initiative in these matters but in so many cases fail to do so."[7]

I realize there are many reasons why you may be hesitating to take that step of getting married. If you are concerned about providing financially for a wife and family, may I assure you that there is no shame in a couple having to scrimp and save. It is generally during these challenging times that you will grow closer together as you learn to sacrifice and to make difficult decisions. Perhaps you are afraid of making the wrong choice. To this I say that you need to exercise faith. Find someone with whom you can be compatible. Realize that you will not be able to anticipate every challenge which may arise, but be assured that almost anything can be worked out if you are resourceful and if you are committed to making your marriage work.

Perhaps you are having a little too much fun being single, taking extravagant vacations, buying expensive cars and toys and just generally enjoying the carefree life with your friends. I've encountered groups of you running around together, and I admit that I've wondered why you aren't out with fine young ladies.

Brethren, there is a point at which it's time to think seriously about marriage and to seek a companion with whom you want to spend eternity. If you choose wisely, and if you are committed to the success of your marriage, there is nothing in this life which will bring you greater happiness.

When you marry, you will wish to marry in the house of the Lord. For you who hold the priesthood, there should be no other option. Be careful, lest you destroy your eligibility to be so married. You can keep your courtship within proper bounds while still having a wonderful time.

Now, brethren, I turn to another subject about which I feel impressed to address you. In the three years since I was sustained as President of the Church, I believe the saddest and most discouraging responsibility I have is the handling of cancellations of sealings. Each one was preceded by a joyous marriage in the house of the Lord, where a loving couple was beginning a new life together and looking forward to spending the rest of eternity with each other. And then months and years go by and, for one reason or another, love dies. It may be the result of financial problems, lack of communication, uncontrolled tempers, interference from in-laws, entanglement in sin. There are any number of reasons. In most cases, divorce does not have to be the outcome.

The vast majority of requests for cancellations of sealings come from women who tried desperately to make a go of the marriage but who, in the final analysis, could not overcome the problems.

Choose a companion carefully and prayerfully; and when you are married, be fiercely loyal one to another. Priceless advice comes from a small framed plaque I once saw in the home of an uncle and aunt. It read: "Choose your love; love your choice." There is great wisdom in those few words. Commitment in marriage is absolutely essential.

Your wife is your equal. In marriage neither partner is superior nor inferior to the other. You walk side by side as a son and a daughter of God. She is not to be demeaned or insulted but should be respected and loved. Said President Gordon B. Hinckley, "Any man in this Church who . . . exercises unrighteous dominion over [his wife] is unworthy to hold the priesthood. Though he may have been ordained, the heavens will withdraw, the Spirit of the Lord will be grieved, and it will be amen to the authority of the priesthood of that man."[8]

President Howard W. Hunter said this about marriage: "Being happily and successfully married is generally not so much a matter of marrying the right person as it is *being the right person*. . . . The conscious effort to do one's part fully is the greatest element contributing to success."[9]

Many years ago in the ward over which I presided as the bishop, there lived a couple who often had very serious, very heated disagreements. Each of the two was certain of his or her position. Neither would yield to the other. When they weren't arguing, they maintained what I would call an "uneasy truce."

One morning at two A.M. I had a telephone call from the couple. They wanted to talk to me, and they wanted to talk right then. I dragged myself from bed, dressed and went to their home. They sat on opposite sides of the room, not speaking to each other. The wife communicated with her husband by talking to me. He replied to her by talking to me. I thought, "How in the world are we going to get this couple together?"

I prayed for inspiration, and the thought came to me to ask them a question. I said, "How long has it been since you have been to the temple and witnessed a temple sealing?" They admitted it had been a long time. They were otherwise worthy people who held temple recommends and who went to the temple and did ordinance work for others.

I said to them, "Will you come with me to the temple on Wednesday morning at eight o'clock? We will witness a sealing ceremony there." In unison they asked, "Whose ceremony?" I responded, "I don't know. It will be for whomever is getting married that morning."

On the following Wednesday at the appointed hour we met at the Salt Lake Temple. The three of us went into one of the beautiful sealing rooms, not knowing a soul in the room except Elder ElRay L. Christiansen, then an Assistant to the Quorum of the Twelve, a general authority position which existed at that time. Elder Christiansen was scheduled to perform a sealing ceremony for a bride and groom in that room that morning. I am confident the bride and her family thought, "These must be friends of the groom," and that the groom's family thought, "These must be friends of the bride." My couple was seated on a little bench with about a foot of space between them.

Elder Christiansen began by providing counsel to the couple who were being married, and he did so in a beautiful fashion. He mentioned how a husband should love his wife, how he should treat her with respect and courtesy, honoring her as the heart of the home. Then he talked to the bride about how she should honor her husband as the head of the home and be of support to him in every way.

I noticed that as Elder Christiansen spoke to the bride and the groom, my couple moved a little closer together. Soon they were seated right next to one another. What pleased me is that they had both moved at about the same rate. By the end of the ceremony, my couple were sitting as close to each other as though *they* were the newlyweds. Each was smiling.

We left the temple that day and no one ever knew who we were or why we had come, but my friends were holding hands as they walked out the front door. Their differences had been set aside. I had not had to say one word. You see, they remembered their own wedding day and the covenants they had made in the house of God. They were committed to beginning again and trying harder this time around.

If any of you is having difficulty in your marriage, I urge you to do all that you can to make whatever repairs are necessary, that you might be as happy as you were when your marriage started out. We who are married in the house of the Lord do so for time and for all eternity, and then we must put forth the necessary effort to make it so. I realize that there are situations where marriages cannot be saved, but I feel strongly that for the most part they can be and should be. Do not let your marriage get to the point where it is in jeopardy.

It is up to each of us who holds the priesthood of God to discipline ourselves so that we stand above the ways of the world. It is essential, however, that we be honorable and decent men. Our actions must be above reproach.

The words we speak, the way we treat others and the way we live our lives all impact our effectiveness as men and boys holding the priesthood.

The gift of the priesthood is priceless. It carries with it the authority to act as God's servants, to administer to the sick, to bless our families and to bless others as well. Its authority can reach beyond the veil of death, on into the eternities. There is nothing else to compare with it in all this world. Safeguard it, treasure it, live worthy of it.

My beloved brethren, may righteousness guide our every step as we journey through life. Today and always may we be worthy recipients of the divine power of the priesthood we bear. May it bless our lives, and may we use it to bless the lives of others, as did He who lived and died for us—even Jesus Christ, our Lord and Savior. This is my prayer, in His sacred and holy name, amen.

NOTES

1. Doctrine and Covenants 121:36–37.
2. Exodus 20:7.
3. Isaiah 1:18.
4. Doctrine and Covenants 58:42.
5. See Doctrine and Covenants 49:5; John 17:14.
6. "President Harold B. Lee's General Priesthood Address," *Ensign*, January 1974, 100.
7. "What God Hath Joined Together," *Ensign*, May 1991, 71.
8. "Personal Worthiness to Exercise the Priesthood," *Ensign*, May 2002, 54.
9. *The Teachings of Howard W. Hunter*, Clyde J. Williams, ed. (1997), 130; emphasis in original.

15

THE HOLY TEMPLE—A BEACON TO THE WORLD

General Conference Sunday Morning Session
April 3, 2011

$\mathbf{M}$Y BELOVED BROTHERS AND SISTERS, I extend my love and greetings to each of you and pray that our Heavenly Father will guide my thoughts and inspire my words as I speak to you today.

May I begin by making a comment or two concerning the fine messages we have heard this morning from Sister Allred and Bishop Burton pertaining to the Church's welfare program. As indicated, this year marks the 75th anniversary of this inspired program which has blessed the lives of so many. It was my privilege to know personally some of those who pioneered this great endeavor—men of compassion and foresight.

As both Bishop Burton and Sister Allred mentioned, the bishop of the ward is given the responsibility to care for those in need who reside within the boundaries of his ward. Such was my privilege when I presided as a young bishop in Salt Lake City over a ward of 1,080 members, including 84 widows. There were many who needed assistance. How grateful I was for the welfare program of the Church and for the help of the Relief Society and the priesthood quorums.

I declare that the welfare program of The Church of Jesus Christ of Latter-day Saints is inspired of Almighty God.

Now my brothers and sisters, this conference marks three years since I was sustained as President of the Church. Of course they have been busy years, filled with many challenges but also with countless blessings. The opportunity I have had to dedicate and rededicate temples has been among the most enjoyable and sacred of these blessings, and it is concerning the temple that I wish to speak to you today.

During the October general conference in 1902, Church President Joseph F. Smith expressed in his opening address the hope that one day we would have "temples built in the various parts of the [world] where they are needed for the convenience of the people."[1]

During the first 150 years following the organization of the Church, from 1830 to 1980, 21 temples were built, including the temples in Kirtland, Ohio, and Nauvoo, Illinois. Contrast that with the 30 years since 1980 during which 115 temples were built and dedicated. With the announcement yesterday of three new temples, there are additionally 26 temples either under construction or in pre-construction stages. These numbers will continue to grow.

The goal President Joseph F. Smith hoped for in 1902 is becoming a reality. Our desire is to make the temple as accessible as possible to our members.

One of the temples currently under construction is in Manaus, Brazil. Many years ago I read of a group of over a hundred members who left Manaus, located in the heart of the Amazon rain forest, to travel to what was then the closest temple, located in São Paulo, Brazil—nearly twenty-five hundred miles from Manaus. Those faithful Saints journeyed by boat for four days on the Amazon River and its tributaries. After completing this journey by water, they boarded buses for another three days of travel over bumpy roads, with very little to eat and with nowhere comfortable to sleep. After seven days and nights, they arrived at the temple in São Paulo, where ordinances eternal in nature were performed. Of course their return journey was just as difficult. However, they had received the ordinances and blessings of the temple, and although their purses were empty, they, themselves, were filled with the spirit of the temple and with gratitude for the blessings they had received.[2] Now, many years later, our members in Manaus are rejoicing as they watch their own temple take shape on the banks of the Rio Negro River. Temples bring joy to our faithful members wherever they are built.

Reports of the sacrifices made in order to receive the blessings found only in temples of God never fail to touch my heart and bring to me a renewed sense of thankfulness for temples.

May I share with you the account of Tihi and Tararaina Mou Tham and their ten children. The entire family joined the Church in the early 1960s when missionaries came to their island, located about one hundred miles south of Tahiti. Soon they began to desire the blessings of an eternal family sealing in the temple.

At that time, the nearest temple to the Mou Tham family was the Hamilton New Zealand Temple, more than twenty-five hundred miles to the southwest, accessible only by expensive airplane travel. The large Mou Tham family, which eked out a meager living on a small plantation, had no money for airplane fare, nor was there any opportunity for employment on their Pacific island. So Brother Mou Tham and his son Gerard made the difficult decision to join another son who was working in the nickel mines of New Caledonia, three thousand miles to the west. The employer provided his employees paid passage to the mines but provided no transportation back home.

The three Mou Tham men labored for four years in the tropical nickel mines, digging and loading the heavy ore.

117

Brother Mou Tham alone returned home for a brief visit once a year, leaving his sons in New Caledonia.

After four years of backbreaking labor, Brother Mou Tham and his sons had saved enough money to take the family to the New Zealand temple. All went except for one daughter. They were sealed for time and eternity, an indescribable and joyful experience.

Brother Mou Tham returned from the temple directly to New Caledonia, where he worked for two more years to pay for the passage of the one daughter who had not been at the temple with them—a married daughter and her child and husband.

In their later years, Brother and Sister Mou Tham desired to serve in the temple. By that time the Papeete Tahiti Temple had been constructed and dedicated, and they served two missions there.[3]

My brothers and sisters, temples are more than stone and mortar. They are filled with faith and fasting. They are built of trials and testimonies. They are sanctified by sacrifice and service.

The first temple to be built in this dispensation was the temple at Kirtland, Ohio. The Saints at the time were impoverished, and yet the Lord had commanded that a temple be built, so build it they did. Wrote Elder Heber C. Kimball of the experience, "The Lord only knows the scenes of poverty, tribulation, and distress which we passed through to accomplish it."[4] And then, after all that had been painstakingly completed, the Saints were forced to leave Ohio and their beloved temple. They eventually found refuge—although it would be temporary—on the banks of the Mississippi River in the state of Illinois. They named their settlement Nauvoo and, willing to give their all once again, and with their faith intact, they erected another temple to their God. Persecutions raged, however, and with the Nauvoo Temple barely completed, they were driven from their homes once again, seeking refuge in a desert place no one else wanted.

The struggle and the sacrifice began once again as they labored for forty years to erect the Salt Lake Temple, which stands majestically on the block just south of those of us who are here today in the Conference Center.

Some degree of sacrifice has ever been associated with temple building and with temple attendance. Countless are those who have labored and struggled in order to obtain for themselves and for their families the blessings which are found in the temples of God.

Why are so many willing to give so much in order to receive the blessings of the temple? Those who understand the eternal blessings which come from the temple know that no sacrifice is too great, no price too heavy, no struggle too difficult in order to receive those blessings. There are never too many miles to travel, too many obstacles to overcome or too much discomfort to endure. They understand that the saving ordinances received in the temple that permit us to someday return to our Heavenly Father in an eternal family relationship and to be endowed with blessings and power from on high are worth every sacrifice and every effort.

Today most of us do not have to suffer great hardships in order to attend the temple. Eighty-five percent of the membership of the Church now live within two hundred miles of a temple, and for a great many of us, that distance is much shorter.

If you have been to the temple for yourselves, and if you live within relatively close proximity to a temple, your sacrifice could be setting aside the time in your busy lives to visit the temple regularly. There is much to be done in our temples in behalf of those who wait beyond the veil. As we do the work for them, we will know that we have accomplished what they cannot do for themselves. President Joseph F. Smith, in a mighty

119

declaration, stated: "Through our efforts in their behalf their chains of bondage will fall from them, and the darkness surrounding them will clear away, that light may shine upon them and they shall hear in the spirit world of the work that has been done for them by their children here, and will rejoice with you in your performance of these duties."[5] My brothers and sisters, the work is ours to do.

In my own family, some of our most sacred and treasured experiences have occurred when we have joined together in the temple to perform sealing ordinances for our deceased ancestors.

If you have not yet been to the temple, or if you *have* been but currently do not qualify for a recommend, there is no more important goal for you to work toward than being worthy to go to the temple. Your sacrifice may be bringing your life into compliance with what is required to receive a recommend, perhaps by forsaking long-held habits which disqualify you. It may be having the faith and the discipline to pay your tithing. Whatever it is, qualify to enter the temple of God. Secure a temple recommend and regard it as a precious possession, for such it is.

Until you have entered the house of the Lord and have received all the blessings which await you there, you have not obtained everything the Church has to offer. The all-important and crowning blessings of membership in the Church are those blessings which we receive in the temples of God.

Now, my young friends who are in your teenage years, always have the temple in your sights. Do nothing which will keep you from entering its doors and partaking of the sacred and eternal blessings there. I commend those of you who already go to the temple regularly to perform baptisms for the dead, arising in the early hours of the morning so you can participate in such baptisms before school begins. I can think of no better way to start a day.

To you parents of young children, may I share with you some sage advice from President Spencer W. Kimball. Said he: "It . . . would be a fine thing if . . . parents would have in every bedroom in their house a picture of the temple so [their children], from the time [they are] infants, could look at the picture every day [until] it becomes a part of [their] life. When [they] reach the age that [they] need to make [the] very important decision [concerning going to the temple], it will have already been made."[6]

Our children sing in Primary:

> *I love to see the temple,*
> *I'll go inside someday.*
> *I'll cov'nant with my Father;*
> *I'll promise to obey.*[7]

I plead with you to teach your children of the temple's importance.

The world can be a challenging and difficult place in which to live. We are often surrounded by that which would drag us down. As you and I go to the holy houses of God, as we remember the covenants we make within, we will be more able to bear every trial and to overcome each temptation. In this sacred sanctuary we will find peace; we will be renewed and fortified.

Now, my brothers and sisters, may I mention one more temple before I close. In the not-too-distant future, as new temples take shape around the world, one will rise in a city which came into being over twenty-five hundred years ago. I speak of the temple which is now being built in Rome, Italy.

Every temple is a house of God, filling the same functions and with identical blessings and ordinances. The Rome Temple, uniquely, is being built in one of the most historic locations in the world, a city where the ancient apostles Peter and Paul preached the gospel of Christ and where each was martyred.

Last October, as we gathered on a lovely pastoral site in the northeast corner of Rome, it was my opportunity to offer a prayer of dedication as we prepared to break ground. I felt impressed to call upon Italian Senator Lucio Malan and Rome's vice mayor Giuseppe Ciardi to be among the first to turn a shovelful of earth. Each had been a part of the decision to allow us to build a temple in their city.

The day was overcast but warm, and although rain threatened, not more than a drop or two fell. As the magnificent choir sang, in Italian, the beautiful strains of "The Spirit of God," one felt as though heaven and earth were joined in a glorious hymn of praise and gratitude to Almighty God. Tears could not be restrained.

In a coming day, the faithful in this, the "Eternal City," will receive ordinances eternal in nature in a holy house of God.

I express my undying gratitude to my Heavenly Father for the temple now being built in Rome and for all of our temples, wherever they are. Each one stands as a beacon to the world, an expression of our testimony that God our Eternal Father lives, that He desires to bless us and, indeed, to bless His sons and daughters of all generations. Each of our temples is an expression of our testimony that life beyond the grave is as real and as certain as is our life here on earth.

My beloved brothers and sisters, may we make whatever sacrifices are necessary to attend the temple and to have the spirit of the temple in our hearts and in our homes. May we follow in the footsteps of our Lord and Savior, Jesus Christ, who made the ultimate sacrifice for us, that we might have eternal life and exaltation in our Heavenly Father's kingdom, I pray, in the name of Jesus Christ, amen.

NOTES

1. In Conference Report, October 1902, 3.
2. See *Church News*, March 13, 1993, 6.
3. See *Church News*, March 16, 1996, 16.

4. Orson F. Whitney, *Life of Heber C. Kimball,* (1945), 67–68.
5. In Conference Report, October 1916, 6.
6. *The Teachings of Spencer W. Kimball,* ed. Edward L. Kimball (1982), 301.
7. "I Love to See the Temple," *Children's Songbook,* 95.

16

DARE TO STAND ALONE

General Conference Priesthood Session
October 1, 2011

M<small>Y BELOVED BRETHREN</small>, it is a tremendous privilege to be with you tonight. We who hold the priesthood of God form a great bond and brotherhood.

We read in the Doctrine and Covenants, section 121, verse 36, "that the rights of the priesthood are inseparably connected with the powers of heaven." What a wonderful gift we have been given—to hold the priesthood, which is "inseparably connected with the powers of heaven." This precious gift, however, brings with it not only special blessings but also solemn responsibilities. We must conduct our lives so that we are ever worthy of the priesthood we bear. We live in a time when we are surrounded by much that is intended to entice us into paths which may lead to our destruction. To avoid such paths requires determination and courage.

I recall a time—and some of you here tonight will also—when the standards of most people were very similar to our standards. No longer is this true. I recently read an article in *The New York Times* concerning a study which took place during the summer of 2008. A distinguished Notre Dame sociologist led a research team in conducting in-depth interviews with 230 young adults across America. I believe we can safely assume that the results would be similar in most parts of the world.

I share with you just a portion of this very telling article:

"The interviewers asked open-ended questions about right and wrong, moral dilemmas and the meaning of life. In the rambling answers, . . . you see the young people groping to say anything sensible on these matters. But they just don't have the categories or vocabulary to do so.

"When asked to describe a moral dilemma they had faced, two-thirds of the young people either couldn't answer the question or described problems that are not moral at all, like whether they could afford to rent a certain apartment or whether they had enough quarters to feed the meter at a parking spot."

The article continues:

"The default position, which most of them came back to again and again, is that moral choices are just a matter of individual taste. 'It's personal,' the respondents typically said. 'It's up to the individual. Who am I to say?'

"Rejecting blind deference to authority, many of the young people have gone off to the other extreme, [saying]: 'I would do what I thought made me happy or how I felt. I have no other way of knowing what to do but how I internally feel.'"

Those who conducted the interviews emphasized that the majority of the young people with whom they spoke had "not been given the resources—by schools, institutions [or] families—to cultivate their moral intuitions."[1]

Brethren, none within the sound of my voice should be in any doubt concerning what is moral and what is not, nor should any be in doubt about what is expected of us as holders of the priesthood of God. We have been and continue to be taught God's laws. Despite what you may see or hear elsewhere, these laws are unchanging.

As we go about living from day to day, it is almost inevitable

125

that our faith will be challenged. We may at times find ourselves surrounded by others and yet standing in the minority or even standing alone concerning what is acceptable and what is not. Do we have the moral courage to stand firm for our beliefs, even if by so doing we must stand alone? As holders of the priesthood of God, it is essential that we are able to face—with courage—whatever challenges come our way. Remember the words of Tennyson: "My strength is as the strength of ten, because my heart is pure."[2]

Increasingly, some celebrities and others who—for one reason or another—are in the public eye have a tendency to ridicule religion in general and, at times, the Church in particular. If our testimonies are not firmly enough rooted, such criticisms can cause us to doubt our own beliefs or to waver in our resolves.

In Lehi's vision of the tree of life, found in 1 Nephi chapter 8, Lehi sees, among others, those who hold to the iron rod until they come forth and partake of the fruit of the tree of life, which we know is a representation of the love of God. And then, sadly, after they partake of the fruit, some are ashamed because of those in the "great and spacious building," who represent the pride of the children of men, who are pointing fingers at them and scoffing at them; and they fall away into forbidden paths and are lost.[3] What a powerful tool of the adversary is ridicule and mockery! Again, brethren, do we have the courage to stand strong and firm in the face of such difficult opposition?

I believe my first experience in having the courage of my convictions took place when I served in the United States Navy near the end of World War II.

Navy boot camp was not an easy experience for me, nor for anyone who endured it. For the first three weeks I was convinced my life was in jeopardy. The navy wasn't trying to train me; it was trying to kill me.

I shall ever remember when Sunday rolled around after the first week. We received welcome news from the chief petty officer. Standing at attention on the drill ground in a brisk California breeze, we heard his command: "Today everybody goes to church—everybody, that is, except for me. I am going to relax!" Then he shouted, "All of you Catholics, you meet in Camp Decatur—and don't come back until three o'clock. Forward, march!" A rather sizeable contingent moved out. Then he barked out his next command: "Those of you who are Jewish, you meet in Camp Henry—and don't come back until three o'clock. Forward, march!" A somewhat smaller contingent marched out. Then he said, "The rest of you Protestants, you meet in the theaters at Camp Farragut—and don't come back until three o'clock. Forward, march!"

Instantly there flashed through my mind the thought, "Monson, you are not a Catholic; you are not a Jew; you are not a Protestant. You are a Mormon, so you just stand here!" I can assure you that I felt completely alone. Courageous and determined, yes—but alone.

And then I heard the sweetest words I ever heard that chief petty officer utter. He looked in my direction and asked, "And just what do you guys call yourselves?" Until that very moment I had not realized that anyone was standing beside me or behind me on the drill ground. Almost in unison, each of us replied, "Mormons!" It is difficult to describe the joy that filled my heart as I turned around and saw a handful of other sailors.

The chief petty officer scratched his head in an expression of puzzlement but finally said, "Well, you guys go find somewhere to meet. And don't come back until three o'clock. Forward, march!"

As we marched away, I thought of the words of a rhyme I had learned in Primary years before:

> Dare to be a Mormon;
> Dare to stand alone.
> Dare to have a purpose firm;
> Dare to make it known.

Although the experience turned out differently from what I had expected, I had been willing to stand alone, had such been necessary.

Since that day, there have been times when there was no one standing behind me and so I *did* stand alone. How grateful I am that I made the decision long ago to remain strong and true, always prepared and ready to defend my religion, should the need arise.

Lest we at any time feel inadequate for the tasks ahead for us, brethren, may I share with you a statement made in 1987 by then-Church President Ezra Taft Benson as he addressed a large group of members in California. Said President Benson:

"In all ages, prophets have looked down through the corridors of time to our day. Billions of the deceased and those yet to be born have their eyes on us. Make no mistake about it—you are a marked generation. . . .

"For nearly six thousand years, God has held you in reserve to make your appearance in the final days before the second coming of the Lord. Some individuals will fall away; but the kingdom of God will remain intact to welcome the return of its Head—even Jesus Christ.

"While this generation will be comparable in wickedness to the days of Noah, when the Lord cleansed the earth by flood, there is a major difference this time: [it is that] God has saved for the final inning some of His strongest . . . children, who will help bear off the kingdom triumphantly."[4]

Yes, brethren, we represent some of His strongest children. Ours is the responsibility to be worthy of all the glorious blessings our Father in Heaven has in store for us. Wherever we go, our priesthood goes with us. Are we standing in holy places? Please, before you put yourself and your priesthood in jeopardy by venturing into places or participating in activities which are not worthy of you or of that priesthood, pause to consider the consequences. Each of us has had conferred upon him the Aaronic Priesthood. In the process, each received the power which holds the keys to the ministering of angels. Said President Gordon B. Hinckley:

"You cannot afford to do anything that would place a curtain between you and the ministering of angels in your behalf.

"You cannot be immoral in any sense. You cannot be dishonest. You cannot cheat or lie. You cannot take the name of God in vain or use filthy language and still have the right to the ministering of angels."[5]

If any of you has stumbled in your journey, I want you to understand without any question whatsoever that there is a way back. The process is called repentance. Our Savior gave His life to provide you and me that blessed gift. Despite the fact that the repentance path is not easy, the promises are real. We have been told: "Though your sins be as scarlet, they shall be as white as snow."[6] "And I will remember [them] no more."[7] What a statement. What a blessing. What a promise.

There may be those of you who are thinking to yourselves, "Well, I'm not living all the commandments, and I'm not doing everything I should, and yet my life is going along just fine. I think I can have my cake and eat it too." Brethren, I promise you that this will not work in the long run.

Not too many months ago I received a letter from a man who once thought he could have it both ways. He has now repented and has brought his life into compliance with gospel principles and commandments. I want to share with you a paragraph from his letter, for it represents the reality of flawed thinking: "I have had to learn for myself (the hard way) that the Savior was absolutely correct when He said, 'No man can serve two masters: for either he will hate the one, and love the other; or else he will hold to the one, and despise the other. Ye cannot serve God and mammon.'[8] I tried, about as hard as anyone ever has, to do both. In the end, I had all of the emptiness, darkness, and loneliness that Satan provides to those who believe his deceptions, illusions, and lies."

In order for us to be strong and to withstand all the forces pulling us in the wrong direction or all the voices encouraging us to take the wrong path, we must have our own testimony. Whether you are 12 or 112—or anywhere in between—you can know for yourself that the gospel of Jesus Christ is true. Read the Book of Mormon. Ponder its teachings. Ask Heavenly Father if it is true. We have the promise that "if ye shall ask with a sincere heart, with real intent, having faith in Christ, he will manifest the truth of it unto you, by the power of the Holy Ghost."[9]

When we know the Book of Mormon is true, then it follows that Joseph Smith was indeed a prophet and that he saw God the Eternal Father and His Son, Jesus Christ. It also follows that the gospel was restored in these latter days through Joseph Smith—including the restoration of both the Aaronic and Melchizedek Priesthoods.

Once we have a testimony it is incumbent upon us to share that testimony with others. Many of you brethren have served as missionaries throughout the world. Many of you young men will yet serve. Prepare yourselves now for that opportunity. Make certain you are worthy to serve.

If we are prepared to share the gospel, we are ready to respond to the counsel of the Apostle Peter, who urged, "Be ready always to give an answer to every man that asketh you a reason of the hope that is in you."[10]

We will have opportunities throughout our lives to share our beliefs, although we don't always know when we will be called upon to do so. Such an opportunity came to me in 1957, when I worked in the publishing business and was asked to go to Dallas, Texas, sometimes called "the city of churches," to address a business convention. Following the conclusion of the convention, I took a sightseeing bus ride through the city's suburbs. As we passed the various churches, our driver would comment, "On the left you see the Methodist church," or "There on the right is the Catholic cathedral."

As we passed a beautiful red brick building situated upon a hill, the driver exclaimed, "That building is where the Mormons meet." A lady in the rear of the bus called out, "Driver, can you tell us something more about the Mormons?"

The driver pulled the bus over to the side of the road, turned around in his seat, and replied, "Lady, all I know about the Mormons is that they meet in that red brick building. Is there anyone on this bus who knows anything about the Mormons?"

I waited for someone to respond. I gazed at the expression on each person's face for some sign of recognition, some desire to comment. I realized it was up to me to do as the Apostle Peter suggested, to "be ready always to give an answer to every man that asketh you a reason for the hope that is in you." I also realized the truth of the adage "When the time for decision arrives, the time for preparation is past."

For the next 15 or so minutes, I had the privilege of sharing with those on the bus my testimony concerning the Church and our beliefs. I was grateful for my testimony and grateful that I was prepared to share it.

With all my heart and soul, I pray that every man who holds the priesthood will honor that priesthood and be true to the trust which was conveyed when it was conferred. May each of us who holds the priesthood of God know what he believes. May we ever be courageous and prepared to stand for what we believe, and if we must stand alone in the process, may we do so courageously, strengthened by the knowledge that in reality we are never alone when we stand with our Father in Heaven.

As we contemplate the great gift we have been given—"the rights of the priesthood . . . inseparably connected with the powers of heaven"[11]—may our determination ever be to guard and defend it and to be worthy of its great promises. Brethren, may we follow the Savior's instruction to us, found in the book of Third Nephi: "Hold up your light that it may shine unto the world. Behold I am the light which ye shall hold up—that which ye have seen me do."[12]

That we may ever follow that light and hold it up for all the world to see is my prayer and my blessing upon all who hear my voice, in the name of Jesus Christ, amen.

NOTES

1. David Brooks, "If It Feels Right . . . ," *New York Times*, September 12, 2011, nytimes.com.
2. Alfred, Lord Tennyson, "Sir Galahad," in *Poems of the English Race*, sel. Raymond Macdonald Alden (1921), 296 [Stanza 1, Lines 3–4].
3. See 1 Nephi 8:26–28.
4. Ezra Taft Benson, "In His Steps" (Church Educational System fireside, Anaheim, California, February 8, 1987); see also "In His Steps," in *1979 Devotional Speeches of the Year: BYU Devotional and Fireside Addresses* (1980), 59.
5. Gordon B. Hinckley, "Personal Worthiness to Exercise the Priesthood," *Ensign*, May 2002, 52.
6. Isaiah 1:18.
7. Jeremiah 31:34.
8. Matthew 6:24.
9. Moroni 10:4.
10. 1 Peter 3:15.
11. Doctrine and Covenants 121:36.
12. 3 Nephi 18:24.

17

STAND IN HOLY PLACES

General Conference Sunday Morning Session
October 2, 2011

M𝚈 BELOVED BROTHERS AND SISTERS, we have heard fine messages this morning, and I commend each who has participated. We're particularly delighted to have Elder Robert D. Hales with us once again and feeling improved. We love you, Bob.

As I have pondered what I would like to say to you this morning, I have felt impressed to share certain thoughts and feelings which I consider to be pertinent and timely. I pray that I may be guided in my remarks.

I have lived on this earth for 84 years now. To give you a little perspective, I was born the same year Charles Lindbergh flew the first solo nonstop flight from New York to Paris in a single-engine, single-seat monoplane. Much has changed during the 84 years since then. Man has long since been to the moon and back. In fact, yesterday's science fiction has become today's reality. And that reality, thanks to the technology of our times, is changing so fast we can barely keep up with it—if we do at all. For those of us who remember dial telephones and manual typewriters, today's technology is more than merely amazing.

133

Also evolving at a rapid rate has been the moral compass of society. Behaviors which once were considered inappropriate and immoral are now not only tolerated but also viewed by ever so many as acceptable.

I recently read in the *Wall Street Journal* an article by Jonathan Sacks, Britain's chief rabbi. Among other things, he writes: "In virtually every Western society in the 1960s there was a moral revolution, an abandonment of its entire traditional ethic of self-restraint. All you need, sang the Beatles, is love. The Judeo-Christian moral code was jettisoned. In its place came [the adage]: *[Do] whatever works for you.* The Ten Commandments were rewritten as the Ten Creative Suggestions."

Rabbi Sacks goes on to lament, "We have been spending our moral capital with the same reckless abandon that we have been spending our financial capital. . . . There are large parts of [the world] where religion is a thing of the past and there is no counter-voice to the culture of buy it, spend it, wear it, flaunt it, because you're worth it. The message is that morality is passé, conscience is for wimps, and the single overriding command is 'Thou shalt not be found out.'"[1]

My brothers and sisters, this—unfortunately—describes much of the world around us. Do we wring our hands in despair and wonder how we'll ever survive in such a world? No. Indeed, we have in our lives the gospel of Jesus Christ, and we know that morality is not passé, that our conscience is there to guide us, and that we are responsible for our actions.

Although the world has changed, the laws of God remain constant. They have not changed; they will not change. The Ten Commandments are just that—commandments. They are *not* suggestions. They are every bit as requisite today as they were when God gave them to the children of Israel. If we but listen, we hear the echo of God's voice, speaking to us, here and now:

Thou shalt have no other gods before me.

Thou shalt not make unto thee any graven image.

Thou shalt not take the name of the Lord thy God in vain.

Remember the sabbath day, to keep it holy.

Honor thy father and thy mother.

Thou shalt not kill.

Thou shalt not commit adultery.

Thou shalt not steal.

Thou shalt not bear false witness.

Thou shalt not covet.[2]

Our code of conduct is definitive; it is not negotiable. It is found not only in the Ten Commandments but also in the Sermon on the Mount, given to us by the Savior when He walked upon the earth. It is found throughout His teachings. It is found in the words of modern revelation.

Our Father in Heaven is the same yesterday, today, and forever. The prophet Mormon tells us that God is "unchangeable from all eternity to all eternity."[3] In this world where nearly everything seems to be changing, His constancy is something on which we can rely, an anchor to which we can hold fast and be safe, lest we be swept away into uncharted waters.

It may appear to you at times that those out in the world are having much more fun than you are. Some of you may feel restricted by the code of conduct to which we in the Church adhere. My brothers and sisters, I declare to you, however, that there is *nothing* which can bring more joy into our lives or more peace to our souls than the spirit which can come to us as we follow the Savior and keep the commandments. That spirit cannot be present at the kinds of activities in which so much of the world participates. The Apostle Paul declared the truth, "The natural man receiveth not the things of the Spirit of God: for they are foolishness unto him: neither can he know them, because they are spiritually discerned."[4] The term "natural man" can refer to any of us if we allow ourselves to be so. We must be vigilant in a world which has moved so far from that which is spiritual. It is essential that we reject anything that does not conform to our standards, refusing in the process to surrender that which we desire most—eternal life in the kingdom of God. The storms will still beat at our doors from time to time, for they are an inescapable part of our experience in mortality. We, however, will be far better equipped to deal with them, to learn from them and to overcome them if we have the gospel at our core and the love of the Savior in our hearts. The prophet Isaiah declared, "The work of righteousness shall be peace; and the effect of righteousness quietness and assurance for ever."[5]

As a means of being *in* the world but not being *of* the world, it is necessary that we communicate with our Heavenly Father through prayer. He wants us to do so; He'll answer our prayers. The Savior admonished us, as recorded in Third Nephi, chapter 18, to "Watch and pray always lest ye enter into temptation; for Satan desireth to have you. . . . Therefore ye must always pray unto the Father in my name; and whatsoever ye shall ask the Father in my name, which is right, believing that ye shall receive, behold it shall be given unto you."[6]

I gained my testimony of the power of prayer when I was about 12 years old. I had worked hard to earn some money and had managed to save five dollars. This was during the Great Depression, when five dollars was a substantial sum of money— especially for a boy of 12. I gave all my coins, which totaled five dollars, to my father, and he gave me in return a five-dollar bill. I know there was something specific I planned to purchase with the five dollars, although all these years later I can't recall what it was. I just remember how important that money was to me.

At the time we did not own a washing machine, so my mother would send to the laundry each week our clothes which needed to be washed. After a couple of days, a load of what we called "wet wash" would be returned to us, and Mother would hang the items on our clothesline out back to dry.

I had tucked my five-dollar bill into the pocket of my jeans and, as you can probably guess, my jeans were sent to the laundry with the money still in the pocket. When I realized what had happened, I was sick with worry. I knew that pockets were routinely checked at the laundry prior to washing. If my money were not discovered and taken during that process, I knew it was almost certain the money would be dislodged during washing and would be claimed by a laundry worker who would have no idea to whom the money should be returned, even if he had the inclination to do so. The chances of getting my five dollars back were extremely remote—a fact which my dear mother confirmed when I told her I had left the money in my pocket.

I wanted that money; I needed that money; I had worked very hard to earn that money. I realized there was only one thing I could do. In my extremity I turned to my Father in Heaven and pleaded with Him to keep my money safe in that pocket somehow until our wet wash came back.

Two very long days later, when I knew it was about time for the delivery truck to bring our wash, I sat by the window waiting. As the truck pulled up to the curb, my heart was pounding. As soon as the wet clothes were in the house, I grabbed my jeans and ran to my bedroom. I reached into the pocket with trembling hands. When I didn't find anything immediately, I thought all was lost. And then my fingers touched that wet five-dollar bill. As I pulled it from the pocket, relief flooded over me. I offered a heartfelt prayer of gratitude to my Father in Heaven, for I knew that He had answered my prayer.

Since that time I have had countless prayers answered. Not a day has gone by that I have not communicated with my Father in Heaven through prayer. It is a relationship I cherish—one I would literally be lost without. If you do not now have such a relationship with your Father in Heaven, I urge you to work toward that goal. As you do so, you will be entitled to His inspiration and guidance in your life—necessities for each of us if we are to survive spiritually during our sojourn here on earth. Such inspiration and guidance are gifts He freely gives if we but seek them. What treasures they are!

I am always humbled and grateful when my Heavenly Father communicates with me through His inspiration. I have learned to recognize it, to trust it, and to follow it. Time and time again I have been the recipient of such inspiration. One rather dramatic experience took place in August of 1987 during the dedication of the Frankfurt Germany Temple. President Ezra Taft Benson had been with us for the first day or two of the dedication but had returned home, and so it became my opportunity to conduct the remaining sessions.

On Saturday we had a session for our Dutch members who were in the Frankfurt Temple district. I was well acquainted with one of our outstanding leaders from the Netherlands, Brother Peter Mourik. Just prior to the session, I had the distinct impression that Brother Mourik should be called upon to speak to his fellow Dutch members during the session and that, in fact, he should be the first speaker. Not having seen him in the temple that morning, I passed a note to Elder Carlos E. Asay, our Area President, asking whether Peter Mourik was in attendance at the session. Just prior to standing up to begin the session, I received a note back from Elder Asay indicating that Brother Mourik was actually *not* in attendance, that he was involved elsewhere and that he was planning to attend the dedicatory session in the temple the following day with the servicemen stakes.

As I stood at the pulpit to welcome the people and to outline the program, I received unmistakable inspiration once again that I was to announce Peter Mourik as the first speaker. This was counter to all my instincts, for I had just heard from Elder Asay that Brother Mourik was definitely *not* in the temple. Trusting in the inspiration, however, I announced the choir presentation, the prayer, and then indicated that our first speaker would be Brother Peter Mourik.

As I returned to my seat, I glanced toward Elder Asay and saw on his face a look of alarm. He later told me that when I had announced Brother Mourik as the first speaker, he couldn't believe his ears. He said he knew that I had received his note and that I indeed had read it, and he couldn't fathom why I would then announce Brother Mourik as a speaker, knowing he wasn't anywhere in the temple.

During the time all of this was taking place, Peter Mourik was in a meeting at the Area Offices in Porthstrasse. As his meeting was going forward, he suddenly turned to Elder Hawkes, who was then the Regional Representative, and asked, "How fast can you get me to the temple?"

Elder Hawkes, who was known to drive rather rapidly in his small sports car, answered, "I can have you there in ten minutes! But why do you need to go to the temple?"

Brother Mourik admitted he did not know why he needed to go to the temple, but that he knew he had to get there. The two of them set out for the temple immediately.

During the magnificent choir number, I glanced around, thinking that at any moment I would see Peter Mourik. I did not. Remarkably, however, I felt no alarm. I had a sweet, undeniable assurance that all would be well.

Brother Mourik entered the front door of the temple just as the opening prayer was concluding, still not knowing why he was there. As he hurried down the hall, he saw my image on the monitor and heard me announce, "We will now hear from Brother Peter Mourik."

To the astonishment of Elder Asay, Peter Mourik immediately walked into the room and took his place at the podium.

Following the session, Brother Mourik and I discussed that which had taken place prior to his opportunity to speak. I have pondered the inspiration which came that day not only to me but also to Brother Peter Mourik. That remarkable experience has provided an undeniable witness to me of the importance of being worthy to receive such inspiration and then trusting it—and following it—when it comes. I know without question that the Lord intended for those who were present at that session of the Frankfurt Temple Dedication to hear the powerful, touching testimony of His servant, Brother Peter Mourik.

My beloved brothers and sisters, communication with our Father in Heaven—including our prayers to Him and His inspiration to us—is necessary in order for us to weather the storms and trials of life. The Lord invites us: "Draw near unto me and I will draw near unto you; seek me diligently and ye shall find me."[7] As we do so, we will feel His spirit in our lives, providing us the desire and the courage to stand strong and firm in righteousness—to "stand . . . in holy places, and be not moved."[8]

As the winds of change swirl around us and the moral fiber of society continues to disintegrate before our very eyes, may we remember the Lord's precious promises to those who trust in Him: "Fear thou not; for I am with thee: be not dismayed; for I am thy God: I will strengthen thee; yea, I will help thee; yea, I will uphold thee with the right hand of my righteousness."[9]

May such be our blessing, I pray, in the sacred name of our Lord and Savior, Jesus Christ, amen.

NOTES

1. Jonathan Sacks, *The Wall Street Journal,* August 20, 2011. Lord Sacks is the chief rabbi of the United Hebrew Congregations of the Commonwealth.
2. See Exodus 20:3, 4, 7, 8, 12–17.
3. Moroni 8:18.
4. 1 Corinthians 2:14.
5. Isaiah 32:17.
6. 3 Nephi 18:18–20.
7. Doctrine and Covenants 88:63.
8. Doctrine and Covenants 87:8.
9. Isaiah 41:10.

18

WILLING AND WORTHY
TO SERVE

General Conference Priesthood Session
March 31, 2012

MY BELOVED BRETHREN, how good it is to meet with you once again. Whenever I attend the general priesthood meeting, I reflect on the teachings of some of the most noble of God's leaders who have spoken in the general priesthood meetings of the Church. Many have passed to their eternal reward, and yet from the brilliance of their minds, from the depths of their souls, and from the warmth of their hearts they have given us inspired direction. I share with you tonight some of their teachings concerning the priesthood.

From the Prophet Joseph Smith: "Priesthood is an everlasting principle, and existed with God from eternity, and will to eternity, without beginning of days or end of years."[1]

From the words of President Wilford Woodruff we learn: "The Holy Priesthood is the channel through which God communicates and deals with man upon the earth; and the heavenly messengers that have visited the earth to communicate with man are men who held and honored the priesthood while in the flesh; and everything that God has caused to be done for the salvation of man, from the coming of man upon the earth to the redemption of the world, has been and will be by virtue of the everlasting priesthood."[2]

President Joseph F. Smith further clarified: "The priesthood is . . . the power of God delegated to man by which man can act in the earth for the salvation of the human family, in the name of the Father and the Son and the Holy Ghost, and act legitimately; not assuming that authority, not borrowing it from generations that are dead and gone, but authority that has been given in this day in which we live by ministering angels and spirits from above, *direct from the presence of Almighty God.*"[3]

And finally from President John Taylor: "What is the priesthood? It is the Government of God, whether on earth or in the heavens, for it is by that power, agency, or principle that all things are governed on earth and in the heavens, and by that power that all things are upheld and sustained. It governs all things—it directs all things—it sustains all things—and has to do with all things that God and truth are associated with."[4]

How blessed we are to be here in these last days, when the priesthood of God is upon the earth. How privileged we are to bear that priesthood. The priesthood is not so much a gift as it is a commission to serve, a privilege to lift, and an opportunity to bless the lives of others.

With these opportunities come responsibilities and duties. I love and cherish the noble word *duty* and all that it implies.

In one capacity or another, in one setting or another, I have been attending priesthood meetings for the past 72 years—since I was ordained a deacon at the age of 12. Time certainly marches on. Duty keeps cadence with that march. Duty does not dim nor diminish. Catastrophic conflicts come and go, but the war waged for the souls of men continues without abatement. Like a clarion call comes the word of the Lord to you, to me, and to priesthood holders everywhere: "Wherefore, now let every man learn his duty, and to act in the office in which he is appointed, in all diligence."[5]

The call of duty came to Adam, to Noah, to Abraham, to Moses, to Samuel, to David. It came to the Prophet Joseph Smith and to each of his successors. The call of duty came to the boy Nephi when he was instructed by the Lord, through his father Lehi, to return to Jerusalem with his brothers to obtain the brass plates from Laban. Nephi's brothers murmured, saying it was a hard thing which had been asked of them. What was Nephi's response? Said he, "I will go and do the things which the Lord hath commanded, for I know that the Lord giveth no commandments unto the children of men, save he shall prepare a way for them that they may accomplish the thing which he commandeth them."[6]

When that same call comes to you and to me, what will be our response? Will we murmur, as did Laman and Lemuel, and say, "This is a hard thing required of us"? Or will we, with Nephi, individually declare, "I will go. I will do"? Will we be willing to serve and to obey?

At times the wisdom of God appears as being foolish or just too difficult, but one of the greatest and most valuable lessons we can learn in mortality is that when God speaks and a man obeys, that man will always be right.

When I think of the word *duty* and how performing our duty can enrich our lives and the lives of others, I recall the words penned by a renowned poet and author:

> *I slept and dreamt*
> *That life was joy.*
> *I awoke and saw*
> *That life was duty.*
> *I acted, and behold—*
> *Duty was joy.*[7]

Robert Louis Stevenson put it another way. Said he: "I know what pleasure is, for I have done good work."

As we perform our duties and exercise our priesthood, we

will find true joy. We will experience the satisfaction of having completed our tasks.

We have been taught the specific duties of the priesthood which we hold, whether it be the Aaronic or the Melchizedek Priesthood. I urge you to contemplate those duties and then do all within your power to fulfill them. In order to do so, each must be worthy. Let us have ready hands, clean hands, and willing hands, that we may participate in providing what our Heavenly Father would have others receive from Him. If we are not worthy, it is possible to lose the power of the priesthood, and if we lose it, we have lost the essence of exaltation. Let us be worthy to serve.

President Harold B. Lee, one of the great teachers in the Church, said: "When one becomes a holder of the priesthood, he becomes an agent of the Lord. He should think of his calling as though he were on the Lord's errand."[8]

During World War II, in the early part of 1944, an experience involving the priesthood took place as United States marines were taking Kwajalein Atoll, part of the Marshall Islands and located in the Pacific Ocean about midway between Australia and Hawaii. What took place in this regard was related by a correspondent—not a member of the Church—who worked for a newspaper in Hawaii. In the 1944 newspaper article he wrote following the experience, he explained that he and other correspondents were in the second wave behind the marines at Kwajalein Atoll. As they advanced, they noticed a young marine floating face down in the water, obviously badly wounded. The shallow water around him was red with his blood. And then they noticed another marine moving toward his wounded comrade. The second marine was also wounded, with his left arm hanging helplessly by his side. He lifted up the head of the one who was floating in the water in order to keep him from drowning. In a panicky voice he called for help. The correspondents looked again at the boy he was supporting and called back, "Son, there is nothing anyone can do for this boy."

"Then," wrote the correspondent, "I saw something that I had never seen before. This boy, badly wounded himself, made his way to the shore with the seemingly lifeless body of his fellow marine. He put the head of his companion on his knee. What a picture that was—these two mortally wounded boys—both . . . clean, wonderful-looking young men, even in their distressing situation. And the one boy bowed his head over the other and said, 'I command you, in the name of Jesus Christ and by the power of the priesthood, to remain alive until I can get medical help.'" The correspondent concluded his article, "The three of us, [the two marines and I], are here in the hospital. The doctors don't know . . . [how they made it alive], but I know."[9]

Miracles are everywhere to be found when the priesthood is understood, its power is honored and used properly, and faith is exerted. When faith replaces doubt, when selfless service eliminates selfish striving, the power of God brings to pass His purposes.

The call of duty can come quietly as we who hold the priesthood respond to the assignments we receive. President George Albert Smith, that modest but effective leader, declared, "It is your duty first of all to learn what the Lord wants and then by the power and strength of His holy Priesthood to magnify your calling in the presence of your fellows in such a way that the people will be glad to follow you."[10]

Such a call of duty—a much less dramatic call but one which nonetheless helped to save a soul—came to me in 1950 when I was a newly called bishop. My responsibilities as a bishop were many and varied, and I tried to the best of my ability to do all that was required of me. The United States was engaged in a different war by then. Because many of our members were serving in the armed services, an assignment came from Church headquarters for all bishops to provide each serviceman a subscription to the *Church News* and the *Improvement Era,* the Church's magazine at that time. In addition, each bishop was asked to write a personal, monthly letter to each serviceman from his ward. Our ward had 23 men in uniform. The priesthood quorums, with effort, supplied the funds for the subscriptions to the publications. I undertook the task, even the duty, to write 23 personal letters each month. After all these years I still have copies of many of my letters and the responses received. Tears come easily when these letters are reread. It is a joy to learn again of a soldier's pledge to live the gospel, a sailor's decision to keep faith with his family.

One evening I handed to a sister in the ward the stack of 23 letters for the current month. Her assignment was to handle the mailing and to maintain the constantly changing address list. She glanced at one envelope and, with a smile, asked, "Bishop, don't you ever get discouraged? Here is another letter to Brother Bryson. This is the seventeenth letter you have sent to him without a reply."

I responded, "Well, maybe this will be the month." As it turned out, that *was* the month. For the first time, he responded to my letter. His reply is a keepsake, a treasure. He was serving far away on a distant shore, isolated, homesick, alone. He wrote: "Dear Bishop, I ain't much at writin' letters." (I could have told him *that* several months earlier.) His letter continued, "Thank you for the *Church News* and magazines, but most of all thank you for the personal letters. I have turned over a new leaf. I have been ordained a priest in the Aaronic Priesthood. My heart is full. I am a happy man."

Brother Bryson was no happier than was his bishop. I had learned the practical application of the adage, "Do your duty; that is best. Leave unto the Lord the rest."

Years later, while attending the Salt Lake Cottonwood Stake when James E. Faust served as its president, I related that account in an effort to encourage attention to our servicemen. After the meeting, a fine-looking young man came forward. He took my hand in his and asked, "Bishop Monson, do you remember me?"

I suddenly realized who he was. "Brother Bryson!" I exclaimed. "How are you? What are you doing in the Church?"

With warmth and obvious pride, he responded, "I'm fine. I serve in the presidency of my elders quorum. Thank you again for your concern for me and the personal letters which you sent and which I treasure."

Brethren, the world is in need of our help. Are we doing all we should? Do we remember the words of President John Taylor: "If you do not magnify your callings, God will hold you responsible for those whom you might have saved had you done your duty"?[11]

There are feet to steady, hands to grasp, minds to encourage, hearts to inspire, and souls to save. The blessings of eternity await you. Yours is the privilege to be not spectators but participants on the stage of priesthood service. Let us hearken to the stirring reminder found in the epistle of James: "Be ye doers of the word, and not hearers only, deceiving your own selves."[12]

Let us learn and contemplate our duty. Let us be willing and worthy to serve. Let us in the performance of our duty follow in the footsteps of the Master. As you and I walk the pathway Jesus walked, we will discover He is more than the Babe in Bethlehem, more than the carpenter's son, more than the greatest teacher ever to live. We will come to know Him as the Son of God, our Savior and our Redeemer. When to Him came the call of duty, He answered, "Father, thy will be done, and the glory be thine forever."[13] May each of us do likewise, I pray, in His holy name, amen.

NOTES

1. *Teachings of Presidents of the Church: Joseph Smith* (2007), 104.
2. *Teachings of Presidents of the Church: Wilford Woodruff* (2004), 38.
3. Joseph F. Smith, *Gospel Doctrine,* 5th ed. (1939), 139–40; emphasis added.
4. *Teachings of Presidents of the Church: John Taylor* (2001), 119.
5. Doctrine and Covenants 107:99.
6. See 1 Nephi 3:1–7.
7. Rabindranath Tagore, in William Jay Jacobs, *Mother Teresa: Helping the Poor* (1991), 42.
8. Harold B. Lee, *Stand Ye in Holy Places* (1974), 255.
9. In Ernest Eberhard, Jr., "Giving Our Young Men the Proper Priesthood Perspective," typescript, July 19, 1971, 4–5, Church History Library.
10. In Conference Report, April 1942, 14.
11. *Teachings: John Taylor,* 164.
12. James 1:22.
13. Moses 4:2.

19

THE RACE OF LIFE

General Conference Sunday Morning Session
April 1, 2012

My beloved brothers and sisters, this morning I wish to speak to you of eternal truths—those truths which will enrich our lives and see us safely home.

Everywhere, people are in a hurry. Jet-powered aircraft speed their precious human cargo across broad continents and vast oceans so that business meetings might be attended, obligations met, vacations enjoyed or family visited. Roadways everywhere—including freeways, thruways and motorways—carry millions of automobiles, occupied by more millions of people, in a seemingly endless stream and for a multitude of reasons as we rush about the business of each day.

In this fast-paced life do we ever pause for moments of meditation—even thoughts of timeless truths?

When compared to eternal verities, most of the questions and concerns of daily living are really rather trivial. What should we have for dinner? What color should we paint the living room? Should we sign Johnny up for soccer? These questions and countless others like them lose their significance when times of crisis arise, when loved ones are hurt or injured, when sickness enters the house of good health, when life's candle dims and darkness threatens. Our thoughts become focused, and we are easily able to determine what is really important and what is merely trivial.

I recently visited with a woman who has been battling a life-threatening disease for over two years. She indicated that prior to her illness, her days were filled with activities such as cleaning her house to perfection and filling it with beautiful furnishings. She visited her hairdresser twice a week and spent money and time each month adding to her wardrobe. Her grandchildren were invited to visit infrequently, for she was always concerned that what she considered her precious possessions might be broken or otherwise ruined by tiny and careless hands.

And then she received the shocking news that her mortal life was in jeopardy and that she might have very limited time left here. She said that at the moment she heard the doctor's diagnosis, she knew immediately that she would spend whatever time she had remaining with her family and friends and with the gospel at the center of her life, for these represented what was most precious to her.

Such moments of clarity come to all of us at one time or another, although not always through so dramatic a circumstance. We see clearly what it is that really matters in our lives and how we should be living.

Said the Savior, "Lay not up for yourselves treasures upon earth, where moth and rust doth corrupt, and where thieves break through and steal: But lay up for yourselves treasures in heaven, where neither moth nor rust doth corrupt, and where thieves do not break through nor steal: For where your treasure is, there will your heart be also."[1]

In our times of deepest reflection or greatest need, the soul of man reaches heavenward, seeking a divine response to life's greatest questions: *Where did we come from? Why are we here? Where do we go after we leave this life?*

Answers to these questions are not discovered within the covers of academia's textbooks or by checking the Internet. These questions transcend mortality. They embrace eternity.

Where did we come from? This query is inevitably thought, if not spoken, by every human being.

The Apostle Paul told the Athenians on Mars' Hill that we are "the offspring of God."[2] Since we know that our physical bodies are the offspring of our mortal parents, we must probe for the meaning of Paul's statement. The Lord has declared that "the spirit and the body are the soul of man."[3] Thus it is the spirit which is the offspring of God. The writer of Hebrews refers to Him as "the Father of spirits."[4] The spirits of all men are literally His "begotten sons and daughters."[5]

We note that inspired poets have, for our contemplation of this subject, written moving messages and recorded transcendent thoughts. William Wordsworth penned the truth:

> *Our birth is but a sleep and a forgetting;*
> *The soul that rises with us, our life's star,*
> *Hath had elsewhere its setting,*
> *And cometh from afar:*
> *Not in entire forgetfulness,*
> *And not in utter nakedness,*
> *But trailing clouds of glory do we come*
> *From God, who is our home:*
> *Heaven lies about us in our infancy!*[6]

Parents ponder their responsibility to teach, to inspire, and to provide guidance, direction, and example. And while parents ponder, children—and particularly youth—ask the penetrating question: "Why are we here?" Usually it is spoken silently to the soul and phrased: "Why am *I* here?"

How grateful we should be that a wise Creator fashioned an

earth and placed us here, with a veil of forgetfulness of our previous existence, so that we might experience a time of testing, an opportunity to prove ourselves in order to qualify for all that God has prepared for us to receive.

Clearly, one primary purpose of our existence upon the earth is to obtain a body of flesh and bones. We have also been given the gift of agency. In a thousand ways we are privileged to choose for ourselves. Here we learn from the hard taskmaster of experience. We discern between good and evil. We differentiate as to the bitter and the sweet. We discover that there are consequences attached to our actions.

By obedience to God's commandments we can qualify for that "house" spoken of by Jesus when He declared: "In my Father's house are many mansions. . . . I go to prepare a place for you . . . that where I am, there ye may be also."[7]

Although we come into mortality "trailing clouds of glory," life moves relentlessly forward. Youth follows childhood, and maturity comes ever so imperceptibly. From experience we learn the need to reach heavenward for assistance as we make our way along life's pathway.

God, our Father, and Jesus Christ, our Lord, have marked the way to perfection. They beckon us to follow eternal verities and to become perfect, as they are perfect.[8]

The Apostle Paul likened life to a race. To the Hebrews he urged: "Let us lay aside . . . the sin which doth so easily beset us, and let us run with patience the race that is set before us."[9]

In our zeal, let us not overlook the sage counsel from Ecclesiastes: "The race is not to the swift, nor the battle to the strong."[10] Actually, the prize belongs to him who endures to the end.

When I reflect on the race of life, I remember another type of race, even from childhood days. My friends and I would take pocketknives in hand and, from the soft wood of a willow tree, fashion small toy boats. With a triangular-shaped cotton sail in place, each would launch his crude craft in the race down the relatively turbulent waters of Utah's Provo River. We would run along the river's bank and watch the tiny vessels sometimes bobbing violently in the swift current and at other times sailing serenely as the water deepened.

During a particular race, we noted that one boat led all the rest toward the appointed finish line. Suddenly, the current carried it too close to a large whirlpool, and the boat heaved to its side and capsized. Around and around it was carried, unable to make its way back into the main current. At last it came to an uneasy rest amid the flotsam and jetsam that surrounded it, held fast by the tentacles of the grasping, green moss.

The toy boats of childhood had no keel for stability, no rudder to provide direction, and no source of power. Inevitably their destination was downstream—the path of least resistance.

Unlike toy boats, we have been provided divine attributes to guide our journey. We enter mortality not to float with the moving currents of life, but with the power to think, to reason, and to achieve.

Our Heavenly Father did not launch us on our eternal voyage without providing the means whereby we could receive from Him guidance to ensure our safe return. I speak of prayer. I speak, too, of the whisperings from that still, small voice; and I do not overlook the holy scriptures, which contain the word of the Lord and the words of the prophets—provided to us to help us successfully cross the finish line.

At some period in our mortal mission, there appears the faltering step, the wan smile, the pain of sickness—even the fading of summer, the approach of autumn, the chill of winter, and the experience we call death.

Every thoughtful person has asked himself the question best phrased by Job of old: "If a man die, shall he live again?"[11]

Try as we might to put the question out of our thoughts, it always returns. Death comes to all mankind. It comes to the aged as they walk on faltering feet. Its summons is heard by those who have scarcely reached midway in life's journey. At times it hushes the laughter of little children.

But what of an existence beyond death? Is death the end of all? Robert Blatchford, in his book *God and My Neighbor*, attacked with vigor accepted Christian beliefs, such as God, Christ, prayer, and particularly immortality. He boldly asserted that death was the end of our existence and that no one could prove otherwise. Then a surprising thing happened. His wall of skepticism suddenly crumbled to dust. He was left exposed and undefended. Slowly he began to feel his way back to the faith he had ridiculed and abandoned. What had caused this profound change in his outlook? His wife died. With a broken heart, he went into the room where lay all that was mortal of her. He looked again at the face he loved so well. Coming out, he said to a friend, "It is she, and yet it is not she. Everything is changed. Something that was there before is taken away. She is not the same. What can be gone if it be not the soul?"

Later he wrote: "Death is not what some people imagine. It is only like going into another room. In that other room we shall find . . . the dear women and men and the sweet children we have loved and lost."[12]

My brothers and sisters, we know that death is not the end. This truth has been taught by living prophets throughout the ages. It is also found in our holy scriptures. In the Book of Mormon we read specific and comforting words: "Now, concerning the state of the soul between death and the resurrection—Behold, it has been made known unto me by an angel, that the spirits of all men, as soon as they are departed from this mortal body, yea, the spirits of all men, whether they be good or evil, are taken home to that God who gave them life.

"And then shall it come to pass, that the spirits of those who are righteous are received into a state of happiness, which is called paradise, a state of rest, a state of peace, where they shall rest from all their troubles and from all their care, and sorrow."[13]

After the Savior was crucified and his body had lain in the tomb for three days, the spirit again entered. The stone was rolled away, and the resurrected Redeemer walked forth clothed with an immortal body of flesh and bones.

The answer to Job's question, "If a man die, shall he live again?" came when Mary and others approached the tomb and saw two men in shining garments who spoke to them: "Why seek ye the living among the dead? He is not here, but is risen."[14]

As the result of Christ's victory over the grave, we shall all be resurrected. This is the redemption of the soul. Paul wrote: "There are . . . celestial bodies, and bodies terrestrial: but the glory of the celestial is one, and the glory of the terrestrial is another."[15]

It is the celestial glory which we seek. It is in the presence of God we desire to dwell. It is a forever family in which we want membership. Such blessings are earned through a lifetime of striving, seeking, repenting and finally succeeding.

Where did we come from? Why are we here? Where do we go after this life? No longer need these universal questions remain unanswered. From the depths of my soul, and in all humility, I testify that those things of which I have spoken are true.

Our Heavenly Father rejoices for those who keep His commandments. He is concerned also for the lost child, the tardy teenager, the wayward youth, the delinquent parent. Tenderly the Master speaks to these, and indeed to all: "Come back. Come up. Come in. Come home. Come unto me."

In one week we will celebrate Easter. Our thoughts will turn to the Savior's life, His death and His resurrection. As His special witness, I testify to you that He lives and that He awaits our triumphant return. That such a return will be ours, I pray in His holy name—even Jesus Christ, our Savior and Redeemer, amen.

NOTES

1. Matthew 6:19–21.
2. Acts 17:29.
3. Doctrine and Covenants 88:15.
4. Hebrews 12:9.
5. Doctrine and Covenants 76:24.
6. William Wordsworth, *Ode: Intimations of Immortality from Recollections of Early Childhood* (1884), 23–24.
7. John 14:2–3.
8. See Matthew 5:48; 3 Nephi 12:48.
9. Hebrews 12:1.
10. Ecclesiastes 9:11.
11. Job 14:14.
12. See *More Things in Heaven and Earth: Adventures in Quest of a Soul* (1925), 11.
13. Alma 40:11–12.
14. Luke 24:5–6.
15. 1 Corinthians 15:40.

SECTION TWO

OTHER CLASSIC MESSAGES

The Blessings of Service

20

ANONYMOUS

I ONCE APPROACHED THE RECEPTION desk of a large hospital to learn the room number of a patient I had come to visit. This hospital, like almost every other in the land, was undergoing a massive expansion. Behind the desk where the receptionist sat was a magnificent plaque which bore an inscription of thanks to donors who had made possible the expansion. The name of each donor who had contributed $100,000 appeared in a flowing script, etched on an individual brass placard suspended from the main plaque by a glittering chain.

The names of the benefactors were well-known. Captains of commerce, giants of industry, professors of learning—all were there. I felt gratitude for their charitable benevolence. Then my eyes rested on a brass placard which was different—it contained no name. One word, and one word only, was inscribed: "Anonymous." I smiled and wondered who the unnamed contributor could have been. Surely he or she experienced a quiet joy unknown to any other.

My thoughts turned backward in time—back to the Holy Land; back to Him who redeemed from the grave all mankind;

161

back to Him who on that special mountain taught His disciples the true spirit of giving when He counseled, "Take heed that ye do not your alms before men, to be seen of them. . . .

"But when thou doest alms, let not thy left hand know what thy right hand doeth."[1]

Then, as though to indelibly impress on their souls the practical application of this sacred truth, He came down from the mountain with a great multitude following Him. "And, behold, there came a leper and worshipped him, saying, Lord, if thou wilt, thou canst make me clean.

"And Jesus put forth his hand, and touched him, saying, I will; be thou clean. And immediately his leprosy was cleansed.

"And Jesus saith unto him, See thou tell no man."[2] The word *anonymous* had a precious meaning then. It still has.

The classics of literature, as well as the words from holy writ, teach us the endurability of anonymity. A favorite of mine is Charles Dickens's *Christmas Carol.* I can picture the trembling Ebenezer Scrooge seeing in vision the return of his former partner, Jacob Marley, though Jacob had been dead for seven years. The words of Marley penetrate my very soul, as he laments, "Not to know that any Christian spirit working kindly in its little sphere, whatever it may be, will find its mortal life too short for its vast means of usefulness. Not to know that no space of regret can make amends for one life's opportunities misused! Yet such was I!"

After a fretful night—wherein Scrooge was shown by the Ghost of Christmas Past, the Ghost of Christmas Present, and the Ghost of Christmas Yet to Come the true meaning of living, loving, and giving—he awakened to discover anew the freshness of life, the power of love, and the spirit of a true gift. He remembered the plight of the Bob Cratchit family, arranged with a lad to purchase the giant turkey (the size of a boy), and sent the gift to the Cratchits. Then, with supreme joy, the reborn Ebenezer Scrooge exclaims to himself, "He shan't know who sends it." Again the word *anonymous*.

The sands flow through the hourglass, the clock of history moves on; yet the divine truth prevails undiminished, undiluted, unchanged.

When the magnificent ocean liner *Lusitania* plunged to the bottom of the Atlantic, many lives were lost with the vessel. Unknown are many deeds of valor performed by those who perished. One man who went down with the *Lusitania* gave his life preserver to a woman, though he could not swim a stroke. It didn't really matter that he was Alfred Vanderbilt, the American multimillionaire. He did not give of worldly treasure; he gave his life. Said Emerson, "Rings and other jewels are not gifts, but apologies for gifts. The only gift is a portion of thyself."[3]

On another occasion, a modern jetliner faltered after take-off and plunged into the icy Potomac River. Acts of bravery and feats of heroism were in evidence that day, the most dramatic of which was one witnessed by the pilot of a rescue helicopter. The rescue rope was lowered to a struggling survivor. Rather than grasping the lifeline to safety, the man tied the line to another, who was then lifted to safety. The rope was lowered again, and yet another was saved. Five were rescued from the icy waters. Among them was not found the anonymous hero. Unknown by name, he "left the vivid air signed with [his] honor."[4]

It is not only in dying that one can show forth the true gift. Opportunities abound in our daily lives to demonstrate our adherence to the Master's lesson. Let me share in capsule form just three:

(1) On a winter's morn, a father quietly awakened his two sons and whispered to them, "Boys, it snowed last night. Get dressed, and we'll shovel the snow from our neighbors' walks before daylight."

The party of three, dressed warmly, and under cover of darkness, cleared the snow from the approaches to several homes. Father had given but one instruction to the boys: "Make no noise, and they will not know who helped them." Again, the word *anonymous*.

(2) At a nursing home in our valley, two young men prepared the sacrament. While doing so, an elderly patient in a wheelchair spoke aloud the words, "I'm cold." Without a moment's hesitation, one of the young men walked over to her, removed his own jacket, placed it about the patient's shoulders, gave her a loving pat on the arm, and then returned to the sacrament table. The sacred emblems were then blessed and passed to the assembled patients.

Following the meeting, I said to the young man, "What you did here today I shall long remember."

He replied, "I worried that without my jacket I would not be properly dressed to bless the sacrament."

I responded, "Never was one more properly dressed for such an occasion than were you."

I know not his name. He remains anonymous.

(3) In far-off Europe, beyond a curtain of iron and a wall called "Berlin," I visited, with a handful of members, a small cemetery. It was a dark night, and a cold rain had been falling throughout the entire day.

We had come to visit the grave of a missionary who many years before had died while in the service of the Lord. A hushed silence shrouded the scene as we gathered about the grave. With a flashlight illuminating the headstone, I read the inscription:

Joseph A. Ott
Born: 12 December 1870—Virgin, Utah
Died: 10 January 1896—Dresden, Germany

Then the light revealed that this grave was unlike any other in the cemetery. The marble headstone had been polished, weeds such as those which covered other graves had been carefully removed, and in their place was an immaculately edged bit of lawn and some beautiful flowers that told of tender and loving care. I asked, "Who has made this grave so attractive?" My query was met by silence.

At last a 12-year-old deacon acknowledged that he had wanted to render this unheralded kindness and, without prompting from parents or leaders, had done so. He said that he just wanted to do something for a missionary who gave his life while in the service of the Lord. I thanked him; and then I asked all there to safeguard his secret, that his gift might remain anonymous.

Perhaps no one in my reading has portrayed this teaching of the Master quite so memorably or so beautifully as Henry Van Dyke in his never-to-be-forgotten "The Mansion." In this classic is featured one John Weightman, a man of means, a dispenser of political power, a successful citizen. His philosophy toward giving can be gained from his own statement: "Of course you have to be careful how you give, in order to secure the best results—no indiscriminate giving—no pennies in beggars' hats! . . . Try to put your gifts where they can be identified and do good all around."[5]

One evening, John Weightman sat in his comfortable chair at his library table and perused the papers before him spread. There were descriptions and pictures of the Weightman wing of the hospital and the Weightman Chair of Political Jurisprudence, as well as an account of the opening of the Weightman Grammar School. John Weightman felt satisfied.

He picked up the family Bible which lay on the table, turned to a passage and read to himself the words: "Lay not up for yourselves treasures upon earth, where moth and rust doth corrupt, and where thieves break through and steal:

"But lay up for yourselves treasures in heaven."[6]

The book seemed to float away from him. He leaned

forward upon the table, his head resting on his folded hands. He slipped into a deep sleep.

In his dream, John Weightman was transported to the Heavenly City. A guide met him and others whom he had known in life and advised that he would conduct them to their heavenly homes.

The group paused before a beautiful mansion and heard the guide say, "This is the home for you, Dr. McLean. Go in; there is no more sickness here, no more death, nor sorrow, nor pain; for your old enemies are all conquered. But all the good that you have done for others, all the help that you have given, all the comfort that you have brought, all the strength and love that you bestowed upon the suffering, are here; for we have built them all into this mansion for you."[7]

A devoted husband of an invalid wife was shown a lovely mansion, as were a mother, early widowed, who reared an outstanding family, and a paralyzed young woman who had lain for 30 years upon her bed—helpless but not hopeless—succeeding by a miracle of courage in her single aim: never to complain, but always to impart a bit of her joy and peace to everyone who came near her.

By this time, John Weightman was impatient to see what mansion awaited him. As he and the Keeper of the Gate walked on, the homes became smaller—then smaller. At last they stood in the middle of a dreary field and beheld a hut, hardly big enough for a shepherd's shelter. Said the guide, "This is your mansion, John Weightman."

In desperation, John Weightman argued, "Have you not heard that I have built a schoolhouse; a wing of a hospital; . . . three . . . churches."

"Wait," the guide cautioned. " . . . They were not ill done. But they were all marked and used as foundations for the name and mansion of John Weightman in the world. . . . Verily, you have had your reward for them. Would you be paid twice?"

A sadder but wiser John Weightman spoke more lowly: "What is it that counts here?"

Came the reply, "Only that which is truly given. Only that good which is done for the love of doing it. Only those plans in which the welfare of others is the master thought. Only those labors in which the sacrifice is greater than the reward. Only those gifts in which the giver forgets himself."[8]

John Weightman was awakened by the sound of the clock chiming the hour of seven. He had slept the night through. As it turned out, he yet had a life to live, love to share, and gifts to give.

May we look upward as we press forward in the service of our God and our fellowmen. And may we incline an ear toward Galilee, that we might hear perhaps an echo of the Savior's teachings: "Do not your alms before men, to be seen of them."[9] "Let not thy left hand know what thy right hand doeth."[10] And of our good deeds: "See thou tell no man."[11] Our hearts will then be lighter, our lives brighter, and our souls richer.

Loving service anonymously given may be unknown to man—but the gift and the giver are known to God. Of this truth I testify.

NOTES

1. Matthew 6:1, 3.
2. Matthew 8:2–4.
3. "Gifts," in *The Complete Writings of Ralph Waldo Emerson* (1929), 286.
4. Stephen Spender, "I think continually of those—" in James Dalton Morrison, ed., *Masterpieces of Religious Verse* (1948), 291.
5. "The Mansion," in *Unknown Quantity: A Book of Romance and Some Half-told Tales* (1918), 337, 339.
6. Matthew 6:19–20.
7. "The Mansion," 361–62.
8. "The Mansion," 364–68.
9. Matthew 6:1.
10. Matthew 6:3.
11. Matthew 8:4.

21

THE LONG LINE OF THE LONELY

TODAY I DESIRE TO PREACH no sermon or deliver no formal message. Rather, may I simply share with you my innermost thoughts. President David O. McKay referred to such as "heart petals." I open to your view a window to my soul.

The Epistle of James has long been a favorite book of the Holy Bible. I find his brief message heartwarming and filled with life. Each of us can quote that well-known passage, "If any of you lack wisdom, let him ask of God, that giveth to all men liberally, and upbraideth not; and it shall be given him."[1] How many of us, however, remember his definition of religion? "Pure religion and undefiled before God and the Father is this, To visit the fatherless and widows in their affliction, and to keep himself unspotted from the world."[2]

The word *widow* appears to have had a most significant meaning to our Lord. He cautioned His disciples to beware the example of the scribes, who feigned righteousness by their long apparel and their lengthy prayers, but who devoured the houses of widows.[3]

To the Nephites came the direct warning, "I will come near

to you to judgment; and I will be a swift witness against . . . those that oppress the . . . widow."[4]

To the Prophet Joseph Smith He directed, "The storehouse shall be kept by the consecrations of the church; and widows and orphans shall be provided for, as also the poor."[5]

Such teachings were not new then. They are not new now. Consistently the Master has taught, by example, His concern for the widow. To the grieving widow at Nain, bereft of her only son, He came personally and to the dead son restored the breath of life—and to the astonished widow her son. To the widow at Zarephath, who with her son faced imminent starvation, He sent the prophet Elijah with the power to teach faith as well as provide food.

We may say to ourselves, "But that was long ago and ever so far away." I respond, "Is there a city called Zarephath near your home? Is there a town known as Nain?" We may know our cities as Columbus or Coalville, Detroit or Denver. Whatever the name, there lives within each city the widow deprived of her companion and often her child. The need is the same. The affliction is real.

The widow's home is generally not large or ornate. Frequently it is modest in size and humble in appearance. Often it is tucked away at the top of the stairs or the back of the hallway and consists of but one room. To such homes He sends you and me.

There may exist an actual need for food, clothing—even shelter. Such can be supplied. Almost always there remains the hope for that special hyacinth to feed the soul.

> Go gladden the lonely, the dreary;
> Go comfort the weeping, the weary;
> Go scatter kind deeds on your way.
> Oh, make the world brighter today![6]

The ranks of those in special need grow larger day by day. Note the obituary page of your newspaper. Here the drama of life unfolds to our view.

After the funeral flowers fade and the well wishes of friends become memories, the prayers offered and words spoken grow dim in the corridors of the mind. Those who grieve frequently join that vast throng I have entitled "The Long Line of the Lonely." Missed is the laughter of children, the commotion of teenagers, and the tender, loving concern of a departed companion. The clock ticks more loudly, time passes more slowly, and four walls do indeed a prison make.

I think, for example, of Mattie, a dear friend and an older widow whom I had known for many years and whose bishop I had been. Each time I visited her, my heart grieved at her utter loneliness. One of her sons lived many miles away, halfway across the country, but he rarely visited her. He would come to Salt Lake, take care of business matters, see his brothers and sisters, and leave for his home without visiting his mother. When I would call to see this widowed mother, she would make an excuse for her boy and tell me just how busy he was. Her words did not carry power or conviction. They simply masked her disappointment and grief.

The years passed. The loneliness deepened. Then one afternoon I received a telephone call. That special son was in Salt Lake City. A change had occurred in his life. He had become imbued with a desire to help others, to adhere more faithfully to God's commandments. He was proud of his newfound ability to cast off the old man and become new and useful. He wanted to come immediately to my office, that he might share with me the joy in service that he now felt. With all my heart I wanted to welcome him and to extend my personal congratulations. Then I thought of his grieving mother, that lonely widow, and suggested, "Dick, I can see you at four o'clock this afternoon, provided you visit your dear mother before coming here." He agreed.

Just before our appointment, a call came to me. It was that same mother. There was an excitement in her voice that words cannot adequately describe. She exuded enthusiasm even over the phone, and declared proudly, "Bishop, you'll never guess who has just visited me." Before I could answer, she exclaimed, "Dick was here! My son Dick has spent the past hour with me. He is a new man. He has found himself. I'm the happiest mother in the world!" Then she paused and quietly spoke, "I just knew he would not really forget me."

As we resolve to minister more diligently to those in need, let us remember to include our children in these learning lessons of life.

I have many memories of my boyhood days. Anticipating Sunday dinner was one of them. Just as we children hovered at our so-called starvation level and sat anxiously at the table with the aroma of roast beef filling the room, Mother would say to me, "Tommy, before we eat, take this plate I've prepared down the street to Old Bob and hurry back."

I could never understand why we couldn't first eat and later deliver his plate of food. I never questioned aloud but would run down to his house and then wait anxiously as Bob's aged feet brought him eventually to the door. Then I would hand him the plate of food. He would present to me the clean plate from the previous Sunday and offer me a dime as pay for my services. My answer was always the same: "I can't accept the money. My mother would tan my hide." He would then run his wrinkled hand through my blond hair and say, "My boy, you have a wonderful mother. Tell her thank you." You know, I think I never did tell her. I sort of felt Mother didn't need to be told. She seemed to sense his gratitude. I remember, too, that Sunday dinner always seemed to taste a bit better after I had returned from my errand.

171

Old Bob came into our lives in an interesting way. He was a widower in his eighties when the house in which he was living was to be demolished. I heard him tell my grandfather his plight as the three of us sat on the old front porch swing. With a plaintive voice, he said to Grandfather, "Mr. Condie, I don't know what to do. I have no family. I have no place to go. I have no money." I wondered how Grandfather would answer. Slowly Grandfather reached into his pocket and took from it that old leather purse from which, in response to my hounding, he had produced many a penny or nickel for a special treat. This time he removed a key and handed it to Old Bob. Tenderly he said, "Bob, here is the key to that house I own next door. Take it. Move in your things. Stay as long as you like. There will be no rent to pay and nobody will ever put you out again."

Tears welled up in the eyes of Old Bob, coursed down his cheeks, then disappeared in his long, white beard. Grandfather's eyes were also moist. I spoke no word, but that day my grandfather stood ten feet tall. I was proud to bear his given name. Though I was but a boy, that lesson has influenced my life.

Each of us has his own way of remembering. At Christmastime I take delight in visiting the widows and widowers from the ward where I served as bishop. On such visits, I never know what to expect; but this I do know: visits like these provide for me the Christmas spirit, which is, in reality, the Spirit of Christ.

Come with me, and we'll together make a call or two. There's the nursing home on West Temple where four widows reside. You never walk up the pathway but what you notice the parted curtain, as one inside waits hour after hour for the approaching step of a friend. What a welcome! Good times are remembered, perhaps a gift given, a blessing provided; but then it is time to leave. Never could I depart without first responding to the request of a widow almost 100 years of age. Though she was blind, she would say, "Bishop, you're to speak at my funeral and recite from memory Tennyson's poem, 'Crossing the Bar.' Let's hear you do it right now!" I would proceed:

> *Sunset and evening star,*
> *And one clear call for me,*
> *And may there be no moaning of the bar,*
> *When I put out to sea, . . .*
>
> *Twilight and evening bell,*
> *And after that the dark!*
> *And may there be no sadness of farewell,*
> *When I embark;*
>
> *For tho' from out our bourne of Time and Place*
> *The flood may bear me far,*
> *I hope to see my Pilot face to face*
> *When I have crossed the bar.*[7]

Tears came easily, and then, with a smile, she would say, "Tommy, that was pretty good, but see that you do it a wee bit better at the funeral!" I later honored her request.

At another nursing home on First South, we might interrupt, as I did a few years ago, a professional football game. There, before the TV, were seated two widows. They were warmly and beautifully dressed—absorbed in the game. I asked, "Who's winning?" They responded, "We don't even know who's playing, but at least it's company." I sat between those two angels and explained the game of football. I enjoyed the best contest I can remember. I may have missed a meeting, but I harvested a memory.

Let's hurry along to Redwood Road. There is a much larger home here where many widows reside. Most are seated in the well-lighted living room. But in her bedroom, alone, is one on whom I must call. She hasn't spoken a word since a devastating stroke some years ago. But then, who knows what she hears?—so I speak of good times together. There isn't a flicker of recognition, not a word spoken. In fact, an attendant asks if I am aware that this patient hasn't uttered a word for years. It made no difference. Not only had I enjoyed my one-sided conversation with her—I had communed with God.

One evening at Christmastime, my wife and I visited a nursing home facility in Salt Lake City. We looked in vain for a 95-year-old widow whose memory had become clouded and who could not speak a word. An attendant led us in our search, and we found Nell in the dining room. She had eaten her meal; she was sitting silently, staring into space. She did not show us any sign of recognition. As I reached to take her hand, she withdrew it. I noticed that she held firmly to a Christmas greeting card. The attendant smiled and said, "I don't know who sent that card, but she will not lay it aside. She doesn't speak but pats the card and holds it to her lips and kisses it." I recognized the card. It was one my wife, Frances, had sent to Nell the week before. We left the nursing home more filled with the Christmas spirit than when we entered. We kept to ourselves the mystery of that special card and the life it had gladdened and the heart it had touched. Heaven was nearby.

Frequently, the need of the widow is not one of food or shelter but of feeling a part of ongoing events. President Horace Richards of Salt Lake City brought to my office a sweet widow whose husband had passed away during a full-time mission they were serving. President Richards explained that her financial resources were adequate and that she desired to contribute to the Church's General Missionary Fund the proceeds of two insurance policies on the life of her departed husband. I could not restrain my tears when she meekly advised me, "This is what I wish to do. It is what my missionary-minded husband would like." The gift was received and entered as a most substantial donation to missionary service. I saw the receipt made in her name, but I believe in my heart it was also recorded in heaven. I invited her and President Richards to follow me to the unoccupied First Presidency Council room in the Church Administration Building. The room is beautiful and peaceful. I asked this sweet widow to sit in the chair usually occupied by our missionary-minded Church President. I felt he would not mind, for I knew his heart. As she sat ever so humbly in the large leather chair, she gripped each armrest with a hand and declared, "This is one of the happiest days of my life." It was also such for President Richards and for me.

During the administration of President George Albert Smith, there lived in our ward an impoverished widow who cared for her three mature daughters, each of whom was an invalid. They were large in size and almost totally helpless. To this dear woman fell the task to bathe, to feed, to dress, and to care for her girls. Means were limited. Outside help was non-existent. Then came the blow that the house she rented was to be sold. What was she to do? Where would she go? The bishop came to the Church Office Building to inquire if there were some way the house could be purchased. It was so small, the price so reasonable. The request was considered, then denied.

A heartsick bishop was leaving the front door of the building when he met President George Albert Smith. After the exchange of greetings, President Smith inquired, "What brings you to the headquarters building?" He listened carefully as the bishop explained, but said nothing. He then excused himself for a few minutes. He returned wearing a smile and directed, "Go upstairs to the fourth floor. A check is waiting there for you. Buy the house!"

"But the request was denied."

Again he smiled and said, "It has just been reconsidered and approved." The home was purchased. That dear widow lived there and cared for her daughters until each of them had passed away. Then she, too, went home to God and to her heavenly reward.

The leadership of this Church is mindful of the widow, the widower, the lonely. Can we be less concerned?

We remember that during the meridian of time a bright, particular star shone in the heavens. Wise men followed it and found the Christ child. Today wise men still look heavenward and again see a bright, particular star. It will guide you and me to our opportunities. The burden of the downtrodden will be lifted, the cry of the hungry stilled, the lonely heart comforted. And souls will be saved—yours, theirs, and mine.

If we truly listen, we may hear that voice from far away say to us, as it spoke to another, "Well done, thou good and faithful servant."[8]

NOTES

1. James 1:5.
2. James 1:27.
3. See Mark 12:38, 40.
4. 3 Nephi 24:5.
5. Doctrine and Covenants 83:6.
6. Mrs. Frank A. Breck, "Make the World Brighter," in *Best-Loved Poems of the LDS People* (1996), 288.
7. Alfred, Lord Tennyson, "Crossing the Bar," in *Best-Loved Poems of the LDS People* (1996), 61.
8. Matthew 25:21.

22

To the Rescue

Not long ago I read a book entitled *The Somme,* which detailed one of the most devastating battles of World War I. Years ago I stood on a very old bridge which spanned the River Somme as it made its steady but unhurried way through the heartland of France. I realized that many decades had come and gone since the signing of the Armistice of 1918 and the termination of World War I. I tried to imagine what the River Somme had looked like all those years before. I wondered how many thousands of soldiers had crossed the same bridge on which I was standing. Some of those soldiers had come back. For others, the Somme was truly a river of no return, for many of the battlefields took a hideous toll of human life.

I gazed on the acres of neat, white crosses which serve as an unforgettable reminder of those who did not return.

> *In Flanders fields the poppies blow*
> *Between the crosses, row on row,*
> *That mark our place; and in the sky*

The larks, still bravely singing, fly
Scarce heard amid the guns below.

We are the Dead. Short days ago
We lived, felt dawn, saw sunset glow,
Loved and were loved, and now we lie
In Flanders fields.[1]

As a boy I enjoyed reading the account of the "lost battalion." The "lost battalion" was a unit of the 77th Infantry Division in World War I. During the Meuse-Argonne offensive, a major led this battalion through a gap in the enemy lines, but the troops on the flanks were unable to advance. An entire battalion was surrounded. Food and water were short; casualties could not be evacuated. Repeated attacks were hurled back. Notes from the enemy requesting the battalion to surrender were ignored. Newspapers heralded the battalion's tenacity. Men of vision pondered its fate. After a brief but desperate period of total isolation, other units of the 77th Division advanced and relieved the "lost battalion." Correspondents noted in their dispatches that the relieving forces seemed bent on a crusade of love to rescue their comrades in arms. Men volunteered more readily, fought more gallantly, and died more bravely. A fitting tribute echoed from that ageless sermon preached on the Mount of Olives: "Greater love hath no man than this, that a man lay down his life for his friends."[2]

Forgotten is the plight of the "lost battalion." Unremembered is the terrible price paid for its rescue. But let us turn from the past and survey the present. Are there "lost battalions" even today? If so, what is our responsibility to rescue them? Their members may not wear clothes of khaki brown nor march to the sound of drums. But they share the same doubt, feel the same despair and know the same disillusionment that isolation brings.

Consider the "lost battalions" of the aged, the widowed, the sick. All too often they are found in the parched and desolate wilderness of isolation called loneliness. When youth departs, when health declines, when vigor wanes, when the light of hope flickers ever so dimly, the members of these vast "lost battalions" can be succored and sustained by the hand that helps and the heart that knows compassion.

In Brooklyn, New York, there once presided in a branch of the Church a young man who, as a boy of 13 living in Salt Lake City, Utah, led a successful rescue of such persons. He and his companions lived in a neighborhood in which resided many elderly widows of limited means. I was their bishop. All the year long, the boys had saved and planned for a glorious Christmas party. They were thinking of themselves until the Christmas spirit prompted them to think of others. Frank, the future branch president, suggested to his companions that the funds they had accumulated so carefully be used not for the planned party, but rather for the benefit of three elderly widows who resided together. The boys made their plans. As their bishop, I needed but to follow.

With the enthusiasm of a new adventure, the boys purchased a giant roasting chicken, the potatoes, the vegetables, the cranberries, and all that comprises the traditional Christmas feast. To the widows' home they went, carrying their gifts of treasure. Through the snow and up the path to the tumbledown porch they came: a knock at the door, the sound of slow footsteps, and then they met.

In the unmelodic voices characteristic of 13-year-olds, the boys sang "Silent night, holy night; all is calm, all is bright." They then presented their gifts. Angels on that glorious night of long ago sang no more beautifully, nor did wise men present gifts of greater meaning.

I gazed at the faces of those wonderful women and thought to myself: "Somebody's mother." I then looked on the countenances of those noble boys and reflected: "Somebody's son."

THE BLESSINGS OF SERVICE

There then passed through my mind the words of a poem written by Mary Dow Brine:

> *The woman was old and ragged and gray*
> *And bent with the chill of the Winter's day.*
> *The street was wet with a recent snow,*
> *And the woman's feet were aged and slow.*
> *She stood at the crossing and waited long,*
> *Alone, uncared for, amid the throng*
> *Of human beings who passed her by,*
> *Nor heeded the glance of her anxious eye.*
>
> *Down the street, with laughter and shout,*
> *Glad in the freedom of "school let out,"*
> *Came the boys like a flock of sheep,*
> *Hailing the snow piled white and deep.*
> *One paused beside her and whispered low,*
> *"I'll help you cross, if you wish to go? . . .*
> *She's somebody's mother, boys, you know,*
> *For all she's aged, and poor, and slow;*
>
> *"And I hope some fellow will lend a hand*
> *To help my mother, you understand,*
> *If ever she's poor and old and gray,*
> *When her own dear boy is far away."*
> *And "somebody's mother" bowed low her head*
> *In her home that night, and the prayer she said*
> *Was, "God be kind to the noble boy,*
> *Who is somebody's son, and pride and joy."*[3]

There are other "lost battalions" comprised of mothers and fathers, sons and daughters who have, through thoughtless comment, isolated themselves from one another. An account of how such a tragedy was narrowly averted occurred in the life of a lad we shall call Jack.

Throughout Jack's life, he and his father had many serious

arguments. One day, when he was 17, they had a particularly violent one. Jack said to his father: "This is the straw that breaks the camel's back. I'm leaving home, and I shall never return." So saying, he went to the house and packed a bag. His mother begged him to stay, but he was too angry and upset to listen. He left her crying at the doorway.

As he left the yard and was about to pass through the gate, he heard his father call to him: "Jack, I know that a large share of the blame for your leaving rests with me. For this I am deeply sorry. But I want you to know that if you should ever wish to return to our home, you'll always be welcome. And I'll try to be a better father to you. I want you to know that I'll always love you."

Jack said nothing, but went to the bus station and bought a ticket to a distant point. As he sat in the bus watching the miles go by, he commenced to think about the words of his father. He began to realize how much love it had required for his father to do what he had done. Dad had apologized. He had invited him back and had left the words ringing in the summer air, "I love you."

It was then that Jack realized that the next move was up to him. He knew that the only way he could ever find peace with himself was to demonstrate to his father the same kind of maturity, goodness, and love that Dad had demonstrated toward him. Jack got off the bus. He bought a return ticket to home and went back.

He arrived shortly before midnight. He entered the house and turned on the light. There in the rocking chair sat his father, his head in his hands. As he looked up and saw Jack, he rose from the chair and they rushed into each other's arms. Jack often said, "Those last years that I was home were among the happiest of my life."

We could say, "Here was a boy who overnight became a man. Here was a father who, suppressing passion and bridling pride, rescued his son before he became one of that vast "lost battalion" resulting from fractured families and shattered homes. Love was the binding balm. Love—so often felt, so seldom expressed.

From Mt. Sinai there thunders in our ears, "Honor thy father and thy mother."[4] And later, from that same God, the injunction, "Live together in love."[5]

There are additional "lost battalions." Some struggle in the jungles of sin, while others wander in the wilderness of fear or apathy or ignorance. For whatever reason, they have isolated themselves from activity in the Church. And they will almost certainly remain unrescued unless there is awakened in us—the active members of the Church—a desire to rescue and to save.

May I share with you a portion of a letter I received some time ago, written by a man who strayed from the Church. It typifies too many of our members. After describing how he had become inactive, he wrote:

"I had so much and now have so little. I am unhappy and feel as though I am failing in everything. The gospel has never left my heart, even though it has left my life. I ask for your prayers.

"Please don't forget those of us who are out here—the lost Latter-day Saints. I know where the Church is, but sometimes I think I need someone else to show me the way, encourage me, take away my fear and bear testimony to me."

While reading this letter, I returned in my thoughts to a visit to one of the great art galleries of the world—even the famed Victoria and Albert Museum in London. Many of you have, no doubt, visited that very museum. There, exquisitely framed, is a masterpiece painted in 1831 by Joseph Turner. The painting features heavy-laden black clouds and the fury of a turbulent sea portending danger and death. A light from a stranded vessel gleams far off. In the foreground, tossed high by incoming waves of foaming water, is a large lifeboat. The men pull mightily on the oars as the lifeboat plunges into the tempest. On the shore there stand a wife and two children, wet with rain and whipped by wind. They gaze anxiously seaward. In my mind I abbreviated the name of the painting. To me it became "To the Rescue."

Amidst the storms of life, danger lurks; and men and women, boys and girls, find themselves stranded and facing destruction. Who will man the lifeboats, leaving behind the comforts of home and family, and go to the rescue?

When the Master ministered among men, He called fishermen at Galilee to leave their nets and follow Him, declaring, "I will make you fishers of men."[6] May we join the ranks of the "fishers of men" and women, that we might provide whatever help we can.

Ours is the duty to reach out to rescue those who have left the safety of activity, that such might be brought to the table of the Lord to feast on His word and to enjoy the companionship of His spirit and be "no more strangers and foreigners, but fellowcitizens with the saints, and of the household of God."[7]

I have found that two fundamental reasons largely account for a return to activity, for changes of attitudes, of habits, and of actions. First, individuals have been shown their eternal possibilities and have made the decision to achieve them. They can't really long rest content with mediocrity once they see excellence is within their reach.

Second, others have followed the admonition of the Savior and have loved their neighbors as themselves and helped to bring their neighbors' dreams to fulfillment and their ambitions to realization.

The catalyst in this process has been—and will continue to be—the principle of love.

Another principle of truth which can guide us is that people can change. I'm reminded of a famous American prison warden named Clinton T. Duffy, who became the warden at California's San Quentin Prison in 1940. When he was appointed, he began one of the most dramatic housecleaning jobs in prison history. He fired the brutish captain of guards and six of his lieutenants. He closed up a dungeon of airless, lightless, unfurnished, iron-doored stone cells into which convicts were thrown as punishment for even the most trivial offenses. Before he became warden, men were being fed from buckets. He installed a cafeteria and hired a dietitian. To the horror of his staff, he strolled, unarmed, into the prison yard and chatted with convicts. To their infinite surprise, he strolled out again—unharmed. He established a broad program of vocational training. He was the first warden to let prisoners listen to radios in their cells. He encouraged athletics, inaugurated a prison newspaper to which he contributed a regular column, and established the first prison chapter of Alcoholics Anonymous. In cleaning up San Quentin, he became one of the best-known, most admired prison administrators ever. But the most eloquent acclaim came from inside the walls, from the prisoners themselves, who truly respected him.

A critic who knew of Warden Duffy's efforts to rehabilitate the men said to him, "Don't you know that leopards can't change their spots?"

Responded Warden Duffy, "You should know that I don't work with leopards. I work with men, and men change every day."

There are those in every ward or branch who seem to have a special skill and aptitude to penetrate the outer shell and reach the heart. Such was Raymond L. Egan, who served as my counselor in the bishopric. He loved to befriend and activate fathers of families and thereby bring into the fold wives and children as well. This wonderful phenomenon occurred many times right up until Brother Egan departed mortality.

There are also other ways by which one might lift and serve. On one occasion, I was speaking with a retired executive I had known for a long time. I asked him, "Ed, what are you doing in the Church?" He replied, "I have the best assignment in the ward. My responsibility is to help men who are unemployed find permanent employment. This year I have helped 12 of my brethren who were out of work to obtain good jobs. I have never been happier in my entire life." Short in stature, "Little Ed," as we affectionately called him, stood tall that evening as his eyes glistened and his voice quavered. He showed his love by helping those in need. He restored human dignity. He opened doors for those who did not know how to do so themselves.

I believe that those who have the ability to reach out and to lift up have found the formula descriptive of Brother Walter Stover—a man who spent his life in service to others. At Brother Stover's funeral, his son-in-law paid tribute to him in these words: "Walter Stover had the ability to see Christ in every face he encountered, and he treated each person accordingly." Legendary are his acts of compassionate help and his talent to lift heavenward every person whom he met.

Acquire the language of the Spirit. It is not learned from textbooks written by men of letters, nor is it acquired through reading and memorization. The language of the Spirit comes to him who seeks with all his heart to know God and keep His divine commandments. Proficiency in this "language" permits one to breach barriers, overcome obstacles, and touch the human heart.

In a day of danger or a time of trial, such knowledge, such hope, such understanding bring comfort to a troubled soul and a grieving heart. Shadows of despair are dispelled by rays of hope; sorrow yields to joy; and the feeling of being lost in the crowd of life vanishes with the certain knowledge that our Heavenly Father is mindful of us.

In closing, I return to the painting by Turner. In a very real sense, those persons stranded on the vessel which had run aground in the storm-tossed sea are like many of our less-active members who await rescue by those who man the lifeboats. Their hearts yearn for help. Mothers and fathers pray for their sons and daughters. Wives plead to heaven that their husbands may be reached. Sometimes it's the children who pray for their parents.

It is my prayer that we might have a desire to rescue the lost battalions of the inactive, to bring them back to the joy of the gospel of Jesus Christ, that they might partake, with us, of all that full fellowship has to offer.

May we remember the words of the Savior when He declared: "If a man have an hundred sheep, and one of them be gone astray, doth he not leave the ninety and nine, and goeth into the mountains, and seeketh that which is gone astray? And if so be that he find it, verily I say unto you, he rejoiceth more of that sheep, than of the ninety and nine which went not astray."[8]

I pray that we may reach out to rescue the lost battalions which surround us: the aged, the widowed, the sick, the handicapped, the less active. Extend to them the hand that helps and the heart that knows compassion. By doing so we will bring joy into their hearts. We ourselves will experience the rich satisfaction which comes to us when we help another along the pathway to eternal life.

NOTES

1. John McCrae, "In Flanders Fields," in *Best-Loved Poems of the LDS People* (1996), 214.
2. John 15:13.
3. Mary Dow Brine, "Somebody's Mother," in *Best-Loved Poems of the LDS People* (1996), 282.
4. Mosiah 13:20.
5. Doctrine and Covenants 42:45.
6. Matthew 4:19.
7. Ephesians 2:19.
8. Matthew 18:12–13.

23

Only a Teacher

Often we hear the expression, "Times have changed." And perhaps they have. Our generation has witnessed enormous strides in the fields of medicine, transportation, communication, and exploration, to name but a few. But there are those isolated islands of constancy midst the vast sea of change. For instance, boys are still boys. And they continue to make the same boyish boasts.

Some time ago I overheard what I am confident is an oft-repeated conversation. Three very young boys were discussing the relative virtues of their fathers. One spoke out: "My dad is bigger than your dad," to which another replied, "Well, my dad is smarter than your dad." The third boy countered: "My dad is a doctor"; then, turning to one boy, he taunted in derision, "and your dad is only a teacher."

The call of a mother terminated the conversation, but the words continued to echo in my ears. Only a teacher. Only a teacher. Only a teacher. One day, each of those small boys will come to appreciate the true worth of inspired teachers and will acknowledge with sincere gratitude the indelible imprint which such teachers will leave on their personal lives.

"A teacher," as Henry Brook Adams observed, "affects eternity; he can never tell where his influence stops." This truth pertains to each of our teachers: first, the teacher in the home; second, the teacher in the school; third, the teacher in the Church.

Perhaps the teacher you and I remember best is the one who influenced us most. She may have used no chalkboard nor possessed a college degree, but her lessons were everlasting and her concern genuine. Yes, I speak of mother. And in the same breath, I also include father. In reality, every parent is a teacher.

The pupil in such a teacher's divinely commissioned classroom—indeed the baby who comes to your home or to mine—is "a sweet new blossom of humanity, fresh fallen from God's own home to flower on earth."[1]

Such a thought may have prompted the poet to pen the words:

> *I took a piece of plastic clay*
> *And idly fashioned it one day—*
> *And as my fingers pressed it, still*
> *It moved and yielded to my will.*
>
> *I came again when days were past;*
> *The bit of clay was hard at last.*
> *The form I gave it, still it bore,*
> *And I could change that form no more!*
>
> *I took a piece of living clay,*
> *And gently fashioned it day by day,*
> *And molded with my power and art*
> *A young child's soft and yielding heart.*
>
> *I came again when years were gone:*
> *It was a man I looked upon.*

He still that early impress bore,
And I could fashion it never more.[2]

Prime time for teaching is fleeting. Opportunities are perishable. Sad will be the parent who procrastinates the pursuit of his responsibility as a teacher.

Should a parent need added inspiration to commence his God-given teaching task, let him remember that the most powerful combination of emotions in the world is not called out by any grand cosmic event nor found in novels or history books—but merely by a parent gazing down upon a sleeping child. "Created in the image of God," that glorious Biblical truth, acquires new and vibrant meaning as a parent repeats this experience. Home becomes a haven called heaven, and loving parents teach their children "to pray, and to walk uprightly before the Lord."[3] Never does such an inspired parent fit the description, "only a teacher."

Next, let us consider the teacher in the school. Inevitably, there dawns that tearful morning when home yields to the classroom part of its teaching time. Johnny and Nancy join the happy throng which each day wends its way from the portals of home to the classrooms of school. There a new world is discovered. Our children meet their teachers.

The teacher not only shapes the expectations and ambitions of her pupils, but she also influences their attitudes toward their future and themselves. If she is unskilled, she leaves scars on the lives of youth, cuts deeply into their self-esteem, and distorts their image of themselves as human beings. But if she loves her students and has high expectations of them, their self-confidence will grow, their capabilities will develop, and their future will be assured.

The teacher's contributions often go unheralded and unacknowledged. The story is told of a group of men who were talking about people who had influenced their lives and for whom they were grateful. One man thought of a high school teacher who had introduced him to Tennyson. He decided to write and thank her. In time, written in a feeble scrawl, came the teacher's reply:

"My dear Willie:

"I can't tell you how much your note meant to me. I am in my 80s, living alone in a small room, cooking my own meals, lonely and like the last leaf lingering behind. You will be interested to know that I taught school for 50 years, and yours is the first note of appreciation I have ever received. It came on a blue, cold morning, and it cheered me as nothing has for years."

We owe an eternal debt of gratitude to those teachers, past and present, who have given so much of themselves, that we might have so much for ourselves.

Unfortunately, there are those few teachers who delight to destroy faith, rather than build bridges to the good life. Ever must we remember that the power to lead is also the power to mislead, and the power to mislead is the power to destroy.

In the words of President J. Reuben Clark: "He wounds, maims, and cripples a soul who raises doubts about or destroys faith in the ultimate truths. God will hold such a one strictly accountable; and who can measure the depths to which one shall fall who wilfully shatters in another the opportunity for celestial glory."[4]

Since we cannot control the classroom, we can at least prepare the pupil. You ask: "How?" I answer: "Provide a guide to the glory of the celestial kingdom of God; even a barometer to distinguish between the truths of God and the theories of men."

Several years ago I held in my hand such a guide. It was a volume of scripture we commonly call the triple combination, containing the Book of Mormon, Doctrine and Covenants, and Pearl of Great Price. The book was a gift from a loving father to a beautiful, blossoming daughter who followed carefully his advice. On the flyleaf page her father had written these inspired words:

April 9, 1944
To My Dear Maurine:
That you may have a constant measure by which to judge between truth and the errors of man's philosophies, and thus grow in spirituality as you increase in knowledge, I give you this sacred book to read frequently and cherish throughout your life.
Lovingly your father,
Harold B. Lee

I ask the question: "Only a teacher?"

Finally, let us turn to the teacher we usually meet on Sunday—the teacher in the Church. In such a setting, the history of the past, the hope of the present, and the promise of the future all meet. Here especially, the teacher learns it is easy to be a Pharisee; difficult to be a disciple. The teacher is judged by his students—not alone by what and how he teaches, but also by how he lives.

The Apostle Paul counseled the Romans: "Thou . . . which teachest another, teachest not thyself? thou that preachest a man should not steal, dost thou steal? Thou that sayest a man should not commit adultery, dost thou commit adultery?"[5]

Paul, that inspired and dynamic teacher, provides us a good example. Perhaps his success secret is revealed through his experience in the dreary dungeon which held him prisoner. Paul knew the tramp, tramp of the soldiers' feet and the clank, clank of the chains which bound him captive. When the prison warden, who seemed to be favorably inclined toward Paul, asked him whether he needed advice as to how to conduct himself before the emperor, Paul said he had an adviser—the Holy Spirit.

This same Spirit guided Paul as he stood in the midst at Mars Hill, read the inscription "To the Unknown God," and declared, "Whom therefore ye ignorantly worship, him declare I unto you. God that made the world and all things therein . . . dwelleth not in temples made with hands; . . . he giveth to all life, and breath, and all things; for in him we live, and move, and have our beings; . . . For we are also his offspring."[6]

Again the question, "Only a teacher?"

In the home, the school, or the house of God, there is one Teacher whose life overshadows all others. He taught of life and death, of duty and destiny. He lived not to be served, but to serve; not to receive, but to give; not to save His life, but to sacrifice it for others. He described a love more beautiful than lust, a poverty richer than treasure. It was said of this teacher that He taught with authority and not as do the scribes. In to-day's world, when many men are greedy for gold and for glory, and dominated by a teaching philosophy of "publish or perish," let us remember that this teacher never wrote—once only He wrote on the sand, and wind destroyed forever His handwriting. His laws were not inscribed upon stone, but upon human hearts. I speak of the master teacher, even Jesus Christ, the Son of God, the Savior and Redeemer of all mankind.

When dedicated teachers respond to His gentle invitation, "Come learn of me," they learn, but they also become partakers of His divine power.

It was my experience as a small boy to come under the influence of such a teacher. In our Sunday School class, she taught us concerning the creation of the world, the fall of Adam, the atoning sacrifice of Jesus. She brought to her classroom as honored guests Moses, Joshua, Peter, Thomas, Paul, and even Christ. Though we did not see them, we learned to love, honor, and emulate them. Well could we have echoed the words of the disciples on the way to Emmaus: "Did not our heart burn within us . . . while [she] opened to us the scriptures?"[7]

I return to the dialogue mentioned earlier. When the boy heard the taunts: "My dad is bigger than yours," "My dad is smarter than yours," "My dad is a doctor," well could he have replied: "Your dad may be bigger than mine; your dad may be smarter than mine; your dad may be a pilot, an engineer or a doctor; but my dad, *my dad is a teacher.*"

May each of us ever merit such a sincere and worthy compliment.

NOTES

1. Gerald Massey.
2. Author unknown, "I Took a Piece of Plastic Clay," in *Best-Loved Poems of the LDS People* (1996), 312.
3. Doctrine and Covenants 68:28.
4. *Improvement Era,* January 1946, 14–15, 60–63.
5. Romans 2:21–22.
6. Acts 17:23–25, 28.
7. Luke 24:32.

24

My Brother's Keeper

As Latter-day Saints, we take most seriously the admonition from the Lord found in the New Testament: "For I was an hungred, and ye gave me meat: I was thirsty, and ye gave me drink: I was a stranger, and ye took me in: Naked, and ye clothed me: I was sick, and ye visited me: I was in prison, and ye came unto me. . . . Verily I say unto you, Inasmuch as ye have done it unto one of the least of these my brethren, ye have done it unto me."[1]

Each time we watch the news on television or pick up a newspaper, we learn of terrible human suffering as a result of tornadoes, floods, fires, drought, hurricanes, earthquakes, conflicts of war. Human suffering surrounds us. I ask the question: Do we have a responsibility to do something about it?

Long years ago a similar question was posed and preserved in Holy Writ, even the Bible. I quote from the book of Genesis: "And Cain talked with Abel his brother: and it came to pass, when they were in the field, that Cain rose up against Abel his brother, and slew him. And the Lord said unto Cain, Where is Abel thy brother? And he said, I know not: Am I my brother's keeper?"[2] The answer to that vital question is: Yes, we are our brothers' keepers.

Countless are the examples of those who take seriously this admonition and do so much to assist their fellow man. Brother Junius Burt, who many years ago worked in the Streets Department in Salt Lake City, related a touching and inspirational experience. Brother Burt reported that on a cold winter morning, the street-cleaning crew of which he was a member was removing large chunks of ice from the street gutters. The regular crew was assisted by temporary laborers who desperately needed the work. One such wore only a lightweight sweater and was suffering from the cold. A slender man with a well-groomed beard stopped by the crew and addressed this particular worker: "You need more than a sweater on a morning like this. Where is your coat?" The man replied that he had no coat to wear. The visitor then removed his own overcoat, handed it to the man, and said, "This coat is yours. It is heavy wool and will keep you warm. I just work across the street." The street was South Temple. The Good Samaritan who walked into the Church Administration Building to his daily work and without his coat was President George Albert Smith. His selfless act of generosity revealed his tender heart. Surely he was his brother's keeper.

As you know, the funding of the operation of the Church worldwide is based on tithing, where members contribute ten percent of their increase, as set forth by the Old Testament prophet Malachi. In addition, we have fast offerings, wherein we fast once a month and contribute the equivalent of the meals not eaten—and any amount in addition we would like— as a fast offering to help the poor and the needy.

Long years ago I served as the bishop of the Sixth-Seventh Ward in Salt Lake City. In our ward were 84 widows and 1,080 members. Late one evening during this time, my telephone rang. I heard a voice say, "Bishop Monson, this is the hospital calling. Kathleen McKee, a member of your congregation, has

THE BLESSINGS OF SERVICE

just passed away. Our records reveal that she had no next of kin, but your name is listed as the one to be notified in the event of her death. Could you come to the hospital right away?"

Upon arriving at the hospital, I was presented with a sealed envelope which contained a key to the modest apartment in which Kathleen McKee had lived. A childless widow 73 years of age, she had enjoyed but few of life's luxuries and possessed scarcely sufficient of its necessities. In the twilight of her life, she had become a member of The Church of Jesus Christ of Latter-day Saints. As she was a quiet and overly reserved person, little was known about her life.

That same night I entered her tidy basement apartment, turned the light switch, and in a moment discovered on her kitchen table a handwritten note on which rested two Alka-Seltzer bottles filled with quarters. The note contained this message: "Bishop, here is my fast offering. I am square with the Lord." A spirit of peace filled that room. A silent sermon had been delivered.

Bishops' prayers are answered when they humbly seek the spirit of the Lord to lead them to those who are in need.

On a cold winter's night in 1951, there was a knock at my door. A German brother from Ogden, Utah, Carl Guertler, announced himself and said, "Are you Bishop Monson?" I answered in the affirmative. He began to weep, and said, "My brother Hans Guertler, his wife, Karla, and their family are coming here from Germany. They are going to live in your ward. Will you come with us to see the apartment we have rented for them?"

On the way to the apartment, he told me he had not seen his brother for many years. Yet all through the holocaust of World War II, his brother had been faithful to the Church, serving as a branch president before the war took him to the Russian front.

I looked at the apartment. It was cold and dreary. The paint was peeling, the wallpaper soiled, the cupboards empty.

A 40-watt bulb hanging from the living room ceiling revealed a linoleum floor covering with a large hole in the center. I was heartsick. I thought, "What a dismal welcome for a family which has endured so much."

My thoughts were interrupted by the brother's statement, "It isn't much, but it's better than they have in Germany." With that, the key was left with me, along with the information that the family would arrive in Salt Lake City in three weeks—just two days before Christmas.

Sleep was slow in coming to me that night. The next morning was Sunday. In our ward welfare committee meeting, one of my counselors said, "Bishop, you look worried. Is something wrong?" I recounted to those present my experience of the night before, the details of the uninviting apartment. There were a few moments of silence. Then the group leader of the high priests said, "Bishop, did you say that apartment was inadequately lighted and that the kitchen appliances were in need of replacement?" I answered in the affirmative. He continued, "I am an electrical contractor. Would you permit the high priests of this ward to rewire that apartment? I would also like to invite my suppliers to contribute a new stove and a new refrigerator. Do I have your permission?" I answered with a glad "Certainly."

Then the seventies president responded: "Bishop, as you know I'm in the carpet business. I would like to invite my suppliers to contribute some carpet, and the seventies can easily lay it and eliminate that worn linoleum."

Then the president of the elders quorum spoke up. He was a painting contractor. He said, "I'll furnish the paint. May the elders paint and wallpaper that apartment?" The Relief Society president was next to speak: "We in the Relief Society cannot stand the thought of empty cupboards. May we fill them?"

The next three weeks are ever to be remembered. It seemed that the entire ward joined in the project. The days passed, and at the appointed time Hans and Karla Guertler and their family arrived from Germany. Again at my door stood the brother from Ogden. With an emotion-filled voice, he introduced to me his brother, wife, and their family. Then he asked, "Could we go visit the apartment?" As we walked up the staircase to the apartment, he repeated, "It isn't much, but it's more than they have had in Germany." Little did he know what a transformation had taken place and that many who participated were inside waiting for our arrival.

The door opened to reveal a literal newness of life. We were greeted by the aroma of freshly painted woodwork and newly papered walls. Gone was the 40-watt bulb, along with the worn linoleum it had illuminated. We stepped on carpet deep and beautiful. A walk to the kitchen presented to our view a new stove and refrigerator. The cupboard doors were still open; however, they now revealed that every shelf was filled with food. The Relief Society as usual had done its work.

In the living room we began to sing Christmas hymns. We sang "Silent night! Holy night! All is calm, all is bright." We sang in English; they sang in German. At the conclusion, Hans Guertler, realizing that all of this was his, took me by the hand to express his thanks. His emotion was too great. He buried his head in my shoulder and repeated the words, "*Mein Bruder, mein Bruder, mein Bruder.*"

President J. Reuben Clark, former diplomat and then first counselor in the First Presidency, made this landmark statement: "The real long-term objective of the Welfare Plan is the building of character in the members of the Church, givers and receivers, rescuing all that is finest down deep inside of them, and bringing to flower and fruitage the latent richness of the spirit, which after all is the mission and purpose and reason for being of this Church."[3]

One who demonstrated such character came forward long years ago when a severe drought struck the Salt Lake Valley. The commodities at the storehouse on Welfare Square had not been their usual quality, nor were they found in abundance. Many products were missing, especially fresh fruit. As a young bishop, worrying about the needs of the many widows in my ward, my prayer one evening is especially sacred to me. I pleaded with the Lord, explaining that these widows, who were among the finest women I knew in mortality and whose needs were simple and conservative, had no resources on which they might rely.

The next morning I received a call from a ward member, a proprietor of a produce business situated in our ward. "Bishop," he said, "I would like to send a semitrailer filled with oranges, grapefruit, and bananas to the bishops' storehouse to be given to those in need. Could you make arrangements?" Could I make arrangements! The storehouse was alerted, and then each bishop in the Salt Lake Valley was telephoned and the entire shipment distributed to those in need. God blesses those who respond so generously to the Spirit's promptings.

May I say a word or two concerning humanitarian aid as compared to conventional welfare aid. The term *humanitarian aid* is a designation for help extended beyond the Church's basic welfare program. The Prophet Joseph Smith stated, "A man filled with the love of God, is not content with blessing his family alone, but ranges through the whole world, anxious to bless the whole human race."[4]

An early example of humanitarian aid took place nearly 54 years ago when World War II came to a close and Europe lay devastated. Hunger stalked the streets, infectious diseases were everywhere to be found, and the people had given up hope. A call came for aid, and President George Albert Smith, then President of The Church of Jesus Christ of Latter-day Saints, went to see President Harry Truman to get permission to send aid to the starving people throughout Europe. President Truman listened to President Smith and then said, "I like what you plan to do. How long will it take you to assemble the goods you would like to send and prepare them for shipment?"

President Smith responded, "President Truman, the goods are all assembled. One nod from you and the trains will roll, and ships will sail, and those supplies will be on their way."

It happened exactly that way, with Ezra Taft Benson, then a member of the Council of the Twelve, delivering the supplies in behalf of the Church.

I was in Zwickau, Germany, several years ago dedicating a chapel. A man came up to me and said, "President Monson, I want you to tell President Ezra Taft Benson that the food he brought after the war—food sent by the Church—kept me and my family from starving. It gave us hope for the future." I was deeply touched as I listened to his expressions of gratitude.

We are often asked about the extent and nature of Church humanitarian assistance. Perhaps a few examples taken from many will be appropriate.

In 1985, as the suffering of famine-stricken Ethiopia became apparent, our members in the United States and Canada were invited to participate in two special fast days. The contributions went to this cause. The proceeds received from these two fast days exceeded 11 million dollars and provided much-needed aid to the people in Ethiopia, Chad, and other sub-Saharan nations.

On August 24, 1992, a devastating hurricane named Andrew slammed into the Florida coast south of Miami, leaving a path of ruin behind it, with homes battered, roofs gone, people hungry. Wind gusts exceeded two hundred miles per hour. It became the most costly disaster in United States history. Eighty-seven thousand homes were destroyed, leaving 150,000 homeless. Damages exceeded 30 billion dollars. One hundred seventy-eight member homes were damaged, with 46 of them destroyed.

A spearhead unit was deployed from the Church welfare facility in Atlanta before the storm hit, and it arrived at its appointed location just as the winds abated. The truck carried food, water, bedding, tools, and medical supplies—the first relief shipment to arrive in the disaster area.

Local priesthood and Relief Society leaders organized rapidly to assess injuries and damage and to assist in the cleanup effort. Three large waves of member volunteers, numbering over five thousand, labored shoulder to shoulder with disaster-stricken residents, helping to repair three thousand homes, a Jewish synagogue, a Pentecostal church, and two schools. Forty-six missionaries from the Florida Fort Lauderdale Mission worked full-time for more than two weeks unloading supply trucks, serving as interpreters, providing security and traffic control, and assisting with repairs. It mattered not the faith or color of the person who occupied the damaged homes.

In 1998, when Hurricane Mitch devastated Honduras and other areas of Central America, we undertook a similar initiative to relieve suffering and want. In his message at the First Presidency Christmas Devotional on December 6, 1998, President Hinckley mentioned that he would like to send some candy to a newly orphaned two-year-old girl he had met during a recent visit to Honduras. Within the week, the Welfare Department took calls from a number of major candy companies wanting to help out. After looking at several options, the Welfare Department made arrangements with two of the companies to send four thousand pounds of candy to Central America. The Church also sent toys, children's clothing, and other needed supplies. Within two weeks of the broadcast, a total of thirteen 40-thousand-pound containers were shipped to the hurricane-ravaged areas.

Far away in the foothills on the western slopes of Mt. Kenya, along the fringe of the colossal Rift Valley, pure water is now coming to the thirsty people. A potable water project has changed the lives of more than 1,100 families. When we originally became aware of the need for pure water, we were able to identify engineers in our Church who responded to a call to go to Africa.

They were asked to stay as long as necessary to complete the project. They worked in cooperation with TechnoServe, a private volunteer organization. Drinkable water now flows through 25 miles of pipes to waiting homes in a 15-village area. The simple blessing of safe drinking water recalls to mind the words of the Lord, "I was thirsty, and ye gave me drink."[5]

In 2004, a 9-plus-magnitude undersea earthquake struck off the coast of Sumatra, generating tsunamis that took the lives of nearly 300,000 people. The Church immediately sent 102,000 pounds of medical supplies, over 40,000 hygiene kits, and 50,000 body bags. In addition, local hygiene supplies, kitchen sets, and medical equipment and supplies were purchased by the Church. We also provided trauma counseling to survivors. The Church continued to provide long-term assistance, focusing on vital needs and helping people to help themselves, constructing homes, schools, and medical centers and rebuilding water systems in 20 villages to provide sanitary water to families.

The day after the tsunami hit, Elder Subandriyo, an Area Seventy living in Indonesia, called upon several Saints he knew he could trust. One call he made was to the district Young Women president, Bertha Suranto. He asked her to purchase the materials for 3,000 hygiene kits. Then he asked her to help make arrangements to unload a cargo plane.

A few days later, Sister Suranto volunteered to travel to the areas hardest hit by the tsunami. She arrived in the northern Sumatra city of Medan, where she immediately began purchasing building materials, tents, food, clothing, kitchen stoves, school uniforms, and materials for thousands of additional hygiene kits.

Sister Suranto joined other members of the Church who worked from early morning until late at night filling over 40 trucks, each 40 feet long, with tens of thousands of needed items. As each truck was filled, Bertha phoned ahead to her husband who was with another group of Saints in Banda Aceh, one of the hardest hit areas. He received the trucks his wife had filled and helped to distribute the items among those in need—99 percent of whom were Muslim.

In many cases the boxes—each labeled, "A Gift from The Church of Jesus Christ of Latter-day Saints"—were stacked inside the mosques. Everywhere our volunteers went, townspeople ran out to greet and welcome them. "We felt as though we were movie stars," Sister Suranto said. "Often we arrived in villages, towns, and refugee camps that had not received help from anyone else."

Each time they met with village leaders, they asked, "What is it you most need?" One village chief said that more than anything else, his village needed copies of the Koran because theirs had been swept away in the tsunami. A few days later, the Church presented the village with 700 copies of the Koran.

As trucks from the Church were unloaded into mosques and city squares, the word rang out, "We have received another donation from the Jesus Church!" And hundreds of grateful mothers, fathers, and children lined up to receive the life-sustaining goods. Heads of villages and heads of families smiled whenever Sister Suranto and the other members of the Church came. "You are a different church," they said. "You don't want anything in return—only to serve. You are our brothers and sisters."

As for Sister Suranto, her outlook on life changed as well. She said, "Before the tsunami, I didn't want to associate with those of other faiths. The people we helped probably felt the same way. Very few of them had ever heard of our Church or knew anything about us. We were strangers to each other. Today, things are different. Today, we feel a close bond. We know we are brothers and sisters."

Far too numerous to mention are all the examples of welfare and humanitarian aid the Church has distributed to those in need. However, I should like to highlight just a few more. One concerns a product we produce which in the past several years has saved thousands upon thousands of lives. It's called

Atmit, and it is specifically formulated for malnourished children and others who cannot digest regular food. It consists of oat flour, powdered milk, and sugar, and it is fortified with vitamin and mineral supplements. Since 2003, over 2,000 tons of Atmit have been manufactured in Salt Lake City at the Church's Welfare Services dairy processing facility. It has been sent to Ethiopia, Uganda, Sudan, South Africa, Niger, Haiti, Gaza/Palestine, Bangladesh, Indonesia, Sri Lanka, India, Paraguay, and many other locations. Starving, malnourished children, and others who cannot digest regular food, who otherwise would die, are being given this life-saving, easy-to-digest formula. Vivid in my mind are two photographs I was shown of an eight-year-old girl. In the first, she weighed only 20 pounds and was literally skin and bones. One wondered how she could possibly survive. The second photograph was of the same girl six months later after supplemental feedings of Atmit. She looked perfectly normal. Her sweet smile in the second photograph was a heartwarming testament to the miracles Atmit has brought about. This girl is typical of hundreds of thousands of children in the areas to which Atmit has been sent.

The Church has collaborated in hundreds of humanitarian projects with over 35 other agencies, including the Red Cross (American and International), Catholic Relief Services, Islamic Relief Worldwide, the Children's Hunger Fund, African Christian Relief, Inc., and so on. Hunger knows no ecclesiastical boundary. We can provide hope; we can preserve life.

Beginning in 1988, the Church has joined with Rotary International in the PolioPlus program, with the goal being to eliminate that dreaded disease. As a young man in high school I witnessed firsthand the start of the polio epidemic in Salt Lake City. Every day it seemed that someone at school came down with polio. If one has ever seen an iron lung or a child who has suffered from the devastating infirmities of polio, he understands what blessings have come because of the PolioPlus program. The Church has purchased sufficient polio serum to immunize hundreds of thousands of children and also has helped place gas and electric refrigerators in rural health outposts to keep vaccines viable until they are administered to the children. Between PolioPlus's inception in 1985, through June 2006, more than two billion children have received oral polio vaccine. As of that date, and as a result of the program, 210 countries, territories, and areas around the world are polio free. One never goes wrong by helping a child.

In many emerging countries, measles is a deadly killer. It is a disease dimly remembered by most Americans, but in some areas of the world, measles takes an estimated 500,000 lives each year, most of them children. In 2003, the Church made a major commitment to the International Red Cross to provide funds and labor to help immunize a million children each year. As part of this commitment, Church Humanitarian Services asked Terry and Danne Morris to travel to Africa and help coordinate the vaccinations. Although Terry, a retired dentist, had a medical background, and although he and his wife had served a previous humanitarian mission in Indonesia, they weren't sure what they would do once they arrived in Africa. It wasn't long before they discovered they weren't alone in their efforts.

Local members of the Church were organized and made a major effort, going door to door to tell people about the opportunity to have their children vaccinated. In all, more than 2,000 members assisted in the campaign, donating nearly 95,000 hours of their time. They helped put up more than 70,000 posters and distributed more than 200,000 flyers.

Said Brother Morris, "It's difficult to tell who benefited the most—those who received the vaccinations or those who gave of themselves to serve others."

Brother Lyatuh of Tanzania spent countless hours going door-to-door to tell the people of the vaccinations, and then, when the medical personnel arrived, he would take the bus each day to the end of the line and would then walk two hours to the vaccination station, where he worked ten hours assisting the medical specialists there. Then he walked two more hours back to the bus and made the long trip home again.

Brother and Sister Morris said, "At first we wondered what we could do to make a difference, but now we know that not only were many families spared the heartbreak of a dreaded disease, but those who gave of themselves grew stronger as a result of their service."

In 2006 alone, the Church participated with immunization campaigns in nine African countries. In each campaign, we mobilize our members to volunteer in getting the word out and assisting at the immunization locations. Last October, the Church mobilized 10,000 members to assist in a measles campaign in Nigeria.

From 2001 through 2006, the Church distributed nearly 200,000 wheelchairs in 97 countries. In 2006 alone, 54,840 wheelchairs were distributed in 54 countries.

The wheelchair program is ongoing. An observer who witnessed the delivery of 500 wheelchairs to Uganda recorded: "The wheelchairs were lined up in all sizes from child to adult. Parents had brought their handicapped children there to receive the long-awaited and much-needed gift, one they would never be able to afford in a lifetime. There are not words to describe the scene. The recipients were joyous as they wheeled themselves around, mobile and independent for the first time in their lives."

In the world today, 1.1 billion people do not have access to a sanitary water supply. From 2002 through 2006 the Church has provided clean water for more than three and a half million people in 2,615 communities. In Ghana, one of our senior missionary couples, Neil and Marjorie Darlington, helped drill new wells and refurbish others, bringing potable water to an estimated 190,000 people in villages and refugee camps throughout the country.

"We were always on the front line of disaster," Brother

Darlington says. "In areas of famine, disease, and social unrest, we were there as representatives of the Church, extending a helping hand to the destitute, the hungry, the distressed."

The Ghana National Disaster Management Organization, the primary council on disaster relief, invited the Darlingtons to serve as members of their organization. Said Brother Darlington, "They liked the way we handled responses to disasters. They came to us frequently because we could often respond within a week, whereas others sometimes took months." Village leaders would often say to the Darlingtons, "Many people come here and promise to come back, but we never see them again. You did what you said you would do. You came back."

Of the many remarkable experiences the Darlingtons had in Ghana, one stands out in their minds. In one of the villages, after drilling a new well, they met with the tribal council. The chief and the elders of the village were there—each dressed in regal tribal attire. After receiving their expressions of gratitude for the new well, this missionary couple began singing the classic, "I Am a Child of God." The chief listened, tears streaming down his face. Said the Darlingtons, "He not only received water that day, but he also tasted of the love of the Savior."

Nearly three decades ago I was called to be a member of President Ronald Reagan's Task Force on Private Sector Initiatives. He knew much concerning our welfare program. On one occasion when we were meeting together in the White House for breakfast, he said to others, pointing to me, "In Elder Monson's church, the members frequently donate their time to can tomatoes and put up corn and other produce for the needy. Wouldn't it be great if all of us did that?"

In September of 1982, President Reagan paid a visit to our welfare cannery in Ogden, Utah. As is always the case in such situations, security was extremely tight. President Reagan and those who were with him observed a production line where about 20 women were canning tomatoes, with each of them having been cleared by the FBI prior to the visit. President Reagan stopped beside the production line and was praising the operation and our entire welfare program when I noticed that each one of the women on that production line was holding a paring knife with a four-inch blade, to be used for peeling tomatoes. After all the security checks and clearances, President Reagan was in a room filled with women holding knives!

David and Marva Coombs, from Washington, Utah, served a humanitarian mission in Thailand. Once, while Marva was getting her hair done, David decided he would cross the street to a local hospital to see if there was anything the Church could do to help.

"You are Mormons, aren't you?" the hospital administrator asked. "Christians?"

David gave an affirmative reply.

"And you know we are Buddhists?" the administrator asked.

"Yes," David replied.

The administrator asked, "Then why are you offering to help us?"

David replied, "Because of our love for the people of Thailand and our desire to serve our Father in Heaven."

Overjoyed, the administrator explained that he had a cancer ward for children and that during the last year they had lost five patients because they didn't have the proper diagnostic equipment. Elder and Sister Coombs went to work and submitted a request to purchase the equipment the hospital needed.

Finally the day arrived when the equipment had been purchased, set up, and was ready to use. The hospital administrator called a press conference inviting nationwide TV stations to cover the event. He placed a plaque in the hospital commemorating the donation of the Church and said, "What a beautiful example of how Buddhists and Christians can work together. We are grateful you are here."

David and Marva Coombs also worked in Sri Lanka, since

their mission covered that area as well. They supplied furniture for orphanages, clean water for villages, and even rebuilt a Catholic chapel. One day a Catholic priest, who had been an enemy of the Church and who had led marches through the streets warning the people not to listen to the Mormons, spoke to a group of his fellow priests. He said, "I have said for years that Mormons aren't Christians. I need to repent. They are some of the finest Christians I have ever met."

When we can work together cooperatively to lift the level of life for so many people, we can accomplish anything. When we do so, we eliminate the weakness of one person standing alone and substitute the strength of many serving together. While we may not be able to do everything, we can and must do something.

May I share just one more example of the miracles which can result from service and sharing. In the Republic of Belarus, beneath the city of Minsk, a series of tunnels honeycomb in what is called a "cellar." This bomb shelter was built in the 1960s and '70s for use in case of a nuclear attack. The tunnels were intended for tens of thousands of citizens to huddle together and wait for the devastation of nuclear war to settle itself upon the surface, giving them a chance to survive.

But today the bomb shelter is used for an entirely different purpose than the one for which it was built. Says Alexander Mikhalchenko, chairman of the State Committee on Archival Record Keeping of the Republic of Belarus, "We are using these shelters to store humanitarian shipments from The Church of Jesus Christ of Latter-day Saints—blankets, quilts, medical supplies, food, hygiene kits, wheelchairs, textbooks.

"All the assistance that comes to us is passed along into the hands of the people who need it the most. It goes to children in orphanages, patients in hospitals, old people in homes. Charitable dinners are arranged. Everything goes—one hundred percent—to those purposes for which it is intended. Not one drop of the assistance goes anywhere else."

Over the last few years, a bond of friendship and trust has developed between the Church and many of the people in Belarus. Halfway around the world from Belarus, the LDS Humanitarian Center prepares shipments for countries throughout the world.

In a wonderful twist of irony, the building that houses the humanitarian center in Salt Lake City was originally built as a factory that made munitions for World War II. What a remarkable and miraculous age in which to live—where an old munitions factory in the United States and an austere bomb shelter in the former Soviet Union can be linked together by a single thread—the thread of compassion. But perhaps, after all, that is the wonder of unselfish love. More than any other element in the world, it has the ability to soften animosity, transform enemies into friends, and make us realize that in the end, we are brothers and sisters and not so very different after all.

God bless all who endeavor to be their brother's keeper, who give to ameliorate suffering, who strive with all that is good within them to make a better world. Have you noticed that such individuals have a brighter smile? Their footsteps are more certain. They have an aura about them of contentment and satisfaction, even dedication, for one cannot participate in helping others without experiencing a rich blessing himself.

I pray we may have the spirit of giving and the spirit of serving, today and always, in the name of Jesus Christ, our Lord and Savior who gave His all.

NOTES

1. Matthew 25:35–36, 40.
2. Genesis 4:8–9.
3. Quoted in Spencer W. Kimball, "The Gospel in Action," *Ensign,* November 1977, 77.
4. *Teachings of Presidents of the Church: Joseph Smith* (2007), 424.
5. Matthew 25:35.

25

A Sacred Gift

I HAVE THOUGHT REPEATEDLY of the blessing which is ours to be bearers of the sacred priesthood of God. When we look at the world as a whole, with a population of over six and one-half billion people, we realize that we comprise a very small, select group. We who hold the priesthood are, in the words of the Apostle Peter, "a chosen generation, a royal priesthood."[1]

President Joseph F. Smith defined the priesthood as "the power of God delegated to man by which man can act in the earth for the salvation of the human family, . . . by which [men] may speak the will of God as if the angels were here to speak it themselves; by which men are empowered to bind on earth and it shall be bound in heaven, and to loose on earth and it shall be loosed in heaven." President Smith added, "[The priesthood] is sacred, and it must be held sacred by the people."[2]

My brethren, the priesthood is a gift which brings with it not only special blessings but also solemn responsibilities. It is our responsibility to conduct our lives so that we are ever worthy of the priesthood we bear. We live in a time when we are surrounded by much that is intended to entice us into paths which may lead to our destruction. To avoid such paths requires determination and courage.

Courage counts. This truth came to me in a most vivid and dramatic manner many years ago. I was serving as a bishop at the time. The general session of our stake conference was being held in the Assembly Hall on Temple Square in Salt Lake City. Our stake presidency was to be reorganized. The Aaronic Priesthood, including members of bishoprics, were providing the music for the conference. As we concluded singing our first selection, President Joseph Fielding Smith, our conference visitor, stepped to the pulpit and read for sustaining approval the names of the new stake presidency. He then mentioned that Percy Fetzer, who became our new stake president, and John Burt, who became the first counselor—each of whom had been counselors in the previous presidency—had been made aware of their new callings before the conference began. However, he indicated that I, who had been called to be second counselor in the new presidency, had no previous knowledge of the calling and was hearing of it for the first time as my name was read for sustaining vote. He then announced, "If Brother Monson is willing to respond to this call, we will be pleased to hear from him now."

As I stood at the pulpit and gazed out on that sea of faces, I remembered the song we had just sung. It pertained to the Word of Wisdom and was titled "Have Courage, My Boy, to Say No." That day I selected as my acceptance theme "Have Courage, My Boy, to Say Yes." The call for courage comes constantly to each of us—the courage to stand firm for our convictions, the courage to fulfill our responsibilities, the courage to honor our priesthood.

Wherever we go, our priesthood goes with us. Are we standing in "holy places"?[3] Said President J. Reuben Clark Jr., who served for many years as a counselor in the First Presidency, "The Priesthood is not like a suit of clothes that you can lay off and take back on. . . . Depending upon ourselves, [it is] an everlasting endowment." He continued, "If we really had that . . . conviction . . . that we could not lay [the priesthood] aside, and that God would hold us responsible if we [demeaned] it, it would save us from doing a good many things, save us from going a good many places. If, every time we started a little detour away from the straight and narrow, we would remember, 'I am carrying my Priesthood here. Should I?' it would not take us long to work back into the straight and narrow."[4]

President Spencer W. Kimball said: "There is no limit to the power of the priesthood which you hold. The limit comes in you if you do not live in harmony with the Spirit of the Lord and you limit yourselves in the power you exert."[5]

My brethren of the priesthood—from the youngest to the oldest—are you living your life in accordance with that which the Lord requires? Are you worthy to bear the priesthood of God? If you are not, make the decision here and now, muster the courage it will take, and institute whatever changes are necessary so that your life is what it should be. To sail safely the seas of mortality, we need the guidance of that eternal mariner— even the great Jehovah. If we are on the Lord's errand, we are entitled to the Lord's help.

His help has come to me on countless occasions throughout my life. During the final phases of World War II, I turned 18 and was ordained an elder—one week before I departed for active duty with the navy. A member of my ward bishopric was at the train station to bid me farewell. Just before train time, he placed in my hand a book. Its title: *The Missionary's Hand Book*. I laughed and commented, "I'll be in the navy—not on a mission." He answered, "Take it anyway. It may come in handy."

It did. During basic training our company commander instructed us concerning how we might best pack our clothing in a large seabag. He then advised, "If you have a hard, rectangular object you can place in the bottom of the bag, your clothes will stay more firm." I thought, "Where am I going to find a hard, rectangular object?" Suddenly I remembered just the right rectangular object—*The Missionary's Hand Book.* And thus it served for 12 weeks at the bottom of that seabag.

The night preceding our Christmas leave, our thoughts were, as always, on home. The barracks were quiet. Suddenly I became aware that my buddy in the adjoining bunk—a member of the Church, Leland Merrill—was moaning in pain. I asked, "What's the matter, Merrill?"

He replied, "I'm sick. I'm really sick."

I advised him to go to the base dispensary, but he answered knowingly that such a course would prevent him from being home for Christmas. I then suggested he be quiet so that we didn't awaken the entire barracks.

The hours lengthened; his groans grew louder. Then, in desperation, he whispered, "Monson, aren't you an elder?" I acknowledged this to be so, whereupon he pleaded, "Give me a blessing."

I became very much aware that I had never given a blessing. I had never received such a blessing; I had never witnessed a blessing being given. My prayer to God was a plea for help. The answer came: "Look in the bottom of the seabag." Thus, at 2:00 A.M. I emptied on the deck the contents of the bag. I then took to the night-light that hard, rectangular object, *The Missionary's Hand Book,* and read how one blesses the sick. With about 120 curious sailors looking on, I proceeded with the blessing. Before I could stow my gear, Leland Merrill was sleeping like a child.

The next morning, Merrill smilingly turned to me and said, "Monson, I'm glad you hold the priesthood!" His gladness was only surpassed by my gratitude—gratitude not only for the priesthood but for being worthy to receive the help I required in a time of desperate need and to exercise the power of the priesthood.

Brethren, our Lord and Savior said, "Come, follow me."[6]

214

When we accept His invitation and walk in His footsteps, He will direct our paths.

In April of 2000, I felt such direction. I had received a phone call from Rosa Salas Gifford, whom I did not know. She explained that her parents had been visiting from Costa Rica for a few months and that just a week prior to her call, her father, Bernardo Agusto Salas, had been diagnosed with liver cancer. She indicated that the doctors had informed the family that her father would live just a few more days. Her father's great desire, she explained, was to meet me before he died. She left her address and asked if I could come to her home in Salt Lake City to visit with her father.

Because of meetings and obligations, it was rather late when I left my office. Instead of going straight home, however, I felt impressed that I should drive farther south and visit Brother Salas that very evening. With the address in hand, I attempted to locate the residence. In rather heavy traffic and with dimming light, I drove past the location where the road to the house should have been. I could see nothing. I drove around the block and came back. Still nothing. One more time I tried and still saw no sign of the road. I began to feel that I would be justified in turning toward home. I had made a gallant effort but had been unsuccessful in finding the address. Instead, I offered a silent prayer for help. The inspiration came that I should approach the area from the opposite direction. I drove a distance and turned the car around so that I was now on the other side of the road. Going this direction, the traffic was much lighter. As I neared the location once again, I could see, through the faint light, a street sign that had been knocked down—it was lying on its side at the edge of the road—and a nearly invisible, weed-covered track leading to a small apartment building and a single, tiny residence some distance from the main road. As I drove toward the buildings, a small girl in a white dress waved to me, and I knew that I had found the family.

I was ushered into the home and then to the room where

Brother Salas lay. Surrounding the bed were three daughters and a son-in-law, as well as Sister Salas. All but the son-in-law were from Costa Rica. Brother Salas's appearance reflected the gravity of his condition. A damp rag with frayed edges—not a towel or a washcloth but a damp rag with frayed edges—rested upon his forehead, emphasizing the humble economic circumstances of the family.

With some prompting, Brother Salas opened his eyes, and a wan smile graced his lips as I took him by the hand. I spoke the words, "I have come to meet you." Tears welled up in his eyes and in mine.

I asked if a blessing would be desired, and the unanimous answer from the family members was affirmative. Since the son-in-law did not hold the priesthood, I proceeded by myself to provide a priesthood blessing. The words seemed to flow freely under the direction of the Spirit of the Lord. Following the blessing, I offered a few words of comfort to the grieving family members. I spoke carefully so that they could understand my English. And then, with my limited Spanish language ability, I let them know that I loved them and that our Heavenly Father would bless them.

I asked for the family Bible and directed their attention to 3 John, verse 4: "I have no greater joy than to hear that my children walk in truth." I said to them, "This is what your husband and father would have you remember as he prepares to depart this earthly existence."

With tears streaming down her face, Brother Salas's sweet wife then asked if I would write down the reference for the scripture I had shared with them so that the family might read it again. Not having anything handy on which I could write, Sister Salas reached into her purse and drew from it a slip of paper. As I took it from her, I noticed it was a tithing receipt. My heart was touched as I realized that, despite the extremely humble circumstances in which the family lived, they were faithful in paying their tithes.

After a tender farewell, I was escorted to my car. As I drove homeward, I reflected on the special spirit we had felt. I experienced, as well, as I have many times before, a sense of gratitude that my Heavenly Father had answered another person's prayer through me.

My brethren, let us ever remember that the priesthood of God which we bear is a sacred gift which brings to us and to those we serve the blessings of heaven. May we, in whatever place we may be, honor and protect that priesthood.

NOTES

1. 1 Peter 2:9.
2. *Gospel Doctrine,* 5th ed. (1939), 139–40.
3. Doctrine and Covenants 45:32; 87:8; 101:22.
4. In Conference Report, October 1951, 169.
5. *The Teachings of Spencer W. Kimball,* ed. Edward L. Kimball (1982), 498.
6. Luke 18:22.

26

GOAL BEYOND VICTORY

Y EARS AGO, MANY OF US participated as players or observers in the all-Church basketball tournaments and later in the softball tournaments. The most coveted prize was not to be adjudged first-place winner, but rather to receive the sportsmanship award. The applause of the audience was louder and longer, the smiles broader and more universal. A goal beyond victory had been won.

Lately we have received at the Office of the First Presidency letters which tell of serious arguments on the sports floor or playing field, name calling by parents, abuse of referees, and all that characterizes poor sportsmanship. We have room for improvement, and improve we must.

In the videotape produced by the Church and entitled *The Church Sports Official,* there is featured this truth from the First Presidency: "Church sports activities have a unique central purpose much higher than the development of physical prowess, or even victory itself. It is to strengthen faith, build integrity, and develop in each participant the attributes of his maker."

It is difficult to achieve this objective if winning overshadows participation. The recreation halls in our many buildings are constructed through the tithes of the members of the Church. It is only fair that all worthy young men and young women have an opportunity to play, to learn, to develop and to achieve.

It is not our objective to produce clones of Larry Bird or Magic Johnson—or even John Wooden or Pat Riley. *When you put a player in a suit, put him in the game.* Let our teams of young men and young women be counseled appropriately. And a word or two for the spectators and coaches would not be amiss.

If I might add a personal touch, I share with you an experience that embarrassed, a game that was lost, and a lesson in not taking ourselves too seriously.

First, in a basketball game when the outcome was in doubt, the coach sent me onto the playing floor right after the second half began. I took an in-bounds pass, dribbled the ball toward the key, and let the shot fly. Just as the ball left my fingertips, I realized why the opposing guards did not attempt to stop my drive: I was shooting for the wrong basket! I offered a silent prayer: "Please, Father, don't let that ball go in." The ball rimmed the hoop and fell out.

From the bleachers came the call: "We want Monson, we want Monson, we want Monson—*out!*" The coach obliged.

I never was a basketball star. What timing—to be a freshman at the University of Utah when all-Americans Arnie Ferrin and Vern Gardner dominated the boards.

I fared much better at fast-pitch softball. My most memorable experience in softball was a 13-inning game I pitched in Salt Lake City on a hot Memorial Day. The game was scheduled for just seven innings, but the tied score could not be broken. In the last of the thirteenth, with two men out and a runner on third, the batter hit a high pop fly to left field. The catch was certain, I thought. And yet the ball fell through the hands of the left fielder. For 38 years I have teased my friend who dropped the ball. I promised myself I would never do so again.

I'm not even going to mention his name. After all, he, too, remembers. It was only a game.

On another occasion, while pitching a game at Pioneer Park, I was absolutely stunned to see that the other team had placed a one-armed batter at the plate. Now, how does a pitcher deliver the pitch to such an opponent? I tossed a gentle lob over the plate. To my amazement, the batter knocked a single, right over the second baseman's head. My temper flared. The next batter was a returned missionary from Mexico, Homer Proctor, six foot two and about 210 pounds. I pitched him fast, high, and inside. On the first pitch, he lifted the ball right out of the park for a home run. I shall ever remember the smile of that one-armed runner, Bernell Hales, as he passed second and third and gleefully streaked for home. I felt like crying, but I broke out laughing, as did each player on both sides. We had a wonderful time.

Let's take the necessary steps to rekindle sportsmanship, to emphasize participation, and to strive for the development of a Christlike character in each individual.

Now, there are other phases of the Lord's work in which all members can participate, where the growth of character is assured and the promise of life eternal bestowed. One such endeavor is referred to as the welfare program. Actually, the language of King Benjamin from the Book of Mosiah provides a perfect scriptural description, even a solemn charge to each of us: "For the sake of retaining a remission of your sins from day to day, that ye may walk guiltless before God—I would that ye should impart of your substance to the poor, every man according to that which he hath, such as feeding the hungry, clothing the naked, visiting the sick and administering to their relief, both spiritually and temporally."[1]

President Marion G. Romney spoke concerning the funding of caring for the needy when he said: "It has been, and now is, the desire and the objective of the Church to obtain from fast offerings the necessary funds to meet the cash needs of the welfare program. . . . At the present time we are not meeting this objective. We can, we ought, and we must do better. If we will increase our fast offerings, we shall increase our own prosperity, both spiritually and temporally. This the Lord has promised, and this has been the record."[2]

Are we generous in the payment of our fast offerings? That we should be so was taught by President Joseph F. Smith. He declared that it is incumbent upon every Latter-day Saint to give to his bishop on fast day an amount equivalent to the food that he and his family would consume for the day and, if possible, a liberal donation to be so reserved and donated to the poor.[3]

President Spencer W. Kimball suggested that, in our generosity, we go beyond a minimum amount. He urged that we "give, instead of the amount saved by our two or more meals of fasting, perhaps much more—ten times more where we are in a position to do it."[4]

Today, in lands far away, and right here in Salt Lake City, there are those who suffer hunger, who know want and are acquainted with poverty. Ours is the opportunity and the sacred privilege to relieve this hunger, to meet this want, to eliminate this poverty.

The Lord provided the way when He declared: "And the storehouse shall be kept by the consecrations of the church; and widows and orphans shall be provided for, as also the poor."[5] Then the reminder, "But it must needs be done in mine own way."[6]

In the vicinity where I once lived and served, we operated a poultry project. Most of the time it was an efficiently operated project, supplying to the storehouse thousands of dozens of fresh eggs and hundreds of pounds of dressed poultry. On a few occasions, however, the experience of being volunteer city farmers provided not only blisters on the hands, but also frustration of heart and mind. For instance, I shall ever remember the time we gathered together the Aaronic Priesthood young men to really give the project a spring-cleaning treatment. Our enthusiastic and energetic throng assembled at the project, and in a speedy fashion uprooted, gathered, and burned large quantities of weeds and debris. By the light of the glowing bonfires, we ate hot dogs and congratulated ourselves on a job well done. The project was now neat and tidy. However, there was just one disastrous problem: The noise and the fires had so disturbed the fragile and temperamental population of five thousand laying hens that most of them went into a sudden molt and ceased laying. Thereafter we tolerated a few weeds, that we might produce more eggs.

No member of the Church who has canned peas, topped beets, hauled hay or watered corn in such a cause ever forgets or regrets the experience of helping provide for those in need.

One recipient of such help was a dear friend of mine, Louis McDonald. Louis never married. Because of a crippling disease, he had never known a day without pain nor many days without loneliness. One winter's day, as I visited him, he was slow in answering the doorbell's ring. I entered his well-kept home; the temperature in save but one room—the kitchen—was a chilly 40 degrees. The reason? Not sufficient money to heat any other room. The walls needed papering, the ceilings needed to be lowered, the cupboards needed to be filled.

I was troubled by Louis's needs. A bishop was consulted, and a miracle of love, prompted by testimony, took place. The members of the ward—particularly the young adults—were organized and the labor of love begun.

A month later, my friend Louis called and asked if I would come and see what had happened to him. I did and indeed beheld a miracle. The sidewalks which had been uprooted by large poplar trees had been replaced, the porch of the home rebuilt, a new door with glistening hardware installed, the ceilings lowered, the walls papered, the woodwork painted, the roof replaced, and the cupboards filled. No longer was the home chilly and uninviting. It now seemed to whisper a warm welcome.

Louis saved until last showing me his pride and joy: there on his bed was a beautiful plaid quilt bearing the crest of his McDonald family clan. It had been made with loving care by the women of the Relief Society. Before leaving, I discovered that each week the young adults would bring in a hot dinner and share a home evening. Warmth had replaced the cold; repairs had transformed the wear of years; but more significantly, hope had dispelled despair and now love reigned triumphant.

Sharing with others that which we have is not new to our generation. We need but to turn to the account found in 1 Kings to appreciate anew the principle that when we follow the counsel of the Lord, when we care for those in need, the outcome benefits all. There we read that a most severe drought had gripped the land. Famine followed. Elijah the prophet received from the Lord what to him must have been an amazing instruction: "Get thee to Zarephath . . . : behold, I have commanded a widow woman there to sustain thee." When he had found the widow, Elijah declared, "Fetch me, I pray thee, a little water in a vessel, that I may drink.

"And as she was going to fetch it, he called to her, and said, Bring me, I pray thee, a morsel of bread in thine hand."

Her response described her pathetic situation as she explained that she was preparing a final and scanty meal for her son and for herself, and then they would die.

How implausible to her must have been Elijah's response: "Fear not; go and do as thou hast said: but make me thereof a little cake first, and bring it unto me, and after make for thee and for thy son.

"For thus saith the Lord God of Israel, The barrel of meal shall not waste, neither shall the cruse of oil fail, until the day that the Lord sendeth rain upon the earth.

"And she went and did according to the saying of Elijah: and she, and he, and her house, did eat many days.

"And the barrel of meal wasted not, neither did the cruse of oil fail."[7] This is the faith that has ever motivated and inspired the welfare plan of the Lord.

Industry, thrift, and self-reliance continue as guiding principles of this effort. As a people, we should avoid unreasonable debt. In a message which Elder Ezra Taft Benson delivered at a general conference in 1957, he instructed: "In the book of Kings we read about a woman who came weeping to . . . the prophet [of the Lord]. Her husband had died, and she owed a debt that she could not pay; and the creditor was on his way to take her two sons and sell them as slaves.

"By a miracle, [the prophet] enabled her to acquire a goodly supply of oil. And he said to her: 'Go, sell the oil, and pay thy debt, and live.'"[8]

"Pay thy debt, and live."[9] What wise counsel for us today! Remember, the wisdom of God may appear as foolishness to men, but the greatest single lesson we can learn in mortality is that when God speaks and a man obeys, that man will always be right.

We should remember that the best storehouse system would be for every family to have a year's supply of needed food, clothing, and, where possible, the other necessities of life. In the early Church, Paul wrote to Timothy: "If any provide not for his own, and specially for those of his own house, he hath denied the faith, and is worse than an infidel."[10]

It is our sacred duty to care for our families. Often we see what might be called "parent neglect." Too frequently the emotional, social, and, in some instances, even the material essentials of life are not provided by children to their aged parents. This is displeasing to the Lord.

The Lord's storehouse includes the time, talents, skills, compassion, consecrated material, and financial means of faithful Church members. These resources are available to the bishop in assisting those in need. Our bishops have the responsibility to learn how to use properly these resources.

May I suggest in summary form five basic guidelines:

1. A bishop is to seek out the poor, as the Lord has commanded, and administer to their needs.
2. In caring for the needy, a bishop exercises discernment, sound judgment, balance, and compassion. Church resources represent a sacred trust.
3. Those receiving welfare assistance are to work to the extent of their ability for that which is received.
4. The assistance given by the bishop is temporary, rather than ongoing.
5. The bishop assists with basic life-sustaining goods and services. He sustains lives rather than lifestyles.

Let me illustrate with a sacred experience which brought these guidelines together in blessing the lives of those in need.

While serving as a bishop, one cold winter day I visited an elderly couple who lived in a two-room duplex. The modest home was heated by a small coal-burning Heatrola. As I approached the home, I met the 82-year-old husband, his aged body bent in the driving snow as he gathered a few pieces of wet coal from his exposed supply of fuel. I helped him with his burden but made a solemn resolve to do more.

I prayed and pondered, seeking a solution. Step by step the inspiration came. In the ward was an unemployed carpenter. He had no fuel for his furnace but was too proud to receive the stoker slack he needed to keep his house warm. I suggested to the carpenter a way he could work for the help he received. Would he build a coal shed for a couple in need? "Of course," he replied.

Now, where were we to obtain the materials? I approached

the proprietors of a local lumberyard from whom we frequently purchased products. I remember saying to the men, "How would the two of you like to paint a bright spot on your souls this winter day?" Not knowing exactly what I meant, they agreed readily. They were invited to donate the lumber and hardware for the coal shed.

Within days the project was completed. I was invited to inspect the outcome. The coal shed was simply beautiful in its sleek covering of battleship-gray paint. The carpenter, who was a high priest, testified that he had actually felt inspired as he labored on this modest shed.

My older friend, with obvious appreciation, stroked the wall of the sturdy structure. He pointed out to me the wide door, the shiny hinges, and then opened to my view the supply of dry coal which filled the shed. In a voice filled with emotion, he said in words I shall ever treasure, "Bishop, take a look at the finest coal shed a man ever had." Its beauty was surpassed only by the pride in the builder's heart. And the elderly recipient labored each day at the ward chapel, dusting the benches, vacuuming the carpet runners, arranging the hymnbooks. He, too, worked for that which he had received.

Once again, the welfare plan of the Lord had blessed the lives of His children.

May our Heavenly Father guide the priesthood of this Church, that we may be obedient to the revelation of the Lord to the Prophet Joseph in which we are charged to "remember in all things the poor and the needy, the sick and the afflicted, for he that doeth not these things, the same is not my disciple."[11]

We will qualify as His disciples when we hear and heed the counsel from Isaiah describing the true fast, the spirit and the promise of the welfare effort:

"Is it not to deal thy bread to the hungry, and that thou bring the poor that are cast out to thy house? when thou seest the naked, that thou cover him; and that thou hide not thyself from thine own flesh?

"Then shall thy light break forth as the morning, and thine health shall spring forth speedily: and thy righteousness shall go before thee; the glory of the Lord shall be thy rereward.

"Then shalt thou call, and the Lord shall answer; thou shalt cry, and he shall say, Here I am. . . .

"And the Lord shall guide thee continually, and satisfy thy soul in drought, . . . and thou shalt be like a watered garden, and like a spring of water, whose waters fail not."[12]

NOTES

1. Mosiah 4:26.
2. "Basics of Church Welfare," talk given to the Priesthood Board, March 6, 1974, 10.
3. See *Improvement Era,* December 1902, 148.
4. In Conference Report, April 1974, 184.
5. Doctrine and Covenants 83:6.
6. Doctrine and Covenants 104:16.
7. 1 Kings 17:9–11, 13–16 (see also v. 12).
8. In Conference Report, April 1957, 53.
9. 2 Kings 4:7.
10. 1 Timothy 5:8.
11. Doctrine and Covenants 52:40.
12. Isaiah 58:7–9, 11.

27

IS THERE A DOCTOR IN THE HOUSE?

SOME YEARS AGO I WAS in the office of then Elder Spencer W. Kimball and he asked me if I had a moment to speak with him. He inquired, "Brother Monson, are you superstitious?"

I said, "No, but I never walk under a ladder."

He said, "I wasn't superstitious until this morning. Let me tell you about it."

I sat back in my chair, and he continued. "I had three marriages in a row this morning in the Salt Lake Temple. They were to be performed in the same room, with an anticipated capacity crowd for each one.

"During the first marriage, I heard a gasp from the group and turned around to find that one of the witnesses had passed out. Instinctively I asked, 'Is there a doctor in the house?' Since no one in the room responded, we opened the door into the hallway, where the second group was assembling. After I repeated the question, one man came forward and said, 'I am a doctor.' He hurried into the room, produced some smelling salts, and revived the witness who had fainted. With the witness back in place, I finished the ceremony."

Brother Kimball continued, "When that second group came into the room, I again thanked the doctor for helping us. I was proceeding with the second ceremony when suddenly the bride fainted at the altar! The same doctor rushed to her aid, with the same beneficial result, and the ceremony went forward.

"As the second group was leaving and the third group preparing to come in, I said to the doctor, 'Would you mind remaining for the third marriage?' He did. Thank heaven his services were not needed for that ceremony."

Brother Kimball had a nice smile on his face as he indicated he felt divine intervention had placed a doctor there who had helped alleviate many hearts on that special day.

I think of the noble service rendered by so many fine doctors, ofttimes without a fee and, in certain instances, making the difference between life and death. I believe they will never know the full effect of many of the services they render in a variety of situations.

I should like to mention a few cases tonight, with the outcome known fully only to our Heavenly Father.

In August of 1990, Elder Russell M. Nelson brought to my office a young boy from Bulgaria who had come to Salt Lake City for medical treatment. He was eight-year-old Evgeny Christov, and he had come to Primary Children's Medical Center for urological surgery, having been born with malformed urinary organs. Reconstructive surgery was performed here.

Elder Nelson had first learned of this youngster's circumstance about six months earlier when he had an assignment to Sofia, Bulgaria. Since there was no doctor in Bulgaria who could perform the surgery Evgeny needed, Elder Nelson, upon his return to Salt Lake City, had made arrangements for the young boy, whose father was an official in the Bulgarian government, to come to Salt Lake City.

In addition to Elder Nelson, the young boy was accompanied to my office by an uncle who was able to interpret for us. Young Evgeny was doing well, and we visited for a time. I told him how brave he had been to come such a long distance from his home and to undergo this difficult surgery. As I spoke with him, I tried to think of something I could give him as a souvenir of our visit. I remembered a commemorative medallion I had received when Rex Lee was inaugurated as president of Brigham Young University. It was in a drawer in my desk in a beautiful little box with a velvet lining.

I took the box from my drawer and, through the interpreter, told Evgeny that I wanted him to have this medal for bravery. As he opened the box and saw the medallion, his eyes lit up and he smiled broadly.

When it was time for him to leave, Evgeny did so clutching tightly his medal for bravery.

Missionary work now continues on a more even keel in Bulgaria.

Incidentally, when I later told Rex Lee of this meeting, he sent six additional boxes containing medallions and promised more when those ran out.

Dr. Gary R. Hunter is one who has shared his skills in faraway places, leaving his demanding practice, accompanied by his wife and daughter as his nurses. Together they journeyed to Africa and there, with local doctors, performed plastic surgery on those whose lives were thereafter improved and changed.

In the late 1960s, J. Vernon Monson served as president of the Rarotonga Mission in the Cook Islands. During his first few months there, he observed a great need for an eye specialist and eye surgeon. Several of the members of the Church were in dire need of eye surgery, along with numerous others not members of the Church. No service was available in the islands.

President Vernon Monson approached the medical people in Rarotonga, as well as the Premier, The Honorable Albert

Henry, and was given every encouragement that if he could get an eye specialist to come for a few weeks, he would have every cooperation.

Vernon Monson decided he would write to his nephew, Dr. Odeen Manning, an ophthalmologist. He did so, outlining the following conditions:

1. There would be no remuneration.
2. Dr. Manning would pay his own expenses.
3. He would be away from his own very profitable practice in Woodland Hills, California, for a period of two months.
4. He would bring his own surgical instruments.
5. Dr. Manning and his wife would be furnished free room and board at the mission home.

Upon receiving the letter from Vernon Monson, Dr. Manning sent off an airmail letter stating, "I accept!"

During the next six months, the necessary planning and arrangements were taken care of, and the Mannings arrived on April 15, 1969. The members gave them a reception the evening they arrived, and the next morning they went to work.

The government provided a car and driver who picked them up each morning and returned them to the mission home each night. They also provided two or three doctors, not ophthalmologists, and several trained nurses, as well as an operating room and hospital facilities. The government also provided, for many who were in serious need of eye care, transportation from some of the outer islands.

All in all, 284 patients were examined, with most being fitted or refitted for glasses. There were 53 patients who had serious eye operations, 20 of whom were members of the Church.

As Dr. Manning's stay came to an end, the entire island responded with thanks. The doctors and medical staff at the hospital gave a farewell reception and bestowed gifts. The patients and friends gave a special *umakai* (a luau) with 300 people present—and more gifts. And to top it off, the government of the Cook Islands gave a farewell function at the Hotel Rarotonga with 200 invited guests, including the entire cabinet and their wives. And more gifts.

The program provided benefits beyond improved eyesight to those in need. The members of the Church were buoyed up and received a new pride in being members of the Church that brought this medical service to the islands.

Dr. Ralph Montgomery is a prominent dentist in Salt Lake City, now retired. Several years ago, Dr. Montgomery helped to organize the Salt Lake Donated Dental Services, where dentists in the Salt Lake Valley could donate their time and talents in behalf of the homeless and others who, because of their circumstances, are unable to afford any dental care. Dr. Montgomery and numerous other dentists in the Valley have rotated in providing services at the clinic. In addition, their dental hygienists and assistants also donate their time and talents.

Dr. Montgomery spent a great amount of time, prior to opening the clinic in Salt Lake City, in providing dental service, free of charge, in countries such as the Philippines and China.

Among others who have been benefitted by the Salt Lake Donated Dental Services are the many mothers who find it necessary to work in order to support their family and who, without such dental work, would find their opportunities for employment foreclosed.

For our next case, I present an illustration involving many people, some speaking Portuguese and some speaking English, with extensive communications between two nations.

When Ricardo Santana was just a young boy in Brazil, his family joined the Church, and so Ricardo was essentially raised in the Church.

Ricardo's father was a noncommissioned officer in the Brazilian Army, and when he was old enough, Ricardo applied to Brazil's Military Academy—their equivalent of West Point—and was accepted. Ricardo did extremely well. Not only did he play on the Academy basketball team, but he also was a student cadet corps leader. He was six feet six inches tall—a handsome black man, quiet, gentle, soft-voiced, yet showing a fierce determination when necessary. When he graduated high in his class, his future as an officer seemed bright.

Then, in 1987, Ricardo was injured in an automobile accident, suffering a severe fracture of his femur. The Brazilian doctors pinned it, but it wouldn't heal and eventually became infected. The doctors removed some of the infected bone, but still there remained many problems. Finally, the army doctors in Brazil decided they should amputate the leg, since the infection was spreading and the situation was becoming life threatening.

Ricardo went to his local Church leaders and received a blessing. Elder Dallas N. Archibald, who was in the Area Presidency there, heard about the situation and talked with Ricardo in an attempt to find out if something more could be done. Brother Archibald said he had to be very careful not to criticize the Brazilian doctors, but he felt Ricardo needed medical attention in the United States. He was able to get copies of Ricardo's X-rays and medical reports, and he and Elder Camargo determined they would take the medical records to Salt Lake City with them when they attended April conference in 1989.

The records were delivered to Dr. George Veasy at LDS Hospital in Salt Lake City. Dr. Veasy saw that the problem was extremely severe and indicated that there was little hope of saving the leg. He had, however, heard of a physician doing actual bone regeneration research—a Dr. Eric Johnson at UCLA Medical Center. He suggested that maybe Dr. Johnson could help.

So Elder Camargo contacted attorney Roger Beitler, former president of the Brazil São Paulo South Mission, who was practicing law in Glendora, California, to see if he could reach Dr. Johnson in an attempt to get help for Ricardo Santana. Elder Camargo sent him a full set of X-rays and medical reports in English to share with Dr. Johnson.

Brother Beitler made an appointment to meet with Dr. Eric Johnson, a young orthopedic surgeon doing cutting-edge surgical research on bone repair and rejuvenation. When Brother Beitler described Ricardo's serious problems, Dr. Johnson indicated this was exactly the kind of injuries he had been experimenting with and that he and a Russian surgeon had developed surgical methods he thought would be successful with Ricardo. Dr. Johnson commented that he was always amazed at how the Mormon church could put together a network to take care of its own. Only after he had agreed to help Ricardo did Dr. Johnson mention that he, too, was a member of the Church. No one had known this beforehand.

Brother Beitler contacted Elder Camargo, who was back in Brazil by this time, and told him of Dr. Johnson's willingness to help. The brethren there in Brazil were able to get a round-trip ticket for Ricardo to travel to Los Angeles and back. On Saturday, August 19, 1989, Ricardo arrived at the Los Angeles International Airport.

On Monday, August 21, 1989, the Beitlers took Ricardo to UCLA and turned him over to Dr. Johnson. Brother Beitler made arrangements with his former mission secretary, John McClurg, and his wife, whose small apartment was only two blocks from the UCLA orthopedic clinic, to take care of Ricardo during the testing and examination stage. The McClurgs were thrilled to help. President Howard Anderson of the Los Angeles Stake had organized a special committee to assist people being treated at the UCLA Medical Center, and these members, as well, went into high gear to take care of Ricardo.

Ricardo finally went into the UCLA Hospital for a surgery

and therapy period. Afterward, Dr. Johnson wanted Ricardo to rest for several weeks before going through a second surgery and treatment period, during which time Ricardo needed to be near UCLA for outpatient drug therapy. A former Brazilian missionary, Michael Fletcher, lived nearby and had a spare basement apartment which he offered, so Ricardo went there and was cared for by the Fletchers as though he were one of their own.

When Dr. Johnson reexplored Ricardo's thigh in an attempt to clean out any residual infection and possibly place a bone graft into the "defect areas" to prevent future fracture, he found the condition of the tissues and bone unbelievable. There was no evidence of infection anywhere in the leg, no evidence of acute inflammation.

Ricardo returned to the UCLA Hospital for the second series of operations in late October. Dr. Johnson said that he had never seen such rapid conversion of an infected femur to a viable bone in the weeks since the operation. He indicated that these types of bone infections require years to remodel and change. He was amazed. The first X-rays had looked as if a giant shark had taken a bite of the bone, leaving only a small connection. The new X-rays looked regular; the bone was whole and complete. There were no indications of any weakness, damage, or disease.

Dr. Johnson said, "The course and healing of Brother Santana's left leg was beyond the expertise that I possess and was of a divine nature."

A year or two after the surgery, I met Ricardo Santana by chance in Salt Lake City. He had recently married the daughter of Elder Helvecio Martins, who was then a member of the Second Quorum of the Seventy, and the family had traveled to Salt Lake City for general conference. This sweet, humble young man walked perfectly and expressed heartfelt gratitude to his Heavenly Father and to Dr. Eric Johnson for the healing miracle he had experienced.

Today Ricardo, a high priest, lives in Brazil with his wife, Marisa, and his six-year-old daughter, where he serves faithfully in the Santo Andre Second Ward.

Knowing of the service so many doctors render unheralded by many but ofttimes having life-changing consequences, I reflect for a moment on the experience of Peter and John at the Gate Beautiful of the temple. One sympathizes with the plight of the man lame from birth who each day was carried to the temple gate that he might ask alms of all who entered. That he asked alms of Peter and John as they approached him indicates he regarded them no differently from others who must have passed by him each day. I love Peter's simple and direct instruction: "Look on us."[1] The lame man gave heed to them.

"Then Peter said, Silver and gold have I none; but such as I have give I thee: In the name of Jesus Christ of Nazareth rise up and walk. And he took him by the right hand, and lifted him up: . . . He . . . stood, and walked, and entered with them into the temple."[2]

When men and women lay aside the frantic schedules they are required to keep and the many demands of their profession to reach out in the types of endeavors I have highlighted today, they will discover a resurgence of their desire to help, and in each instance they will realize that they have returned with no diminution of ability but with a heart filled with gratitude, for they will find they have been on the Lord's errand and have been the beneficiaries of His help and blessings.

NOTES
1. Acts 3:4.
2. Acts 3:6–8.

28

PREPARATION PRECEDES PERFORMANCE

In the races we ran as schoolboys, we would signal the start of the race with the expression, "Ready, get set, go!" And we were off and running. Later, when I was a young man training for service in the navy, one element of that training involved a grueling day at the rifle range. Over and over again we would hear the command, "Ready, aim, fire!" No one returned to the barracks until all had qualified.

In a very real sense, all of you who hold the Aaronic Priesthood are entering into the most exciting and challenging period of your young lives, even the race of life. Danger abounds, enemies lurk; but God is near to guide your way and insure your victory. May I suggest four guidelines which, when followed, will assure your success in every endeavor you undertake:

1. Grow in wisdom.
2. Walk by faith.
3. Teach through testimony.
4. Serve with love.

Let us for a few minutes discuss each of these guides to your success.

First, **grow in wisdom.** There is but little recorded concerning the boyhood of the Master, even the Lord Jesus Christ. We marvel at His experience in the temple and His response when His loved ones "found him in the temple, sitting in the midst of the doctors, both hearing them, and asking them questions.

"And all that heard him were astonished at his understanding and answers.

"And when they saw him, they were amazed: and his mother said unto him, Son, why hast thou thus dealt with us? behold, thy father and I have sought thee sorrowing.

"And he said unto them, How is it that ye sought me? wist ye not that I must be about my Father's business?. . . .

"And Jesus increased in wisdom and stature, and in favour with God and man."[1] I think it most interesting that Jesus was 12 years old when this event transpired—the identical age when you were ordained deacons.

As you who hold the Aaronic Priesthood prepare yourselves in the classrooms of learning, that you can better meet the challenges of life, please remember the advice of Henry Ford, the American industrialist, who said: "An educated man is not one whose memory is trained to carry a few dates in history. He is one who can accomplish things. A man who cannot think is not an educated man, however many college degrees he may have acquired. Thinking is the hardest work anyone can do, which is probably the reason why we have so few thinkers."[2]

It is hazardous in the extreme to count on a situation typical of one I read about some years ago pertaining to a large, ecclesiastically oriented college in the eastern part of America, where every student had to enroll in a class called Religion 1. The professor of that particular class had been there many years and loved the writings and teachings of the Apostle

Paul. He loved them with such a vigor that that is about all he taught in Religion 1. Consequently, he would tell the class at the beginning of the semester, "I will not give any examinations during the semester except the final. The result of the final examination will determine your grade for the course."

Now, that would be kind of overwhelming, except that every semester for 21 years he had given the same examination in every class of Religion 1. The examination consisted of one question. And for all those years, the question had been the same. Can you believe it? What a snap class! The question had always been: *Describe the travels and teachings of the Apostle Paul.*

Some young people would come to class the first day and get their name on the record. That was about it until the final examination. Then they would come, having boned up on an answer to that question.

One particular semester, three young men who had followed that practice of registering and then absenting themselves until the end of the semester sat with their pencils poised as the professor went to the chalkboard and said, "I shall place on the board the question on which your entire grade will depend." To their great astonishment he did not write the usual question. Instead, he wrote, "Criticize the Sermon on the Mount."

One young man said, "I don't even know what book it is in." He closed his test book and left the room.

The second one thought for a moment. He didn't know anything about the Sermon on the Mount because he had prepared for a different test question. He left the room, anticipating a failing grade.

The third one of this trio stayed in the class. He wrote line after line and page after page. His friends were outside in the hallway, looking through the door window, wondering what he was writing. They knew that he had no more knowledge of the

Sermon on the Mount than did they, that he had prepared for the question that was not asked. They wondered what he was writing in that test book.

He didn't tell them until the day the papers were examined and returned. They all huddled around to see what grade he had received. He had an "A" on the test and in the course. As he opened the cover of the exam book, there was the instruction: "Criticize the Sermon on the Mount." And here is what this enterprising young man had written: "I will leave it to someone far more knowledgeable and experienced than I am to criticize the greatest sermon from the greatest life ever lived. As for me, I would prefer to describe the travels and teachings of the Apostle Paul."

A clever response is rarely an effective substitute for proper preparation, however. One lesson I learned well during my teenage years is the truth of the statement: "Something for nothing" is usually "nothing for something." Let me explain. During the time I was growing up, there was, at the Brighton and Lagoon resorts in Utah, as well as at the pier at Ocean Park, California, a glass-enclosed case displaying all sorts of gifts—a few of them more valuable than the rest. One put a coin in the slot and then operated mechanical claws which could be maneuvered in place to pick up a gift. Inevitably, when one of the more valuable gifts was captured, it would fall out of the claws before it was placed in position where it could be grasped by the person operating the machine and thus become his. Time would run out, the crane would return to its resting place and the tray which every boy imagined his gift would occupy lay empty.

That which we seek in life requires effort, preparation, study, and perseverance—and the determination to choose the right when a choice is placed before us.

Just because men can think the right thing does not mean that they will heed it. We remember Pierre, one of the central

240

characters in Tolstoy's monumental work *War and Peace.* Torn by spiritual agonies, Pierre cries out to God, "Why is it that I know what is right and I do what is wrong?" We can *know* what is right, but we don't always have the will to *do* what is right.

In a little different category, let us turn to a favorite of every boy—even Huckleberry Finn—as he, through the pen of Samuel Clemens, better known as Mark Twain, taught us a lesson. Huckleberry Finn is talking:

"It made me shiver. And I about made up my mind to pray and see if I couldn't try to quit being the kind of boy I was and be better. So I kneeled down. But the words wouldn't come. Why wouldn't they? It warn't no use to try and hide it from Him. . . . I knowed very well why they wouldn't come. It was because my heart warn't right; it was because I warn't square; it was because I was playing double. I was letting *on* to give up sin, but away inside of me I was holding on to the biggest one of all. I was trying to make my mouth *say* I would do the right and the clean thing . . . ; but deep down in me, I knowed it was a lie, and He knowed it. You can't pray a lie—I found that out."[3]

I know of no better formula to help each of us to grow in wisdom than is found in the seventeenth chapter of Alma:

"And now it came to pass that as Alma was journeying from the land of Gideon southward, away to the land of Manti, behold, to his astonishment, he met with the sons of Mosiah journeying towards the land of Zarahemla.

"Now these sons of Mosiah were with Alma at the time the angel first appeared unto him; therefore Alma did rejoice exceedingly to see his brethren; and what added more to his joy, they were still his brethren in the Lord; yea, and they had waxed strong in the knowledge of the truth; for they were men of a sound understanding and they had searched the scriptures diligently, that they might know the word of God.

"But this is not all; they had given themselves to much

prayer, and fasting; therefore they had the spirit of prophecy, and the spirit of revelation, and when they taught, they taught with power and authority of God."[4]

Second, **walk by faith.** A deacon with whom I became acquainted is not with us tonight. I speak of Aaron Daniel Bower, who died of the ravages of spina bifida and leukemia at home a few months ago. Aaron was really a living miracle. In his short lifetime of 13 years, his small body underwent 33 major surgeries, radiation, and chemotherapy, along with innumerable lab tests and diagnostic procedures. Aaron, however, taught us valuable lessons. He always chose to do the loving deed, to speak the kind word, and he was a friend to everyone he met. His smile lit up the world. He taught us courage, compassion, and unconditional love.

Aaron treasured the Aaronic Priesthood which he held, and even though it was difficult for him to climb stairs, he was still able to accept an assignment to take the sacrament to those on the stand. When he became confined to a wheelchair, Aaron was able to hold the bread or water trays on his lap. The other deacons would seek for the privilege of wheeling Aaron around during the sacrament. He was a superb example of one who "walked" by faith. He was a model, fashioned by courage and faith, worthy for others to follow.

Third, **teach through testimony.** Elder Mark E. Petersen was fond of reciting a short poem which contained these words:

> *Give me the old time religion,*
> *Give me the old time religion,*
> *Give me the old time religion,*
> *It's good enough for me.*
>
> *It was taught by Paul and Peter,*
> *It was taught by Paul and Peter,*
> *It was taught by Paul and Peter,*
> *And it's good enough for me.*

What did the Apostle Paul say about teaching through testimony? How about the Apostle Peter? What did he teach? Paul declared to the Romans: "For I am not ashamed of the gospel of Christ: for it is the power of God unto salvation to every one that believeth."[5] The late Elder Delbert L. Stapley often taught that if we are not ashamed of the gospel of Christ, we should not be ashamed to teach it; and if we are not ashamed to teach it, we should not be ashamed to live it.

Some years ago I attended a stake conference in the southern part of the United States, where Elder Stapley served as a missionary in his youth. After the conference concluded, a sister came forward and opened for my view a rather old copy of the Book of Mormon. She asked, "Do you know the man who inscribed this book when he was a missionary and presented it to my grandparents?"

I looked at the signature, immediately recognized its authenticity, and replied, "Yes, I serve with Elder Stapley."

She then asked, "Would you please take this book to Elder Stapley with our love and tell him that his testimony and this book guided my entire family to become members of the Church."

I wholeheartedly assented to her request. However, I waited for an appropriate opportunity when neither of us was hurried, and then I went to Elder Stapley's office, told him of my experience, and handed him the copy of the Book of Mormon he had presented many years before. He read the inscription he had written on the title page of the book and saw his name; then great tears came to his eyes and coursed down his cheeks. Teaching through testimony had brought to him indescribable joy and profound gratitude.

Fourth, **serve with love.** As bearers of the Aaronic Priesthood, you have weekly, if not daily, opportunities to serve with love. I hope each of you will live the teachings of the Lord and keep His commandments so you can qualify to be worthy to fill a mission. Until that day dawns, you will have the privilege as a deacon, as a teacher, as a priest to prepare for such divine service.

Bishops, may I suggest that you guide the footsteps of every deacon, that he may receive a spiritual awareness of the sacredness of his ordained calling. In my life this was accomplished when the bishopric asked that I, as a deacon, take the sacrament to a shut-in who lived about a half mile from the chapel. That special Sunday morning, as I knocked on the door of Brother Wright's humble home, I heard his feeble reply, "Come in." I entered not only his humble cottage but also a room filled with the Spirit of the Lord. I approached his bedside and carefully placed a piece of the bread to his lips. I then held the cup of water, that he might drink. As I departed, I saw him smile, and he moved his fingers through my blond hair and said, "God bless you, my boy." And God did bless me with an appreciation which continues even today for the sacred emblems.

Is every ordained teacher given the assignment to home teach? What an opportunity to prepare for a mission. What a privilege to learn the discipline of duty. A boy will automatically turn from concern for self when he is assigned to "watch over" others.[6]

And what of the priests? These young men have the opportunity to bless the sacrament, to continue their home teaching duties, and to participate in the sacred ordinance of baptism.

My dear brethren, do you with me remember the name of a popular ballad of our time, "I Did It My Way"? May I suggest that there is really a better way—even the Lord's way. Let us learn of Him, let us follow in His footsteps, let us live by His precepts. By so doing, we will be prepared for any service He calls us to perform. This is His work. This is His Church. Indeed, He is our captain, the King of Glory, even the Son of God, of whom I testify that He lives.

NOTES

1. Luke 2:46–48, 52.
2. In Thomas S. Monson, *Favorite Quotations from the Collection of Thomas S. Monson* (1985), 235.
3. Mark Twain, *The Adventures of Huckleberry Finn* (1965), 205; emphasis added.
4. Alma 17:1–3.
5. Romans 1:16.
6. Doctrine and Covenants 20:53.

The Worth of Souls

29

LABELS

THE NATIONAL GALLERY at Trafalgar Square in London, England, is one of the truly great museums of art in all the world. The gallery proudly proclaims its Rembrandt Room and Constable Corner and urges all to take the tour of Turner's masterpieces. Visitors come from every corner of the earth. They depart uplifted and inspired.

During a recent visit to the National Gallery, I was surprised to see displayed in a most prominent location magnificent portraits and landscapes which featured the name of no artist. Then I noticed a large placard which provided this explanation:

"This exhibition is drawn from the large number of paintings that hang in a public but somewhat neglected area of the Gallery—the lower floor. The exhibition is intended to encourage visitors to look at the paintings without being too worried about who painted them. In several instances, we do not precisely know.

"The information on labels on paintings can often affect, half unconsciously, our estimate of them; and here labeling has been deliberately subordinate in the hope that visitors will read

249

only after they have looked and made their own assessment of each work."

Like the labels on paintings are the outward appearances of some men—often misleading. The Master declared to one group: "Woe unto you, scribes and Pharisees, hypocrites! for ye are like unto whited sepulchres, which indeed appear beautiful outward, but are within full of dead men's bones, and of all uncleanness. . . . Ye . . . outwardly appear righteous unto men, but within ye are full of hypocrisy and iniquity."[1]

Then there are those who may outwardly appear impoverished, without talent, and doomed to mediocrity. A classic label appeared beneath a picture of the boy Abraham Lincoln as he stood in front of his humble birthplace—a simple log cabin. The words read: "Ill-housed, ill-clothed, ill-fed." Unanticipated, unspoken, and unprinted was the real label of the boy: "Destined for immortal glory."

As the poet expressed:

> Nobody knows what a boy is worth;
> We'll have to wait and see.
> But every man in a noble place
> A boy once used to be.[2]

At another time, and in a distant place, the boy Samuel must have appeared like any lad his age as he ministered unto the Lord before Eli. As Samuel lay down to sleep and heard the voice of the Lord calling him, Samuel mistakenly thought it was aged Eli calling and responded, "Here am I."[3] However, after Eli had listened to the boy's account and told him it was of the Lord, Samuel followed Eli's counsel and subsequently responded to the Lord's call with the memorable reply, "Speak; for thy servant heareth."[4] The record then reveals that "Samuel grew, and the Lord was with him, . . . and all Israel from Dan even to Beer-sheba knew that Samuel was established to be a prophet of the Lord."[5]

The years rolled by, as they relentlessly do, and prophecy came to fulfillment when a lowly manger cradled a newborn child. No label could describe this event. With the birth of the babe in Bethlehem, there emerged a great endowment, a power stronger than weapons, a wealth more lasting than the coins of Caesar. This child, born in such primitive circumstances, was to be the "King of kings, and Lord of lords,"[6] the promised Messiah—even Jesus Christ, the Son of God.

As a boy, Jesus was found in the temple, "sitting in the midst of the doctors, both hearing them, and asking them questions. And all that heard him were astonished at his understanding and answers." And when Joseph and His mother saw Him, "they were amazed."[7] To the learned doctors in the temple, the boy's outward label may have conveyed brightness of intellect but certainly not "Son of God and future Redeemer of all mankind."

The Messianic words of the prophet Isaiah convey a special meaning: "He hath no form nor comeliness; and when we shall see him, there is no beauty that we should desire him."[8] Such was the foretold description of our Lord.

Matthew records the apparent necessity of that wicked multitude of sinners who would seek after the life of the Lord to conspire with the betrayer Judas, that he might point out to them who of the apostolic group was the Jesus whom they sought. These chilling verses from sacred writ torment the reader: "Now he that betrayed him gave them a sign, saying, Whomsoever I shall kiss, that same is he: hold him fast.

"And forthwith he came to Jesus, and said, Hail, master; and kissed him.

"And Jesus said unto him, Friend, wherefore art thou come? Then came they, and laid hands on Jesus, and took him."[9]

The label of a traitor's kiss had identified the Master. Judas now wore his own label of inescapable shame and revulsion.

Sometimes cities and nations bear special labels of identity. Such was a cold and very old city in eastern Canada. The missionaries called it "Stony Kingston." There had been but one convert to the Church in six years, even though missionaries had been continuously assigned there during the entire interval. No one baptized in Kingston. Just ask any missionary who labored there. Time in Kingston was marked on the calendar like days in prison. A missionary transfer to another place—anyplace—would be uppermost in thoughts, even in dreams.

While I was praying about and pondering this sad dilemma, for my responsibility then as a mission president required that I pray and ponder about such things, my wife called to my attention an excerpt from the book, *A Child's Story of the Prophet Brigham Young,* by Deta Petersen Neeley. She read aloud that Brigham Young entered Kingston, Ontario, on a cold and snow-filled day. He labored there 30 days and baptized 45 souls.[10] Here was the answer. If the missionary Brigham Young could accomplish this harvest, so could the missionaries of today.

Without providing an explanation, I withdrew the missionaries from Kingston, that the cycle of defeat might be broken. Then the carefully circulated word: "Soon a new city will be opened for missionary work, even the city where Brigham Young proselyted and baptized 45 persons in 30 days." The missionaries speculated as to the location. Their weekly letters pleaded for the assignment to this Shangri-la. More time passed. Then four carefully selected missionaries—two of them new, two of them experienced—were chosen for this high adventure. The members of the small branch pledged their support. The missionaries pledged their lives. The Lord honored both.

In the space of three months, Kingston became the most productive city of the Canadian Mission. The gray limestone buildings still stood, the city had not altered its appearance, the population remained constant. The change was one of attitude. The label of doubt had yielded to the label of faith.

The branch president of the Kingston Branch of the Church wore his own identifying label. Gustav Wacker was from the old country. He spoke English with a thick accent. He never owned or drove a car. He plied the trade of a barber. The highlight of his day would be when he had the privilege to cut the hair of a missionary. Never would there be a charge. Indeed, he would reach deep into his pockets and give the missionaries all of his tips for the day. If it were raining, as it often does in Kingston, President Wacker would call a taxi and send the missionaries to their apartment by taxi, while he himself, at day's end, would lock the small shop and walk home—in the driving rain.

I first met Gustav Wacker when I noticed that his tithing paid was far in excess of that expected from his potential income. My efforts to explain that the Lord required no more than ten percent as tithing fell on attentive but unconvinced ears. He simply responded that he loved to pay all he could to the Lord. It amounted to about half his income. His dear wife felt exactly as he did. Their unique manner of tithing payment continued throughout their earning lives.

Gustav and Margarete Wacker established a home that was a heaven. They were not blessed with children but mothered and fathered their many church visitors. A sophisticated and learned leader from Ottawa told me, "I like to visit President Wacker. I come away refreshed in spirit and determined to ever live close to the Lord."

Did our Heavenly Father honor such abiding faith? The branch prospered. The membership outgrew the rented Slovakian Hall and moved into a modern and lovely chapel of their own. President and Sister Wacker had their prayers answered by serving a proselyting mission to their native Germany and later a temple mission to the beautiful temple in Washington, D.C. While they were serving that temple mission, Gustav Wacker passed away peacefully while being held in the loving arms of his eternal companion. Only one label appears fitting for such an obedient and faithful servant: "Who honors God, God honors."[11]

A label that often keeps people from making connections and participating in the joy of the gospel is "less active." Many years ago, as a bishop, I worried about any members of the ward who wore this label. Such was my thought one day as I drove down the street where Ben and Emily lived. The aches and pains of advancing years had caused them to withdraw from activity to the shelter of their home—isolated, detached, shut out from the mainstream of daily life and association. Ben and Emily had not been in our sacrament meeting for many years. Ben, who had, many years before served as a bishop in another ward, loved to sit in his front room reading the New Testament.

I was en route from my uptown sales office to our plant. For some reason I had driven down First West, a street I never had traveled before to reach the destination of our plant. Then I felt the unmistakable prompting to park my car and visit Ben and Emily, even though I was on my way to a meeting. I did not heed the impression at first but drove on for two more blocks; however, when the impression came again, I returned to their home.

I approached the door to their home and knocked. Emily opened the door and, upon seeing me—her bishop—she exclaimed, "All day long I have waited for my phone to ring. It has been silent. I hoped that the postman would deliver a letter. He brought only bills. Bishop, how did you know today is my birthday?"

I answered, "Our Heavenly Father knows, Emily, for He loves you. I don't know why I was directed here today, but He knows. Let's kneel in prayer and ask Him."

Ben came into the room, and the three of us knelt in prayer. The reason for my visit was made clear as I felt impressed to invite both Ben and Emily to join us in our Church meetings, asking each of them to respond to a particular assignment. Each accepted and began regular attendance once again at Church, remaining active for the rest of their lives. That day of my visit with Ben and Emily, hearts were touched and souls saved. A label that had held them back was replaced with the joy of full fellowship.

Another label frequently seen and grudgingly borne is one which reads: "Handicapped."

Years ago, President Spencer W. Kimball shared with President Gordon B. Hinckley, Elder Bruce R. McConkie, and me an experience he had in the appointment of a patriarch for the Shreveport Louisiana Stake of the Church. President Kimball described how he interviewed, how he searched, and how he prayed, that he might learn the Lord's will concerning the selection. For some reason, none of the suggested candidates was the man for this assignment at this particular time.

The day wore on. The evening meetings began. Suddenly President Kimball turned to the stake president and asked him to identify a particular man seated perhaps two-thirds of the way back from the front of the chapel. The stake president replied that the individual was James Womack, whereupon President Kimball said, "He is the man the Lord has selected to be your stake patriarch. Please have him meet with me in the high council room following the meeting."

Stake president Charles Cagle was startled, for James Womack did not wear the label of a typical man. He had sustained terrible injuries while in combat during World War II. He lost both hands and one arm, as well as most of his eyesight and part of his hearing. Nobody had wanted to let him in law school when he returned, yet he finished third in his class at Louisiana State University. James Womack simply refused to wear the label "Handicapped."

That evening as President Kimball met with Brother

Womack and informed him that the Lord had designated him to be the patriarch, there was a protracted silence in the room. Then Brother Womack said, "Brother Kimball, it is my understanding that a patriarch is to place his hands on the head of the person he blesses. As you can see, I have no hands to place on the head of anyone."

Brother Kimball, in his kind and patient manner, invited Brother Womack to make his way to the back of the chair on which Brother Kimball was seated. He then said, "Now, Brother Womack, lean forward and see if the stumps of your arms will reach the top of my head." To Brother Womack's joy, they touched Brother Kimball, and the exclamation came forth, "I can reach you! I can reach you!"

"Of course you can reach me," responded Brother Kimball. "And if you can reach me, you can reach any whom you bless. I will be the shortest person you will ever have seated before you."

President Kimball reported to us that when the name of James Womack was presented to the stake conference, "the hands of the members shot heavenward in an enthusiastic vote of approval."

Like a golden thread woven through the tapestry of life is the message on the label of a humble heart. It was true of the boy Samuel, it was the experience of Jesus, it was the testimony of Gustav Wacker, it marked the calling of James Womack. May it ever be the label which identifies each of us: "Lord, here am I."

NOTES

1. Matthew 23:27–28.
2. Author unknown, "Nobody Knows What a Boy Is Worth," in *Best-Loved Poems of the LDS People* (1996), 19.
3. 1 Samuel 3:4.
4. 1 Samuel 3:10.
5. 1 Samuel 3:19–20.
6. 1 Timothy 6:15.

7. Luke 2:46–48.

8. Isaiah 53:2.

9. Matthew 26:48–50.

10. Deta Petersen Neeley, *A Child's Story of the Prophet Brigham Young* (1959), 36.

11. See 1 Samuel 2:30.

30

———◆———

Yellow Canaries with Gray on Their Wings

I WAS CALLED AS A YOUNG MAN to serve as the bishop of a large ward in Salt Lake City. The magnitude of the calling was overwhelming and the responsibility frightening. My inadequacy humbled me. But my Heavenly Father did not leave me to wander in darkness and in silence, uninstructed or uninspired. In His own way, He revealed the lessons He would have me learn.

One evening, at a late hour, my telephone rang. I heard a voice say, "Bishop Monson, this is the hospital calling. Kathleen McKee, a member of your congregation, has just passed away. Our records reveal that she had no next of kin, but your name is listed as the one to be notified in the event of her death. Could you come to the hospital right away?"

Upon arriving there, I was presented with a sealed envelope which contained a key to the modest apartment in which Kathleen McKee, a childless widow 73 years of age, had lived. That same night I entered her tidy basement apartment, turned the light switch, and in a moment discovered a letter written ever so meticulously in Kathleen McKee's own hand. It rested face up on a small table and read:

"Bishop Monson,

"I think I shall not return from the hospital. In the dresser drawer is a small insurance policy which will cover funeral expenses. The furniture may be given to my neighbors.

"In the kitchen are my three precious canaries. Two of them are beautiful, yellow-gold in color, and are perfectly marked. On their cages I have noted the names of friends to whom they are to be given. In the third cage is 'Billie.' He is my favorite. Billie looks a bit scrubby, and his yellow hue is marred by gray on his wings. Will you and your family make a home for him? He isn't the prettiest, but his song is the best."

In the days that followed, I learned much more about Kathleen McKee. She had befriended many neighbors in need. She had given cheer and comfort almost daily to a cripple who lived down the street. Indeed, she had brightened each life she touched. Kathleen McKee was much like "Billie," her prized yellow canary with gray on its wings. She was not blessed with beauty, gifted with poise, nor honored by posterity. Yet her song helped others to more willingly bear their burdens and more ably shoulder their tasks.

The world is filled with yellow canaries with gray on their wings. The pity is that so precious few of them have learned to sing. Perhaps the clear notes of proper example have not sounded in their ears or found lodgment in their hearts.

Some are young people who don't know who they are, what they can be or even want to be. They are afraid, but they don't know of what. They are angry, but they don't know at whom. They are rejected, and they don't know why. All they want is to be somebody.

Others are stooped with age, burdened with care, or filled with doubt—living lives far below the level of their capacities.

All of us are prone to excuse our own mediocre performance. We blame our misfortunes, our disfigurements, or our so-called handicaps. Victims of our own rationalization, we say silently to ourselves: "I'm just too weak," or "I'm not cut out for better things." Others soar beyond our meager accomplishments. Envy and discouragement then take their toll.

To live greatly, we must develop the capacity to face trouble with courage, disappointment with cheerfulness, and triumph with humility. You ask, "How might we achieve these goals?" I answer, "By getting a true perspective of who we really are!" We are sons and daughters of a living God in whose image we have been created. Think of that truth: "Created in the image of God." We cannot sincerely hold this conviction without experiencing a profound new sense of strength and power, even the strength to live the commandments of God, the power to resist the temptations of Satan.

True, we live in a world where moral character ofttimes is relegated to a position secondary to facial beauty or personal charm. We read and hear of local, national, and international beauty contests. Throngs pay tribute to Miss America, Miss World, and Miss Universe. Athletic prowess, too, has its following. The winter games, the world Olympics, the tournaments of international scope bring forth the adoring applause of the enthralled crowd. Such are the ways of men!

But what are the inspired words of God? From a time of long ago, the counsel of Samuel the prophet echoes in our ears: "The Lord seeth not as man seeth; for man looketh on the outward appearance, but the Lord looketh on the heart."[1]

Sham and hypocrisy found no place with the Lord Jesus Christ. He denounced the scribes and Pharisees for their vanity and shallow lives, their pretense and feigned righteousness. They, like the beautiful yellow canaries, were outwardly handsome, but a true song came not from their hearts.

To their counterparts on this continent, God's prophet declared: "For behold, ye do love money, and your substance, and your fine apparel, and the adorning of your churches, more than ye love the poor and the needy, the sick and the afflicted. . . .

Why are ye ashamed to take upon you the name of Christ? . . .
Why do ye adorn yourselves with that which hath no life, and yet
suffer the hungry, and the needy, and the naked, and the sick
and the afflicted to pass by you, and notice them not?"[2]

The Master could be found mingling with the poor, the
downtrodden, the oppressed, and the afflicted. He brought
hope to the hopeless, strength to the weak, and freedom to the
captive. He taught of the better life to come—even eternal life.
This knowledge ever directs those who receive the divine injunction: "Follow thou me." It guided Peter. It motivated Paul. It can
determine our personal destiny. Can we make the decision to
follow in righteousness and truth the Redeemer of the world?
With His help a rebellious boy can become an obedient man, a
wayward girl can cast aside the old self and begin anew. Indeed,
the gospel of Jesus Christ can change men's lives.

In his epistle to the Corinthians, the Apostle Paul taught:
"God hath chosen the weak things of the world to confound
the things which are mighty."[3]

When the Savior sought a man of faith, He did not select
him from the throng of self-righteous who were found regularly
in the synagogue. Rather, He called him from among the fishermen of Capernaum.

While teaching on the seashore, He saw two ships standing
by the lake. He entered one and asked its owner to put it out
a little from the land so He might not be pressed upon by the
crowd. After teaching further, He said to Simon, "Launch out
into the deep, and let down your nets."

Simon answered: "Master, we have toiled all the night, and
have taken nothing: nevertheless at thy word I will let down the
net. And when they had this done, they inclosed a great multitude of fishes. . . . When Simon Peter saw it, he fell down at Jesus'
knees, saying, Depart from me; for I am a sinful man, O Lord."[4]

Came the reply: "Follow me, and I will make you fishers of
men."[5] Simon the fisherman had received his call. Doubting,

disbelieving, unschooled, untrained, impetuous Simon did not find the way of the Lord a highway of ease nor a path free from pain. He was to hear the rebuke: "O thou of little faith,"[6] and likewise the denunciation, "Get thee behind me, Satan: thou art an offence unto me."[7] Yet, when the Master asked him, "Whom say ye that I am?" Peter answered: "Thou art the Christ, the Son of the living God."[8]

Simon, man of doubt, had become Peter, apostle of faith. A yellow canary with gray on his wings qualified for the Master's full confidence and abiding love.

When the Savior was to choose a missionary of zeal and power, He found him not among his advocates, but amidst his adversaries. Saul of Tarsus made havoc of the Church and breathed out threatenings and slaughter against the disciples of the Lord. But this was before the experience of Damascus Way. Of Saul, the Lord declared: "He is a chosen vessel unto me, to bear my name before the Gentiles, and kings, and the children of Israel: . . . I will shew him how great things he must suffer for my name's sake."[9]

Like the yellow canary with gray on his wings, Saul, who became Paul, also had his blemishes. He himself said: "And lest I should be exalted above measure through the abundance of the revelations, there was given to me a thorn in the flesh, the messenger of Satan to buffet me. . . . For this thing I besought the Lord thrice, that it might depart from me. And he said unto me, My grace is sufficient for thee: for my strength is made perfect in weakness."[10]

Both Paul and Peter were to expend their strength and forfeit their lives in the cause of truth. The Redeemer chose imperfect men to teach the way to perfection. He did so then. He does so now—even yellow canaries with gray on their wings.

He calls you and me to serve Him here below and sets us to the tasks He would have us fulfill. The commitment is total. There is no conflict of conscience. And in our struggle, should we stumble, then let us plead: "Lead us, oh lead us, great Molder of men; out of the darkness to strive once again."[11]

Our appointed task may appear insignificant, unnecessary, unnoticed. We may be tempted to question:

> "Father, where shall I work today?"
> And my love flowed warm and free.
> Then he pointed out a tiny spot
> And said, "Tend that for me."
> I answered quickly, "Oh no, not that!
> Why, no one would ever see,
> No matter how well my work was done.
> Not that little place for me."
> And the word he spoke, it was not stern;
> He answered me tenderly:
> "Ah, little one, search that heart of thine;
> Art thou working for them or for me?
> Nazareth was a little place,
> And so was Galilee."[12]

My prayer is that we indeed will follow that Man of Galilee. May we praise His name, and so order our lives so as to reflect our love. May we remember that to us God our Father gave His Son, and that for us Jesus Christ gave His life. I testify that He lives and pray we may be worthy of such a divine gift.

NOTES

1. 1 Samuel 16:7.
2. Mormon 8:37–39.
3. 1 Corinthians 1:27.
4. Luke 5:4–6, 8.
5. Matthew 4:19.
6. Matthew 14:31.
7. Matthew 16:23.
8. Matthew 16:15–16.
9. Acts 9:15–16.
10. 2 Corinthians 12:7–9.
11. From the "Fight Song," Yonkers High School.
12. Meade MacGuire, "Father, Where Shall I Work Today?" in *Best-Loved Poems of the LDS People* (1996), 152.

31

AN APOSTOLIC ODYSSEY

ONE DAY MANY YEARS AGO, I removed from my desk calendar a sheet bearing the date: February 28, 1985. History tugged at my heartstrings as I pondered the thought that 150 years earlier, in February of 1835, members of the first Quorum of the Twelve of this dispensation were chosen and ordained.

I reflected on my own calling to the Twelve in October of 1963. There coursed through my mind that solemn charge found in the 107th section of the Doctrine and Covenants, where the Lord declared: "The Twelve are a Traveling Presiding High Council, to officiate in the name of the Lord, under the direction of the Presidency of the Church, agreeable to the institution of heaven; to build up the church, and regulate all the affairs of the same in all nations."[1]

My ordination has taken me to many nations, spanning wide oceans, and a staggering number of miles in fulfillment of these divine words of revelation. I invite you to travel with me in thought on an apostolic odyssey as we revisit faithful people and beautiful lands and attend meetings where two or more were gathered in His name, and His Spirit was present and felt.

264

Let us begin with an example of simple faith and answered prayer in the small town of Vidor, Texas. In a routine manner I received the assignment to attend the Beaumont Texas Stake Conference and, upon arriving in Beaumont, learned that I would be privileged to dedicate a lovely chapel for a small branch of dedicated members in Vidor. The chapel was filled. Hearts were overflowing with gratitude that special night when it seemed heaven was so very close.

The branch president welcomed me with a wide smile and said, "Glad you are here, Brother Monson. We prayed y'all here." He then explained that after the sacrifice on the part of the members to build a chapel of their own, a meeting was held and a vote taken by the people concerning the General Authority visitor they would like to have attend their dedicatory services. My name was chosen. I was the most recently ordained General Authority. Perhaps they wanted to look me over. The branch president led his members in a prayer that Brother Monson be assigned to come. Brother Monson came. No phone call or letter initiated the assignment. These were not needed, for simple faith and humble prayer sufficed.

Let us now board the transcontinental jet that will take us to far-off Australia. Sydney is our assignment. Marye Nielsen, who travels with us as a member of the Primary general board, is nervous about staying at the home of the stake Primary president, for the husband in the home is not a member of the Church and is even a bit antagonistic. Sister Nielsen asked me what she should do. I replied, "Let's wait until we meet the James Lord family and then decide where you will stay."

At the airport the stake Primary president welcomed Sister Nielsen and invited her to stay at her home. She pointed to a large pillar in the airport lobby and said, "My husband is standing behind the pillar—out of view."

We proceeded to meet the nonmember husband, and I then said to Marye, "Stay in their home, and the Lord will bless you and bless them." Like a disappointed child trudging off to the bedroom, Sister Nielsen departed to her unknown fate.

Three years later I attended a conference in Sydney, Australia, to divide a stake and to appoint a new stake presidency and high council. Sunday evening, as I placed my hands on the head of a newly sustained high councilor to ordain him a high priest and set him apart to his assignment, I repeated his name, "James Lord," and then asked him, "Haven't I met you before?"

He responded, "Yes, Brother Monson. I am the nonmember husband who was hiding behind the pillar in the Sydney Airport three years ago. Would you thank Marye Nielsen for staying in our home? Her example and sweet spirit prompted me to commence my study and to become a member."

Let's now take the short flight to Brisbane and then the long one to a mining village called Mt. Isa. When the mission president and I landed in this remote outpost, we were surprised to see a young mother and her two children waiting for our arrival. How they knew we were coming I never learned. The mother introduced herself as Judith Louden, and then we met her children. She said that her husband was not a member of the Church and that she and her children were the only members in the town. She said, "Won't you meet with us for a few minutes? We need your strength." We held a home teaching visit there in the small airport. I urged that she continue faithful with her study of the scriptures and the teaching of her children. I outlined how she could hold a home Primary. Our flight was called, and we prepared to leave the lonesome trio. Sister Louden pleaded, "Don't go yet. Surely we can spend a few more minutes together." Then we heard the announcement that, due to a mechanical problem, the flight would be delayed thirty minutes. Did our Father look down in tender mercy on this mother and her children? I know that He did.

Later, I sent to Sister Louden the lesson manuals for a home

Primary, a few missionary tracts, and a letter of encouragement. I also sent to her a subscription to the *Children's Friend.*

Years later, while attending a priesthood leadership meeting in Brisbane, Australia, I related this experience at isolated Mt. Isa and mused, "I wonder what ever happened to Judith Louden, her two children, and her nonmember husband. I suppose I shall never know."

A brother raised his hand and said, "Brother Monson, I can answer your question, for my wife is Judith Louden. Those two children are mine. I am now a member of the Church and a president of the stake seventies quorum."

That night in my personal prayer I thanked God for faithful women who make something of us men.

Now for a short flight across the Tasman Sea to beautiful New Zealand. My assignment? To ordain the first local patriarchs in the land. Only one patriarch resided in New Zealand, he being Heber Jensen, president of the New Zealand Temple and a native of Western Canada. In President and Sister Jensen's home that evening I asked President Jensen how many patriarchal blessings he had given in the six months he had been in New Zealand. I was not prepared for his reply. He responded, "I have given 503 blessings."

I was amazed and asked, "Who has done the massive amount of typing required?"

"I typed them myself," he replied.

In addition to this prodigious workload, he had personally performed the bulk of all the sealings in the New Zealand Temple during this period. Never a complaint—just an expression of gratitude for the privilege to serve. The word of the Lord came to me: "If ye have desires to serve God ye are called to the work."[2]

Our small plane now takes us to the peoples of Polynesia—first to Nukualofa, Tonga. A visit by a General Authority is rare. The gratitude of the people is reflected in their smiles.

On Saturday evening the tiny son of mission president John H. Groberg and his wife, Jean, is taken seriously ill. The medical facilities are primitive, the ailment not diagnosed. What to do? Through a variety of communication means the word goes forth throughout the islands concerning the health of John Enoch Groberg. The next day Tongan runners bring the message: "All the members are fasting and praying for John Enoch. God will heal him." And John Enoch began his long improvement. Today he is strong and well—a grown man. He has been told many times by grateful parents of the night during which hundreds—even thousands—of Tongan Saints joined in a united and fervent plea in his behalf. Is it any wonder that the Groberg family members love the Lord and serve Him faithfully? The years pass, but the miracle of God is remembered still.

At Papeete, Tahiti, we meet a distinguished yet humble man, extraordinarily blessed with the gift of love. He is 84-year-old Tahauri Hutihuti from the island of Takaroa in the Tuamotu island group. A faithful Church member all his life, he had longed for the day when there would be in the Pacific a holy temple of God. He had a love for the sacred ordinances he knew could only be performed in such a house. Patiently, and with purpose, he carefully saved his meager earnings as a pearl diver. When the New Zealand Temple was completed and opened, he took from beneath his bed his life savings of $600, accumulated over a 40-year span; and together with loved ones, he journeyed to the temple and thereby brought a fond dream to final fulfillment.

As I said a tender good-bye to the Tahitians, each one came forward, placed an exquisite shell lei about my neck, and left an affectionate kiss upon my cheek. Tahauri, who did not speak English, stood by my side and spoke to me through an interpreter. The interpreter listened attentively and then, turning to me, reported: "Tahauri says he has no gift to bestow except the love of a full heart." Tahauri clasped my hand and kissed my cheek. Of all the gifts received that memorable night, the gift of this faithful man remains the brightest.

During another stop in the South Pacific, my wife, Frances, and I met with a large gathering of small children—nearly 200 of them. At the conclusion of our messages to these shy but beautiful youngsters, I suggested to the native Samoan teacher that we go forward with the closing exercises. As he announced the final hymn, the distinct impression came to me that I should personally greet each of these children. My watch revealed that the time was too short for such a privilege, so I discounted the impression.

Before the benediction was to be spoken, I again felt this strong impression to shake the hand of each child. This time I made the desire known to the instructor, who displayed a broad and beautiful smile. He spoke in Samoan to the children, and they beamed their approval of his comments.

The instructor then revealed to me the reason for his and their joy. He said, "When we learned that President McKay had assigned a member of the Council of the Twelve to visit us in faraway Samoa, I told the children if they would each one earnestly and sincerely pray and exert faith like the Bible accounts of old, that the Apostle would visit our tiny village at Sauniatu, and through their faith, he would be impressed to greet each child with a personal handclasp."

Tears could not be restrained as each of those precious boys and girls walked shyly by and whispered softly to us a sweet *talofa lava*. Their prayers had been answered.

The clock tells us we must hurry along. Let us take the long flight from the islands of the Pacific northward to Japan and observe the pure faith of a convert.

After a stake conference in this beautiful land, a young Japanese convert, perhaps 26 years of age, drives us to the hotel where we are to stay. He is so neat and meticulous in all he does. The car is polished to a brightness seldom seen. He even wears white gloves. I engage him in conversation, for his English is adequate for the vocabulary used. As a result of the conversation, I learn that he has a girlfriend who is a member. I asked him if he loved her. He replied, "Oh, yes, Brother Monson."

My next question was obvious: "Does she love you?"

"Oh, yes, Brother Monson."

I then suggested, "Why don't you ask her to marry you?"

"Oh, I am too shy to ask," he responded.

I then recited the words of the hymn, "Come, Come, Ye Saints," with emphasis on the phrase, "Fresh courage take. Our God will never us forsake."

Some months later I received a lovely letter from my Japanese friend and his sweet wife. They thanked me for my urging and added, "Our favorite hymn is 'Come, Come, Ye Saints.' We took fresh courage. God did not us forsake. Thank you."

We could linger in the Orient, but we must make a European stop or two, so it's off to Germany for the concluding leg of our odyssey.

May I introduce you to one of the dearest friends I have ever known—a modern Paul, a fearless Peter, and a guileless Nathaniel. I speak of the late Percy K. Fetzer. At the call of the Church, Brother Fetzer left his home, his business, and his family to nurture and care for our faithful Church members in the countries of Eastern Europe. He loved the people. He spoke the language of the heart. He had been ordained a patriarch to give blessings to worthy members in a host of nations.

During the long period of his service, Brother Fetzer made dozens of flights to Europe, blessing the members, instructing the priesthood holders, and providing an example of faith, of works, and of love.

While on an assignment in the land of Poland, he gave

blessings to a number of German-speaking members who, due to the new geographical boundaries dictated by World War II, found themselves in a nation whose language they did not speak, isolated from the conferences of the Church. Upon his return to Salt Lake City, Brother Fetzer called me on the telephone and, with some anxiety, asked to come to my office. When he arrived, we embraced as old and dear friends do. I then asked him to explain his anxiety and concern.

Brother Fetzer related this account: "Brother Monson, I have just returned from Poland, where I gave patriarchal blessings to the Erich Konietz family." His voice wavered and tears began to course down his cheeks. He continued: "I try to live close to the Lord so that He will inspire the blessings I give. I have given blessings to the Konietz family which are impossible of fulfillment. I have promised Brother and Sister Konietz that, because of their faith, they will enter the temple of the Lord and have their entire family sealed to them for eternity as well as time. Brother Monson, they cannot leave their country. It is forbidden for them to do so. What have I done?"

I knew the heart and soul of Percy Fetzer. I responded, "If you made these promises as you did, let us now kneel down before God and ask for them to be fulfilled in His own time and in His own way."

As we prayed, a perfect peace filled our hearts. The matter was left with God. Several years later, and without fanfare or notice, there was announced a pact between the German Federal Republic and Poland to the effect that native Germans, trapped behind the Polish border following the war, could now emigrate to Germany. The Konietz family and most other member families in that land came home to their native Germany.

Let us witness together a celestial scene. The setting is the Swiss Temple of the Church at Zollikofen, Switzerland. We are seated in a beautiful sealing room. The Erich Konietz family is to be joined for all eternity. Tears cannot be restrained: tears

271

of gratitude for the Lord's help; tears of love for one another; tears of quiet amazement at the power of heaven. They look up into the kind and smiling face of the temple president who will now perform these sacred ordinances. The temple president is Percy K. Fetzer. The patriarch who, years before, pronounced patriarchal blessings, will now bring to fulfillment the prophetic promises made. The words from Proverbs provide the answer to the unspoken question, "How has this been possible?" "Trust in the Lord with all thine heart; and lean not unto thine own understanding. In all thy ways acknowledge him, and he shall direct thy paths."[3]

Our journey is complete for the time being, but the work of our Father goes on. How grateful we all can be that it reaches "every nation, and kindred, and tongue, and people."[4]

NOTES
1. Doctrine and Covenants 107:33.
2. Doctrine and Covenants 4:3.
3. Proverbs 3:5–6.
4. Doctrine and Covenants 133:37.

32

ANXIOUSLY ENGAGED

T HERE ARE VAST NUMBERS of priesthood bearers who, for whatever reason, have drifted from their duties and have chosen to pursue other pathways. The Lord speaks rather plainly to us to reach out and rescue such individuals and bring them and theirs to the table of the Lord. We well could pay heed to the Lord's divine instructions when He declared, "Wherefore, now let every man learn his duty, and to act in the office in which he is appointed, in all diligence."[1] He added:

"For behold, it is not meet that I should command in all things; for he that is compelled in all things, the same is a slothful and not a wise servant; wherefore he receiveth no reward.

"Verily I say, men should be anxiously engaged in a good cause, and do many things of their own free will, and bring to pass much righteousness;

"For the power is in them, wherein they are agents unto themselves. And inasmuch as men do good they shall in nowise lose their reward."[2]

I have observed in studying the life of the Master that His lasting lessons and His marvelous miracles usually occurred when he was doing His Father's work. On the way to Emmaus He appeared with a body of flesh and bones. He partook of food and testified of His divinity. All of this took place after he had exited the tomb.

At an earlier time, it was while He was on the road to Jericho that He restored sight to one who was blind.

The Savior was ever up and about—teaching, testifying, and saving others. Such is our individual duty as members of priesthood quorums today.

I share with you tonight two experiences from my life—one which took place when I was a boy, and the other pertaining to a friend of mine who was a husband and father of children.

Not long after my ordination as a teacher in the Aaronic Priesthood, I was called to serve as president of the quorum. Our adviser, Harold, was interested in us, and we knew it. One day he said to me, "Tom, you enjoy raising pigeons, don't you?"

I responded with a warm, "Yes."

Then he proffered, "How would you like me to give you a pair of purebred Birmingham Roller pigeons?"

This time I answered, "Yes, Sir!" You see, the pigeons I had were just the common variety, trapped on the roof of the Grant Elementary School.

He invited me to come to his home the next evening. The following day was one of the longest in my young life. I was awaiting my adviser's return from work an hour before he arrived home. He took me to his pigeon loft, which was in the upper area of a small barn located at the rear of his yard. As I looked at the most beautiful pigeons I had yet seen, he said, "Select any male, and I will give you a female which is different from any other pigeon in the world." I made my selection. He then placed in my hand a tiny hen pigeon. I asked what made her so different. He responded, "Look carefully, and you'll notice that she has but one eye." Sure enough, one eye was missing, a cat having done the damage. "Take them home to your loft," he counseled. "Keep them in for about 10 days, and then turn them out to see if they will remain at your place."

I followed Harold's instructions. Upon his release, the male pigeon strutted about the roof of the loft, then returned inside to eat. But the one-eyed female was gone in an instant. I called Harold and asked, "Did that one-eyed pigeon return to your loft?"

"Come on over," he said, "and we'll have a look."

As we walked from his kitchen door to the loft, my adviser commented, "Tom, you are the president of the teachers quorum." This, of course, I already knew. Then he added, "What are you going to do to activate Bob, who is a member of your quorum?"

I answered, "I'll have him at quorum meeting this week."

Then he reached up to a special nest and handed me the one-eyed pigeon. "Keep her in a few days and try again." This I did, and once more she disappeared. Again the experience, "Come on over, and we'll see if she returned home." Came the comment as we walked to the loft: "Congratulations on getting Bob to priesthood meeting. Now what are you and Bob going to do to activate Bill?"

"We'll have him there next week," I volunteered.

This experience was repeated over and over again. I was a grown man before I fully realized that indeed Harold, my adviser, had given me a special pigeon, the only pigeon in his loft he knew would return every time she was released. It was his inspired way of having an ideal personal priesthood interview with the teachers quorum president every two weeks. I owe a lot to that one-eyed pigeon. I owe more to that quorum adviser. He had the patience and the skill to help me prepare for responsibilities which lay ahead.

Fathers, grandfathers, we have an even greater responsibility to guide our precious sons and grandsons. They need our help, they need our encouragement, they need our example. It has been wisely said that our youth need fewer critics and more models to follow.

Now for the illustration pertaining to those men whose habits and lives include but little Church attendance or Church activity of any kind. The ranks of these prospective elders have grown larger. This is because of those younger boys of the Aaronic Priesthood quorums who are lost along the Aaronic Priesthood pathway and also those grown men who are baptized but do not persevere in activity and faith so that they might be ordained elders.

Many years ago, Marvin O. Ashton, who served as a counselor in the Presiding Bishopric, gave an illustration I'd like to share with you. Picture with me, if you will, a farmer driving a large open-bed truck filled with sugar beets en route to the sugar refinery. As the farmer drives along a bumpy dirt road, some of the sugar beets bounce from the truck and are strewn along the roadside. When he realizes he has lost some of the beets, he instructs his helpers, "There's just as much sugar in those which have slipped off. Let's go back and get them!"

In my application of this illustration, the sugar beets represent the quorum members for whom we are responsible; and those that have fallen out of the truck represent those who, for whatever reason, have fallen from the path of activity. Paraphrasing the farmer's comments concerning the sugar beets, I say of those men: "There's just as much value in those who have slipped off. Let's go back and get them!"

I not only reflect on the hearts and souls of such individual men, but also sorrow for their sweet wives and growing children. These men await a helping hand, an encouraging word, and a personal testimony of truth expressed from a heart filled with love and a desire to lift and to build.

Shelley, my friend, was such a person. His wife and children were fine members, but all efforts to motivate him toward baptism and then priesthood blessings had failed.

But then Shelley's mother died. Shelley was so sorrowful that he retired to a special room at the mortuary where the funeral was being held. We had wired the proceedings to this room so that he might mourn alone and where no one could see him weep with sorrow. As I comforted him in that room before going to the pulpit, he gave me a hug, and I knew a tender chord had been touched.

Time passed. Shelley and his family moved to another part of the city. I was called to preside over the Canadian Mission and, together with my family, moved to Toronto, Canada, for a three-year period.

When I returned and after I was called to the Twelve, Shelley telephoned me. He said, "Bishop, will you seal my wife, my family, and me in the Salt Lake Temple?"

I answered hesitantly, "But Shelley, you first must be baptized a member of the Church."

He laughed and responded, "Oh, I took care of that while you were in Canada. I sort of snuck up on you. There was this home teacher who called on us regularly and taught me the truths of the Church. He was a school crossing guard and helped the small children across the street each morning when they went to school and each afternoon when they went home. He asked me to help him. During the intervals when there was no child crossing, he gave me additional instruction pertaining to the Church."

I had the privilege to see this miracle with my own eyes and feel the joy with my heart and soul. The sealings were performed; a family was united. Shelley died not too long after this period. I had the privilege of speaking at his funeral services. I shall ever see, in memory's eye, the body of my friend Shelley lying in his casket dressed in his temple clothing. I readily admit the presence of tears, tears of gratitude, for the lost had been found.

Those who have felt the touch of the Master's hand somehow cannot explain the change which comes into their lives. There is a desire to live better, to serve faithfully, to walk humbly, and to be more like the Savior. Having received their spiritual eyesight and glimpsed the promises of eternity, they echo the words of the blind man to whom Jesus restored sight: "One thing I know, that, whereas I was blind, now I see."[3]

How can we account for these miracles? Why the upsurge of activity in men long dormant? The poet, speaking of death, wrote, "God . . . touch'd him, and he slept."[4] I say, speaking of this new birth, "God touched them, and they awakened."

Two fundamental reasons largely account for these changes of attitudes, of habits, of actions.

First, men have been shown their eternal possibilities and have made the decision to achieve them. They cannot really long rest content with mediocrity once excellence is within their reach.

Second, other men and women and, yes, young people have followed the admonition of the Savior and have loved their neighbors as themselves and helped to bring their neighbors' dreams to fulfillment and their ambitions to realization.

The catalyst in this process has been the principle of love.

The passage of time has not altered the capacity of the Redeemer to change men's lives. As He said to the dead Lazarus, so He says to you and me: "Come forth."[5] I add: Come forth from the despair of doubt. Come forth from the sorrow of sin. Come forth from the death of disbelief. Come forth to a newness of life.

As we do and direct our footsteps along the paths which Jesus walked, let us remember the testimony Jesus gave: "Behold, I am Jesus Christ, whom the prophets testified shall come into the world. . . . I am the light and . . . life of the world."[6] "I am the first and the last; I am he who liveth, I am he who was slain; I am your advocate with the Father."[7]

There are quorum members and those who should be our quorum members who require our help. John Milton wrote in his poem "Lycidas": "The hungry sheep look up, and are not fed."[8] The Lord Himself said to Ezekiel the prophet, "Woe be to the shepherds of Israel that . . . feed not the flock."[9]

My brethren of the priesthood, the task is ours. Let us

remember and never forget, however, that such an undertaking is not insurmountable. Miracles are everywhere to be seen when priesthood callings are magnified. When faith replaces doubt, when selfless service eliminates selfish striving, the power of God brings to pass His purposes.

NOTES

1. Doctrine and Covenants 107:99.
2. Doctrine and Covenants 58:26–28.
3. John 9:25.
4. Alfred, Lord Tennyson, "In Memoriam A. H. H.," section 85, stanza 5, line 4.
5. John 11:43.
6. 3 Nephi 11:10–11.
7. Doctrine and Covenants 110:4.
8. John Milton, "Lycidas," line 125.
9. Ezekiel 34:2–3.

33

THEY WILL COME

SEVERAL YEARS AGO AN unusual motion picture swept the theaters in this and in other lands. It was entitled *Field of Dreams* and was the story of a young man who revered the baseball players of his youth and, from this foundation, carved out a large section from his cornfield and located there a full-blown baseball diamond. People mocked his foolishness and ridiculed his lack of common sense. The film goes on to show the many challenges he faced in completing the project and readying the baseball diamond for view. His was not an easy task. During the period of doubt as to the future success of his dream, he was driven by the reassuring words, "If you build it, they will come." And come they did. Travelers by the thousands visited this unique place which was filled with baseball's many memories.

Lately I have reflected on the importance of building a bridge to the heart of a person. I think of the nearly 55,000 full-time missionaries from our faith who are assigned over much of the world with the divine commission to teach, to testify, and to baptize. Theirs is a bridge-building task awesome to behold and somewhat overwhelming to contemplate. With God's mandate ringing in their ears, with the Lord's instruction penetrating their hearts, they move forward in their lofty callings. They ponder the Lord's words: "Go ye therefore, and teach all nations, baptizing them in the name of the Father, and of the Son, and of the Holy Ghost: Teaching them to observe all things whatsoever I have commanded you: and, lo, I am with you alway, even unto the end of the world."[1]

When Utah marked the centennial anniversary of its statehood, many ambassadors from other countries made a visit to our state capitol and also to the Church Administration Building. Many also toured the Missionary Training Center at Provo, Utah. They visited the classes of learning; they heard the testimonies of those going to their respective fields of labor. They marveled at the language proficiency, faith, and love exhibited by the missionaries. One ambassador stated: "I observed a sense of purpose, a commitment to prepare and to serve, and a joyful heart in each missionary."

These missionaries go forward with faith. They know their duty. They understand that they are a vital link between the persons they will meet as missionaries and the teaching and testifying they will experience as they bring others to the truth of the gospel.

They yearn for more persons to teach. They pray for the essential help each member can give to the conversion process.

The decision to change one's life and come unto Christ is perhaps the most important decision of mortality. Such a dramatic change is taking place daily throughout the world.

The Book of Mormon prophet Alma describes this personal miracle: "And behold . . . a mighty change was . . . wrought in their hearts, and they humbled themselves and put their trust in the true and living God."[2]

The covenant of baptism spoken of by Alma causes all of us to probe the depths of our souls: "Now, as ye are desirous to come into the fold of God, and to be called his people, and are willing to bear one another's burdens, that they may be light; Yea, and are willing to mourn with those that mourn; yea, and comfort those that stand in need of comfort, and to stand as witnesses of God at all times and in all things, and in all places. . . . Now I say unto you, if this be the desire of your hearts, what have you against being baptized in the name of the Lord, as a witness before him that ye have entered into a covenant with him, that ye will serve him and keep his commandments, that he may pour out his Spirit more abundantly upon you?"[3]

Our studies reveal that most of those who embrace the message of the missionaries have had other exposures to The Church of Jesus Christ of Latter-day Saints—perhaps hearing the magnificent Tabernacle Choir perform, maybe reading and viewing press reports of our well-traveled President Gordon B. Hinckley and his skillful participation in broad-ranging interviews, or just in knowing another person who is a member and for whom respect exists. We as members should be at our best. Our lives should reflect the teachings of the gospel and our hearts and voices ever be ready to share the truth.

Many have come into the Church—or at least have come to know and respect the Church—because someone made the effort to reach outward. I share with you a treasured family experience which had its beginning back in 1959 when I was called to preside over the Canadian Mission, headquartered in Toronto.

Our daughter, Ann, turned five shortly after we arrived in Canada. She saw the missionaries going about their work and she, too, wanted to be a missionary. My wife demonstrated understanding by permitting Ann to take to class a few copies of the *Children's Friend*. That wasn't sufficient for Ann. She also wanted to take with her a copy of the Book of Mormon so that she might talk to her teacher, Miss Pepper, about the Church. I think it rather thrilling that just a few years ago, long years after our return from Toronto, we came home from a vacation and found in our mailbox a note from Miss Pepper which read:

"Dear Ann:

"Think back many years ago. I was your school teacher in Toronto, Canada. I was impressed by the copies of the *Children's Friend* which you brought to school. I was impressed by your dedication to a book called *The Book of Mormon.*

"I made a commitment that one day I would come to Salt Lake City and see why you talked as you did and why you believed in the manner you believed. Today I had the privilege of going through your visitors' center on Temple Square. Thanks to a five-year-old girl who had an understanding of that which she believed, I now have a better understanding of The Church of Jesus Christ of Latter-day Saints."

Something as simple as a child's gesture can make a significant difference in the life of an individual.

Fellowshipping of the investigator should begin well before baptism. The teachings of the missionaries often need the second witness of a new convert to the Church. It has been my experience that such a witness, borne from the heart of one who has undergone this mighty change himself, brings resolve and commitment. When I served as mission president in Eastern Canada, we found that in Toronto, as well as in most of the cities of Ontario and Quebec, there was no dearth of willing helpers to accompany the missionaries and to fellowship the investigators, welcome them to meetings, and introduce them to the ward or branch officers and members. Fellowshipping, friendshipping, and reactivating are ongoing in the daily life of a Latter-day Saint.

Each new convert should be provided a calling in the Church. Such brings interest, stability, and growth. The task may be somewhat simple, such as that given to Jacob de Jager when he and his family became members in Toronto. He held lofty posts in business, but his first calling in the Church was to put the hymnbooks in place along the pews. He took his assignment seriously. In recollecting this first calling, he said, "I had to be present each week, or the hymnbooks would remain undistributed." As you know, Elder de Jager later served many years as a member of the First Quorum of the Seventy. Though he had many demanding responsibilities as a General Authority, he never forgot his first calling in the Church.

The unseen hand of the Lord guides the efforts of those who strive to learn and live the truth of the gospel. As a mission president, I received a weekly letter from each missionary. One that pleased me greatly came from a young elder serving in Hamilton. He and his companion were working with a lovely family, a young couple with two children. The couple felt that the message was true, and they could not deny their desire to be baptized. The wife, however, worried about her mother and father in faraway western Canada, fearing she and her husband would be disowned by her parents for joining the Church. She took pen in hand and jotted a note to her parents in Vancouver. The note read something like this:

"Dear Mother and Father,

"I want to thank you with all of my heart for your kindness and for your understanding and for the teachings which you gave me in my youth. John and I have come across a great truth, The Church of Jesus Christ of Latter-day Saints. We have studied the discussions, and our baptism will take place next Saturday night. We hope you will understand. In fact, we hope that you will welcome the missionaries in your home as we welcomed them in ours."

The letter was sealed with a tear, a stamp was affixed, and it was mailed to Vancouver. On the very day it was received in Vancouver, the couple in Hamilton received a letter from the wife's mother and father. They wrote:

"We are far away from you, or we would surely talk to you in person. We want you to know that missionaries from The

Church of Jesus Christ of Latter-day Saints have called at our home, and we cannot deny the validity of their message. We have set a date for our baptism to take place next week. We hope you will understand and not be unduly critical of our decision. This gospel means so much to us and has brought such happiness into our lives that we pray someday you might also agree to learn more about it."

Can you imagine what happened when the couple in Hamilton received that letter from the wife's parents? They phoned Mother and Dad, and there were many tears of joy shed. I am sure there was a long-distance embrace, for both families became members of the Church.

You see, our Heavenly Father knows who we are, His sons and daughters. He wants to bring into our lives the blessings for which we qualify, and He can do it. He can accomplish anything.

A visible and tender act of fellowshipping was witnessed in the ancient city of Rome. Some years ago Sister Monson and I met with over 500 members there in a district conference. The presiding officer at that time was Leopoldo Larcher, a wonderful Italian. His brother had been working as a guest employee in the auto plants in Germany when two missionaries taught him the gospel. He went back to Italy and taught the gospel to his brother. Leopoldo accepted and sometime later became the president of the Italy Rome Mission and then the Italy Catania Mission.

During that district conference meeting, I noticed that in the throng were many who were wearing white carnations. I said to Leopoldo, "What is the significance of the white carnation?"

He said, "Those are new members. We provide a white carnation to every member who has been baptized since our last district conference. Then all the members and the missionaries know that these people are especially to be fellowshipped."

I watched those new members being embraced, being greeted, being spoken to. They were no more strangers nor foreigners; they were "fellowcitizens with the saints, and of the household of God."[4]

Beyond the new convert to the Church are some who have drifted from that pathway which upward leads and, for one reason or another, have become less active for months, even years. Perhaps they were not fellowshipped; maybe friends departed from their lives. Whatever the reason, the fact remains: we need them, and they need us. Missionaries can effectively visit the homes where these individuals reside. When they approach, those within the shelter of home may come to remember the glorious feelings which came over them when they first heard the principles of the gospel taught to them. The missionaries can teach such individuals and witness the changes which come into their lives as they return to activity.

They need friends with testimonies. They need to know that we truly care for the one.

Aaronic Priesthood quorum advisers and Young Women teachers are on the line of battle, and miracles are within their grasp. Who is the teacher you best remember from your youth? I would guess that in all probability it was the one who knew your name, who welcomed you to class, who was interested in you as a person and who truly cared. When a leader walks the pathway of mortality with a precious youth alongside, there develops a bond of commitment between the two that shields the youth from the temptations of sin and keeps him or her walking steadfastly on the path that leads onward, upward, and unswervingly to eternal life. Build a bridge to each youth.

Let me share with you visits to two stake conferences where I evidenced the miracle which can take place when we take to heart the words of the pioneer hymn, "Put your shoulder to the wheel."[5]

One visit was to the Millcreek Stake in Salt Lake City some

years ago. Just over one hundred brethren who were prospective elders had been ordained elders during the preceding year. I asked President James Clegg the secret of his success. He was too modest to take the credit. His counselor revealed that President Clegg, recognizing the challenge, had undertaken to personally call and arrange a private appointment between him and each prospective elder. During the appointment, President Clegg would mention the temple of the Lord, the saving ordinances and covenants emphasized there, and would conclude with this question: "Wouldn't you desire to take your sweet wife and your children to the house of the Lord, that you might be a forever family throughout the eternities?" An acknowledgment followed, the reactivation process was pursued, and the goal was obtained.

The other visit was to the North Carbon Stake in Price, Utah, many years ago. I noted during my visit that they had rescued 86 men from the prospective elders in one year and had taken them and their wives to the Manti Temple. I said to Cecil Broadbent, the president of the stake, "How did you do it, President?"

He said, "I didn't. My counselor, President Judd, did."

President Judd was a large, ruddy-faced Welsh coal miner. I said to him, "President Judd, will you tell me how you were able to rescue 86 brethren in one year?"

I sat anticipating his answer, and he said, "No!"

I was stunned. I'd never had anyone say *no* so directly in my life. I asked, "Why not?"

He said, "Then you'll tell the other stake presidents you visit, and we won't lead the Church in reactivation." He was smiling, though, so I knew I was halfway there. He said, "I'll make a deal with you, Brother Monson. I'll tell you how we rescued 86 men in one year if you'll get me two tickets to general conference."

I said, "You're on!" And so he told me. What he didn't tell

me is that he intended to collect interest every conference for the next ten years. He came faithfully every six months for his two tickets.

In both the Millcreek and the North Carbon Stake, as well as in others which have been successful in this phase of the work, four principles have prevailed:

1. The reactivation opportunity was handled at the ward level.
2. The bishop of the ward was involved.
3. Qualified and inspired teachers were provided.
4. Attention was given to each individual.

In building a bridge to the investigator, the new convert, or the less-active member, when we do our part, the Lord does His. I testify concerning this truth.

When I served as a bishop, I noted one Sunday morning that one of our priests was missing from priesthood meeting. I left the quorum in the care of the adviser and visited Richard's home. His mother said he was working at the West Temple Garage.

I drove to the garage in search of Richard and looked everywhere, but I could not find him. Suddenly I had the inspiration to gaze down into the old-fashioned grease pit situated at the side of the station. From the darkness I could see two shining eyes. Then I heard Richard say, "You found me, Bishop! I'll come up." After that he rarely missed a priesthood meeting.

The family moved to a nearby stake. Time passed, and I received a phone call informing me that Richard had been called to serve a mission in Mexico, and I was invited by the family to speak at his farewell testimonial. At the meeting, when Richard responded, he mentioned that the turning point in his determination to fill a mission came one Sunday morning—not in the chapel, but as he gazed up from the depths of a dark grease pit and found his quorum president's outstretched hand.

Through the years Richard has stayed in touch with me, telling of his testimony, his family, and his faithful service in the Church, including his calling as a bishop.

My beloved brethren, let us, with faith unwavering and with love unstinting, be bridge builders to the hearts of those with whom we labor. As in the movie *Field of Dreams,* if we build it, they will come.

NOTES
1. Matthew 28:19–20.
2. Alma 5:13.
3. Mosiah 18:8–10.
4. Ephesians 2:19.
5. *Hymns,* no. 252.

34

THE SERVICE THAT COUNTS

WHILE DRIVING TO THE office one morning, I passed a dry-cleaning establishment which had a sign by the side of the front door. It read, "It's the Service That Counts." I suppose in a highly competitive field such as the dry-cleaning business and many others, the differentiating factor which distinguishes one store from another is, in actual fact, service.

The message from the small sign simply would not leave my mind. Suddenly I realized why. In actual fact it *is* the service that counts—the Lord's service.

All of us admire and respect that noble king of Book of Mormon fame—even King Benjamin. How respected he must have been for the people to gather in such great numbers to hear his words and receive his counsel. I think it most interesting that the multitude "pitched their tents round about the temple, every man having his tent with the door thereof towards the temple, that thereby they might remain in their tents and hear the words which king Benjamin should speak unto them."[1] Even a high tower had to be erected that the people might hear his words.

In the true humility of an inspired leader, King Benjamin recounted his desire to serve his people and lead them in paths of righteousness. He then declared to them:

"Because I said unto you that I had spent my days in your service, I do not desire to boast, for I have only been in the service of God.

"And behold, I tell you these things that ye may learn wisdom; that ye may learn that when ye are in the service of your fellow beings ye are only in the service of your God."[2]

This is the service that counts—the service to which all of us have been called, the service of the Lord Jesus Christ.

Our Father in Heaven loves all of His children, and we serve Him best by helping our brothers and sisters to return to Him. In a revelation to Joseph Smith the Prophet, Oliver Cowdery, and David Whitmer, the Lord taught:

"Remember the worth of souls is great in the sight of God;

"For, behold, the Lord your Redeemer suffered death in the flesh; wherefore he suffered the pain of all men, that all men might repent and come unto him. . . .

"And how great is his joy in the soul that repenteth!

"Wherefore, you are called to cry repentance unto this people.

"And if it so be that you should labor all your days in crying repentance unto this people, and bring, save it be one soul unto me, how great shall be your joy with him in the kingdom of my Father!

"And now, if your joy will be great with one soul that you have brought unto me into the kingdom of my Father, how great will be your joy if you should bring many souls unto me!"[3]

Some years ago, at a priesthood leadership session of the Monument Park West Stake conference, this scripture became the theme for the visitor from the Welfare Committee, my former stake president, Paul C. Child. In his accustomed style, Brother Child left the stand and began to walk down the aisle among the assembled priesthood brethren. He quoted the verse, "Remember the worth of souls is great in the sight of God." Then he asked the question, "Who can tell me the worth of a human soul?"

Every man in attendance began to think of an answer in the event Brother Child were to call on him. I had grown up under his leadership, and I knew he would never call on a high councilor or member of a bishopric; rather, he would select one who would least expect to be called. Sure enough, he called from a list he carried the name of an elders quorum president. Thunderstruck, the brother stammered as he asked, "Would you repeat the question, please?" The question was repeated, followed by an even longer pause. Suddenly the response came forth, "The worth of a human soul is its capacity to become as God."

Brother Child closed his scripture, walked back to the pulpit, and, while passing me, whispered, "A profound reply; a profound reply."

With this perspective firmly in our minds, we are prepared to serve in the great mission of bringing souls unto Him.

Following Thanksgiving time a year or so ago, I received a letter from a widow whom I had known in the stake where I served in the presidency. She had just returned from a dinner sponsored by her bishopric. Her words reflect the peace she felt and the gratitude which filled her heart:

"Dear President Monson,

"I am living in Bountiful now. I miss the people of our old stake, but let me tell you of a wonderful experience I have had. In early November all the widows and older people received an invitation to come to a lovely dinner. We were told not to worry about transportation since this would be provided by the older youth in the ward.

"At the appointed hour, a very nice young man rang the bell and took me and another sister to the stake center. He stopped the car, and two other young men walked with us to the chapel where the young ladies took us to where we removed our wraps—then into the cultural hall, where we sat and visited for a few minutes. Then they took us to the tables, where we were seated on each side by either a young woman or a young man. Then we were served a lovely Thanksgiving dinner and afterward provided a choice program.

"After the program we were given our dessert—either apple or pumpkin pie. Then we left, and on the way out we were given a plastic bag with sliced turkey and two rolls. Then the young men took us home. It was such a nice, lovely evening. Most of us shed a tear or two for the love and respect we were shown.

"President Monson, when you see young people treat others like these young people did, I feel the Church is in good hands."

I add my own commendation: God bless the leaders, the young men, and the young women who so unselfishly brought such joy to the lonely and such peace to their souls. Through their experience, they learned the meaning of service and felt the nearness of the Lord.

One of the great missionaries of pioneer times was Joseph Millett, who served a mission to the Maritime Provinces of Canada when but 18 years of age. His mission was marked by discouragement, yet punctuated by faith-promoting experiences—even miraculous intervention by the Lord. This lifelong servant of the Lord, who learned on his mission, and never forgot, what it is like to be in need and how to give, leaves us with this final picture of himself, taken from his personal journal and using his own words:

"One of my children came in, said that Brother Newton Hall's folks were out of bread. Had none that day. I put . . . our flour in [a] sack to send up to Brother Hall's. Just then Brother Hall came in. Says I, 'Brother Hall, how are you out for flour.'

'Brother Millett, we have none.' 'Well, Brother Hall, there is some in that sack. I have divided and was going to send it to you. Your children told mine that you were out.' Brother Hall began to cry. Said he had tried others. Could not get any. Went to the cedars and prayed to the Lord and the Lord told him to go to Joseph Millett. 'Well, Brother Hall, you needn't bring this back if the Lord sent you for it. You don't owe me for it.'"

His journal continued: "You can't tell how good it made me feel to know that the Lord knew that there was such a person as Joseph Millett."[4]

May I share with you an account of an opportunity of service which came to me unexpectedly and in an unusual manner. I received a telephone call from a granddaughter of an old friend. She asked, "Do you remember Francis Brems who was your Sunday School teacher?" I told her that I did. She continued, "He is now one hundred and five years of age. He lives in a small care center but meets with the entire family each Sunday, where he delivers a Sunday School lesson. Last Sunday, Grandpa announced to us, 'My dears, I am going to die this week. Will you please call Tommy Monson and tell him this. He'll know what to do.'"

I visited Brother Brems the very next evening. I could not speak to him, for he was deaf. I could not write a message for him to read, for he was blind. What was I to do? I was told that his family communicated with him by taking the finger of his right hand and then tracing on the palm of his left hand the name of the person visiting and then any message. I followed the procedure and spelled T-O-M-M-Y M-O-N-S-O-N. Brother Brems became excited and, taking my hands, placed them on his head. I knew his desire was to receive a priesthood blessing. The driver who had taken me to the care center joined me as we placed our hands on the head of Brother Brems and provided the desired blessing. Afterward, tears streamed from his sightless eyes. He grasped our hands, and we read the movement of his lips. The message: "Thank you so much."

Within that week, just as Brother Brems had predicted, he passed away. I received the telephone call and then met with the family as funeral arrangements were made. How thankful I am that a response to render service was not delayed.

The Lord knows each of us. Do you think for a moment that He who notes the sparrow's fall would not be mindful of our needs and our service? We simply cannot afford to attribute to the Son of God the same frailties which we find in ourselves.

Sometimes the Lord puts an opportunity for service in place long before the service is actually rendered. Such was the case with Brother Edwin Q. Cannon, Jr., who was a missionary to Germany in 1938, where he loved the people and served faithfully. At the conclusion of his mission, he returned home to Salt Lake City. He married and commenced his own business.

Forty years passed by. One day Brother Cannon came to my office and said he had been pruning his missionary photographs. Among those photographs he had kept since his mission were several which he could not specifically identify. Every time he had planned to discard them, he had been impressed to keep them, although he was at a loss as to why. They were photographs taken by Brother Cannon during his mission when he served in Stettin, Germany, and were of a family—a mother, a father, a small girl, a small boy. He knew their surname was Berndt but could remember nothing more about them. He indicated that he understood there was a Berndt who was a Church leader in Germany, and he thought, although the possibility was remote, that this Berndt might have some connection with the Berndts who had lived in Stettin and who were depicted in the photographs. Before disposing of the photos, he thought he would check with me.

I told Brother Cannon I was leaving shortly for Berlin,

where I anticipated that I would see Dieter Berndt, the Church leader, and that I would show the photographs to him to see if there were any relationship and if he wanted them. There was a possibility I would also see Brother Berndt's sister, who was married to Dietmar Matern, a stake president in Hamburg.

The Lord didn't even let me get to Berlin before His purposes were accomplished. I was in Zurich, Switzerland, boarding the flight to Berlin, when who should also board the plane but Dieter Berndt. He sat next to me, and I told him I had some old photographs of people named Berndt from Stettin. I handed them to him and asked if he could identify those shown in the photographs. As he looked at them carefully, he began to weep. He said, "Our family lived in Stettin during the war. My father was killed when an Allied bomb struck the plant where he worked. Not long afterward, the Russians invaded Poland and the area of Stettin. My mother took my sister and me and fled from the advancing enemy. Everything had to be left behind, including any photographs we had. Brother Monson, I am the little boy pictured in these slides, and my sister is the little girl. The man and woman are our dear parents. Until today, I have had no photographs of our childhood in Stettin or of my father."

Wiping away my own tears, I told Brother Berndt the photographs were his. He placed them carefully and lovingly in his briefcase.

At the next general conference, when Dieter Berndt visited Salt Lake City, he paid a visit to Brother and Sister Edwin Cannon, Jr., that he might express in person his gratitude for the inspiration that came to Brother Cannon to retain these precious photographs and that he followed that inspiration in keeping them for forty years.

William Cowper penned the lines:

> *God moves in a mysterious way*
> *His wonders to perform;*

He plants his footsteps in the sea
And rides upon the storm. . . .

Judge not the Lord by feeble sense,
But trust him for his grace;
Behind a frowning providence
He hides a smiling face.[5]

A while back, my good friend G. Marion Hinckley from Utah County, my fellow trail rider, came to the office with two grandsons who were brothers, one having served an honorable mission in Japan and the other in Scotland. Brother Hinckley said, "Let me share with you a wonderful experience which came to these grandsons of mine." His buttons were almost bursting with pride.

In faraway Japan, a commercial street photographer stopped one of the brothers, having taken a picture of him holding a small child. He offered the print for sale to the missionary and his companion. They explained that they were on a tight budget, that they were missionaries, and they directed the photographer's attention to their nameplates. They didn't purchase the picture.

Some months later, the brother serving in Scotland was asking two missionaries why they had arrived late for a zone meeting, when they told this story: A most persistent street photographer had attempted to sell them a picture of a missionary in Japan holding a small child. They had no interest in the picture, but to avoid arriving even later at their zone meeting, they purchased it.

"A likely story," responded Elder Lamb, whereupon they handed him the picture. He could not believe his eyes. It was a photograph of his own brother in faraway Japan.

That day in my office they presented to my view the picture and, with their grandfather beaming his approval, they declared, "The Lord surely is mindful of his servants the missionaries."

As they departed my office, I thought, "Yes, the Lord is mindful of his missionaries—and their fathers, their mothers, their grandparents, and all who sacrifice for their support, that precious souls may be taught and provided His gospel."

Now, many are not on the front line of missionary service in the Church callings they fill. Does God remember them also? Is He mindful of their needs and the yearnings of their hearts? What about those who have been in the limelight but grown old with faithful service, have been released and have slipped into the anonymity of the vast congregation of Church members? To all such individuals, I testify that He does remember and He does bless.

Many years ago I was assigned to divide the Modesto California Stake. The Saturday meetings had been held, the new stake presidencies selected, and preparations concluded for the announcements to be made the following morning in the Sunday session of conference.

As the Sunday session was about to begin, there went through my mind the thought that I had been in Modesto before. But when? I let my mind search back through the years for a confirmation of the thought I was thinking. Suddenly I remembered. Modesto, years before, had been a part of the San Joaquin Stake. The stake president was Clifton Rooker. I had stayed in his home during that conference. But that was many years earlier. Could my thoughts be playing tricks on my mind? I said to the stake presidency as they sat on the stand, "Is this the same stake over which Clifton Rooker once presided?"

The brethren answered, "Yes, it is. He was our former president."

"It's been many years since I was last here," I said. "Is Brother Rooker with us today?"

They responded, "Oh, yes. We saw him early this morning as he came to conference."

I asked, "Where is he seated on this day when the stake will be divided?"

"We don't know exactly," they replied. The response was a good one, for the building was filled to capacity.

I stepped to the pulpit and asked, "Is Clifton Rooker in the audience?" There he was—way back in the recreation hall, hardly in view of the pulpit. I felt the inspiration to say to him publicly, "Brother Rooker, we have a place for you on the stand. Would you please come forward?"

With every eye watching him, Clifton Rooker made that long walk from the rear of the building right up to the front and sat by my side. It became my opportunity to call upon him, one of the pioneers of that stake, to bear his testimony and to tell the people whom he loved that he was the actual beneficiary of the service he had rendered his Heavenly Father and which he had provided the stake members.

After the session was concluded, I said, "Brother Rooker, how would you like to step with me into the high council room and help me set apart the two new presidencies of these stakes?"

He replied, "That would be a highlight for me."

We proceeded to the high council room. There, with his hands joining my hands and the hands of the outgoing stake presidency, we set apart to their callings the two new stake presidencies. Brother Rooker and I embraced as he said good-bye and went to his home.

Early the next morning, after I had returned to my home, I had a telephone call from the son of Clifton Rooker. "Brother Monson," he said, "I'd like to tell you about my dad. He passed away this morning; but before he did so, he said that yesterday was the happiest day of his entire life."

As I heard that message from Brother Rooker's son, I paused to thank God for the inspiration which came to me to invite this good man, while he was yet alive and able to enjoy them, to come forward and receive the plaudits of the stake members whom he had served.

To all those who serve the Lord by serving their fellow men, and to those who are the recipients of this selfless service, the Redeemer seems to be speaking to you when He declared:

"When the Son of man shall come in his glory, and all the holy angels with him, then shall he sit upon the throne of his glory:

"And before him shall be gathered all nations: and he shall separate them one from another, as a shepherd divideth his sheep from the goats:

"And he shall set the sheep on his right hand, but the goats on the left.

"Then shall the King say unto them on his right hand, Come, ye blessed of my Father, inherit the kingdom prepared for you from the foundation of the world:

"For I was an hungred, and ye gave me meat: I was thirsty, and ye gave me drink: I was a stranger, and ye took me in:

"Naked, and ye clothed me: I was sick, and ye visited me: I was in prison, and ye came unto me.

"Then shall the righteous answer him, saying, Lord, when saw we thee an hungred, and fed thee? or thirsty, and gave thee drink?

"When saw we thee a stranger, and took thee in? or naked, and clothed thee?

"Or when saw we thee sick, or in prison, and came unto thee?

"And the King shall answer and say unto them, Verily I say unto you, Inasmuch as ye have done it unto one of the least of these my brethren, ye have done it unto me."[6]

That each of us may qualify for this blessing from our Lord is my prayer.

NOTES

1. Mosiah 2:6.
2. Mosiah 2:16–17.
3. Doctrine and Covenants 18:10–11, 13–16.
4. Quoted in Eugene England, "Without Purse or Scrip: A 19-Year-Old Missionary in 1853," *New Era,* July 1975, 28.
5. "God Moves in a Mysterious Way," in John Newton, *Twenty-six Letters on Religious Subjects* (1774).
6. Matthew 25:31–40.

35

MIRACLES—THEN AND NOW

ALMOST FORTY YEARS AGO I received an invitation to meet with President J. Reuben Clark, Jr., a counselor in the First Presidency of the Church, a statesman of towering stature, and a scholar of international renown. My profession then was in the field of printing and publishing. President Clark made me welcome in his office and then produced from his old rolltop desk a large sheaf of handwritten notes, many of them made when he was a law student long years before. He proceeded to outline for me his goal of producing a harmony of the Gospels. This goal was achieved with his monumental work, *Our Lord of the Gospels.*

Recently I took down from my library shelf a personally inscribed, leather-bound copy of this classic treatment of the life of Jesus of Nazareth. As I perused the many pages, I paused at the section entitled "The Miracles of Jesus." I remembered as though it were yesterday President Clark asking me to read to him several of these accounts while he sat back in his large leather chair and listened. This was a day in my life never to be forgotten.

President Clark asked me to read aloud the account found in Luke concerning the man filled with leprosy. I proceeded to read:

"And it came to pass, when he was in a certain city, behold a man full of leprosy: who seeing Jesus fell on his face, and besought him, saying, Lord, if thou wilt, thou canst make me clean.

"And he put forth his hand, and touched him, saying, I will: be thou clean. And immediately the leprosy departed from him."[1]

He asked that I continue reading from Luke concerning the man afflicted with palsy and the enterprising manner in which he was presented for the attention of the Lord:

"And, behold, men brought in a bed a man which was taken with a palsy: and they sought means to bring him in, and to lay him before him.

"And when they could not find by what way they might bring him in because of the multitude, they went upon the housetop, and let him down through the tiling with his couch into the midst before Jesus.

"And when he saw their faith, he said unto him, Man, thy sins are forgiven thee."[2]

There followed snide comment from the Pharisees concerning who had the right to forgive sins. Jesus silenced their bickering by saying: "Whether is easier, to say, Thy sins be forgiven thee; or to say, Rise up and walk?

"But that ye may know that the Son of man hath power upon earth to forgive sins, (he said unto the sick of the palsy,) I say unto thee, Arise, and take up thy couch, and go into thine house.

"And immediately he rose up before them, and took up that whereon he lay, and departed to his own house, glorifying God."[3]

President Clark removed from his pocket a handkerchief

and wiped the tears from his eyes. He commented, "As we grow older, tears come more frequently." After a few words of good-bye, I departed from his office, leaving him alone with his thoughts and his tears.

As I reflect on this experience, my heart fills with gratitude to the Lord for His divine intervention to relieve the suffering, heal the sick, and raise the dead. I grieve, however, for the many, similarly afflicted, who knew not how to find the Master, to learn of His teachings, and to become the beneficiaries of His power. I remembered that President Clark himself suffered heartache and pain in the tragic death at Pearl Harbor of his son-in-law, Mervyn S. Bennion, captain of the battleship *West Virginia*. That day there had been no ram in the thicket, no steel to stop the shrapnel, no miracle to heal the wounds of war. But faith never wavered, and answered prayers provided the courage to carry on.

So it is today. In our lives, sickness comes to loved ones, accidents leave their cruel marks of remembrance, and tiny legs that once ran are imprisoned in a wheelchair.

Mothers and fathers who anxiously await the arrival of a precious child sometimes learn that all is not well with this tiny infant. A missing limb, sightless eyes, a damaged brain, or the term "Down syndrome" greets the parents, leaving them baffled, filled with sorrow, and reaching out for hope.

There follows the inevitable blaming of oneself, the condemnation of a careless action, and the perennial questions: "Why such a tragedy in our family?" "Why didn't I keep her home?" "If only he hadn't gone to that party." "How did this happen?" "Where was God?" "Where was a protecting angel?" *If, why, where, how*—those recurring words—do not bring back the lost son, the perfect body, the plans of parents, or the dreams of youth. Self-pity, personal withdrawal, or deep despair will not bring the peace, the assurance, or help which are needed. Rather, we must go forward, look upward, move onward, and rise heavenward.

It is imperative that we recognize that whatever has happened to us has happened to others. They have coped and so must we. We are not alone. Heavenly Father's help is near.

My thoughts turn to a place far distant and to a time long ago—even to a pool called Bethesda. The book of John describes what occurred there:

"Now there is at Jerusalem by the sheep market a pool, which is called in the Hebrew tongue Bethesda, having five porches.

"In these lay a great multitude of impotent folk, of blind, halt, withered, waiting for the moving of the water.

"For an angel went down at a certain season into the pool, and troubled the water: whosoever then first after the troubling of the water stepped in was made whole of whatsoever disease he had.

"And a certain man was there, which had an infirmity thirty and eight years.

"When Jesus saw him lie, and knew that he had been now a long time in that case, he saith unto him, Wilt thou be made whole?

"The impotent man answered him, Sir, I have no man, when the water is troubled, to put me into the pool: but while I am coming, another steppeth down before me.

"Jesus saith unto him, Rise, take up thy bed, and walk.

"And immediately the man was made whole, and took up his bed, and walked."[4]

Who can count the boys and girls, the men and women, where sickness has left its mark, rendering strong limbs lifeless and causing loved ones to shed tears of sorrow and offer prayers of faith for them?

Illness is not the only culprit that intrudes and alters our lives. In our hectic and fast-moving world, accidents can in an

305

instant inflict pain, destroy happiness, and curtail our future. Such was the experience of young Robert Hendricks. Healthy and carefree three years ago, a sudden, three-car accident left him with brain damage, limited use of his limbs, and impaired speech. Summoned to his side by his mother, who pleaded her despair, I gazed at his almost-lifeless form as he lay on the white hospital bed in the critical care unit. Life supports functioning, his head swathed in bandages, his future was not only in doubt, but death appeared certain.

The hoped-for miracle, however, did occur. Heavenly help was forthcoming. Robert lived. His recovery has been labored and slow—but steady. A devoted friend, who was bishop at the time of the accident, has cared for Robert each week, getting him ready and driving him to Sunday church meetings—always patient, ever faithful.

One day Robert's former bishop brought him to my office, since Robert wanted to meet with me, not having remembered that I saw him that night of crisis in the hospital. He and the dedicated bishop sat down, and Robert "talked" with me through a small electronic machine on which he spelled out his thoughts and they were then printed on strips of paper. He spelled out on the machine the love he has for his mother, his thanks for helping hands and willing hearts which have aided him, and his gratitude to a kind and caring Heavenly Father who has sustained him through his prayers. Here are some of his less private and personal messages: "I'm coming along pretty good, considering what I've been through." Another: "I know that I will be able to help people and make some difference in people's lives, and that's great." Another: "I don't really know just how fortunate I am, but in my prayers I am told to just keep pushing on."

At the conclusion of our visit, the bishop said, "Robert would like to surprise you." Robert stood and, with considerable effort, said aloud, "Thank you." A broad smile crossed his face. He was on the way back. "Thanks be to God" were the only words I could utter. Later I prayed aloud, "Thanks be also for loving bishops, kind teachers, and skilled specialists."

Today, Robert, through the help of his former bishop, his current bishop, and others, has been to the temple. He has learned the computer. He is enrolled in computer study at college. He was also aided along the way by Deseret Industries helpers who provided encouragement and taught him essential skills. Now, with the support of a cane, Robert walks. He has learned to talk, though in halting phrases and with great effort. His progress has been phenomenal.

After the tears of a day of despair, a night of sorrow, "joy cometh in the morning."[5]

Just two years ago, Eve Gail McDaniel and her parents, Bishop and Sister Jerry Lee McDaniel of the Reedsport Oregon Ward, came to my office and presented as a contribution to the Church Historical Department a copy of the Book of Mormon which Eve had written, by hand, and placed in three large binders. Eve, then 28, was born September 18, 1962. A case of meningitis when she was a baby resulted in brain damage. She cannot read; but she copied the entire Book of Mormon, letter by letter, over a period of about 18 months. In doing so, she learned to recognize certain words and phrases, such as *commandments* and *nevertheless*. Her favorite—and she glowed as she repeated the phrase—was "And it came to pass." Eve reflected the joy of accomplishment, even the smile of success. Her parents rejoiced in her gladness of heart and buoyancy of spirit. Heaven was very near.

On another occasion, near the Christmas season, I had the opportunity to meet in the Church Office Building with a group of handicapped children. There were about 60 in the group. My heart literally melted as I met with them. They sang for me "I Am a Child of God," "Rudolph, the Red-nosed Reindeer," and "As I Have Loved You, Love One Another."

There was such an angelic expression on their faces and such a simple trust expressed in their comments that I felt I was on sacred ground. They presented to me a beautiful booklet where each one had prepared a special page illustrating those blessings for which he or she was most thankful at Christmastime. I commend the many teachers and families who work behind the scenes in bringing a measure of comfort, purpose, and joy to these special children. They brightened my entire day.

Several years ago, Brigham Young University honored with a presidential citation Sarah Bagley Shumway, a truly remarkable woman of our time. The citation contained the words, "It is often within our homes and among our own family members that the eternally significant—but usually unheralded—drama of daily living occur. The people in these plain but important places bring stability to the present and promise to the future. Their lives are filled with struggle and deep feeling as they face circumstances that rarely fit neatly within the formulae of plays, films and newscasts. But their victories, however slight, strengthen the boundaries through which the history of future generations must pass."

Sarah married H. Smith Shumway, then her "friend and sweetheart of nine years," in 1948. The courtship was longer than most because Smith, an infantry officer in World War II, was blinded and severely wounded by a land-mine explosion in the advance on Paris, France. During his long rehabilitation, Sarah learned braille so that she could correspond with him in privacy. She couldn't tolerate the idea of others reading her letters aloud to the man she loved.

Something of the spirit of this young couple comes to us in the simple candor of Smith Shumway's proposal of marriage. Finally home in Wyoming after the war, he told Sarah, "If you will drive the car and sort the socks and read the mail, I will do the rest." She accepted the offer.

Years of study led to a successful career, eight accomplished children, a host of grandchildren, and lives of service. The Shumways, along life's pathway, have faced problems of a child with severe deafness, a missionary son developing cancer, and a twin granddaughter injured at birth.

My family and I had the privilege to meet the entire Shumway clan at an Aspen Grove family camp. It was our joy to be with them. Each wore an identifying T-shirt on which was a map depicting the location of each child and family, along with the names of all. Brother Shumway, with justifiable pride, pointed to the location on his shirt of his precious ones and beamed the smile of gladness. Only then did I ponder that he had never seen any of his children or grandchildren. Or had he? While his eyes had never beheld them, in his heart he knew them and he loved them.

At an evening of entertainment, the Shumway family was on the stage at Aspen Grove. The children were asked, "What was it like growing up in a household with a sightless father?" One daughter smiled and said, "When we were little, occasionally we felt Daddy should not have too much dessert at dinner, so without telling him, we would trade our smaller helping with his larger one. Maybe he knew, but he never complained."

One child touched our hearts when she recounted, "When I was about five years old, I remember my father holding my hand and walking me around the neighborhood, and I never realized he was blind because he talked about the birds and other things. I always thought he held my hand because he loved me more than other fathers loved their children."

Today, Brother Shumway is a patriarch. Who would you guess learned typing skills so as to be able to type the many blessings he gives? You're correct: his beloved wife, Sarah.

Smith and Sarah Shumway and their family are examples of rising above adversity and sorrow, overcoming the tragedy of war-inflicted impairment, and walking bravely the higher road-way of life.

Ella Wheeler Wilcox, the poetess, wrote:

> *It is easy enough to be pleasant*
> *When life flows by like a song,*
> *But the man worth while is one who will smile*
> *When everything goes dead wrong.*
> *For the test of the heart is trouble,*
> *And it always comes with the years,*
> *And the smile that is worth the praises of earth*
> *Is the smile that shines through tears.*[6]

May I conclude with the inspiring example of Melissa Engle of West Valley City, Utah. In the August 1992 issue of the *New Era,* Melissa tells her own story:

"When I was born I only had a thumb on my right hand because the umbilical cord got wrapped around my fingers and [severed them]. My dad wanted to find something I could do to strengthen my hand and make it useful. Playing the violin seemed like a natural because I wouldn't have to finger with both hands, like you would with a flute. . . .

"I've been playing for about eight years now. I take private lessons, and I have to work at things like a paper route to help pay for them. I get to [my violin] lessons by riding a bus across town.

"A highlight [of my life] was Interlochen, located on a lake in Michigan, one of the best music camps in the world for [youth]. I sent in my application for the eight weeks of intensive music training and couldn't believe I [was] accepted.

"The only problem was money. It costs thousands of dollars, and there was no way I [could] . . . make that much before the deadline. So I prayed and prayed, and about a week before I had to send in the money, I was called into the office of a man who had a grant for someone with a handicap who was pursuing the arts. That, to me, was a miracle. . . . I'm really grateful for it."[7]

Melissa, when she received the grant, turned to her mother, who had been anxious not to see her daughter disappointed and had thus attempted to curb her enthusiasm and hope, and said, "Mother, I told you Heavenly Father answers prayers, for look how He has answered mine."

To all who have suffered silently from sickness, to you who have cared for those with physical or mental impairment, who have borne a heavy burden day by day, year by year, and to you noble mothers and dedicated fathers—I salute you and pray God's blessings to ever attend you. To the children, particularly they who cannot run and play and frolic, come the assuring words: "Dearest children, God is near you, Watching o'er you day and night."[8]

There will surely come that day, even the fulfillment of the precious promise from the Book of Mormon:

"The soul shall be restored to the body, and the body to the soul; yea, and every limb and joint shall be restored to its body; yea, even a hair of the head shall not be lost; but all things shall be restored to their proper and perfect frame. . . .

"And then shall the righteous shine forth in the kingdom of God."[9]

From the Psalm echoes the assurance: "My help cometh from the Lord, which made heaven and earth. . . .

"He that keepeth thee will not slumber.

"Behold, he that keepeth Israel shall neither slumber nor sleep."[10]

Through the years the Latter-day Saints have taken comfort from the favorite hymn remembered from our youth:

> *When upon life's billows you are tempest-tossed,*
> *When you are discouraged, thinking all is lost,*
> *Count your many blessings; name them one by one,*
> *And it will surprise you what the Lord has done. . . .*
>
> *Are you ever burdened with a load of care?*
> *Does the cross seem heavy you are called to bear?*

Count your many blessings; ev'ry doubt will fly,
And you will be singing as the days go by. . . .

So amid the conflict, whether great or small,
Do not be discouraged; God is over all.
Count your many blessings; angels will attend,
Help and comfort give you to your journey's end.[11]

To any who from anguish of heart and sadness of soul have silently asked, "Heavenly Father, are you really there? . . . Do you hear and answer every . . . prayer?"[12] I bear to you my witness that He is there. He does hear and answer every prayer. His Son, the Christ, burst the bands of our earthly prisons. Heaven's blessings await us.

NOTES

1. Luke 5:12–13.
2. Luke 5:18–20.
3. Luke 5:23–25.
4. John 5:2–9.
5. Psalm 30:5.
6. Ella Wheeler Wilcox, "Worth While," in *Best-Loved Poems of the LDS People* (1996), 7.
7. Melissa Engle and Lisa A. Johnson, "Something You Really Love," *New Era*, August 1992, 30–31.
8. "Dearest Children, God Is Near You," *Hymns*, no. 96.
9. Alma 40:23, 25.
10. Psalm 121:2–4.
11. "Count Your Blessings," *Hymns*, no. 241.
12. Janice Kapp Perry, "A Child's Prayer," *Children's Songbook*, 12.

36

A LAND OF MIRACLES

PRIOR TO WORLD WAR II, the land that became known as the German Democratic Republic, which some erroneously termed East Germany, was the most productive area of the German-speaking world as pertained to missionary success. The city of Chemnitz, later known as Karl-Marx-Stadt, had as many as six branches of members and was the largest concentration of Latter-day Saints outside of North America. Then came the terrible destruction of World War II. After the bombs ceased and the artillery went silent, the land was left devastated. Then, like moles from the earth came the people, bedraggled, hungry, frightened, lost. In memory one could hear the cry, "Mother, where are you? Father where have you gone?" They were greeted by nothing but a moonscape of shell holes, jagged buildings, and piles of rubble. A nation lay desolate and destroyed.

About that time, the prophet of the Lord determined that one named Ezra Taft Benson would undertake a rescue mission to those people. Elder Benson left his dear wife, whom he treasured with all of his heart, and his precious children, who were tiny at the time, and went on a mission, the length of which was left uncertain. He traversed the land of Germany—East and West. He fed the people. He clothed the people. But more than that, he blessed the people. And he gave them hope. His record of service was a foundation for that which was to come.

Another savior to that country was Walter Stover, a man for whom a residence hall on the campus of Brigham Young University is named. If I had a family member living on campus, I would want him or her to occupy Stover Hall, simply because of the love I have for Walter Stover. At the request of the Church, he went back to his homeland. He provided funds for the building of chapels. Since the Saints were scattered all over the nation, he rented an entire train. He thought big. At every stop, Latter-day Saints would get on the train and proceed to the city of Dresden, where there was held a great open-air meeting. Gratitude filled every heart because the war had ended. Peace could now prevail. When they took the roll call, it was discovered that hundreds of Latter-day Saints had been killed. Many others had been maimed. Others were held as prisoners in the Soviet Union. The Church was no longer the entity that it once was in that country. When they found there were others who had survived, they thanked God for their blessings. They partook of the sacrament on a Sunday morning in a bombed-out nation, but where hope sprang eternal in the breast of every Latter-day Saint.

When I received my initial assignment to supervise the work of the Church in Europe, I had never been to Germany. I knew little concerning the history of the Church there. I did know, however, that the Cold War was on at that time. I knew that Americans were being arrested as spies on trumped-up charges and placed in jails. I knew that there were Soviet soldiers everywhere to be found, along with shepherd dogs, policemen, machine guns. I relayed these facts to Sister Monson as I prepared for my journey. I mentioned to her that I had contacted the

State Department and had been advised that no diplomatic relationships existed with that nation. I was told, "If you go, you go at your own risk." After I explained this to Sister Monson, she came up with a brilliant idea. She said, "Tom, you know we have three young children at home. If you should be arrested and held in jail for I don't know how long in that country, someone should be here to rear the children." And with a smile on her face, she said, "You go, and I'll stay here and pray for you." I went.

It was just as I had read about. It was spooky and difficult. I drove down to the Czech border to a little city called Goerlitz. There I attended my first meeting with the Saints in the German Democratic Republic. We assembled in a small, worn-out hall. There was an ancient little organ for accompaniment. My, how the Saints could sing the hymns of Zion! The German Saints can sing like no other Saints in all the world. Elder Harold B. Lee used to say, "What they may lack in quality, they make up in volume." As the Saints sang, they literally filled the hall with their faith and their devotion. These members love the scriptures. I learned that they had few written materials—just the standard works. Yet, they were the best-informed group of Saints I've ever met. This says something about concentrating one's reading in the standard works. My heart was filled with sorrow, because they had no patriarch; they had no wards or stakes—just branches. They could not receive temple blessings—either endowment or sealing. No official visitor had come from Church headquarters in a long time. The members were forbidden to leave the country. Yet, they trusted in the Lord with all their hearts, and they leaned not to their own understanding. In all their ways they acknowledged Him, and He directed their paths.[1]

I stood at the pulpit, and with tear-filled eyes and a voice choked with emotion, I made a promise to the people: "If you will remain true and faithful to the commandments of God, every blessing any member of the Church enjoys in any other country shall be yours." Then I realized what I had said. That night I dropped to my knees and said to my Heavenly Father, "Father, I'm on Thy errand; This is Thy Church. I have spoken words that came not from me, but from Thee and Thy Son. Wilt Thou, therefore, fulfill the promise in the lives of this noble people."

Thus concluded my first visit to the German Democratic Republic. I must admit that when I departed Checkpoint Charlie and entered West Berlin, I looked with appreciation at my American passport. It never looked so good. When I was met at home by my wife and family, I could say, "Home sweet home! Be it ever so humble, there's no place like home!"

The Lord's promise began to unfold. A patriarch was named—Brother Percy K. Fetzer, who was assigned as a Regional Representative for the area. Then Walter Krause, a native of that country, was ordained a patriarch. To date, he has given 989 patriarchal blessings, and his wife has typed every one of them.

In addition to providing patriarchal service, the great problem confronting us was to get to the branches and districts written material. I had just completed an assignment pertaining to a revision of the General Handbook of Instructions—a slow, detailed, three-year process. While in the temple one Thursday morning, I said to Spencer W. Kimball, Harold B. Lee, and Joseph Fielding Smith, "With all my heart I wish we had one copy of the new General Handbook of Instructions printed in the German language and available in the German Democratic Republic." Brother Kimball said, "Why can't you mail one?" I replied, "The borders are closed. Literature is verboten. There is no way." Then he said, "I have another idea, Brother Monson. Why don't you, since you've worked with the General Handbook of Instructions, memorize it, and then we'll put *you* across the border?" I laughed, and then I looked at him. He was dead serious. The man meant what he said.

I began the difficult assignment of attempting to memorize the General Handbook of Instructions. Now, I didn't commit it to memory. I don't want anyone to believe I have that capacity, but I pretty well had the paragraphs, the chapters and the pages, with their contents, stored away somewhere upstairs. When I crossed the border to East Berlin, I said to our leader there, "Give me a typewriter and a ream of paper and let me work." I sat down at a table in the branch office and began to type the General Handbook. I was about thirty pages into the Handbook when I took time to stand. I noticed on a shelf what appeared to be the General Handbook. I retrieved the volume and discovered that it was, indeed, the new General Handbook, printed in the German language. Someone had smuggled it across the border. All my efforts had been in vain. But for the next few years, until we revised it, I was pretty well an authority on the General Handbook of Instructions.

Time and again I paid visits to that nation. I remember leadership meetings where the priesthood leaders were so eager they would arise and actually run to the front when their names were called, that they might have some printed instructions concerning how a quorum should operate or how a branch should function. I remember going to a conference in the city of Erfurt. There a sweet sister came forward and asked, "Are you an Apostle?" My interpreter said, "Yes, he's a member of the Quorum of the Twelve." She then reached in her purse and brought forth a picture of the Quorum of the Twelve. She said, "Which one are you?" I looked at the picture. The junior member of the Quorum of the Twelve in that picture was John A. Widtsoe. She had not seen a member of the Twelve for a long time!

On another occasion, in the city of Annaberg, as I walked toward the entrance of the chapel, a man ran from the door of the chapel and embraced me. Through an interpreter, he declared, "I've had a dream; I've had a dream; I've had a dream!" He had dreamed that though no visitor was scheduled to his district conference, one would come and that one would be me. Later I saw this brother standing at the rear of the filled hall as we conducted our conference that day. I thought to myself, "Why doesn't someone get up and let that older man have a seat?" I never spoke a word, but a man on the front row, a young man, arose and went to the back and said to that dear man, "My seat is yours. I've been here two hours saving it for you." Then he escorted the elderly man to the front row, where he sat and enjoyed the conference spirit. The Lord was working His purposes upon that people.

Soon a mission organization was established, the first high priest ordained, and then district councils and branches. Then there was organized a stake of Zion—a stake of Zion!—in Freiberg and then another stake in Leipzig. Every member of the Church in the German Democratic Republic was now a member of a stake of Zion. One branch president whom I interviewed had been a branch president for 21 years; he was only 42 years of age. Half his life he had been a branch president, but he was willing to carry on in any assignment. The members eagerly accepted their calls.

While we were interviewing the brethren pertinent to a stake organization, we heard the singing of a magnificent male chorus in the main portion of the rented building we occupied. I said, "Is this the choir preparing for tonight's meeting?" They said, "Oh, no; these are the brethren yet to be interviewed. They simply love to sing."

These remarkable events were preceded by a special dedication of the land in which an earnest appeal to our Heavenly Father was made. Entries from my journal of April 25, 26, and 27, 1975, describe in detail the setting in which that prayer was offered. The response of our Heavenly Father speaks for itself:

Friday, April 25, 1975: Frances and I flew to Copenhagen, and she continued her journey to London and thence to Salt Lake City. I journeyed to Berlin by way of Frankfurt and was there met by President and Sister Gary Schwendiman of the Germany Hamburg Mission. We drove through Checkpoint Charlie and into East Berlin, and thence to the Dresden Mission, where that evening we held a lengthy mission presidency meeting, with the presidency of the Dresden Mission, President Henry Burkhardt, President Walter Krause, and President Gottfried Richter. I mentioned to the brethren that while I was dedicating the land of Portugal, I felt impressed that I should offer a similar prayer, invoking our Heavenly Father's blessings upon the German Democratic Republic. President Burkhardt was assigned to suggest a place where the dedicatory prayer could be offered, perhaps on the Sabbath morning.

Saturday, April 26, 1975: Today was a very busy day, wherein I held conference sessions for the Saints in the German Democratic Republic. At 11:00 A.M. we met with all of the priesthood leaders of the entire mission area. These brethren are eager to learn and represented a most enthusiastic audience. At 1:00 P.M. there was convened a general session for all of the members in the northern part of the mission, there being perhaps 720 in attendance. Following this session, we returned to the hotel for a brief rest and then at 7:00 P.M. held a general leadership meeting for the group that had come from the southern part of the mission. I had no intention to deliver the message which the Lord prompted me subsequently to present. I had in mind discussing leadership principles, but felt a strong and distinct impression to instead provide the leaders

319

assembled personal glimpses into the lives of each member of the First Presidency and Council of the Twelve. They seemed extremely pleased to receive this rather intimate message concerning Brethren whom they revere—many of whom they have never seen in person.

Earlier in the day we visited the charred yet partially restored buildings of the Dresden area. This, of course, was the scene of the great fire bombing during World War II where British and American air forces destroyed much of the city, killing many thousands of persons.

Sunday, April 27, 1975: Last evening we had dinner at the hotel adjacent to the one where we stayed. It is rather spooky to have as your table guests next to you officers of the Russian Army. Conditions have noticeably improved in the German Democratic Republic since I first visited the area several years ago.

At 7:30 A.M., by appointment, the Dresden Mission Presidency and their wives, President Schwendiman and his wife, and I left the hotel en route to Friedensburg, the location which had been selected for the special prayer which I felt prompted to offer in this land. The setting was as beautiful a spot as could be imagined. Though a light rain was falling, we walked through the woods for about 20 minutes into a clearing overlooking the Elbe River, with Meissen on the right and Dresden on the left, Meissen being the home of Karl G. Maeser, the founder of Brigham Young University.

As I explained the purpose of the prayer, the Burkhardts, Krauses and Richters particularly showed keen interest. During the prayer, I mentioned that "Today marks the dawning of a new beginning for the Dresden Mission." As I used these words, we heard the unmistakable sound of a rooster crowing, followed by the pealing of a cathedral bell in the distance. The day had been overcast, with rain falling, but during the prayer the sun shone brilliantly upon us, warming our bodies and giving us the assurance that our Heavenly Father was pleased with the prayer which was being offered.

Following is the text of the prayer of rededication:

"Our beloved Heavenly Father, under the inspiration of Thy Holy Spirit, which we acknowledge freely and appreciate greatly, we assemble on this mountainside on this, Thy Holy Day, to dedicate and rededicate this land for the advancement of the work of The Church of Jesus Christ of Latter-day Saints.

"Thou knowest the faith of the people of this land—the many tens of thousands who have embraced Thy Gospel and have served to build up Thy Church wherever they have been. Thou knowest the sermons which they have preached in song, for they sing with their hearts and echo the feelings of their souls.

"Thou knowest, Heavenly Father, the sufferings of this people, and Thou hast been near to them in times of trouble and in times of joy.

"We express our gratitude unto Thee for the privilege we have of holding meetings here, for bringing to the membership of the Dresden Mission the entire program of the Church; and these blessings were scarcely imaginable a few years ago. We confess before Thee that it has been through Thy intervention that this blessing has been brought to pass. We acknowledge Thy hand in every aspect of our lives and pledge our lives to Thy service.

"In the authority of the Holy Apostleship which I bear, and in the name of Thy Beloved Son, Jesus Christ, the Savior and Redeemer of the world, I dedicate and rededicate this land for the advancement of Thy work.

"I invoke, Heavenly Father, upon this people Thy divine blessings. Wilt Thou bless the membership of the Church. Grant that every member may have a desire to serve Thee and keep Thy commandments. Father, we ask Thee to cause that each one that is called to serve may serve with all of his heart and all of his strength. Grant unto Thy membership here a significant blessing, the blessing mentioned in the Book of Third John, 'I have no greater joy than to hear that my children walk in truth.' Grant that the children of the membership of the Church in the Dresden Mission may be loyal to Thy cause, and the grandchildren, even unto the last generation, before the Second Coming of Thy Beloved Son. Grant, Heavenly Father, that the membership here may receive their patriarchal blessings and live in such a way as to bring the promises to fulfillment.

"Heavenly Father, wilt Thou open up the way that the faithful may be accorded the privilege of going to Thy holy temple, there to receive their holy endowments and to be sealed as families for time and all eternity.

"Heavenly Father, we invoke a blessing upon the nonmembers of this land, that they may be touched in their hearts, that they may respond to the examples which the members set before them. Arouse within them a curiosity concerning the Church, and then cause that this curiosity may turn to a desire to know more, and then that this desire to know more will result in conversion to the Gospel, and that the membership of the Church may stabilize and indeed grow.

"Heavenly Father, wilt Thou intervene in the governmental affairs. Cause that Thy Holy Spirit may dwell with those who preside, that their hearts may be touched and that they may make those decisions which would help in the advancement of Thy work.

"We seek a blessing of peace upon this people, the peace promised by Thy Beloved Son. We look forward to the day when Thy missionaries may again be permitted to preach the everlasting Gospel in this area, for we know there is much of the blood of Israel here.

"Amidst the ringing of Church bells this morning, and the singing of birds in this, the forest which Thou hast created, music fills our souls and gratitude fills our hearts as we humbly acknowledge before Thee that Thou art our Father, that with Thee all things are possible, and that Thy Gospel has been restored upon the earth.

"Let the word go forth from this place, Heavenly Father. In Thy due time grant that many hundreds may seek membership in Thy Church, and that Thy children whom Thou hast preserved may indeed be saved in the Celestial Kingdom of God.

"Our Heavenly Father, wilt Thou bless the president of the Dresden Mission. We know of no man of greater faith in Thy kingdom. And for a man to serve as he has served has required the support of a devoted companion.

"Bless the counselors in the mission presidency who stand by the side of the president and perform a marvelous work and a wonder among this people. Bless their companions and the families of each member of the presidency. Grant unto these men Thy power, for they are men who are righteous in the use of power, and who are resolute and true in defending Thy word.

"Shower down upon us, Heavenly Father, Thy bounteous blessings. Bring to this land Zion, in all of its glory. Bring to the heart of each member a firm testimony of the gospel and grant that, from this day forth, the way may be opened for Thy word to go forward in greater power. Grant that the way may be cleared for the program of the Church in its fulness to come to this people, for they, through their faith, have merited such blessings.

"As Thy humble servant, acknowledging the divine revelation and inspiration of this day, I therefore invoke Thy holy blessings upon Thy work and upon Thy people in the Dresden Mission of The Church of Jesus Christ of Latter-day Saints.

"We as a group acknowledge before Thee our indebtedness to Thee and place in Thee our trust, knowing that Thou issued a holy promise. For thou hast said, 'I, the Lord, am merciful and gracious unto those who fear me, and delight to honor those who serve me in righteousness and in truth unto the end. Great shall be their reward and eternal shall be their glory.'

"With these divine words from the 76th section of the Doctrine and Covenants ringing in our ears, we offer up unto Thee this dedication and rededication prayer, in the name of Thy Beloved Son, Jesus Christ. Amen."

As we returned to our automobiles, the sun disappeared from the sky and the overcast condition which previously existed once again prevailed. I think I have not enjoyed a more spiritual experience as a member of the Council of the Twelve than the experience of offering the prayer in this communist controlled land, invoking the blessings of our Heavenly Father on as faithful a group of Saints as ever existed.

At 10:00 A.M. we held a general session for all of the membership in the greater Dresden area. Two unusual experiences occurred during the general session. I felt

324

impressed to call upon a sister Sabine Baasch, a young 17-year-old blonde-haired member who was singing in the chorus. I felt impressed to call upon her to bear her testimony, even though I knew that President Henry Burkhardt had been asked to designate two young people to speak, and I had no idea whom he had selected. To my surprise, the young lady whom he had selected was none other than Sister Baasch. After she bore her testimony, she rendered a beautiful vocal solo, impromptu, "O My Father." I told her that the Lord had called upon her to speak and bear her testimony in word and song that day. Of this I am certain. Her father was the leader of the chorus and is a professional musician from Leipzig.

At the conclusion of the meeting, the Saints sang the beautiful number, "God Be With You Till We Meet Again. Auf Wiedersehen, auf Wiedersehen." Each person's eyes were filled with tears, and handkerchiefs were everywhere in view as I bade a tender farewell to these, the most wonderful Saints to be found anywhere. As I walked from the pulpit, a lady came up to me and introduced herself and her son, Reinhold Daniel Sommer, from Goerlitz. She said that six years ago when I was in Goerlitz, she had just lost a child, a son, and appealed to me for consolation. I told her that if she were faithful, our Heavenly Father would bless her with another son. She mentioned that she conceived the very next day and that young Reinhold Daniel was the answer to that particular promise and prayer.

We chatted informally in the mission office, and then it was my opportunity to bless a wonderful couple. Benno Kurt Meyer had suffered a stroke and was making progress toward his recovery. Following the blessing which I provided Brother Meyer, I laid my hands upon the head of Hildegaard Lizbeth Meyer. As I began to bless her, I felt impressed to tell her that the loving service she had rendered her husband in his illness had been recorded in heaven and that our Heavenly Father would bless her abundantly for her kindness. As I continued in the blessing, brilliant sunlight came through the window and enveloped us. I felt this was a prompting of our Heavenly Father and felt impressed to promise Sister Meyer that her hip operation would be a success and that the doctors would be inspired of God and that her recovery would be complete. Rare are the occasions when one feels such a strong influence of the spirit as was the case today.

Thus ended my journal entry for Sunday, April 27, 1975—a momentous day in the history of the Church in Germany.

The work moved forward. The blessing we needed was the blessing that worthy members might receive their endowments and their sealings. One day as I returned to my office from a temple meeting, I saw a note which said "For your eyes only." President Spencer W. Kimball and his counselors had requested that I return to the temple. Now the first thought that goes through anyone's mind when the Presidency of this Church says, "Come to the temple and tell no one you're coming," is "What in the world have I done wrong? Where have I made a mistake?" When I arrived there, President Kimball said, "Brother Monson, we know of the love you have for those members in the German Democratic Republic. We know of your desire to provide them their endowments and sealings. We sustain you, and we pray for you, and we now say to you, 'Find a way.' That's all." When the Prophet of the Lord says "Find a way," you must find a way.

We explored every possibility. A trip once in a lifetime to the temple in Switzerland? Not approved by the government. Perhaps father and mother to come to Switzerland, leaving the children behind as hostages? Not right. How do you seal children to parents when they cannot kneel at an altar? It was a tragic situation. Then, through the fasting and the prayers of many members, a breakthrough occurred. In a very interesting discussion with government leaders, they asked the question, "Rather than having our people go to Switzerland or to London to visit a temple, why don't you build a temple in one of the Socialist countries?" I said, "We will." It came out just like that! Their offer had been accepted and we, therefore, went forward and broke ground for a beautiful temple in the city of Freiberg.

A few years later, a temple of God was dedicated. Many of us were in attendance. We felt that heaven was very close that day. This temple is one of the busiest temples for its size in the Church. It's the only temple I know where the stake presidents say, "What can we do? Our home teaching is down because everyone is in the temple!" When I heard that, I thought, "That's not bad—not bad at all!"

Doors long closed began to open. Church officers from Salt Lake City, including General Authorities and members of the Church auxiliary boards, were able to go into the German Democratic Republic, and our leaders there were able to come to general conference sessions in Salt Lake City. A miracle of miracles had taken place.

But there remained one miracle. How can the Church grow without missionaries? How can our numbers increase despite an aging population? A new building in Freiberg, a new stake center in Leipzig, and now a new stake center to be dedicated in Dresden and a new chapel in Zwickau, a new building for Plauen next year and another building for Berlin. But what use are buildings if there are not sufficient members to occupy them?

This dilemma was on my mind as we went forward with another assignment in the German Democratic Republic. We had fasted and we had prayed—Elder Russell M. Nelson,

Elder Hans B. Ringger, and I. We were granted an audience with government leaders, who greeted us with utmost respect. The State Secretary for Religious Affairs, Kurt Loeffler, said to us at a lovely luncheon—with orange juice and water on the table rather than the alcoholic beverages which were usually served—"We want to be helpful to you. We've observed you and your people for 20 years. We know you are what you profess to be—honest men and women. We like your work ethic. We like your emphasis on the family. We love your Article of Faith which says, 'We believe in being subject to kings, presidents, rulers, and magistrates, in obeying, honoring, and sustaining the law.' Let us help you."

From there we went to Dresden, that beautiful city bombed to smithereens during the war. There we had the opportunity to dedicate a magnificent stake center. The Saints sang their hearts out. The government officials were there to tour the building. They said, "We like this building for its functional design and for its beauty." One of the leaders said to the Chief of Architecture, "See that we incorporate in our public buildings the same utility that the Mormons have incorporated into this building."

When the congregation sang that day, "God Be with You Till We Meet Again," we remembered Him, the Prince of Peace, who died on the cross at Calvary. I contemplated our Lord and Savior, as He walked the path of pain, the trail of tears, even the road to righteousness. I thought of His beautiful declaration, "Peace I leave with you, my peace I give unto you: not as the world giveth, give I unto you. Let not your heart be troubled, neither let it be afraid."[2]

I thought, too, of His sad comment, "The foxes have holes, and the birds of the air have nests; but the Son of man hath not where to lay his head."[3] I said to myself and I would make a plea to you: We have many rooms in our homes—a room for sleeping, a room for eating, a room for recreation. Do we have room for Christ? We have time in our lives—time for golf, time for fishing, time for tennis. Do we have time for Christ? Let's open the doorways to our hearts, let's welcome the Prince of Peace, and then we shall have His spirit to be with us. This is the spirit we felt in Dresden. This is what we felt in Zwickau. Our building there was the most beautiful building in the entire city.

Then it was on to Berlin for the crucial meetings with the head of the country, Chairman Erich Honecker. I confess that the Brethren in the temple were remembering us in their prayers. I was surely upon my knees, for I know my limitations. That special morning the sunlight bathed the city of Berlin. It had been raining all night, but now beauty prevailed. We were driven to the chambers of the chief representatives of the government. You had to arrive exactly on time—not a minute early, not a minute late. (That's German efficiency!) I confess to you that while earlier I had been worried and concerned, now I had a calm come into my heart that reminded me of the Prophet Joseph Smith's declaration, and I felt, as did he, calm as a summer's morn.

Beyond the exquisite entry to the government chambers, we were greeted by Chairman Honecker. We presented to him the statuette *First Step*, depicting a mother helping her child take its first step toward its father. He was highly pleased with the statuette. Then he escorted us into his private council room. There, around a large, round table, we were seated. The group included Chairman Erich Honecker and his deputies, Kurt Loeffler, the State Secretary for Religious Affairs, Elders Russell M. Nelson and Hans B. Ringger, President Henry Burkhardt, President Frank Apel, and President Manfred Schutze, and an interpreter.

Chairman Honecker began: "We know you Mormons believe in work; you've demonstrated that. We know you believe in the family; you've demonstrated that. We know you are good citizens in whatever country you may be living. We have observed that. The floor is yours. Make your desires known."

I began modestly: "Chairman Honecker, our young people have not been given an opportunity to hold a conference, a conference of young men and young women. [The government had been very leery of youth gatherings since World War II.] We desire to hold such a conference."

He then said, "Your request is granted."

I continued, "Chairman Honecker, at the dedication and open house for the temple in Freiberg, 89,800 of your countrymen stood in line, at times up to four hours, sometimes in the rain, that they might see a house of God. In the city of Leipzig, at the dedication of the stake center, 12,000 people stood in line to attend an open house. In the city of Dresden there were 29,000 visitors; in the city of Zwickau, 5,300; and every week of the year 1,500 to 1,800 people come to the temple grounds in the city of Freiberg. They want to know what we believe. We would like to tell your countrymen that we believe in the family unit. We would like to tell them that we believe in honoring and obeying and sustaining the law of the land and that we strive to achieve strong family units. These are a few of our beliefs. We cannot answer questions and we cannot convey our feelings because we have no missionary representatives here as we do in other countries."

Then there flashed through my mind a recent experience. I said, "A month ago we had the ambassador from Argentina meeting with us at Church headquarters. We took him to Brigham Young University. There he met and visited with returned missionaries from Argentina. They became the best advocates of Argentina and her people that one could imagine." I said, "The young men and young women which we would like to have come to your country would similarly love your nation and your people. More particularly, they would leave an influence with your people which would be ennobling."

I continued on: "We would like to see young men and young women from your nation have a view of other nations. Some would be called to serve in America, in Canada, and other countries as missionaries. They will return better prepared to assume positions of responsibility in your nation."

He then spoke to me for thirty minutes on what he and his associates had been attempting to achieve. He covered the field from striving for peace to their country's standing in the world summer Olympics. I thought he would never address my critical questions. Then he looked at me and said, "We can trust you. You have the look of an honest man. Permission is granted for your missionary request." My spirit literally soared out of that room. The meeting was concluded. He said, "My administrative aide, Secretary Kurt Loeffler, will work out the details with your representative." (Mr. Loeffler was the man who had already complimented us on our work and had said that things would go well for us.)

As we left those magnificent chambers, Elder Russell Nelson turned to me and said, "Notice how the light of sunshine is penetrating this hall. It's almost as though God were saying, 'I am pleased.'"

We left the building. We were driven to the border. The border was crossed. We boarded our plane and departed. The black darkness of night had ended. The bright light of day had dawned.

As I left Germany and our beloved Saints, I thought of the words of Rudyard Kipling:

> *The tumult and the shouting dies;*
> *The captains and the kings depart.*
> *Still stands thine ancient sacrifice,*
> *An humble and a contrite heart.*
> *Lord God of hosts, be with us yet,*
> *Lest we forget, lest we forget.*[4]

My plea today is that we will remember that if we seek the Lord, as did those Saints in the German Democratic Republic, we shall find Him. He may come "to us as One unknown, as of old, by the lake-side, He came to those men who knew Him not. He speaks the same word: 'Follow thou me!' and sets us to the tasks which [we are to perform in] our time," and whether these tasks be large or small, "He will reveal Himself to us in the [sorrows we] pass through in His fellowship, and . . . [we] shall know in [our] own experience Who He is."[5]

As I reflect on these events, my thoughts turn to the Savior's words, "And in nothing doth man offend God, or against none is his wrath kindled, save those who confess not his hand in all things, and obey not his commandments."[6] I confess the hand of God in the miraculous events pertaining to the Church in the German Democratic Republic. Unto Him and His Son I ascribe all honor, glory, and accomplishment.

I remember the Lord's promise as recorded in the 76th section of the Doctrine and Covenants: "I, the Lord, am merciful and gracious unto those who fear me, and delight to honor those who serve me in righteousness and in truth unto the end. Great shall be their reward and eternal shall be their glory."[7] This is the promise of the Lord to you and to me.

NOTES

1. See Proverbs 3:5–6.
2. John 14:27.
3. Matthew 8:20.
4. "God of Our Fathers, Known of Old," *Hymns*, no. 80.
5. Albert Schweitzer, *The Quest of the Historical Jesus* (1948), 403.
6. Doctrine and Covenants 59:21.
7. Doctrine and Covenants 76:5–6.

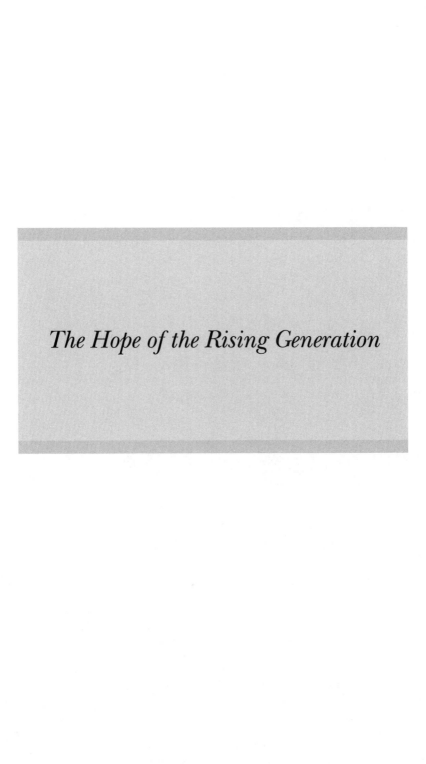

The Hope of the Rising Generation

37

LIFE'S GREATEST QUESTIONS

H ow pleased I am to be with you choice young people tonight. I would like to direct my remarks to three of the most
significant questions you will ever have to consider: What will
be my faith? Whom shall I marry? What will be my life's work?

First, *what will be my faith?* Each one of us has the responsibility to find out for himself whether or not this gospel of
Jesus Christ is true. If we read the Book of Mormon, read the
standard works, and put the teachings to the test, then we shall
know of the doctrine, whether it be of man or whether it be of
God, for this is our promise.

Sometimes the decision of what we believe can have far-
reaching consequences. When I had the privilege to preside
over the Canadian Mission, we had the wonderful opportunity
of working with about 450 of the finest young men and young
women in all the world. I should like to relate an experience
Sister Monson had in Canada which had far-reaching significance. One Sunday she was the only person in an otherwise
very busy mission home. The telephone rang, and the person

who was on the other end of the line spoke with a Dutch accent and asked, "Is this the headquarters of the Mormon church?"

Sister Monson assured him that it was, as far as Toronto was concerned. Then Sister Monson asked, "May I help you?"

The party on the other end said, "Yes, we have come from our native Holland, where we have had an opportunity to learn something about the Mormons, and we would like to know a little more."

Sister Monson, being a good missionary, responded, "We think we can help you."

Then the caller said, "Would you wait just a little while, however, because we have chicken pox in our home. If you could wait until the children are well, we would love to have the missionaries call."

Sister Monson indicated that she would arrange such and that terminated the conversation. Excitedly she told the two missionaries on our staff, "Here is a golden referral," and the missionaries responded excitedly. But, like some missionaries, they decided to procrastinate calling upon the family. Days turned into weeks, and the weeks became several. Finally Sister Monson said, "Elders, are you going to call on that Dutch family?" They responded, "We're too busy tonight, but we're going to get around to it."

A few more days went by. Again Sister Monson said, "What about my Dutch family? Are you going to call on them tonight?"

Again came the reply, "We're too busy tonight, but we're going to work it into our schedule."

Finally, they had crowded Sister Monson too much and she said, "If you aren't going to call on the Dutch family tonight, my husband and I will call on them."

They said, "We'll work it into our schedule tonight."

They called on a lovely family. They taught them the gospel. Each member of the family became a member of the Church. The family was the Jacob de Jager family. Brother de

Jager became the president of our elders quorum. He worked with the gigantic Phillips Electronics Industries. His company transferred him to Mexico and then back to the Netherlands, where he later became the counselor to several mission presidents, including Brother Max Pinegar. He became a Regional Representative of the Twelve, then became a member of the First Quorum of the Seventy, and he served as the Area Supervisor for all missionary work in Southeast Asia.

I ask the question, was it an important decision that was made on the part of the missionaries to call on the de Jagers? Was it an important decision for Sister Monson to say, "Tonight is the night or else?" Was it an important decision for the de Jagers to telephone Walnut 34578 in Toronto, Canada, and say, "Could we have the missionaries come?" I bear testimony that that decision had eternal consequences not only for the de Jagers but for many other people as well; for here is a man who can teach the gospel in English, in Dutch, in German, in Spanish, in Indonesian, and in Chinese. I ask the question, "What will be your faith?"

Maybe your conversion will not be so dramatic as Brother and Sister de Jager's happened to be, but to you it will be equally as long-lasting and equally as far-reaching. That in which we believe is a very important matter. Weigh very carefully your responsibility to search for truth.

Secondly, *whom shall I marry?* I think I should like to take you with me back to my college days. At that time, young people would graduate from high school in Salt Lake City at the age of 16 or 17, and we were enrolled as freshmen at the various universities. I remember at a New Year's Eve party, I was dancing with a girl from West High School when a young lady from East High School danced by with her partner. Her name was Frances Johnson. I didn't know it at the time. I just took one look and decided that there was a young lady I wanted to meet. But she danced away and I didn't see her again for three more months. Then one day, at University Avenue and Second South Street, I looked across the street and couldn't believe my eyes. There was the young lady whom I had seen dancing across the floor. She was standing with another young lady and a young man whom I remembered from grade school days. Unfortunately, I couldn't remember his name. I had a decision to make. What should I do? I found in my heart an appreciation of that phrase that "when the time for decision arrives, the time for preparation is past." I squared my shoulders and plunged toward my opportunity. I walked up to that young man and said, "Hello, my old friend from grade school days."

He said to me, "I can't quite remember your name." I told him my name. He told me his name, and then he introduced me to the girl who later became my wife. That day I made a little note in my student directory to call on Frances Beverly Johnson, and I did. That decision, I believe, was perhaps the most important decision that I have ever made.

You young people have the responsibility to make that same decision. We have an important responsibility in choosing not only whom we shall date, but whom we shall marry. Elder Bruce R. McConkie is the author of a most priceless statement: "Nothing is more important than marrying the right person, at the right time, in the right place, and by the right authority."

We hope you will avoid what we call quick courtships, weekend courtships, which we have seen in some cases. I might report to you that our marriage took place three and one-half years after I made that first acquaintance with Sister Monson. Of course, I'm not here to put cold water on any of you who have plans contrary to three and one-half years. But I think it is important that you become acquainted with the person whom you plan to marry, that you make certain that you are looking down the same pathway, in the same direction, with the same objectives in mind. It is ever so significant that you do this.

I should like to dispel one rumor which is very hard to put

to rest. I know of no mission president in all the world who has ever told a missionary that he had the responsibility to marry within six months after his mission concluded. I think that rumor was commenced by a returned missionary, and if not by a returned missionary, by the girlfriend of a returned missionary. You will know when the right time is here and when the right girl or the right boy is ready for your proposal. I am going to discuss that just a little bit later.

Now may I move to the last subject. *What will be my life's work?* I have counseled many returning missionaries who have asked this question. We find that missionaries like to emulate their mission president. If he is an educator, a preponderant number of missionaries will want to be educators. If he is a businessman, a large number will want to study business. If he is a doctor, a lot of the missionaries will want to be physicians. It's natural for them to want to emulate a man whom they respect and admire.

My counsel to returning missionaries and to each one of you young people is that you should study and prepare for your life's work in a field that you enjoy, because you are going to spend a good share of your life in that field. It should be a field which will challenge your intellect and which will make maximum utilization of your talents and your capabilities. Finally, it should be a field which will provide you sufficient remuneration to provide adequately for your companion and your children. Now that is a big order, but I bear testimony that these criteria are very important in choosing your life's work.

I hope that you are not afraid of tough classes. I hope that you are not afraid of lengthy periods of preparation. I hope that you want to be so well equipped when you leave this institution that you can compete in this world which I have described as a competitive world. I hope that you will learn to take responsibility for your decisions, whether they be in your courses of study which you elect to take or whether they be in the direction of the academic attainments which you strive to achieve.

We find all sorts of people who are willing to alibi or who are willing to make excuse for a failure. During World War II, a vital decision was made by one of the great leaders of the Allied military, Viscount Slim, from Great Britain. He made this statement after a problem which occurred in the Battle for Khartoum in 1940 against the Italians. He said, long after the war, "I could find plenty of excuses but only one reason—myself. When two courses of action were open to me, I had not chosen, as a good commander should, the bolder. I had taken counsel of my fears."

My young brothers and sisters, don't take counsel of your fears. Don't say to yourselves, "I'm not smart enough to study chemical engineering, so I will study this. I'm not wise enough or I can't apply myself sufficiently well to study this difficult subject or in this difficult field, so I shall choose the easier way." I plead with you to choose the hard way and to tax your talent, and our Heavenly Father will make you equal to those decisions.

If you should stumble, if you should take a course and get less than the A grade that you desire, I hope you won't let it become a discouraging thing to you. I hope that you will rise and try again. I think, for example, of Admiral Chester Nimitz. When he graduated as an ensign, he was given an old, decrepit destroyer as his first command. It was named the *Decatur*. It was all he could do to put the old destroyer in shape, and on one of its maiden voyages, Ensign Nimitz ran the ship aground. It resulted in a summary court martial. Fortunately, he was found guilty only of neglect of duty rather than a more serious offense. Now, had Chester Nimitz not been made of the stuff he was, that defeat could have ruined his career. But what did he do? He put that defeat behind him, and he went on to become the commanding admiral of the greatest sea force ever assembled in this world, the Pacific Fleet. He showed one and all that one defeat could not keep a good man down.

I turn to the sports world for another illustration. My wife blames the malfunction of our television set on the many hours watching bowl games. I might say that one of the best bowl games I ever watched and one of the best football games that I ever viewed was the one which taught me the greatest lesson that I have learned from sports. A great quarterback for the New York Giants, Y. A. Tittle, was playing in a critical game. It was down to the final play. The opposing team was three points ahead. Tittle had time for one pass. The sportscaster became very excited when he said, "It looks like the game is about over, but Tittle has one opportunity. He takes the snap from center. He's looking for a receiver, but his receivers are covered. He is fading deeper into his backfield. The linemen are upon him. It looks like it's all over for the New York Giants. But wait. Tittle is eluding tackler after tackler. It looks like he might get the pass away and he does and it's caught in the end zone for the winning touchdown and the game belongs to the New York Giants!" Then, all out of breath the sportscaster said, "That was a great second effort by Y. A. Tittle!"

In this life, where we have opportunities to strive and to achieve, I want to bear witness that we need to make that second effort on occasion—and a third effort, and a fourth effort, and as many degrees of effort as may be required to accomplish what we strive to accomplish.

There is much importance attached to those three questions: What will be my faith? Whom shall I marry? What will be my life's work? I am so grateful that we need not make those decisions without eternal help. Every one of us can have the guidance and the direction of our Heavenly Father if we strive to receive it.

I think that you students should learn and memorize the ninth section of the Doctrine and Covenants. This is a section which is largely overlooked but which has a lesson for each one of you. When you contemplate a decision, go to your Heavenly Father in the manner in which the Prophet Joseph indicated that the Lord advised him: "Behold, you have not understood; you have supposed that I would give it unto you, [meaning the answer] when you took no thought save it was to ask me. But, behold, I say unto you, that you must study it out in your mind; then you must ask me if it be right, and if it is right I will cause that your bosom shall burn within you; therefore, you shall feel that it is right." Then the Lord goes on, "But if it be not right you shall have no such feelings, but you shall have a stupor of thought that shall cause you to forget the thing which is wrong."[1]

Study the thing out in your own mind and then take it to the Lord for that confirmation, that burning feeling in your bosom; and upon bended knee, in the attitude of prayer, you can obtain from Him that feeling within your heart that your decision is right.

Last year I had the privilege of returning to Tahiti to a people whom I dearly love. There I was talking to our mission president, President Raymond Baudin, about the Tahitian people. They are known as some of the greatest seafaring people in all the world. Brother Baudin, who speaks French but little English, was trying to describe to me the secret of the success of the Tahitian sea captains. He said, "They are amazing. The weather may be terrible, the vessels may be leaky, there may be no navigational aids except their inner feelings and the stars in the heavens, but they pray and they go." He repeated it three times, "They pray and they go. They pray and they go. They pray and they go." There is a lesson in that statement. We need to pray and then we need to act. Both are important.

In addition to the importance of prayer, I add a third dimension. Follow the prophets of God. When you follow the prophets, you will be in safe territory. I know that the Lord inspires His prophets, His seers, and His revelators. Years ago, I had the responsibility to go to a stake conference to choose a new president. I interviewed throughout the day. Many names were mentioned. In my final interview, a bishop said to me, "Brother Monson, if you really want to know who would make the finest president of our stake, it's Edgar M. Denny." I had never met Brother Denny, but I want to bear testimony that I didn't hear any bells, I didn't see any lights flash, but I knew that Edgar Denny was to be the president of that stake.

I had President Stanford Smith call him on the telephone. Sister Denny answered and said, "Brother Denny is not here. He's in Florida." She then said: "Just a moment, President Smith, someone is at the door." She went to the door, and there stood her husband. She said, "Come in. The stake president wants you. You're not supposed to be home until tomorrow."

He said, "I just felt that I should come."

The Dennys came over to the office, and I extended to him the call to serve as president of his stake. At the time he was serving as a second counselor in his ward bishopric. He had been the bishop of the ward, but he felt in his employment that he had to have additional education. He made a decision to enroll evenings in law school, and even with a large family, he graduated with the Order of the Coif from his university with that coveted degree and qualified himself to receive the top job in his field. At that time, he was asked to be the second counselor in the bishopric where he had served as bishop, and he responded cheerfully and willingly and was hidden away in that assignment when the Lord gave me the responsibility to select a president. He knew that Edgar Denny was to be the president.

As I speak of following the prophets, I shall share with you a very intimate experience that I had in my youth. When I desire to achieve, I desire to achieve with all my heart, whether it be in athletics, in school, or in business, or anything else. I served in the United States Navy toward the end of World War II. I was what is called a seaman, the lowest possible rank. Then I qualified to be a seaman first class; then I qualified to be yeoman third class. The war ended, and I was discharged. But I made a decision that if ever I went back into the military, I wanted to go in as a commissioned officer. If you haven't been in the military, I won't take the time to tell you the difference between the apprentice seaman and the commissioned officer. One can only learn that by experience, but once learned, one never forgets. I thought, *no more mess kitchens for me, no more scrubbing of the decks, if I can avoid it,* and I worked like a slave to qualify for that commission.

I joined the United States Naval Reserve. I went to drill every Monday night. I studied hard that I might qualify academically. I took every kind of examination imaginable: mental, physical, and emotional. Finally, there came from Denver, Colorado, the beautiful news, "You have been accepted to receive the commission of an ensign in the United States Naval Reserve." I gleefully showed it to Sister Monson and said, "I made it!" She hugged me and said, "You've worked hard to achieve it."

But then something happened. I got called to be a counselor in my ward bishopric. The bishop's council meeting was on the evening of my drill meeting. I knew that there was a terrible conflict. I knew that I didn't have the time to pursue the naval reserve and my bishopric duties. What was I to do? A decision had to be made. I prayed about it. I then went to see my former stake president, Elder Harold B. Lee. I sat down across the table from him. I told him how much I valued that commission, and then he said to me, "Here's what you should do, Brother Monson. You write a letter to the Bureau of Naval Affairs and tell them that because of your call as a member of the bishopric, you can't accept that commission in the United States Naval Reserve." My heart sank. Then he said, "Write to the commandant of the Twelfth Naval District in San Francisco and tell them that you would like to be discharged from the reserve."

I said, "Brother Lee, you don't understand the military. Of course they will decline to give me that commission if I refuse, but the Twelfth Naval District isn't going to let any noncommissioned officer out of their hands with a war brewing in Korea. I'm stuck to go back in as a noncommissioned officer if I don't accept this commission. Are you sure this is the counsel you want me to receive?"

He put his hand on my shoulder and, in a fatherly way, said, "Brother Monson, have more faith. The military is not for you."

I went to my home. I placed a tear-stained commission back in its envelope with its accompanying letter and declined to accept it. I then wrote a letter to the Twelfth Naval District and requested a discharge from the naval reserve.

My discharge from the naval reserve was in the last group processed before the outbreak of the Korean War. My headquarters outfit was activated, and six weeks after I had been called to be a counselor in a bishopric, I was called to be the bishop of my ward. I would not be standing before you this evening had I not followed the counsel of a prophet, had I not prayed about a decision, had I not come to appreciate an important truth. The wisdom of God ofttimes appears as foolishness to men. But the greatest single lesson we can learn in mortality is that when God speaks and a man obeys, that man will always be right.

My dear brothers and sisters, I pray with all the strength and all the fervor of my conviction that our Heavenly Father will guide and bless you in these important decisions which each one of you will be called upon to make. If you want to see the light of heaven, if you want to feel the inspiration of Almighty God, if you want to have that feeling within your bosom that your Heavenly Father is guiding you to the left or guiding you to the right, follow the instruction from the passage, "stand ye in holy places, and be not moved,"[2] and then the spirit of our Heavenly Father will be yours.

NOTES

1. Doctrine and Covenants 9:7–9.
2. Doctrine and Covenants 87:8.

38

THE FAITH OF A CHILD

When I was a boy, I had a wonderful teacher in Sunday School. From the Bible she would read to us of Jesus, the Redeemer and Savior of the world. One day she taught us how the little children were brought unto Him, that He should put His hands on them and pray. His disciples rebuked those that brought the children. "But when Jesus saw it, he was much displeased, and said unto them, Suffer the little children to come unto me, and forbid them not: for of such is the kingdom of God."[1]

That lesson has never left me. Indeed, just a few months ago I relearned its meaning and partook of its power. My teacher was the Lord. May I share with you this experience.

Far away from Salt Lake City, and some 80 miles from Shreveport, Louisiana, lives the Jack Methvin family. Mother, dad, and the boys are members of The Church of Jesus Christ of Latter-day Saints. Until just recently there was a lovely daughter who, by her presence, graced that home. Her name was Christal. She was but ten years old when death ended her earthly sojourn.

Christal liked to run and play on the spacious ranch where her family lives. She could ride horses skillfully and excelled in 4-H work, winning awards in the local and state fairs. Her future was bright, and life was wonderful. Then there was discovered on her leg an unusual lump. The specialists in New Orleans completed their diagnosis and rendered their verdict: carcinoma. The leg must be removed.

She recovered well from the surgery, lived as buoyantly as ever and never complained. Then the doctors discovered that the cancer had spread to her tiny lungs. The Methvin family did not despair, but rather planned a flight to Salt Lake City. Christal could receive a blessing from one of the General Authorities. The Methvins knew none of the Brethren personally, so opening before Christal a picture of all the General Authorities, a chance selection was made. By sheer coincidence, my name was selected.

Christal never made the flight to Salt Lake City. Her condition deteriorated. The end drew nigh. But her faith did not waver. To her parents, she said, "Isn't stake conference approaching? Isn't a General Authority assigned? And why not Brother Monson? If I can't go to him, the Lord can send him to me."

Meanwhile in Salt Lake City, with no knowledge of the events transpiring in Shreveport, a most unusual situation developed. For the weekend of the Shreveport Louisiana Stake conference, I had been assigned to El Paso, Texas. President Ezra Taft Benson called me to his office and explained that one of the other Brethren had done some preparatory work regarding the stake division in El Paso. He asked if I would mind were another to be assigned to El Paso and I assigned elsewhere. Of course there was no problem—anywhere would be fine with me. Then President Benson said, "Brother Monson, I feel impressed to have you visit the Shreveport Louisiana Stake." The assignment was accepted. The day came. I arrived in Shreveport.

That Saturday afternoon was filled with meetings—one with the stake presidency, one with priesthood leaders, one with the patriarch, then yet another with the general leadership of the stake. Rather apologetically, Stake President Charles F. Cagle asked if my schedule would permit me time to provide a blessing to a ten-year-old girl afflicted with cancer. Her name: Christal Methvin. I responded that, if possible, I would do so, and then inquired if she would be at the conference, or was she in a Shreveport hospital? Knowing the time was tightly scheduled, President Cagle almost whispered that Christal was confined to her home—*more than 80 miles from Shreveport!*

I examined the schedule of meetings for that evening and the next morning—even my return flight. There simply was no available time. An alternative suggestion came to mind. Could we not remember the little one in our public prayers at conference? Surely the Lord would understand. On this basis, we proceeded with the scheduled meetings.

When the word was communicated to the Methvin family, there was understanding but a trace of disappointment as well. Hadn't the Lord heard their prayers? Hadn't He provided that Brother Monson would come to Shreveport? Again the family prayed, asking for a final favor—that their precious Christal would realize her desire.

At the very moment the Methvin family knelt in prayer, the clock in the stake center showed the time to be 7:45. The leadership meeting had been inspirational. I was sorting my notes, preparing to step to the pulpit, when I heard a voice speak to my spirit. The message was brief, the words familiar: "Suffer the little children to come unto me, and forbid them not: for of such is the kingdom of God." My notes became a blur. My thoughts turned to a tiny girl in need of a blessing. The decision was made. The meeting schedule was altered. After all, people are more important than meetings. I turned to Bishop

James Serra and asked that he leave the meeting and advise the Methvins.

The Methvin family had just arisen from their knees when the telephone rang and the message was relayed that early Sunday morning—the Lord's day—in a spirit of fasting and prayer, we would journey to Christal's bedside.

I shall ever remember and never forget that early-morning journey to a heaven the Methvin family calls home. I have been in hallowed places—even holy houses—but never have I felt more strongly the presence of the Lord than in the Methvin home. Christal looked so tiny lying peacefully on such a large bed. The room was bright and cheerful. The sunshine from the east window filled the bedroom with light as the Lord filled our hearts with love.

The family surrounded Christal's bedside. I gazed down at a child who was too ill to rise—almost too weak to speak. Her illness had now rendered her sightless. So strong was the Spirit that I fell to my knees, took her frail hand in mine, and said simply, "Christal, I am here." She parted her lips and whispered, "Brother Monson, I just knew you would come." I looked around the room. No one was standing. Each was on bended knee. A blessing was given. A faint smile crossed Christal's face. Her whispered "thank you" provided an appropriate benediction. Quietly, each filed from the room.

Four days later, on Thursday, as Church members in Shreveport joined their faith with the Methvin family and Christal's name was remembered in a special prayer to a kind and loving Heavenly Father, the pure spirit of Christal Methvin left its disease-ravaged body and entered the paradise of God.

For those of us who knelt that Sabbath day in a sun-filled bedroom, and particularly for Christal's mother and father as they enter daily that same room and remember how she left it, the immortal words of Eugene Field will bring back precious memories:

The little toy dog is covered with dust,
But sturdy and staunch he stands;
And the little toy soldier is red with rust,
And his musket moulds in his hands.
Time was when the little toy dog was new,
And the soldier was passing fair,
And that was the time when our Little Boy Blue
Kissed them and put them there.

"Now, don't you go till I come," he said,
"And don't you make any noise!"
So toddling off to his trundle-bed
He dreamt of the pretty toys.
And as he was dreaming, an angel song
Awakened our Little Boy Blue,—
Oh, the years are many, the years are long,
But the little toy friends are true!

Ay, faithful to Little Boy Blue they stand,
Each in the same old place,
Awaiting the touch of a little hand,
The smile of a little face.
And they wonder, as waiting these long years through,
In the dust of that little chair,
What has become of our Little Boy Blue
Since he kissed them and put them there.[2]

For us there is no need to wonder or to wait. Said the Master, "I am the resurrection, and the life: he that believeth in me, though he were dead, yet shall he live: and whosoever liveth and believeth in me shall never die."[3] To you, Jack and Nancy Methvin, He speaks: "Peace I leave with you, my peace I give unto you: not as the world giveth, give I unto you. Let not your heart be troubled, neither let it be afraid."[4] And from your sweet Christal could well come the comforting expression: "I go to prepare a place for you . . . that where I am, there ye may be also."[5]

To believers everywhere, I bear witness that Jesus of Nazareth does love little children, that He listens to your prayers and responds to them. The Master did indeed utter those words, "Suffer the little children to come unto me, and forbid them not: for of such is the kingdom of God."[6]

I know these are the words He spoke to the throng gathered on the coast of Judea by the waters of Jordan—for I have read them.

I know these are the words He spoke to an Apostle on assignment in Shreveport, Louisiana—for I heard them.

To these truths I bear record.

NOTES

1. Mark 10:14.
2. "Little Boy Blue," *One Hundred and One Famous Poems* (1958), 15.
3. John 11:25–26.
4. John 14:27.
5. John 14:2–3.
6. Mark 10:14.

39

YOUR PATRIARCHAL BLESSING: A LIAHONA OF LIGHT

Have you ever cleaned an attic or rummaged through an old storeroom? One discovers a bit of history and a whole lot of sentiment. A few weeks ago we emptied the attic of our mountain cabin. Seventy years of treasures, each with its own special memory, passed in review. Leading the parade was an old high chair with metal wheels. This was followed by glass milk bottles that once had pasteboard caps, and then a copy of *Life Magazine* with a story from World War II.

Featured in the magazine was an account of a once proud airplane, a mighty bomber, found rather well preserved in an isolated corner of the vast Sahara Desert. The bomber and crew had participated in the famous raid over Romania's Ploiesti oil fields. The craft had been struck by antiaircraft fire, which completely destroyed its communication and navigational equipment. As the stricken plane turned toward its desert landing field, a sudden sandstorm obliterated familiar points of reference. The field's landing lights were shrouded by sand. The plane droned on, even far beyond the landing field, into the desert wastes until, with fuel exhausted, it settled on the Sahara, never to fly again. All crew members perished. Home and the safety and shelter there to be found had been denied. Victory, hopes, dreams—all had been swallowed by the silence of the desert's dust.

Centuries earlier, a righteous and loving father by the name of Lehi took his beloved family into a desert wasteland. He journeyed in response to the voice of the Lord. But the Lord did not decree that such a "flight" be undertaken without heavenly help. The words of Nephi describe the gift provided on the morning of the historic trek:

"And it came to pass that as my father arose in the morning, and went forth to the tent door, to his great astonishment he beheld upon the ground a round ball of curious workmanship; and it was of fine brass. And within the ball were two spindles; and the one pointed the way whither we should go into the wilderness."[1]

War and man-made means of destruction could not confuse or destroy this curious compass. Neither could the sudden desert sandstorms render useless its guiding powers. The prophet Alma explained that this "Liahona," as it was called, was a compass prepared by the Lord. It worked for them according to their faith and pointed the way they should go.[2]

The same Lord who provided a Liahona to Lehi provides for you and for me today a rare and valuable gift to give direction to our lives, to mark the hazards to our safety, and to chart the way, even safe passage—not to a promised land, but to our heavenly home. The gift to which I refer is known as your patriarchal blessing. Every worthy member of the Church is entitled to receive such a precious and priceless personal treasure.

"Patriarchal blessings," wrote the First Presidency in a letter to stake presidents, "contemplate an inspired declaration of the lineage of the recipient and, when so moved upon by the Spirit, an inspired and prophetic statement of the life mission of the recipient, together with such blessings, cautions and admonitions as the patriarch may be prompted to give for the accomplishment of such life's mission, it being always made clear that the realization of all promised blessings is conditioned upon faithfulness to the gospel of our Lord, whose servant the patriarch is."[3]

Who is this man, this patriarch, through whom such seership and priesthood power flow? How is he called? The Quorum of the Twelve Apostles has special responsibility pertaining to the calling of such men. From my own experience I testify that patriarchs are called of God by prophecy. How else could our Heavenly Father reveal those to whom such prophetic powers are to be given? A patriarch holds an ordained office in the Melchizedek Priesthood. The patriarchal office, however, is one of blessing—not of administration. I have never called a man to this sacred office but what I have felt the Lord's guiding influence in the decision. May I share with you one treasured experience?

Many years back I had been assigned to name a patriarch for a stake in Logan, Utah. I found such a man, wrote his name on a slip of paper, and placed the note inside my scriptures. My further review revealed that another worthy patriarch had moved to this same area, making unnecessary the naming of a new patriarch. None was named.

Nine years later I was again assigned a stake conference in Logan. Once more a patriarch was needed for the stake I was to visit. I had been using a new set of scriptures for several years and had them in my briefcase. However, as I prepared to leave my home for the drive to Logan, I took from the bookcase shelf an older set of scriptures, leaving the new ones at home. During the conference I began my search for a patriarch: a worthy man, a blameless servant of God, one filled with faith, characterized by kindness. Pondering these requirements, I opened my scriptures and there discovered the slip of paper placed there long years before. I read the name written on the paper: Cecil B. Kenner. I asked the stake presidency if by chance Brother Kenner lived in this particular stake. I found he did. Cecil B. Kenner was that day ordained a patriarch.

Patriarchs are humble men. They are students of the scriptures. They stand before God as the means whereby the blessings of heaven can flow from that eternal source to the recipient on whose head rest the hands of the patriarch. He may not be a man of letters, a possessor of worldly wealth, or a holder of distinguished office. He, however, must be blessed with priesthood power and personal purity. To reach to heaven for divine guidance and inspiration, a patriarch is to be a man of love, a man of compassion, a man of judgment, a man of God.

A patriarchal blessing is a revelation to the recipient, even a white line down the middle of the road, to protect, inspire, and motivate activity and righteousness. A patriarchal blessing literally contains chapters from your book of eternal possibilities. I say eternal, for just as life is eternal, so is a patriarchal blessing. What may not come to fulfillment in this life may occur in the next. We do not govern God's timetable. "For my thoughts are not your thoughts, neither are your ways my ways, saith the Lord.

"For as the heavens are higher than the earth, so are my ways higher than your ways, and my thoughts than your thoughts."[4]

Your patriarchal blessing is yours and yours alone. It may be brief or lengthy, simple or profound. Length and language do not a patriarchal blessing make. It is the Spirit that conveys the true meaning. Your blessing is not to be folded neatly and tucked away. It is not to be framed or published. Rather, it is to be read. It is to be loved. It is to be followed. Your patriarchal blessing will see you through the darkest night. It will guide you through life's dangers. Unlike the struggling bomber of yesteryear, lost in the desert wastes, the sands and storms of life will not destroy you on your eternal flight.

Your patriarchal blessing is your passport to peace in this life. It is a Liahona of light to guide you unerringly to your heavenly home.

NOTES

1. 1 Nephi 16:10.
2. See Alma 37:38–40.
3. First Presidency letter to stake presidents, 28 June 1958.
4. Isaiah 55:8–9.

40

DECISIONS DETERMINE DESTINY

T HE WAY TO EXALTATION IS not a freeway featuring unlimited vision, unrestricted speeds, and untested skills. Rather, it is known by many forks and turnings, sharp curves, and controlled speeds. Your driving skill will be put to the test. Are you ready? You are driving. You haven't passed this way before. Fortunately, the Master Highway Builder, even our Heavenly Father, has provided a road map showing the route to follow. He has placed markers along the way to guide you to your destination.

Perhaps you may recognize some of His signs:

Honor thy father and thy mother.

Search the scriptures, for they are they which testify of me.

Seek ye first the kingdom of God and His righteousness.

Be ye clean.

That evil one, too, has placed road signs to frustrate your progress and to lead you from the path of truth into detours of sin. His detours all lead to a dead end. Have you noticed his markers:

Times have changed.

My love is mine to give; my life is mine to live.

It can't hurt anyone but me.

Just this once won't matter.

Now we see coming into focus the responsibility to choose, that inevitable crisis at the crossroads of life. He who would lead you down waits patiently for the dark night, a wavering will, a confused conscience, a mixed-up mind. Are you prepared to make the decision at the crossroads?

You may ask, "Are decisions really that important?" Decisions determine destiny. You can't make eternal decisions without eternal consequences.

May I provide a simple formula by which you can measure the choices which confront you. It's easy to remember, sometimes difficult to apply: "You can't be right by doing wrong; you can't be wrong by doing right." Your personal conscience always warns you as a friend before it punishes you as a judge.

The Lord, in a revelation given through Joseph Smith the Prophet at Kirtland, Ohio, May 1831, counseled: "That which doth not edify is not of God, and is darkness. That which is of God is light."[1]

Some foolish persons turn their backs on the wisdom of God and follow the allurement of fickle fashion, the attraction of false popularity, and the thrill of the moment. Their course of conduct so resembles the disastrous experience of Esau, who exchanged his birthright for a mess of pottage.

Where money, rather than morality, dictates one's actions, one is inclined away from God. Turning away from God brings broken covenants, shattered dreams, vanished ambitions, evaporated plans, unfulfilled expectations, crushed hopes, misused drives, warped character, and wrecked lives.

Such a quagmire of quicksand I plead with you to avoid. You are of a noble birthright. Eternal life in the kingdom of our Father is your goal.

Such a goal is not achieved in one glorious attempt, but

rather is the result of a lifetime of righteousness, an accumulation of wise choices, even a constancy of purpose. Like the coveted *A* grade on the report card of a difficult and required college course, the reward of eternal life requires effort.

Responsibility was taught rather effectively in this lesson from World War II. At a large air force base, men were taught to jump from high-flying planes, depending for their lives on the parachute each wore. Some died when chutes failed to open. Those who packed them had not been careful. The result was tragedy. Then a solution was devised. Each packed parachute would bear the number of him who packed it; then periodically, and without prior notice, the base commander would assemble all who had packed the chutes. Each would be handed a parachute he had personally packed. These men would then board a plane and, upon a given signal, while high in the sky would themselves jump, depending for their lives on the very chute each had packed. The results were gratifying. Not a single death occurred—then or later. When we understand the importance of what we are doing, we accept accountability for our actions.

There is a fable told about Euclid and Pharaoh and geometry. It is said that Pharaoh, entranced by some of the explanations and demonstrations of Euclid, wished to learn geometry, and Euclid undertook to teach him. He studied for a brief period and then called in Euclid and said this process was too slow for him. He was a Pharaoh. There must be some shorter road. He did not want to spend all his time to learn geometry. Then Euclid gave voice to this great principle. He said: "Your majesty, there is no royal road to geometry."

There is no royal road to salvation and exaltation. There is no royal road to success in any endeavor. The *A* grade is the result of each theme, each quiz, each class, each examination, each library project, each term paper. So each Sunday School lesson, each Mutual teacher, each prayer, each date, each

360

friend, each dance all precede the goal of temple marriage—that giant step toward an *A* grade on the report card of life.

A short time ago I returned from a journey to the stakes and missions in Germany. As the great jet plane hurtled through the heavens, I gazed out the window and marveled at the stars by which the navigator charted our course. My thoughts were upon you and the opportunity given me to meet with you tonight. I thought of the old saying: "Ideals are like the stars—you can't touch them with your hands, but by following them you reach your destination."[2]

What ideals, when followed, will bring to you those blessings you so much seek, even a quiet conscience, a peace-filled heart, a loving spouse, a healthy family, a contented home?

May I suggest these three:

Choose your friends with caution.

Plan your future with purpose.

Frame your life with faith.

First: Choose your friends with caution.

In a survey which was made in selected wards and stakes of the Church, we learned a most significant fact. Those persons whose friends married in the temple usually married in the temple, while those persons whose friends did not marry in the temple usually did not marry in the temple. The influence of one's friends appeared to be a more dominant factor than parental urging, classroom instruction or proximity to a temple.

We tend to become like those whom we admire. Just as in Nathaniel Hawthorne's classic account, "The Great Stone Face," we adopt the mannerisms, the attitudes, even the conduct of those whom we admire—and they are usually our friends. Associate with those who, like you, are planning not for temporary convenience, shallow goals or narrow ambition, but rather for those things that matter most—even eternal objectives.

How well I remember the challenges confronting the youth

in the ward over which I once presided as a bishop. One evening a lovely teenage girl came to my office with her boyfriend to talk things over with me. The two of them were very much in love, and temptation was beginning to get the best of them.

As we counseled together, each made a pledge to the other to resist temptation and keep uppermost in their minds the goal of a temple marriage. I suggested a course of action to follow and then felt impressed to say: "If you ever find yourselves in a position of compromise and need additional strength, you call me, regardless of the hour."

Early one morning at 1:00 A.M. the telephone rang, and a voice said: "Bishop, this is Susan. Remember how you asked me to call if I found myself being tempted? Well, Bishop, I'm in that situation." I asked where she was, and she described a popular parking spot in the Salt Lake Valley. She and her fiancé had walked to a nearby phone booth to make the call. The setting wasn't ideal for providing counsel, but the need was great, and the young couple was receptive.

I won't mention how often Susan called. However, when the mailman delivered her wedding announcement to our home and Sister Monson read, "Mr. and Mrs. Jones request the pleasure of your company at the wedding reception of their daughter, Susan," she sighed, "Thank heaven!" When I noticed the small print at the bottom which read, "Married in the Salt Lake Temple," I said silently, "Thank heaven for the strength of Latter-day Saint youth."

Inscribed on the wall of Stanford University Memorial Hall is the truth: "We must teach our youth that all that is not eternal is too short, and all that is not infinite is too small."

Choose your friends with caution.

Second: Plan your future with purpose.

The great Thomas Carlyle said: "A man without purpose in life is as a ship without a rudder, a waif, a nothing, a nobody.

Have a purpose in life, and having it, throw such strength of muscle and brain into your work as God has given you."

Some years ago I served as a mission president. I had 450 of the most marvelous missionaries who ever served the Lord. After returning home, my dear wife and I were a little surprised one evening as we ran a tally on our missionaries, to find that there were some sister missionaries who had not as yet found that man "on whose shoulder she might rest her weary head." And so we determined we would do something about it. I said to Sister Monson, "Frances, let's invite three or four of our lovely sister missionaries over to the home and let's plan an activity where they can tell us who of all the returned male missionaries they would like to have invited to a little fireside in our home. Then we will show pictures of the mission, and we will arrange the seating so that they can become well acquainted with one another." This was done, and I might say that the four girls whom we invited eagerly responded to the challenge.

In shoe boxes we maintained individual five-by-seven-inch photographs of every missionary. We had four such boxes with 125 missionary pictures in each. As those four girls sat around our living room, I said to each of them, "Here is a gift. Each of you thumb through a box of 125 pictures and tell me which of all the pictures represents the young man whom you would most like to have invited to come to this fireside." My, that was an interesting scheme. I think that the only way I could adequately describe it is to ask a question. Have you ever seen children on Christmas morning? We went forward and invited four young men to join these four young ladies in our home, and we had a glorious evening. At the conclusion of the evening, I noticed two of them slowly walking down our driveway, and I said to Sister Monson, "This looks promising." They were walking very close together.

It wasn't long after that when I received a telephone call from the young man. He said, "President Monson, do you remember that I promised you that if I ever fell in love I would let you know?" I said, "Yes, sir." He said, "President, I have fallen in love." I said, "Good; with whom?" He said, "You'll never guess in all this world." I was discreet. I didn't guess. I said, "You tell me." And he named the sister missionary with whom he had walked side by side and hand in hand from our party that evening. Today these fine young people are happily married. They have three lovely children. He has obtained his master's degree in engineering. They are serving the Lord and making their mark in their profession and Church activity.

In your quest for the man of your dreams and the dream of your life, you may well heed the counsel given by King Arthur in the popular musical *Camelot.* Faced with a particularly vexing dilemma, King Arthur was speaking to himself, but could well have been speaking to you, when he declared, "We must not let our passions destroy our dreams."

On one occasion the General Sunday School Conference honored several outstanding teachers. It was my privilege to pay a tribute to a Sunday School teacher of my boyhood days: Lucy Gertsch Thomson.

Lucy was lovely and ever so sweet. She was deserving of a worthy companion. Yet success evaded her. The years flew by and Lucy reached the worrisome twenties, the desperate thirties, even the frightful forties—and then she met Dick. It was a case of love at first sight. Just one problem: Dick was not a member of the Church. Did Lucy succumb to the age-old fallacy of marrying out of desperation, with the fleeting hope that one day he would become a member? Not Lucy. She was wiser than this. She simply told Dick, "Dick, I think you're wonderful, but we would never be happy dating together."

"Why not?" he countered.

"Because you're not a Mormon."

"How do I become a Mormon? I want to date you." He studied the gospel. She answered his questions. He was baptized.

Then he said, "Lucy, now that I'm a member, we can be married at last."

Lucy replied, "Oh, Dick, I love you so much. Now that you are a member of the Church you wouldn't be content with anything but a temple marriage."

"How long will that take, Lucy?"

"About a year, if we meet the other requirements." One year later Lucy and Dick entered the house of the Lord.

Plan your future with purpose.

Third: Frame your life with faith.

Amidst the confusion of our age, the conflicts of conscience and the turmoil of daily living, an abiding faith becomes an anchor to our lives. In today's world, some young people don't know who they are, what they can be or even want to be. They are afraid but they don't know of what. They are angry, but they don't know at whom. They are rejected and they don't know why. All they want is to be somebody!

The kind of determination which is required is that set forth by a 21-year-old female college senior, who declared:

"Our generation has been exposed, through every means of communication, to major and minor fears—the little threat of not finding a mate if one does not use a certain mouthwash, or fear of nonacceptance if one does not succumb to a low moral standard because it is 'the nature of the beast.'

"Many of us accept the premises that 'You can't fight City Hall,' 'Live life to its fullest now,' so 'Eat, drink, and make merry'—for tomorrow we will be destroyed by nuclear war.

"I am old-fashioned enough to believe in God, to believe in the dignity and potential of His creature—man, and I am realistic, not idealistic, enough to know that I am not alone in these feelings.

"Some say that unlike other generations we have no threat to our freedom, no cause to propagate, no mission in life—everything has been handed to us. We have not been pampered, but spiritually impoverished. I don't want to live in the poverty of affluence, and I cannot live alone."

Remember that faith and doubt cannot exist in the same mind at the same time, for one will dispel the other.

Should doubt knock at your doorway, just say to those skeptical, disturbing, rebellious thoughts: "I propose to stay with my faith, with the faith of my people. I know that happiness and contentment are there, and I forbid you, agnostic, doubting thoughts to destroy the house of my faith. I acknowledge that I do not understand the processes of creation, but I accept the fact of it. I grant that I cannot explain the miracles of the Bible, and I do not attempt to do so, but I accept God's word. I wasn't with Joseph, but I believe him. My faith did not come to me through science, and I will not permit so-called science to destroy it. When I change my mind about God and His work, only the inspiration of God will change it."[3]

I think of an account I read about the wife of one of our early pioneers. Her name was Catherine Curtis Spencer. Her husband, Orson Spencer, was a sensitive, well-educated man. She had been reared in Boston and was cultured and refined. She and Orson had six children. After leaving Nauvoo, her delicate health declined from exposure and hardship. Elder Spencer wrote to her parents and asked if she could return to live with them while he established a home for her in the West. Their reply: "Let her renounce her degrading faith, and she can come back—but never until she does." Sister Spencer would not renounce her faith. When her parents' letter was read to her, she asked her husband to get his Bible and read to her from the Book of Ruth: "Intreat me not to leave thee, or to return from following after thee: for whither thou goest, I will go; and where thou lodgest, I will lodge: thy people shall be my people, and thy God my God."[4] Outside the storm raged, the wagon covers leaked, and friends held milk pans over Sister Spencer's head to keep her dry. In these conditions, and without a word of complaint, she closed her eyes for the last time.

Though we may not necessarily forfeit our lives in service to our God, we can certainly demonstrate our love for Him by how well we serve Him. He who hears our silent prayers, He who observes our unheralded acts, will reward us openly when the need comes.

Frame your life with faith.

When you, my dear young friends, choose your friends with caution, plan your future with purpose, and frame your life with faith, you will merit the companionship of the Holy Spirit. You will have a perfect brightness of hope.

NOTES

1. Doctrine and Covenants 50:23–24.
2. Carl Schurz, 1859, in John Bartlett, comp., *Bartlett's Familiar Quotations,* 15th ed. (1980), 602.
3. Statement from Stephen L Richards.
4. Ruth 1:16.

41

A LITTLE CHILD SHALL
LEAD THEM

Dᴜʀɪɴɢ ᴛʜᴇ Gᴀʟɪʟᴇᴀɴ ᴍɪɴɪsᴛʀʏ of our Lord and Savior, the disciples came unto Him, saying, "Who is the greatest in the kingdom of heaven?

"And Jesus called a little child unto him, and set him in the midst of them,

"And said, Verily I say unto you, Except ye be converted, and become as little children, ye shall not enter into the kingdom of heaven.

"Whosoever therefore shall humble himself as this little child, the same is greatest in the kingdom of heaven.

"And whoso shall receive one such little child in my name receiveth me.

"But whoso shall offend one of these little ones which believe in me, it were better for him that a millstone were hanged about his neck, and that he were drowned in the depth of the sea."[1]

Recently, as I read the daily newspaper, my thoughts turned to this passage and the firm candor of the Savior's declaration. In one column of the newspaper I read of a custody battle between the mother and father of a child. Accusations were made, threats hurled, and anger displayed as parents moved here and there on the international scene with the child spirited away from one continent to another.

A second story told of a 12-year-old lad who was beaten and set on fire because he refused a neighborhood bully's order to take drugs. Hospitalized, his condition remains critical.

Still a third report told of a father's sexual molestation of his small child.

These are *reported* cases of child abuse. There are many more never reported but equally as serious. A physician revealed to me the large number of children who are brought to the emergency rooms of local hospitals in your city and mine. In many cases guilty parents provide fanciful accounts of the child falling from his high chair or stumbling over a toy and striking his head. Altogether too frequently it is discovered that the parent was the abuser and the innocent child the victim. Shame on the perpetrators of such vile deeds. God will hold such strictly accountable for their actions.

When we realize just how precious children are, we will not find it difficult to follow the pattern of the Master in our association with them. Not long ago, a sweet scene took place at the Salt Lake Temple. Children, who had been ever so tenderly cared for by faithful workers in the temple nursery, were now leaving in the arms of their mothers and fathers. One child turned to the lovely women who had been so kind to them and, with a wave of her arm, spoke the feelings of her heart as she exclaimed, "Good night, angels."

Who among us has not praised God and marveled at His powers when an infant is held in one's arms? That tiny hand, so small yet so perfect, instantly becomes the topic of conversation. No one can resist placing his little finger in the clutching hand of an infant.

When the disciples of Jesus attempted to restrain the children from approaching the Lord, He declared:

"Suffer the little children to come unto me, and forbid them not: for of such is the kingdom of God.

"Verily I say unto you, Whosoever shall not receive the kingdom of God as a little child, he shall not enter therein.

"And he took them up in his arms, put his hands upon them, and blessed them."[2]

What a magnificent pattern for us to follow.

My heart burned warmly within me when the First Presidency approved the allocation of a substantial sum from special fast-offering contributions to join with those funds from Rotary International, that polio vaccine might be provided and the children living in Kenya immunized against this vicious crippler and killer of children.

I thank God for the work of our doctors who leave for a time their own private practices and journey to distant lands to minister to children. Cleft palates and other deformities which would leave a child impaired physically and damaged psychologically are skillfully repaired. Despair yields to hope. Gratitude replaces grief. These children can now look in the mirror and marvel at a miracle in their own lives.

In a recent meeting, I told of a dentist in my ward who each year visits the Philippine islands to work his skills without compensation to provide corrective dentistry for children. Smiles are restored, spirits lifted, and futures enhanced. I did not know the daughter of this dentist was in the congregation to which I was speaking. At the conclusion of my remarks, she came forward and, with a broad smile of proper pride, said, "You have been speaking of my father. How I love him and what he is doing for children!"

In the faraway islands of the Pacific, hundreds who were near-blind now see because a missionary said to his physician brother-in-law, "Leave your wealthy clientele and the comforts of your palatial home and come to these special children of God who need your skills and need them now." The ophthalmologist responded without a backward glance. Today he comments quietly that this visit was the best service he ever rendered and the peace which came to his heart the greatest blessing of his life.

Tears come easily to me when I read of a father who has donated one of his own kidneys in the hope that his son might have a more abundant life. I drop to my knees at night and add my prayer of faith in behalf of a mother in our community who journeyed to Chicago, that she might provide part of her liver to her daughter in a delicate and potentially life-threatening surgery. She who already had gone down into the valley of the shadow of death to bring forth this child into mortality, again put her hand in the hand of God and placed her own life in jeopardy for her child. Never a complaint, but ever a willing heart and a prayer of faith.

Elder Russell M. Nelson, upon returning from Romania, shared with us the pitiable plight of orphan children in that land—perhaps 30 thousand in the city of Bucharest alone. He visited one such orphanage and arranged that the Church might provide vaccine, medical dressings, and other urgently needed supplies. Certain couples will be identified and called to fill special missions to these children. I can think of no more Christlike service than to hold a motherless child in one's arms or to take a fatherless boy by the hand.

We need not be called to missionary service, however, in order to bless the lives of children. Our opportunities are limitless. They are everywhere to be found—sometimes very close to home.

Last summer I received a letter from a woman who has emerged from a long period of Church inactivity. She is ever so anxious for her husband, who as yet is not a member of the Church, to share the joy she now feels.

She wrote of a trip which she, her husband, and their three sons made from the family home to Grandmother's home in

Idaho. While driving through Salt Lake City, they were attracted by the message which appeared on a billboard. The message invited them to visit Temple Square. Bob, the nonmember husband, made the suggestion that a visit would be pleasant. The family entered the visitors' center, and Father took two sons up a ramp that one called "the ramp to heaven." Mother and three-year-old Tyler were a bit behind the others, they having paused to appreciate the beautiful paintings which adorned the walls. As they walked toward the magnificent sculpture of Thorvaldsen's *Christus,* tiny Tyler bolted from his mother and ran to the base of the *Christus,* while exclaiming, "It's Jesus! It's Jesus!" As Mother attempted to restrain her son, Tyler looked back toward her and his father and said, "Don't worry. He likes children."

After departing the center and again making their way along the freeway toward Grandmother's, Tyler moved to the front seat next to his father. Dad asked him what he liked best about their adventure on Temple Square. Tyler smiled up at him and said, "Jesus."

"How do you know that Jesus likes you, Tyler?"

Tyler, with a most serious expression on his face, looked up at his father's eyes and answered, "Dad, didn't you see his face?" Nothing else needed to be said.

As I read this account, I thought of the statement from the book of Isaiah: "And a little child shall lead them."[3]

The words of a Primary hymn express the feelings of a child's heart:

> *Tell me the stories of Jesus I love to hear,*
> *Things I would ask him to tell me if he were here.*
> *Scenes by the wayside, tales of the sea,*
> *Stories of Jesus, tell them to me.*
>
> *Oh, let me hear how the children stood round his knee.*
> *I shall imagine his blessings resting on me;*
> *Words full of kindness, deeds full of grace,*
> *All in the lovelight of Jesus' face.*[4]

I know of no more touching passage in scripture than the account of the Savior blessing the children, as recorded in Third Nephi. The Master spoke movingly to the vast multitude of men, women, and children. Then, responding to their faith and the desire that He tarry longer, He invited them to bring to Him their lame, their blind, and their sick, that He might heal them. With joy they accepted His invitation. The record reveals that "he did heal them every one."[5] There followed His mighty prayer to His Father. The multitude bore record: "The eye hath never seen, neither hath the ear heard, before, so great and marvelous things as we saw and heard Jesus speak unto the Father."[6]

Concluding this magnificent event, Jesus "wept, . . . and he took their little children, one by one, and blessed them, and prayed unto the Father for them. . . .

"And he spake unto the multitude, and said unto them: Behold your little ones.

"And as they looked to behold they cast their eyes towards heaven, and they saw the heavens open, and they saw angels descending out of heaven . . . ; and they came down and encircled those little ones . . . ; and the angels did minister unto them."[7]

Over and over in my mind I pondered the phrase, "Whosoever shall not receive the kingdom of God as a little child, he shall not enter therein."[8]

Peace will be our blessing as we remember and follow the Prince of Peace. That we may do so is my sincere prayer.

NOTES

1. Matthew 18:1–6.
2. Mark 10:14–16.
3. Isaiah 11:6.
4. "Tell Me the Stories of Jesus," *Children's Songbook*, 57.
5. 3 Nephi 17:9.
6. 3 Nephi 17:16.
7. 3 Nephi 17:21, 23–24.
8. Mark 10:15.

42

Primary Days

SOME TIME AGO I JOTTED down from one of our national magazines a short compilation of "Children's Letters to God." I found them most interesting. Little Mark wrote: "Dear God, I keep waiting for spring, but it never did come yet. What's up? Don't forget." Another child stated: "Dear God, if you made the rule for kids to take out the garbage, please change it." Little Beth wrote: "Dear God, if you watch in Church on Sunday, I will show you my new shoes." Jeff wrote: "Dear God, It is great the way you always get the stars in the right place. Why can't you do that with the moon?" Joyce wrote: "Dear God, Thank you for the baby brother, but what I prayed for was a puppy." I like this one from Matthew the best: "Dear God, I read your book and I like it." Then he asked, "I would like to write a book someday with the same kind of stories. Where do you get your ideas? Best wishes."

All of us—teachers, parents, and, of course, priesthood leaders—take for our guide the inspiration of the Lord's statement when He declared: "And now, verily I say unto you, and what I say unto one I say unto all, be of good cheer, little children; for I am in your midst, and I have not forsaken you."[1]

374

I feel to reflect on my own Primary days of long ago. The words of the poet have coursed through my mind:

Backward, turn backward, O Time, in your flight,
Make me a child again just for tonight![2]

I was a boy of the Great Depression. I remember children wearing galoshes because they had no shoes and going hungry because they had no food. These were difficult times. My father was a craftsman—a printer—and he always had employment, although others were not so fortunate during that period. I remember some boys with whom I went to school who had clothing bought only at rummage sales. In one family the same size jacket was to fit four boys of different ages. Occasionally when I would call upon the boys, that we might walk to school together, I observed that they would be having a breakfast of cornflakes with warm water. There was no milk; there was no cream; there was no sugar—only cornflakes and water. On every hand were empty purses, bare cupboards, shattered dreams, and hopeless hearts.

As a bright light of hope shining amidst the pervading gloom of despair was Primary each Wednesday afternoon. I had a marvelous Trekker teacher. She was newly married; she was young; she was vivacious. We 10-year-old boys looked upon her as an ideal. She knew how to motivate boys. She talked to us about our bandolos which we wore about our neck, representing our Trail Builder classification, and about our accomplishments and our objectives. We were dedicated to that teacher. I look back upon that year as my finest in Primary, and I must say it was because of my wonderful teacher. It wasn't necessarily that she was well educated or had many degrees after her name; she had none of those. It wasn't because the boys in the class were particularly enlightened or unusually well motivated and well behaved; on the contrary. But that which cemented the relationship between the teacher and her boys was the fact that she loved us, and she taught us the gospel.

With youthful gusto, we would sing the Primary Trail Builder song. I still remember the words:

> Oh we are the boy trail builders,
> Out West where the sunsets glow;
> Where the brooks flow down like silver
> From the heights of the virgin snow. . . .
> Our light is the light of virtue,
> Our strength is the strength of youth;
> Our trails are the trails of honor,
> For we build with the stones of truth.[3]

During our Primary years, there were those occasional disappointments which would leave us a little bruised—but never in a state of despair. At that time the Primary Children's Hospital in Salt Lake City was located in a remodeled house on North Temple, but a new hospital was soon to be constructed on the Avenues in Salt Lake City. Each Wednesday afternoon in Primary, we would talk about the future Primary Children's Hospital, where little children could be cared for and where skilled physicians could mend broken limbs and ease the effects of sickness.

In our ward we had a cardboard replica of the hospital. It formed a bank with a little slot in the top of it. Each Wednesday we would sing and march to the tune, "'Give,' said the little stream, 'Give, oh! give, give, oh! give.' 'Give,' said the little stream, As it hurried down the hill."[4] To its cadence we would walk by the bank and put our pennies in it. I recall sitting next to a dear friend of mine and saying, "Jack, I've got a good idea. I've got in my pocket a dime and a penny. When we march by and put that penny in the little bank, let's just march right out the front door. We won't go to class at all, but I'll take you over to the Hatch Dairy, and there we'll buy two of those delicious five-cent fudgsicles."

Jack snuggled up to me and said, "Let's see the dime." He was doubting. Financial depression did that to boys. I reached in my pocket, produced the dime, and then carefully returned it to its safe place. Suddenly we heard the strains of the music and stood and marched by the little bank as we sang "'Give,' said the little stream." I reached in my pocket and dropped my coin in the bank, walked out the front door with Jack, and headed for the Hatch Dairy. Just then he said, "Let's see the dime again." I reached into my pocket to show him the dime and produced the penny. The dime had gone to the Primary Children's Hospital. As a disappointed boy, I walked back and put the penny in the bank also. For a long while I felt that I, perhaps, had the most substantial investment in the Primary Children's Hospital—more so than any boy in the entire ward.

At home in a hidden-away corner, I have a small black cane with an imitation silver handle. It once belonged to a distant relative. Why do I keep it for a period now spanning 60 years? There is a special reason. You see, as a Primary boy I participated in a Christmas pageant in our ward. I was privileged to be one of the three wise men. With a bandanna about my head, Mother's precious Chickering piano bench cover draped over my shoulder, and the black cane in my hand, I spoke my assigned lines: "Where is he that is born King of the Jews? for we have seen his star in the east, and are come to worship him."[5] I don't recall all of the words in that pageant, but I vividly remember the feelings of my heart as the three of us wise men looked up, saw the star, journeyed across the stage, found Mary with the young child, Jesus, then fell down and worshipped Him and opened our treasures and presented gifts: gold, frankincense, and myrrh. I especially liked the fact that we did not return to the evil Herod to betray the baby Jesus, but we obeyed God and departed another way.

The years have flown by. The events of a busy life take their proper places in the hallowed halls of memory, but the Christmas cane continues to occupy its special place in my home—and in my heart is a commitment to Christ.

President David O. McKay counseled: "Three influences in

home life awaken reverence in children and contribute to its development in their souls. These are: first, firm but Gentle Guidance; second, Courtesy by parents to each other, and to children; and third, Prayer in which children participate." [6]

Some years ago, in reporting his visit to a six-stake youth conference in the Montpelier, Idaho, area, Elder Vaughn J. Featherstone said, "There was a beautiful spirit in the meetings, and it reached a climax in the afternoon as the meeting was turned over to the youth for testimony bearing.

"One girl about sixteen stood up and said she knew the Church was true, and she could do the greatest missionary work right in her home. She said her father had become very inactive during the past several years, and her mother had compromised into inactivity with him. This girl was working on a way to approach her parents to activate them but hadn't done anything. One day her eight-year-old brother came home from Primary and declared the family was going to have family prayer. That evening all of the family except the father knelt and had family prayer. She said that finally, after four or five nights of family prayer, the father came and knelt down with the rest of the family and had continued to do so."

Reading the New Testament, each parent can appreciate the feelings of Jairus as he sought the Lord Jesus Christ and, upon finding Him, fell at His feet and pleaded, "My little daughter lieth at the point of death: I pray thee, come and lay thy hands on her, that she may be healed; and she shall live."[7]

"While he yet spake, there cometh one from the [ruler's] house, saying to him, Thy daughter is dead; trouble not the Master.

"But when Jesus heard it, he answered him, saying, Fear not: believe only, and she shall be made whole." Parents wept. Others mourned. Jesus declared: "Weep not; she is not dead, but sleepeth." He "took her by the hand, and called, saying, Maid, arise.

"And her spirit came again, and she arose straightway."[8] The Lord had stretched forth His hand to take the hand of another—even the hand of a child.

I recall a letter I received from an old friend, a printer, Sharman Hummell. Some years ago I had worked with him in the printing business in Salt Lake City, and during that long-ago period, I once gave Sharman a ride home from work and asked him how he came to receive his testimony of the gospel. He responded, "It's interesting, Tom, that you asked me that question, for this very week my wife, my children, and I are going to the Manti Temple, there to be sealed for all eternity." He continued his account, "We lived in the East. I was journeying by bus to San Francisco to establish myself in a new printing company, and then I was going to send for my wife and children. All the way from New York City to Salt Lake City the bus trip was uneventful. But in Salt Lake City there entered the bus a girl—a Primary girl—who sat next to me. She was going to Reno, Nevada, there to have a visit with her dear aunt. As we journeyed westward, I noticed a road sign which read, 'Visit the Mormon Sunday School this week.' I said to the little girl, 'I guess there are a lot of Mormons in Utah, aren't there?' She replied, 'Yes, sir.' Then I said to her, 'Are you a Mormon?' Again, 'Yes, sir.'"

He countered: "What do Mormons believe?" And that little girl recited the first Article of Faith, and then she talked about it. Continuing, she gave him the second Article of Faith and talked about it. Then she gave him the third, and the fourth, and the fifth, and the sixth, and all of the Articles of Faith and talked about all of them. She knew them consecutively.

Sharman Hummell said, "When we got to Reno, and we let that little girl off into the arms of her aunt, I was profoundly impressed." He said, "All the way to San Francisco I thought, 'What is it that prompts that little girl to know her doctrine so well?' When I arrived in San Francisco, the very first thing I did was to look through the yellow pages for The Church of

Jesus Christ of Latter-day Saints; I called the mission president, J. Leonard Love, and he sent two missionaries to where I was staying. I became a member of the Church, my wife became a member, all of our children became members, in part because a Primary girl knew her Articles of Faith." Sharman said, "I have but one regret. I never asked for her name. I've never been able to properly thank her."

From Alma we learn, "And now, he imparteth his word by angels unto men, yea, not only men but women also. Now this is not all; little children do have words given unto them many times, which confound the wise and the learned."[9]

The love our Savior has for children knows no bounds. When we as parents, as priesthood leaders, as officers and teachers in the Primary follow His example and heed His words, "Feed my lambs,"[10] boys and girls blossom before our very eyes and grow "in wisdom and stature, and in favour with God and man."[11]

When I was a young boy in Primary, all was not bliss, for boys will be boys. The laughter of the boys and the chatter of the girls at times must have been most disconcerting to our Primary leaders.

One day as we left the chapel for our classrooms, I noted that our Primary president remained behind. I paused and observed her. She sat all alone on the front row of the benches, took out her handkerchief, and began to weep. I walked up to her and said, "Sister Georgell, don't cry."

She said, "I'm sad."

I responded, "What's the matter?"

She said, "I can't control the Trail Builders. Will you help me?"

Of course I answered, "Yes."

She said, "Oh, that would be wonderful, Tommy, if you would."

What I didn't know then is that I was the source of her tears. She had effectively enlisted me to aid in achieving reverence in our Primary. And we did.

The years flew by. When Melissa Georgell was in her nineties, she lived in a nursing facility in the northwest part of Salt Lake City. One year just before Christmas, I determined to visit my beloved Primary president. Over the car radio I heard the music of familiar Christmas carols: "Hark! the Herald Angels Sing," "O Little Town of Bethlehem," and many others. I reflected on the visit made by wise men those long years ago and the visit made by us boys when we portrayed the wise men in the pageant. The wise men brought precious gifts to the Christ child. I brought to Melissa only the gift of love and a desire to say "Thank you."

I found her in the lunchroom. She was staring at her plate of food, teasing it with the fork she held in her aged hand. Not a bite did she eat. As I spoke to her, my words were met by a benign but blank stare. I gently took her fork from her and began to feed her, talking all the time I did so about her service to boys and girls as a Primary worker and the joy which was mine to have served later as her bishop. You know, there wasn't even a glimmer of recognition, far less a spoken word. Two other residents of the nursing home gazed at me with puzzled expressions. At last one of them spoke, saying, "She doesn't know anyone—even her own family. She hasn't said a word for a long, long time."

Luncheon ended. My one-sided conversation wound down. I stood to leave. I held her frail hand in mine and gazed into her wrinkled but beautiful countenance and said, "God bless you, Melissa, and merry Christmas."

Without warning, she spoke the words, "I know you. You're Tommy Monson, my Primary boy. How I love you."

She pressed my hand to her lips and bestowed on it the kiss of love. Tears coursed down her cheeks and bathed our clasped hands. Those hands, that day, were hallowed by heaven and graced by God. The herald angels did sing, for I heard them in my heart.

The words of the Master seemed to have a personal meaning never before fully felt: "Woman, behold thy son!" And to his disciple, "Behold thy mother!"[12]

The words of the poet came to my heart and provided my Christmas gift. James Barrie wrote, "God gave us memories, that we might have June roses in the December of our lives."[13] Memories of Primary days are such beautiful roses. Such a priceless gift will come to each of us as we serve His precious children. May we follow him and do so is my humble prayer.

NOTES

1. Doctrine and Covenants 61:36.
2. Elizabeth Akers Allen, "Backward," in *Best-Loved Poems of the LDS People* (1996), 226.
3. Lyrics by Theodore E. Curtis.
4. "Give, Said the Little Stream," *Children's Songbook,* 236.
5. Matthew 2:2.
6. *Improvement Era,* December 1956, 915.
7. Mark 5:23.
8. Luke 8:49, 50, 52, 54, 55.
9. Alma 32:23.
10. John 21:15.
11. Luke 2:52.
12. John 19:26–27.
13. *Peter's Quotations: Ideas for Our Time,* sel. Laurence J. Peter (1977), 335.

The Power of Self-Mastery

43

Finishers Wanted

O N SUNLIT DAYS DURING THE noon hour, the streets of Salt Lake City abound with men and women who for a moment leave the confines of the tall office buildings and engage in that universal delight called window-shopping. On occasion I, too, am a participant.

One Wednesday I paused before the elegant show window of a prestigious furniture store. That which caught and held my attention was not the beautifully designed sofa nor the comfortable-appearing chair which stood at its side. Neither was it the beautiful chandelier positioned overhead. Rather, my eyes rested upon a small sign which had been placed at the bottom right-hand corner of the window. Its message was brief: "FINISHERS WANTED." The store had need of those persons who possessed the talent and the skill to make ready for final sale the expensive furniture which the firm manufactured and sold. "Finishers wanted." The words remained with me as I returned to the pressing activities of the day.

In life, as in business, there has always been a need for

those persons who could be called finishers. Their ranks are few, their opportunities many, their contributions great.

From the very beginning, to the present time, a fundamental question remains to be answered by each who runs the race of life. Shall I falter, or shall I finish? On the answer await the blessings of joy and happiness here in mortality and eternal life in the world to come.

We are not left without guidance to make this momentous decision. The Holy Bible contains those accounts, even those lessons which, if carefully learned, will serve us well and be as a beacon light to guide our thoughts and influence our actions. As we read, we sympathize with those who falter. We honor those who finish.

The Apostle Paul likened life to a great race when he declared: "Know ye not that they which run in a race run all, but one receiveth the prize? So run, that ye may obtain."[1]

And before the words of Paul fell upon the ears of his listeners, the counsel of the preacher, even the son of David, king in Jerusalem, cautioned: "The race is not to the swift, nor the battle to the strong."[2]

Could the son of David have been referring to his own father? Judged by any standards, the greatest king Israel ever had was David. Anointed by Samuel, he was honored by the Lord.

In the first flush of his incredible triumphs, David rode the crest of popularity. In adoration the people exclaimed: "Behold, we are thy bone and thy flesh."[3] Power he won. Peace he lost.

It happened late one afternoon when David was walking upon the roof of the king's house that he saw from the roof a woman bathing, and the woman was very beautiful. "And David sent and enquired after the woman. And one said, Is not this Bath-sheba, . . . the wife of Uriah the Hittite?" So "David sent messengers, and took her."[4] The gross sin of adultery was followed by yet another: "Set ye Uriah in the forefront of the hottest battle, and retire ye from him, that he may be smitten, and die."[5] Lust and power had triumphed.

David's rebuke came from the Lord God of Israel: "Thou hast killed Uriah the Hittite with the sword, and hast taken his wife to be thy wife. . . . Now therefore the sword shall never depart from thine house."[6] David commenced well the race, then faltered and failed to finish his course.

Lest we lull ourselves into thinking that only the gross sins of life cause us to falter, consider the experience of the rich young man who came running to the Savior and asked the question: "Good Master, what good thing shall I do, that I may have eternal life?" Jesus answered him: "If thou wilt enter into life, keep the commandments. He saith unto him, Which?" To Jesus' enumeration of the commandments, "The young man saith . . . , All these things have I kept from my youth up: what lack I yet? Jesus said unto him, If thou wilt be perfect, go and sell that thou hast, and give to the poor . . . and come and follow me. But when the young man heard that saying, he went away sorrowful: for he had great possessions."[7] He preferred the comforts of earth to the treasures of heaven. He would not purchase the things of eternity by abandoning those of time. He faltered. He failed to finish.

So it was with Judas Iscariot. He commenced his ministry as an apostle of the Lord. He ended it a traitor. For 30 paltry pieces of silver, he sold his soul. At last, realizing the enormity of his sin, Judas, to his patrons and tempters of his crime, shrieked: "I have sinned in that I have betrayed the innocent blood."[8] Remorse had led to despair, despair to madness, and madness to suicide. He had succeeded in betraying the Christ. He had failed to finish the apostolic ministry to which he had been divinely called.

Lust for power, greed of gold, and disdain for honor have ever appeared as faces of failure in the panorama of life. Captivated by their artificial attraction, many noble souls have stumbled and fallen, thus losing the crown of victory reserved for the finisher of life's great race.

May we turn from the lives of those who faltered and consider for a moment some who finished and won the prize.

Following the earthly ministry of the Lord, there were many who, rather than deny their testimony of Him, would forfeit their lives. Such was Paul the Apostle. The impulse of his father to send him to Jerusalem opened the door to Paul's destiny. He would pass through it and help to shape a new world.

Gifted in his capacity to stir, move, and manage groups of men, Paul was a peerless example of one who nobly made the transition from sinner to saint. Though disappointment, heartache, and trial were to beset him, yet Paul, at the conclusion of his ministry, could say: "I have fought a good fight, I have finished my course, I have kept the faith."[9] Paul was a finisher.

He admonished us to "lay aside . . . sin" and to "run with patience the race . . . looking [for an example] unto Jesus the author and finisher of our faith."[10]

Though Jesus was tempted by the evil one, yet He resisted. Though He was hated, yet He loved. Though He was betrayed, yet He triumphed. Not in a cloud of glory or chariot of fire was Jesus to depart mortality, but with arms outstretched in agony upon the cruel cross. The magnitude of His mission is depicted in the simplicity of His words. To His Father He prayed, "The hour is come. . . . I have glorified thee on the earth: I have finished the work which thou gavest me to do."[11] "Into thy hands I commend my spirit."[12] Mortality ended. Eternity began.

Frequently His help comes silently—on occasion with dramatic impact. Such was my experience of some years ago when, as a mission president, I was afforded the privilege to guide the activities of precious young men and women, even missionaries whom He had called. Some had problems, others required motivation; but one came to me in utter despair. He had made his decision to leave the mission field when but at the halfway mark. His bags were packed, his return ticket purchased. He came by to bid me farewell. We talked; we listened; we prayed. There remained hidden the actual reason for his decision to quit.

As we arose from our knees in the quiet of my office, the missionary began to weep almost uncontrollably. Flexing the muscle in his strong right arm, he blurted out, "This is my problem. All through school my muscle power qualified me for honors in football and track, but my mental power was neglected. President Monson, I'm ashamed of my school record. It reveals that 'with effort' I have the capacity to read at but the level of the fourth grade. I can't even read the Book of Mormon. How then can I understand its contents and teach others its truths?"

The silence of the room was broken by my young nine-year-old son, who, without knocking, opened the door and, with surprise, apologetically said, "Excuse me. I just wanted to put this book back on the shelf."

He handed me the book. Its title: *A Child's Story of the Book of Mormon,* by Dr. Deta P. Neeley. I turned to the foreword and read these words: "This book has been written with a scientifically controlled vocabulary to the level of the fourth grade." A sincere prayer from an honest heart had been dramatically answered.

My missionary accepted the challenge to read the book. Half laughing, half crying, he declared: "It will be good to read something I can understand." Clouds of despair were dispelled by the sunshine of hope. He completed an honorable mission. He became a finisher.

In our chosen fields, the obstacles confronting us may be mountainous in their appearance—even impassable in their challenge to our abilities. Press onward we must, for we understand full well that attacking is not solving. Complaining is not thinking. Ridiculing is not reasoning. Accountability is not for the intention but for the deed. No man is proud simply of what he intends to do. Let us not be deceived. Like the mice who voted to place a warning bell around the neck of the cat, we may mistakenly feel that the problem has been taken care of simply because we have discussed it. To put it another way, machines are not creative or imaginative, nor even responsible. They are simply tools, and tools do not work and serve mankind until skilled hands take them up. Because our tools are growing in complexity and in potential usefulness, we must grow in order to use them both profitably and wisely. Let us not be frightened. Rather, let us be challenged. Only the human mind has the capacity for creativity, imagination, insight, vision, and responsibility. Let us use these capacities to run well our race and to be finishers.

Today I think I shall once more walk by that furniture store in our city and again gaze at the small sign in the large show window, that I may indelibly impress upon my mind the true meaning of its words: "FINISHERS WANTED."

I pray humbly that each one of us may be a finisher in the race of life and thus qualify for that precious prize: eternal life with our Heavenly Father in the celestial kingdom.

NOTES

1. 1 Corinthians 9:24.
2. Ecclesiastes 9:11.
3. 2 Samuel 5:1.
4. 2 Samuel 11:3–4.
5. 2 Samuel 11:15.
6. 2 Samuel 12:9–10.
7. Matthew 19:16–18, 20–22.
8. Matthew 27:4.
9. 2 Timothy 4:7.
10. Hebrews 12:1–2.
11. John 17:1, 4.
12. Luke 23:46.

1st Corinthians Chapter 15
verses 20-22

But now is Christ risen from the dead and become the firstfruits of them that slept.

For since by man came death by man came also the resurrection of the dead.

For as in Adam all die, even so in Christ shall all be made alive.

1st Corinthians Chapter 15
verses 20-22

44

MEETING YOUR GOLIATH

FOR MANY EONS, BOTH anciently and in our day, the people of Israel have experienced the trials and tribulations of war. This troubled land has witnessed much conflict; its peoples have suffered terribly. No single battle is better remembered, however, than occurred in the Valley of Elah during the year 1063 B.C. Along the mountains on one side, the feared armies of the Philistines were marshalled to march directly to the heart of Judah and the Jordan Valley. On the other side of the valley, King Saul had drawn up his armies in opposition.

Historians tell us that the opposing forces were about evenly matched in number and in skill. However, the Philistines had managed to keep secret their valued knowledge of smelting and fashioning iron into formidable weapons of war. The sound of hammers pounding upon anvils and the sight of smoke rising skyward from many bellows as the smiths went about the task of sharpening weapons and fashioning new ones, must have struck fear into the hearts of Saul's warriors; for even the most novice of soldiers could know the superiority of iron weapons to those of brass.

As often happened when armies faced each other, individual champions challenged others from the opposing forces to single combat. There was considerable precedent for this sort of fighting; and on more than one occasion, notably during the tenure of Samson as judge, battles had been decided by individual combat.

Now, however, the situation was reversed as far as Israel was concerned, and it was a Philistine who dared to challenge all others—a veritable giant of a man called Goliath of Gath. Old accounts tell us that Goliath was ten feet tall. He wore brass armor and a coat of mail. And the staff of his spear would stagger a strong man merely to lift, let alone hurl. His shield was the longest ever seen or heard of, and his sword a fearsome blade.

This champion from the Philistine camp stood and cried unto the armies of Israel: "Why are ye come out to set your battle in array? am not I a Philistine, and ye servants to Saul? choose you a man for you, and let him come down to me."[1]

His challenge was that if he were overpowered by the Israelite warrior, then all the Philistines would become servants to the Israelites. On the other hand, if he were victorious, the Israelites would become their slaves. Goliath roared: "I defy the armies of Israel this day; give me a man, that we may fight together."[2]

And so, for 40 days came the challenge met only by fear and trembling. And all the men of Israel, when they saw the man Goliath, "fled from him and were sore afraid."

There was one, however, who did not quake with fear nor run in alarm. Rather, he stiffened the spine of Israel's soldiers by his piercing question of rebuke toward them: "Is there not a cause? . . . Let no man's heart fail because of him; thy servant will go and fight with this Philistine."[3] David, the shepherd boy, had spoken. But he did not speak just as a shepherd boy. For the hands of Samuel, God's prophet, had rested upon his head and anointed him; and the Spirit of the Lord had come upon him.

Saul said to David: "Thou art not able to go against this Philistine to fight with him: for thou art but a youth, and he a man of war from his youth."[4] But David persevered and, bedecked with the armor of Saul, prepared to meet the giant. Realizing his helplessness so garbed, David discarded the armor, took instead his staff in his hand, chose him five smooth stones out of the brook and put them in a shepherd's bag; and with his sling in hand, he drew near to the Philistines.

All of us remember the shocked exclamation of Goliath: "Am I a dog, that thou comest to me with staves? . . . Come to me, and I will give thy flesh unto the fowls of the air, and to the beasts of the field."[5]

Then David said: "Thou comest to me with a sword, and with a spear, and with a shield: but I come to thee in the name of the Lord of hosts, the God of the armies of Israel, whom thou hast defied. This day will the Lord deliver thee into mine hand . . . that all the earth may know that there is a God in Israel. And all this assembly shall know that the Lord saveth not with sword and spear: for the battle is the Lord's, and he will give you into our hands.

"And it came to pass, when the Philistine arose, and came and drew nigh to meet David, that David hasted, and ran toward the army to meet the Philistine. And David put his hand in his bag, and took thence a stone, and slang it, and smote the Philistine . . . that the stone sunk into his forehead; and he fell upon his face to the earth. So David prevailed over the Philistine with a sling and with a stone, and smote the Philistine, and slew him."[6]

The battle had thus been fought. The victory had been won. David emerged a national hero, his destiny before him.

Some of us remember David as a shepherd boy divinely commissioned by the Lord through the prophet Samuel.

393

Others of us know him as a mighty warrior; for doesn't the record show the chant of the adoring women following his many victorious battles, "Saul hath slain his thousands, and David his ten thousands"?[7] Or perhaps we look upon him as the inspired poet or as one of Israel's greatest kings. Still others recall that he violated the laws of God and took that which belonged to another—the beautiful Bathsheba. He even arranged the death of her husband, Uriah.

I, however, like to think of David as the righteous lad who had the courage and the faith to face insurmountable odds when all others hesitated, and to redeem the name of Israel by facing that giant in his life—Goliath of Gath.

Well might we look carefully into our own lives and judge our courage, our faith. Is there a Goliath in your life? Is there one in mine? Does he stand squarely between you and your desired happiness? Oh, your Goliath may not carry a sword or hurl a verbal challenge of insult that all may hear and force you to decision. He may not be ten feet tall, but he likely will appear equally as formidable; and his silent challenge may shame and embarrass.

One man's Goliath may be the stranglehold of a cigarette or perhaps an unquenchable thirst for alcohol. To another, his Goliath may be an unruly tongue or a selfish streak which causes him to spurn the poor and the downtrodden. Envy, greed, fear, laziness, doubt, vice, pride, lust, selfishness, discouragement—all spell Goliath.

The giant you face will not diminish in size nor in power or strength by your vain hoping, wishing, or waiting for him to do so. Rather, he increases in power as his hold upon you tightens.

The battle for our immortal souls is no less important than the battle fought by David. The enemy is no less formidable, the help of Almighty God no farther away. What will our action be? Like David of old, "our cause is just." We have been placed upon earth not to fail or fall victim to temptation's snare, but rather to succeed. Our giant, our Goliath, must be conquered.

David went to the brook and carefully selected five smooth stones with which he might meet his enemy. He was deliberate in his selection, for there could be no turning back; no second chance—this battle was to be decisive.

Just as David went to the brook, well might we go to our source of supply—the Lord. What polished stones will you select to defeat the Goliath that is robbing you of your happiness by smothering your opportunities? May I offer suggestions.

The stone of **courage** will be essential to your victory. As we survey the challenges of life, that which is easy is rarely right. In fact, the course which we should properly follow at times appears impossible, impenetrable, hopeless.

Such did the way appear to Laman and Lemuel. When they looked upon their assignment to go unto the house of Laban and seek the records according to God's command, they murmured, saying it was a hard thing which was required of them. Thus, a lack of courage took from them their opportunity; and it was given to courageous Nephi, who responded, "I will go and do the things which the Lord hath commanded, for I know that the Lord giveth no commandments unto the children of men, save he shall prepare a way for them that they may accomplish the thing which he commandeth them."[8] Yes, the stone of courage is needed.

Let us not overlook the stone of **effort**—mental effort and physical effort.

> *The heights by great men reached and kept*
> *Were not obtained by sudden flight,*
> *But they, while their companions slept,*
> *Were toiling upward through the night.* [9]

The decision to overcome a fault or correct a weakness is an actual step in the process of doing so. "Thrust in thy sickle with thy might" was not spoken of missionary work alone.

Then there must be in our selection the stone of **humility**, for haven't we been told through divine revelation that when we are humble, the Lord, our God, will lead us by the hand and give us answer to our prayers?

And who would go forth to battle his Goliath without the stone of **prayer**, remembering that the recognition of a power higher than oneself is in no way debasing; rather, it exalts.

Finally, let us choose the stone of **duty**. Duty is not merely to do the thing we ought to do, but to do it when we should, whether we like it or not.

Armed with this selection of five polished stones to be propelled by the mighty sling of faith, we need then but to take the staff of virtue to steady us; and we are ready to meet the giant Goliath, wherever, and whenever, and however we find him.

The stone of **courage** will melt the Goliath of fear; the stone of **effort** will bring down the Goliaths of indecision and procrastination. And the Goliaths of pride, of envy, of lack of self-respect will not stand before the power of the stones of **humility**, **prayer,** and **duty**.

Above all else, may we ever remember that we do not go forth alone to battle against the Goliaths of our lives. As David declared to Israel, so might we echo the knowledge, "the battle is the Lord's, and he will give [Goliath] into our hands."[10]

The battle must be fought. Victory cannot come by default. So it is in the battles of life. Life will never spread itself in an unobstructed view before us. We must anticipate the approaching forks and turnings in the road.

However, we cannot hope to reach our desired journey's end if we think aimlessly about whether to go east or west. We must make our decisions purposefully. Our most significant opportunities will be found in times of greatest difficulty.

The vast, uncharted expanse of the Atlantic Ocean stood as a Goliath between Christopher Columbus and the New World. The hearts of his comrades became faint, their courage dimmed, hopelessness engulfed them; but Columbus prevailed with his watchword, "Westward, ever Westward, sail on, sail on."

Carthage jail, an angry mob with painted faces, certain death faced the Prophet Joseph Smith. But from the wellsprings of his abundant faith he calmly met the Goliath of death. "I am going like a lamb to the slaughter; but I am calm as a summer's morning; I have a conscience void of offense towards God, and towards all men."[11]

Gethsemane, Golgotha, intense pain and suffering beyond the comprehension of mortal man stood between Jesus the Master and victory over the grave. Yet He lovingly assured us, "I go to prepare a place for you . . . that where I am, there ye may be also."[12]

And what is the significance of these accounts? Had there been no ocean, there would have been no Columbus. No jail, no Joseph. No mob, no martyr. No cross, no Christ!

Should there be a Goliath in our lives or a giant called by any other name, we need not "flee" or be "sore afraid" as we go up to battle against him. Rather we can find assurance and divine help in that inspired psalm of David: "The Lord is my shepherd; I shall not want. . . . Yea, though I walk through the valley of the shadow of death, I will fear no evil: for thou art with me."[13]

May this knowledge be ours, I pray.

NOTES

1. 1 Samuel 17:8.
2. 1 Samuel 17:10.
3. 1 Samuel 17:29, 32.
4. 1 Samuel 17:33.
5. 1 Samuel 17:43–44.
6. 1 Samuel 17:45–50.
7. 1 Samuel 18:7.
8. 1 Nephi 3:7.
9. Henry Wadsworth Longfellow, "The Ladder of St. Augustine," in *Best-Loved Poems of the LDS People* (1996), 336.
10. 1 Samuel 17:47.
11. Doctrine and Covenants 135:4.
12. John 14:2–3.
13. Psalm 23:1, 4.

45

How Firm a Foundation

In 1959, NOT LONG AFTER I began my service as president of the Canadian Mission, headquartered in Toronto, Ontario, Canada, I met N. Eldon Tanner, a prominent Canadian who just months later would be called as an Assistant to the Quorum of the Twelve Apostles, then to the Quorum of the Twelve, and then as a counselor to four Church Presidents.

At the time I met him, President Tanner was president of the vast TransCanada Pipelines, Ltd., and president of the Canada Calgary Stake. During that first meeting, we discussed, among other subjects, the cold Canadian winters, where storms rage, temperatures can linger well below freezing for weeks at a time, and where icy winds lower those temperatures even further. I asked President Tanner why the roads and highways in Western Canada basically remained intact during such winters, showing little or no signs of cracking or breaking, while the road surfaces in many areas where winters are less cold and less severe developed cracks and breaks and potholes.

Said he, "The answer is in the depth of the base of the paving materials. In order for them to remain strong and unbroken, it is necessary to go very deep with the foundation layers. When the foundations are not deep enough, the surfaces cannot withstand the extremes of weather."

Over the years I have thought often of this conversation and of President Tanner's explanation, for I recognize in his words a profound application for our lives. Stated simply, if we do not have a deep foundation of faith and a solid testimony of truth, we may have difficulty withstanding the harsh storms and icy winds of adversity which inevitably come to each of us.

Mortality is a period of testing, a time to prove ourselves worthy to return to the presence of our Heavenly Father. In order for us to be tested, we must face challenges and difficulties. These can break us, and the surface of our souls may crack and crumble—that is, if our foundations of faith, our testimonies of truth are not deeply imbedded within us.

We can rely on the faith and testimonies of others only so long. Eventually we must have our own strong and deeply placed foundation, or we will be unable to withstand the storms of life, which *will* come. Such storms come in a variety of forms. We may be faced with the sorrow and heartbreak of a wayward child who chooses to turn from the pathway leading to eternal truth and rather travel the slippery slopes of error and disillusionment. Sickness may strike us or a loved one, bringing suffering and sometimes death. Accidents may leave their cruel marks of remembrance or may snuff out life.

How can we build a foundation strong enough to withstand such vicissitudes of life? How can we maintain the faith and testimony which will be required, that we might experience the joy promised to the faithful? Constant, steady effort is necessary. Most of us have experienced inspiration so strong that it brings tears to our eyes and a determination to ever remain faithful. I have heard the statement, "If I could keep such feelings with me always, I would never have trouble doing what I should." Such feelings, however, can be fleeting. The inspiration we feel during these conference sessions may diminish and fade as Monday comes and we face the routines of work, of school, of managing our homes and families. Such can easily take our minds from the holy to the mundane, from that which uplifts to that which, if we allow it, will chip away at our testimonies, our strong spiritual foundations.

Of course we do not live in a world where we experience nothing but the spiritual, but we can fortify our foundations of faith, our testimonies of truth, so that we will not falter, we will not fail. How, you may ask, can we most effectively gain and maintain the foundation needed to survive spiritually in the world in which we live?

May I offer three guidelines to help us in our quest.

First, fortify your foundation through prayer. "Prayer is the soul's sincere desire, Uttered or unexpressed."[1]

As we pray, let us really communicate with our Father in Heaven. It is easy to let our prayers become repetitious, expressing words with little or no thought behind them. When we remember that each of us is literally a spirit son or daughter of God, we will not find it difficult to approach Him in prayer. He knows us; He loves us; He wants what is best for us. Let us pray with sincerity and meaning, offering our thanks and asking for those things we feel we need. Let us listen for His answers, that we may recognize them when they come. As we do, we will be strengthened and blessed. We will come to know Him and His desires for our lives. By knowing Him, by trusting His will, our foundations of faith will be strengthened. If any one of us has been slow to hearken to the counsel to pray always, there is no finer hour to begin than now. William Cowper declared, "Satan trembles when he sees the weakest Saint upon his knees."

Let us not neglect our family prayers. Such is an effective deterrent to sin, and thence a most beneficent provider of joy and happiness. The old saying is yet true: "The family that prays together stays together." By providing an example of prayer to our children, we will also be helping them to begin their own deep foundations of faith and testimonies which they will need throughout their lives.

My second guideline: Let us study the scriptures and "meditate therein day and night," as counseled by the Lord in the book of Joshua.[2]

In 2005, hundreds of thousands of Latter-day Saints accepted President Gordon B. Hinckley's challenge to read the Book of Mormon by the end of the year. I believe December of 2005 would set an all-time record for hours devoted to meeting the challenge on time. We were blessed as we completed the task; our testimonies were strengthened, our knowledge increased. I would encourage all of us to continue to read and study the scriptures, that we might understand them and apply in our lives the lessons we find there.

Spending time each day in scripture study will, without doubt, strengthen our foundations of faith and our testimonies of truth.

Recall with me the joy Alma experienced as he was journeying from the land of Gideon southward to the land of Manti and met the sons of Mosiah. Alma had not seen them for some time, and he was overjoyed to discover that they were "still his brethren in the Lord; yea, and they had waxed strong in the knowledge of the truth; for they were men of a sound understanding and they had searched the scriptures diligently, that they might know the word of God."[3]

May we also know the word of God and conduct our lives accordingly.

My third guideline for building a strong foundation of faith and testimony involves service.

Along your pathway of life you will observe that you are not the only traveler. There are others who need your help.

Thirteen years ago it was my privilege to provide a blessing to a beautiful 12-year-old young lady, Jami Palmer. She had just been diagnosed with cancer and was frightened and bewildered.

She subsequently underwent surgery and painful chemotherapy. Today she is cancer free and is a bright, beautiful 26-year-old who has accomplished much in her life. Some time ago, I learned that in her darkest hour, when any future appeared somewhat grim, she learned that her leg where the cancer was situated would require multiple surgeries. A long-planned hike with her Young Women class up a rugged trail to Timpanogos Cave—located in the Wasatch Mountains about 40 miles south of Salt Lake City, Utah—was out of the question, she thought. Jami told her friends they would have to undertake the hike without her. I'm confident there was a catch in her voice and disappointment in her heart. But then the other young women responded emphatically, "No, Jami, you are going with us!"

"But I can't walk," came the anguished reply.

"Then, Jami, we'll carry you to the top!" And they did.

Today, the hike is a memory, but in reality it is much more. None of those precious young women will ever forget that memorable day when a loving Heavenly Father looked down with a smile of approval and was well pleased.

Through the years, the offices I have occupied have been decorated with lovely paintings of peaceful and pastoral scenes. However, there is one picture that always hangs on the wall which I face when seated behind my desk. It is a constant reminder of Him whom I serve, for it is a picture of our Lord and Savior, Jesus Christ. When confronted with a vexing problem or difficult decision, I always gaze at that picture of the Master and silently ask myself the question: "What would He have me do?" No longer does doubt linger, nor does indecision prevail. The way to go is clear, and the pathway before me beckons. Such will also work for each of you as you focus on what the Lord would have you do.

As He enlists us to His cause, He invites us to draw close to Him, and we feel His Spirit in our lives.

As we establish a firm foundation for our lives, let us each one remember His precious promise:

> *Fear not, I am with thee; oh, be not dismayed,*
> *For I am thy God and will still give thee aid.*
> *I'll strengthen thee, help thee, and cause thee to stand,*
> *Upheld by my righteous, omnipotent hand.*[4]

May each of us qualify for this blessing.

NOTES

1. "Prayer Is the Soul's Sincere Desire," *Hymns,* no. 145.
2. Joshua 1:8.
3. Alma 17:2.
4. "How Firm a Foundation," *Hymns,* no. 85.

46

TRUE TO THE FAITH

MANY YEARS AGO, ON AN assignment to the beautiful islands of Tonga, I was privileged to visit our Church school, the Liahona High School, where our youth were taught by teachers with a common bond of faith—providing training for the mind and preparation for life. On that occasion, entering one classroom, I noticed the rapt attention the children gave their native instructor. His textbook and theirs lay closed upon the desks. In his hand he held a strange-appearing fishing lure fashioned from a round stone and large seashells. This, I learned, was a *maka-feke,* or octopus trap. In Tonga, octopus meat is a delicacy.

The teacher explained that Tongan fishermen glide over a reef, paddling their outrigger canoes with one hand and dangling the *maka-feke* over the side with the other. An octopus dashes out from its rocky lair and seizes the lure, mistaking it for a much-desired meal. So tenacious is the grasp of the octopus and so firm is its instinct not to relinquish the precious prize that fishermen can flip it right into the canoe.

It was an easy transition for the teacher to point out to the

eager and wide-eyed youth that the Evil One—even Satan—has
fashioned so-called *maka-fekes* with which to ensnare unsuspecting persons and take possession of their destinies.

Today we are surrounded by the *maka-fekes* which the Evil
One dangles before us and with which he attempts to entice us
and then to ensnare us. Once grasped, such *maka-fekes* are ever
so difficult—and sometimes nearly impossible—to relinquish.
To be safe, we must recognize them for what they are and then
be unwavering in our determination to avoid them.

Constantly before us is the *maka-feke* of immorality. Almost
everywhere we turn there are those who would have us believe
that what was once considered immoral is now acceptable. I
think of the scripture: "Wo unto them that call evil good, and
good evil, that put darkness for light, and light for darkness."[1]
Such is the *maka-feke* of immorality. We are reminded in the Book
of Mormon that chastity and virtue are precious above all things.

Next, the Evil One also dangles before us the *maka-feke* of
pornography. He would have us believe that the viewing of pornography really hurts no one.

Some publishers and printers prostitute their presses by
printing millions of pieces of pornography each day. No expense
is spared to produce a product certain to be viewed, then viewed
again. One of the most accessible sources of pornography today
is the Internet, where one can turn on a computer and instantly
have at his fingertips countless sites featuring pornography.
President Gordon B. Hinckley has said: "I fear this may be going
on in some of your homes. It is vicious. It is lewd and filthy. It is
enticing and habit-forming. It will take [you] down to destruction as surely as anything in this world. It is foul sleaze that makes
its exploiters wealthy, its victims impoverished."[2] Tainted as well
is the movie producer, the television programmer, or the enter-
tainer who promotes pornography. Long gone are the restraints
of yesteryear. So-called realism is the quest, with the result that
today we are surrounded by this filth.

Avoid any semblance of pornography. It will desensitize the spirit and erode the conscience. We are told in the Doctrine and Covenants: "That which doth not edify is not of God, and is darkness."[3] Such is pornography.

I mention next the *maka-feke* of drugs, including alcohol. Once grasped, this *maka-feke* is particularly difficult to abandon. Drugs and alcohol cloud thinking, remove inhibitions, fracture families, shatter dreams and shorten life. They are everywhere to be found and are placed purposely in the pathway of vulnerable youth. Each one of us has a body that has been entrusted to us by a loving Heavenly Father. We have been commanded to care for it. Can we deliberately abuse or injure our bodies without being held accountable? We cannot! May we keep our bodies—our temples—fit and clean and free from harmful substances which destroy our physical, mental, and spiritual well-being.

The final *maka-feke* I wish to mention today is one which can crush our self-esteem, ruin relationships, and leave us in desperate circumstances. It is the *maka-feke* of excessive debt. It is a human tendency to want the things which will give us prominence and prestige. We live in a time when borrowing is easy. We can purchase almost anything we could ever want just by using a credit card or obtaining a loan. Extremely popular are home equity loans, where one can borrow an amount of money equal to the equity he has in his home. What we may not realize is that a home equity loan is equivalent to a second mortgage. The day of reckoning *will* come if we have continually lived beyond our means.

My brothers and sisters, avoid the philosophy that yesterday's luxuries have become today's necessities. They aren't necessities unless we make them so. Many enter into long-term debt only to find that changes occur: people become ill or incapacitated, companies fail or downsize, jobs are lost, natural disasters befall us. For many reasons, payments on large amounts of debt can often no longer be made. Our debt becomes as a Damocles sword hanging over our head and threatening to destroy us.

I urge you to live within your means. One cannot continually spend more than he earns and remain solvent. I promise you that you will then be happier than you would be if you were constantly worrying about how to make the next payment on nonessential debt.

There are, of course, countless other *maka-fekes* which the Evil One dangles before us to lead us from the path of righteousness. However, our Heavenly Father has given us life and with it the capacity to think, to reason, and to love. We have the power to resist any temptation and the ability to determine the path we will take, the direction we will travel. Our goal is the celestial kingdom of God. Our purpose is to steer an undeviating course in that direction.

To all who walk the pathway of life, our Heavenly Father cautions: Beware the detours, the pitfalls, the traps. Cunningly positioned are those cleverly disguised *maka-fekes* beckoning us to grasp them and to lose that which we most desire. Do not be deceived. Pause to pray. Listen to that still, small voice which speaks to the depths of our souls the Master's gentle invitation: "Come, follow me."[4] By doing so, we turn from destruction, from death, and find happiness and life everlasting.

Yet, there are those who do not hear, who will not obey, who listen to the enticings of the Evil One, who grasp those *maka-fekes* until they cannot let go, until all is lost. I think of that person of power, that cardinal of the cloth, even Cardinal Wolsey. The prolific pen of William Shakespeare described the majestic heights, the pinnacle of power to which Cardinal Wolsey ascended. That same pen told how principle was eroded by vain ambition, by expediency, by a clamor for prominence and prestige. Then came the tragic descent, the painful lament of one who had gained everything, then lost all.

To Cromwell, his faithful servant, Cardinal Wolsey speaks:

O Cromwell, Cromwell!
Had I but serv'd my God with half the zeal
I serv'd my king, he would not in mine age
Have left me naked to mine enemies.[5]

That inspired mandate which would have led Cardinal Wolsey to safety was ruined by the pursuit of power and prominence, the quest for wealth and position. Like others before him and many more yet to follow, Cardinal Wolsey fell.

In an earlier time, and by a wicked king, a servant of God was tested. Aided by the inspiration of heaven, Daniel interpreted to King Belshazzar the writing on the wall. Concerning the proffered rewards—even a royal robe and a necklace of gold—Daniel said: "Let thy gifts be to thyself, and give thy rewards to another."[6]

Darius, a later king, also honored Daniel, elevating him to the highest position of prominence. There followed the envy of the crowd, the jealousy of princes, and the scheming of ambitious men.

Through trickery and flattery, King Darius signed a proclamation providing that anyone who made a request of any god or man, except the king, should be thrown into the lion's den. Prayer was forbidden. In such matters, Daniel took direction not from an earthly king but from the King of heaven and earth, his God. Overtaken in his daily prayers, Daniel was brought before the king. Reluctantly, the penalty was pronounced. Daniel was to be thrown into the lion's den.

I love the biblical account which follows:

"The king arose very early in the morning, and went in haste unto the den of lions. And when he came to the den, he cried with a lamentable voice. . . . O Daniel, . . . is thy God, whom thou servest continually, able to deliver thee from the lions? Then said Daniel unto the king. . . . My God hath sent his angel, and hath shut the lions' mouths, that they have not hurt me. . . . Then was the king exceeding glad. . . . Daniel was taken up out of the den, and no manner of hurt was found upon him, because he believed in his God."[7]

In a time of critical need, Daniel's determination to remain true and faithful provided divine protection and a sanctuary of safety.

The clock of history, like the sands of the hourglass, marks the passage of time. A new cast occupies the stage of life. The problems of our day loom ominously before us. Surrounded by the challenges of modern living, we look heavenward for that unfailing sense of direction, that we might chart and follow a wise and proper course. Our Heavenly Father will not leave our sincere petition unanswered.

My brothers and sisters, let us resolve here and now to follow that straight path which leads home to the Father of us all so that the gift of eternal life—life in the presence of our Heavenly Father—may be ours. Should there be those things which need to be changed or corrected in order to do so, I encourage you to take care of them now.

In the words of a familiar hymn, may we ever be . . .

> *True to the faith that our parents have cherished,*
> *True to the truth for which martyrs have perished,*
> *To God's command, Soul, heart, and hand,*
> *Faithful and true we will ever stand.*[8]

NOTES

1. 2 Nephi 15:20; see also Isaiah 5:20.
2. "Great Shall Be the Peace of Thy Children," *Ensign*, November 2000, 51.
3. Doctrine and Covenants 50:23.
4. Luke 18:22.
5. *King Henry the Eighth*, Act 3, scene 2, lines 455–58.
6. Daniel 5:17.
7. Daniel 6:19–23.
8. "True to the Faith," *Hymns*, no. 254.

47

Mercy—The Divine Gift

Not long ago, I read a lengthy report concerning the violence and bloodshed that stalked the land of what was once Yugoslavia. The killing and maiming seemed to go on, despite the efforts put forth to bring peace. The account of a sniper taking deadly aim and snuffing out the life of a small child brought sorrow to my soul. I silently asked: *Where to be found is that divine attribute of mercy?*

The cruelty of war seems to bring forth hatred toward others and disregard for human life. It has ever been so. Yet, in such degradation at times there shines forth the inextinguishable light of mercy.

During the television documentaries shown throughout the fiftieth anniversary of the D-Day invasion of Normandy, the terrible toll in human life was graphically illustrated, and gripping firsthand experiences of soldiers who were there were shared. I particularly remember the comments of an American infantryman who told that, after a day of ferocious fighting, he glanced up from his shallow foxhole to see an enemy soldier with his gun barrel leveled at the American's heart. Said the infantryman: "I felt I was soon to cross over that bridge of death which leads to eternity. Incredibly my enemy, in broken English, said to me, 'Soldier, for you this war is over!' He took me prisoner and thus saved my life. Such mercy I shall remember forever."

At an earlier time, and in a different conflict—namely, the American Civil War—a historically documented account illustrates courage, coupled with mercy.

From December 11 to 13, 1862, the Union forces attacked Marye's Heights, a large hill overlooking the town of Fredericksburg, Virginia, where six thousand Rebels awaited them. The Southern troops were in secure defensive positions behind a stone wall which meandered along the foot of the hill. In addition, they stood four deep on a sunken road behind the wall, out of sight of Union forces.

The Union troops—over forty thousand strong—launched a series of suicidal attacks across open ground. They were mowed down by a scythe of shot; none got closer than 40 yards from the stone wall.

Soon the ground in front of the Confederate positions was littered with hundreds, then thousands, of fallen Union soldiers in their blue uniforms—over twelve thousand before sunset. Crying for help, the wounded lay in the bitter cold throughout that terrible night.

The next day, a Sunday, dawned cold and foggy. As the morning fog lifted, the agonized cries of the wounded could still be heard. Finally, a young Confederate soldier, a 19-year-old sergeant, had had all he could take. The young man's name was Richard Rowland Kirkland. To his commanding officer, Kirkland exclaimed, "All night and all day I have heard those poor people crying for water, and I can stand it no longer. I . . . ask permission to go and give them water." His request was initially denied on the grounds that it was too dangerous. Finally, however, permission was granted, and soon thousands of amazed men on both sides saw the young soldier, with several canteens draped around his neck, climb over the wall and walk to the nearest wounded Union soldier. He raised the stricken man's head, gently gave him a drink, and covered him with his own overcoat. Then he moved to the next of the wounded—and the next and the next. As Kirkland's purpose became clear, fresh cries of "Water, water, for God's sake water" arose all over the field.

The Union soldiers were at first too surprised to shoot. Soon they began to cheer the young Southerner as they saw what he was doing. For more than an hour and a half, Sergeant Kirkland continued his work of mercy.

Tragically, Richard Kirkland was himself killed a few months later at the battle of Chicamauga. His last words to his companions were, "Save yourselves, and tell my pa I died right."

Kirkland's Christlike compassion made his name synonymous with mercy for a post-Civil War generation, both North and South. He became known by soldiers on both sides of the conflict as "the angel of Marye's Heights." His loving errand of mercy is commemorated by a bronze monument which stands today in front of the stone wall at Fredericksburg. It depicts Sergeant Kirkland lifting the head of a wounded Union soldier to give him a drink of refreshing water. A tablet to Kirkland's honor hangs in the Episcopal church in Gettysburg, Pennsylvania. With simple eloquence, it captures the essence of the young soldier's mission of mercy. It reads: "A hero of benevolence, at the risk of his own life, he gave his enemy drink at Fredericksburg."[1]

The words of William Shakespeare describe Kirkland's deed:

> *The quality of mercy is not strain'd,*
> *It droppeth as the gentle rain from heaven*
> *Upon the place beneath: it is twice blest;*
> *It blesseth him that gives, and him that takes: . . .*
> *It is an attribute to God himself.*[2]

412

Two brilliant and faith-filled counselors to President David O. McKay spoke to us everlasting counsel concerning the greatest act of mercy ever known to man. President Stephen L Richards said: "The Savior Himself declared that He came to fulfill the law, not to do away with it, but with the law He brought the principle of mercy to temper its enforcement, and to bring hope and encouragement to [the] offenders for forgiveness through [mercy and] repentance."[3]

President J. Reuben Clark, Jr., testified: "You know, I believe that the Lord will help us. I believe if we go to Him, He will give us wisdom, if we are living righteously. I believe He will answer our prayers. I believe that our Heavenly Father wants to save every one of His children. I do not think He intends to shut any of us off because of some slight transgression, some slight failure to observe some rule or regulation. There are the great elementals that we must observe, but He is not going to be captious about the lesser things.

"I believe that His juridical concept of His dealings with His children could be expressed in this way: I believe that in His justice and mercy, He will give us the maximum reward for our acts, give us all that He can give, and in the reverse, I believe that He will impose upon us the minimum penalty which it is possible for Him to impose."[4]

"I often think that one of the most beautiful things in the Christ's life was His words on the cross, when, suffering under the agony of a death that is said to have been the most painful that the ancients could devise, death on the cross, after He had been unjustly, illegally, contrary to all the rules of mercy, condemned and then crucified, when He had been nailed to the cross and was about to give up His life, He said to His Father in heaven, as those who were within hearing testify, '. . . Father, forgive them; for they know not what they do.' (Luke 23:34)."[5]

In the Book of Mormon, Alma describes beautifully the

foregoing with his words: "The plan of mercy could not be brought about except an atonement should be made; therefore God himself atoneth for the sins of the world, to bring about the plan of mercy, to appease the demands of justice, that God might be a perfect, just God, and a merciful God also."[6]

From the springboard of such knowledge we ask ourselves, Why, then, do we see on every side those instances where people decline to forgive one another and show forth the cleansing act of mercy and forgiveness? What blocks the way for such healing balm to cleanse human wounds? Is it stubbornness? Could it be pride? Maybe hatred has yet to melt and disappear. "Blame keeps wounds open. Only forgiveness heals!"[7]

At times the need for mercy can be found close to home and in simple settings. We have a four-year-old grandson named Jeffrey. One day his 15-year-old brother, Alan, had just completed, on the family computer, a most difficult and rather ingenious design of an entire city. When Alan slipped out of the room for just a moment, little Jeffrey approached the computer and accidentally erased the program. Upon his return, Alan was furious when he observed what his brother had done. Sensing that his doom was at hand, Jeffrey raised his finger and, pointing it toward Alan, declared from his heart and soul, "Remember, Alan, Jesus said, 'Don't hurt little boys.'" Alan began to laugh; anger subsided; mercy prevailed.

There are those among us who torture themselves through their inability to show mercy and to forgive others some supposed offense or slight, however small it may be. At times the statement is made, "I never can forgive [this person or that person]." Such an attitude is destructive to an individual's well-being. It can canker the soul and ruin one's life. In other instances, an individual can forgive another but cannot forgive himself. Such a situation is even more destructive.

Early in my ministry as a member of the Quorum of the

Twelve, I took to President Hugh B. Brown the experience of a fine person who could not serve in a ward position because he could not show mercy to himself. He could forgive others but not himself; mercy was seemingly beyond his grasp. President Brown suggested that I visit with that individual and counsel him along these lines: "I, the Lord, will forgive whom I will forgive, but of you it is required to forgive all men."[8] Then, from the Doctrine and Covenants: "Behold, he who has repented of his sins, the same is forgiven, and I, the Lord, remember them no more."[9]

With a pensive expression on his face, President Brown added: "Tell that man that he should not persist in remembering that which the Lord has said He is willing to forget." Such counsel will help to cleanse the soul and renew the spirit of any who applies it.

The Prophet Joseph urged, "Be merciful and you shall find mercy. Seek to help save souls, not to destroy them: for verily you know, that 'there is more joy in heaven, over one sinner that repents, than there is over ninety and nine just persons [who] need no repentance.'"[10]

At times a small mistake can fester and bring distress and heartache to him or her who harbors and dwells on the matter, leaving it uncorrected. All of us are subject to such an experience. Let me share with you an example with a beautiful ending. I recently received a note, with a key enclosed, which read:

"Dear President Monson,

"Thirteen years ago this summer my husband and I stayed at the Hotel Utah. As a memento of our vacation, I took this hotel key and have felt bad about it [ever since]. I know that the Church owns the former Hotel Utah, and so I am returning this key to you—to the Church—in an effort to set this right. I am so sorry for having taken the key. Please, [please,] forgive me."

I thought to myself, What honesty; what a sweet spirit the writer must possess. I replied as follows:

"Dear Sister,

"Thank you for your thoughtful note and for the Hotel Utah key which you returned. My heart was touched by your sincerity. Though the key itself weighed very little, apparently this has been a heavy burden for you to carry for [such] a long time. Though the key was of very little worth, its return is of far greater value. I am honored to accept the key and know that you are certainly forgiven. Please accept the enclosed gift with my warmest wishes."

The key was returned to her, mounted on an attractive plaque.

One of the most touching examples of mercy and forgiveness is the well-remembered experience in the life of Jesus, when he "went unto the mount of Olives.

"And early in the morning he came again into the temple, and all the people came unto him; and he sat down, and taught them.

"And the scribes and Pharisees brought unto him a woman taken in adultery; and when they had set her in the midst,

"They say unto him, Master, this woman was taken in adultery, in the very act.

"Now Moses in the law commanded us, that such should be stoned: but what sayest thou?

"This they said, tempting him, that they might have to accuse him. But Jesus stooped down, and with his finger wrote on the ground, as though he heard them not.

"So when they continued asking him, he lifted up himself, and said unto them, He that is without sin among you, let him first cast a stone at her.

"And again he stooped down, and wrote on the ground.

"And they which heard it, being convicted by their own conscience, went out one by one, beginning at the eldest, even unto the last: and Jesus was left alone, and the woman standing in the midst.

"When Jesus had lifted up himself, and saw none but the woman, he said unto her, Woman, where are . . . thine accusers? hath no man condemned thee?

"She said, No man, Lord. And Jesus said unto her, Neither do I condemn thee: go, and sin no more."[11]

The sands of time quickly erased what the Savior had written, but forever will be remembered the mercy He showed.

I stand all amazed at the love Jesus offers me,
Confused at the grace that so fully he proffers me.
I tremble to know that for me he was crucified,
That for me, a sinner, he suffered, he bled and died. . . .

I think of his hands pierced and bleeding to pay the debt!
Such mercy, such love and devotion can I forget?
No, no, I will praise and adore at the mercy seat,
Until at the glorified throne I kneel at his feet.[12]

This same Jesus, "seeing the multitudes, he went up into a mountain: and when he was set, his disciples came unto him:

"And he opened his mouth, and taught them, saying, . . .

"Blessed are the merciful: for they shall obtain mercy."[13]

My sincere and humble prayer is that each of us may be the provider and the recipient of mercy—the divine gift.

NOTES

1. *The Battle of Fredericksburg* (1990); "He Gave His Enemy Drink," *CWT Illustrated*, October 1962, 38–39. Information on Richard Kirkland provided by staff of the Fredericksburg and Spotsylvania National Military Park, National Park Service, U.S. Department of the Interior.
2. William Shakespeare, *The Merchant of Venice*, Act 4, scene 1, lines 184–95.
3. In Conference Report, April 3, 1954, 11.
4. In Conference Report, October 3, 1953, 84.
5. J. Reuben Clark, Jr., in Conference Report, September 30, 1955, 24.
6. Alma 42:15.
7. From *O Pioneers!* by Willa Cather.

8. Doctrine and Covenants 64:10.

9. Doctrine and Covenants 58:42.

10. *Teachings of the Prophet Joseph Smith* (1976), 77.

11. John 8:1–11.

12. "I Stand All Amazed," *Hymns,* no. 193.

13. Matthew 5:1–2, 7.

48

PEACE, BE STILL

W HEN I WAS A BOY, we had a chorister who taught us boys
how to sing. We had to sing. Sister Stella Waters would wave the
baton within inches of our noses and beat time with a heavy
foot that made the floor creak.

If we responded properly, Sister Waters let us choose a favorite hymn to sing. Inevitably, the selection was:

> *Master, the tempest is raging!*
> *The billows are tossing high!*
> *The sky is o'ershadowed with blackness.*
> *No shelter or help is nigh.*
> *Carest thou not that we perish?*
> *How canst thou lie asleep*
> *When each moment so madly is threat'ning*
> *A grave in the angry deep?*

Then the assuring chorus:

> *The winds and the waves shall obey thy will:*
> *Peace, be still, peace, be still.*

419

Whether the wrath of the storm-tossed sea
Or demons or men or whatever it be,
No waters can swallow the ship where lies
The Master of ocean and earth and skies.
They all shall sweetly obey thy will:
Peace, be still; peace, be still.
They all shall sweetly obey thy will:
Peace, peace, be still.[1]

As a boy, I could fathom somewhat the danger of a storm-tossed sea. However, I had but little understanding of other demons which can stalk our lives, destroy our dreams, smother our joys, and detour our journey toward the celestial kingdom of God.

A list of destructive demons is lengthy; and each man, young or old, knows the ones with which he must contend. I'll name but a few: the Demon of **Greed**; the Demon of **Dishonesty**; the Demon of **Debt**; the Demon of **Doubt**; the Demon of **Drugs**; and those twin Demons of **Immodesty** and **Immorality**. Each of these demons can wreak havoc with our lives. A combination of them can spell utter destruction.

Concerning **greed**, the counsel from Ecclesiastes speaks caution: "He that loveth silver shall not be satisfied with silver; nor he that loveth abundance with increase."[2]

Jesus counseled, "Take heed, and beware of covetousness: for a man's life consisteth not in the abundance of the things which he possesseth."[3]

We must learn to separate need from greed.

When we speak of the demon of **dishonesty**, we can find it in a variety of locations. One such place is in school. Let us avoid cheating, falsifying, taking advantage of others, or anything like unto it. Let integrity be our standard.

Enticements to embrace the demon of **debt** are thrust upon us many times each day. I quote the counsel from President Gordon B. Hinckley:

"I am troubled by the huge consumer installment debt

which hangs over the people of the nation, including our own people. . . .

"We are beguiled by seductive advertising. Television carries the enticing invitation to borrow up to 125 percent of the value of one's home. But no mention is made of interest. . . .

"I recognize that it may be necessary to borrow to get a home, of course. But let us buy a home that we can afford and thus ease the payments which will constantly hang over our heads without mercy or respite for as long as 30 years."[4]

I would add: We must not allow our yearnings to exceed our earnings.

In discussing the demon of **drugs**, I include, of course, alcohol. Drugs impair our ability to think, to reason, and to make prudent and wise choices. Often they result in violence, child and wife abuse, and they can provoke conduct which brings pain and suffering to those who are innocent. "Just say no to drugs" is an effective statement of one's determination. This can be buttressed by the scripture:

"Know ye not that ye are the temple of God, and that the Spirit of God dwelleth in you?

"If any man defile the temple of God, him shall God destroy; for the temple of God is holy, which temple ye are."[5]

When I consider the demons who are twins—even **immodesty** and **immorality**, I should make them triplets and include **pornography**. They all three go together.

In the interpretation of Lehi's dream, we find a rather apt description of the destructiveness of pornography: "And the mists of darkness are the temptations of the devil, which blindeth the eyes, and hardeneth the hearts of the children of men, and leadeth them away into broad roads, that they perish and are lost."[6]

A modern-day Apostle, Hugh B. Brown, has declared: "Any immodesty inducing impure thoughts is a desecration of the body—that temple in which the Holy Spirit may dwell."[7]

I commend to you tonight a jewel from the *Improvement Era*.

It was published in 1917 but is equally applicable here and now: "The current and common custom of indecency in dress, the flood of immoral fiction in printed literature, in the drama, and notably in [motion] picture[s] . . . , the toleration of immodesty in everyday conversation and demeanor, are doing deadly work in the fostering of soul-destroying vice."[8]

For each of us it is infinitely better to hear and heed the call of conscience. Conscience always warns us as a friend before punishing us as a judge.

There is one responsibility that no one can evade. That is the effect of personal influence.

Our influence is surely felt in our respective families. Sometimes we fathers forget that once we, too, were boys, and boys at times can be vexing to parents.

I recall how much, as a youngster, I liked dogs. One day I took my wagon and placed a wooden orange crate in it and went looking for dogs. At that time dogs were everywhere to be found: at school, walking along the sidewalks, or exploring vacant lots, of which there were many. As I would find a dog and capture it, I placed it in the crate, took it home, locked it in the coal shed, and turned the latch on the door. That day I think I brought home six dogs of varying sizes and made them my prisoners after this fashion. I had no idea what I would do with all these dogs, so I didn't reveal my deed to anyone.

Dad came home from work and, as was his custom, took the coal bucket and went to the coal shed to fill it. Can you imagine his shock and utter consternation as he opened the door and immediately faced six dogs, all attempting to escape at once? As I recall, Dad flushed a little bit, and then he calmed down and quietly told me, "Tommy, coal sheds are for coal. Other people's dogs rightfully belong to them." By observing him, I learned a lesson in patience and calmness.

It is a good thing I did, for a similar event occurred in my life with our youngest son, Clark.

Clark has always liked animals, birds, reptiles—anything that is alive. Sometimes that resulted in a little chaos in our home. One day in his boyhood he came home from Provo Canyon with a water snake, which he named Herman.

Right off the bat Herman got lost. Sister Monson found him in the silverware drawer. Water snakes have a way of being where you least expect them. Well, Clark moved Herman to the bathtub, put a plug in the drain, put a little water in, and had a sign taped to the back of the tub which read, "Don't use this tub. It belongs to Herman." So we had to use the other bathroom while Herman occupied that sequestered place.

But then one day, to our amazement, Herman disappeared. His name should have been *Houdini*. He was gone! So the next day Sister Monson cleaned up the tub and prepared it for normal use. Several days went by.

One evening I decided it was time to take a leisurely bath; so I filled the tub with a lot of warm water, and then I peacefully lay down for a few moments of relaxation. I was lying there just pondering, when the soapy water reached the level of the overflow drain and began to flow through it. Can you imagine my surprise when, with my eyes focused on that drain, Herman came swimming out, right for my face? I yelled out to my wife, "Frances! Here comes Herman!"

Well, Herman was captured again, put in a foolproof box, and we made a little excursion to Vivian Park in Provo Canyon and there released Herman into the beautiful waters of the South Fork Creek. Herman was never again to be seen by us.

I was grateful that day to have my own father's example of patience before me to show me the proper response.

In the performance of our responsibilities, I have learned that when we heed a silent prompting and act upon it without delay, our Heavenly Father will guide our footsteps and bless our lives and the lives of others. I know of no experience more sweet or feelings more precious than to heed a prompting, only to discover that the Lord has answered another's prayer through you.

Perhaps just one example will suffice. One day just over a year ago, after taking care of matters at the office, I felt a strong impression to visit an aged widow who was a patient at St. Joseph Villa. I drove there directly.

When I went to her room, I found it empty. I asked an attendant concerning her whereabouts and was directed to a lounge area. There I found this sweet widow visiting with her sister and another friend. We had a pleasant conversation together.

As we were talking, a man came to the door of the room to obtain a can of soda from the vending machine. He glanced at me and said, "Why, you are Tom Monson."

"Yes," I replied. "And you look like a Hemingway." He acknowledged that he was Stephen Hemingway, the son of Alfred Eugene Hemingway, who had served as my counselor when I was a bishop many years ago and whom I called Gene. Stephen told me that his father was there in the same facility and was near death. He had been calling my name, and the family had wanted to contact me but had been unable to find a telephone number for me.

I excused myself immediately and went with Stephen up to the room of my former counselor, where others of his children were also gathered, his wife having passed away some years previous. The family members regarded my meeting Stephen in the lounge area as a response by our Heavenly Father to their great desire that I would see their father before he died and answer his call. I, too, felt that this was the case, for if Stephen had not entered the room in which I was visiting at precisely the time he did, I would not have known Gene was even in the facility.

We gave a blessing to him. A spirit of peace prevailed. We had a lovely visit, after which I left.

The following morning a phone call revealed that Gene Hemingway had passed away—just 20 minutes after he had received the blessing from his son and me.

I expressed a silent prayer of thanks to Heavenly Father for His guiding influence which prompted my visit to St. Joseph Villa and led me to my dear friend Alfred Eugene Hemingway.

I like to think that Gene Hemingway's thoughts that evening, as we basked in the Spirit's glow, participated in humble prayer, and pronounced a priesthood blessing, echoed the words mentioned in the hymn "Master, the Tempest Is Raging," which I cited at the beginning of my message:

> *Linger, O blessed Redeemer!*
> *Leave me alone no more,*
> *And with joy I shall make the blest harbor*
> *And rest on the blissful shore.*

I still love that hymn and testify to you tonight as to the comfort it offers:

> *Whether the wrath of the storm-tossed sea*
> *Or demons or men or whatever it be,*
> *No waters can swallow the ship where lies*
> *The Master of ocean and earth and skies.*
> *They all shall sweetly obey thy will:*
> *Peace, be still.*[9]

His words in holy writ are sufficient: "Be still, and know that I am God."[10]

NOTES

1. "Master, the Tempest Is Raging," *Hymns,* no. 105.
2. Ecclesiastes 5:10.
3. Luke 12:15.
4. "To the Boys and to the Men," *Ensign,* November 1998, 53.
5. 1 Corinthians 3:16–17.
6. 1 Nephi 12:17.
7. *The Abundant Life* (1965), 65.
8. Joseph F. Smith, "Unchastity the Dominant Evil of the Age," *Improvement Era,* June 1917, 742.
9. *Hymns,* no. 105.
10. Psalm 46:10.

49

HIDDEN WEDGES

In April 1966, at the Church's annual general conference, then-Elder Spencer W. Kimball gave a memorable address. He quoted an account written by Samuel T. Whitman entitled "Forgotten Wedges." Today I, too, have chosen to quote from Samuel T. Whitman, followed by examples from my own life.

Whitman wrote: "The ice storm that winter wasn't generally destructive. True, a few wires came down, and there was a sudden jump in accidents along the highway. Normally, the big walnut tree could easily have borne the weight that formed on its spreading limbs. It was the iron wedge in its heart that caused the damage.

"The story of the iron wedge began years earlier when the white-haired farmer who now inhabited the property on which it stood was a lad on his father's homestead. The sawmill had then only recently been moved from the valley, and the settlers were still finding tools and odd pieces of equipment scattered about. On this particular day it was a [faller's] wedge—wide, flat, and heavy, a foot or more long, and splayed from mighty poundings—which the lad found in the south pasture. [A faller's wedge, used to help fell a tree, is inserted in a cut made by a saw and then struck with a sledgehammer to widen the cut.] Because he was already late for dinner, the young man laid the wedge . . . between the limbs of the young walnut tree his father had planted near the front gate. He would take the wedge to the shed right after dinner, or sometime when he was going that way. He truly meant to, but he never did.

"The wedge was there between the limbs, a little tight, when he attained his manhood. It was there, now firmly gripped, when he married and took over his father's farm. It was half grown over on the day the threshing crew ate dinner under the tree. . . . Grown in and healed over, the wedge was still in the tree the winter the ice storm came.

"In the chill silence of that wintry night . . . one of the three major limbs split away from the trunk and crashed to the ground. This so unbalanced the remainder of the top that it, too, split apart and went down. When the storm was over, not a twig of the once-proud tree remained.

"Early the next morning, the farmer went out to mourn his loss. . . . Then his eyes caught sight of something in the splintered ruin. 'The wedge,' he muttered, reproachfully, 'that I found in the south pasture.' A glance told him why the tree had fallen. Growing edge up in the trunk, the wedge had prevented the limb fibers from knitting together as they should."

My brothers and sisters, there are hidden wedges in the lives of many whom we know—yes, perhaps in our own families.

Let me share with you the account of a lifelong friend, now departed from mortality. His name was Leonard. He was not a member of the Church, although his wife and children were. His wife served as a Primary president; his son served an honorable mission. His daughter and his son married companions in solemn ceremonies and had families of their own.

Everyone who knew Leonard liked him, as did I. He supported his wife and children in their Church assignments. He attended many Church-sponsored events with them. He lived a good and clean life, even a life of service and kindness. His family, and indeed many others, wondered why Leonard had gone through mortality without the blessings the gospel brings to its members.

In Leonard's advanced years, his health declined. Eventually he was hospitalized, and life was ebbing away. In what turned out to be my last conversation with Leonard, he said, "Tom, I've known you since you were a boy. I feel persuaded to explain to you why I have never joined the Church." He then related an experience of his parents which took place many, many years before. Reluctantly, the family had reached a point where they felt it was necessary to sell their farm, and an offer had been received. Then a neighboring farmer asked that the farm be sold to him instead—although for a lesser price—adding, "We've been such close friends. This way, if I own the property, I'll be able to watch over it." At length Leonard's parents agreed, and the farm was sold. The buyer—even the neighbor—held a responsible position in the Church, and the trust this implied helped to persuade the family to sell to him, even though they did not realize as much money from the sale as they would have had they sold to the first interested buyer. Not long after the sale was made, the neighbor sold both his own farm and the farm acquired from Leonard's family in a combined parcel which maximized the value and hence the selling price. The long asked question of why Leonard had never joined the Church had been answered. He always felt that his family had been deceived by the neighbor.

He confided to me following our conversation that he felt a great burden had at last been lifted as he prepared to meet his Maker. The tragedy is that a hidden wedge had kept Leonard from soaring to greater heights.

I am acquainted with a family which came to America from Germany. The English language was difficult for them. They had but little by way of means, but each was blessed with the will to work and with a love of God.

Their third child was born, lived but two months and then died. Father was a cabinetmaker and fashioned a beautiful casket for the body of his precious child. The day of the funeral was gloomy, thus reflecting the sadness they felt in their loss. As the family walked to the chapel, with Father carrying the tiny casket, a small number of friends had gathered. However, the chapel door was locked. The busy bishop had forgotten the funeral. Attempts to reach him were futile. Not knowing what to do, the father placed the casket under his arm and, with his family beside him, carried it home, walking in a drenching rain.

If the family were of lesser character, they could have blamed the bishop and harbored ill feelings. When the bishop discovered the tragedy, he visited the family and apologized. With the hurt still evident in his expression, but with tears in his eyes, the father accepted the apology, and the two embraced in a spirit of understanding. No hidden wedge was left to cause further feelings of anger. Love and acceptance prevailed.

The spirit must be freed from tethers so strong and feelings never put to rest, so that the lift of life may give buoyancy to the soul. In many families, there are hurt feelings and a reluctance to forgive. It doesn't really matter what the issue was. It cannot and should not be left to injure. Blame keeps wounds open. Only forgiveness heals. George Herbert, an early 17th century poet, wrote, "He that cannot forgive others breaks the bridge over which he himself must pass if he would ever reach heaven, for everyone has need of forgiveness."

There are some who have difficulty forgiving themselves and who dwell on all of their perceived shortcomings. I like the account of a religious leader who went to the side of a woman who lay dying, attempting to comfort her—but to no avail. "I am lost," she said. "I have ruined my life and every life around me. There is no hope for me."

The man noticed a framed picture of a lovely girl on the dresser. "Who is this?" he asked.

The woman brightened. "She is my daughter, the one beautiful thing in my life."

"And would you help her if she were in trouble or had made a mistake? Would you forgive her? Would you still love her?"

"Of course I would!" cried the woman. "I would do anything for her. Why do you ask such a question?"

"Because I want you to know," said the man, "that figuratively speaking, Heavenly Father has a picture of you on His dresser. He loves you and will help you. Call upon Him."

A hidden wedge to her happiness had been removed.

In a day of danger or a time of trial, such knowledge, such hope, such understanding will bring comfort to the troubled mind and grieving heart. The entire message of the New Testament breathes a spirit of awakening to the human soul. Shadows of despair are dispelled by rays of hope, sorrow yields to joy, and the feeling of being lost in the crowd of life vanishes with the certain knowledge that our Heavenly Father is mindful of each of us.

The Savior provided assurance of this truth when He taught that even a sparrow shall not fall to the ground unnoticed by our Father. He then concluded the beautiful thought by saying, "Fear ye not therefore, ye are of more value than many sparrows."[1]

Sometimes we can take offense so easily. On other occasions we are too stubborn to accept a sincere apology. Who will subordinate ego, pride and hurt—then step forward with, "I am truly sorry! Let's be as we once were: friends. Let's not pass to future generations the grievances, the anger of our time." Let's remove any hidden wedges that can do nothing but destroy.

Where do hidden wedges originate? Some come from unresolved disputes, which lead to ill feelings, followed by remorse and regret. Others find their beginnings in disappointments, jealousies, arguments, and imagined hurts. We must solve them—lay them to rest and not leave them to canker, fester, and ultimately destroy.

A lovely lady of more than ninety years visited with me one day and unexpectedly recounted several regrets. She mentioned that many years earlier a neighboring farmer with whom she and her husband had occasionally disagreed, asked if he could take a shortcut across her property to reach his own acreage. She paused in her narrative and, with a tremor in her voice, said, "Tommy, I didn't let him cross our property but required him to take the long way around—even on foot—to reach his property. I was wrong and I regret it. He's gone now, but oh, I wish I could say to him 'I'm so sorry.' How I wish I had a second chance."

From Third Nephi in the Book of Mormon comes this inspired counsel: "There shall be no disputations among you. . . . For verily, verily I say unto you, he that hath the spirit of contention is not of me, but is of the devil, who is the father of contention, and he stirreth up the hearts of men to contend with anger, one with another. Behold, this is not my doctrine, to stir up the hearts of men with anger, one against another; but this is my doctrine, that such things should be done away."[2]

Let me conclude with an account of two men who are heroes to me. Their acts of courage were not performed on a national scale, but rather in a peaceful valley known as Midway, Utah.

Long years ago Roy Kohler and Grant Remund served together in Church capacities. They were the best of friends. They were tillers of the soil and dairymen. Then a misunderstanding arose which became somewhat of a rift between them.

Later, when Roy Kohler became grievously ill with cancer and had but a limited time to live, my wife Frances and I visited Roy, and I gave him a blessing. As we talked afterward, Brother Kohler said, "Let me tell you about one of the sweetest experiences I have had during my life." He then recounted to me his misunderstanding with Grant Remund and the ensuing estrangement. His comment was, "We were on the outs with each other.

"Then," continued Roy, "I had just put up our hay for the winter to come, when one night, as a result of spontaneous combustion, the hay caught fire, burning the hay, the barn, and everything in it right to the ground. I was devastated," said Roy. "I didn't know what in the world I would do. The night was dark, except for the dying embers of the fire. Then I saw coming toward me from the road, in the direction of Grant Remund's place, the lights of tractors and heavy equipment. As the 'rescue party' turned in our drive and met me amidst my tears, Grant said, 'Roy, you've got quite a mess to clean up. My boys and I are here. Let's get to it.'" Together they plunged to the task at hand. Gone forever was the hidden wedge which had separated them for a short time. They worked throughout the night and into the next day, with many others in the community joining in.

Roy Kohler has passed away, and Grant Remund is getting older. Their sons have served together in the same ward bishopric. I truly treasure the friendship of these two wonderful families.

My brothers and sisters, may we ever be exemplary in our homes and faithful in keeping all of the commandments, that we may harbor no hidden wedges but rather remember the Savior's admonition: "By this shall all men know that ye are my disciples, if ye have love one to another."[3]

NOTES
1. Matthew 10:31.
2. 3 Nephi 11:28-30.
3. John 13:35.

The Path of a Disciple

50

I Will Serve the Lord

I SUPPOSE EVERY ONE OF US has had a few "heart stoppers" in his or her life, where we just seem to hang by a thread and wonder what the outcome will be. I thought that I might mention a few of the "heart stoppers" in my life.

One of the "heart stoppers" occurred in the Provo Tabernacle. I had no assignment on a particular Sunday morning, and I was driving through Provo and thought I would go to the Tabernacle to see which stake was holding its conference. It happened to be the Provo Utah West Stake, and my good friend Marion Hinckley was the stake president. He saw me and motioned for me to join him on the stand. I did so and remember sitting directly behind the podium. As I sat there, I did as most men do—I had my right leg over my left knee. After a moment or two, I decided it was time to put my left leg over my right knee. I did so just two minutes after I had arrived. I understand it was the second counselor who was speaking at the podium. He had really only begun his message. As I crossed my leg over my knee, the toe of my shoe accidentally touched the back of the leg of the speaker. He misunderstood the touch and simply said, "In the name of Jesus Christ, amen." It was a "heart stopper" for me, and I think it was a "heart stopper" for him—at least it was a "message stopper." From that point on, I have always kept my feet firmly on the floor when I have been seated behind the podium anywhere.

I had another "heart stopper" many years ago in the Tabernacle as a newly called member of the Twelve. The experience came before I was even sustained. President David O. McKay had extended to me the call to the Apostleship. As he extended the call, I could feel the Spirit of the Lord within him, that great leader. He asked that I be confidential, that I reveal the information to no one except my wife, and that I be present the next morning when my name would be read for a sustaining vote.

The following morning I went into the Tabernacle not knowing where to sit. Being a member of the Home Teaching Committee, I determined that I would sit among the members of that committee. As I went five or six rows back in the Tabernacle, I noted a friend of mine by the name of Hugh Smith, who was also a member of the Home Teaching Committee. He motioned for me to sit by him; and as I did so, he said, "I really don't know if you want to sit here or not."

"Why, Brother Smith?" I asked.

He answered, "A strange coincidence: the last two times that a General Authority has been appointed, the fellow was sitting right next to me when his name was read." I couldn't say a thing, but I sat down. In a few moments, the members of the Twelve were sustained and, of course, my name was read. Hugh Smith looked at me and said simply, "Lightning has struck for the third time!" I suppose that was a "heart stopper" for Brother Hugh Smith.

It's a heart-stopping feeling to look at you today and realize the responsibility which rests with me as your speaker. Your time is so valuable, your talents so many, and your future so bright. I earnestly seek our Heavenly Father's help.

As I have contemplated what I would say to you, I have thought of the many challenges which you face. The future is in your hands; the outcome is up to you. To aid you in facing the challenges which lie ahead, I offer the following advice which, as you follow it, will greatly aid you and will help provide the happiness you seek:

Live within your means;

Stand firm for truth;

Find joy in service.

First, **live within your means.** I would like to mention the excessive debt that some of our people are piling up. This is a day of borrowing; this is a day where credit cards by the bushel are sent out in every mailing. You no doubt receive them. According to recent statistics, the average American has 10 credit cards. It's so easy to buy on time, without reading the small print. A fairly low interest rate may apply for the first 60 days or so, but one generally doesn't realize that after that period, the interest rate increases dramatically. As an example of how much interest one pays at such a rate, if a person owed just $500 in credit card debt, had a rate of 18.5% interest, and paid a minimum payment of $10 per month, it would take 7 years and 10 months to pay the debt in full. In addition to paying the principal of $500, one would have paid $430 in interest for the privilege of borrowing the $500.

Listen to the words of President J. Reuben Clark, who for many years served in the First Presidency, as he spoke on this subject:

"It is a rule of our financial and economic life in all the world that interest is to be paid on borrowed money. May I say something about interest?

"Interest never sleeps nor sickens nor dies; it never goes to the hospital; it works on Sundays and holidays; it never takes a vacation; it never visits nor travels; it takes no pleasure; it is never laid off work nor discharged from employment; it never works on reduced hours. . . . Once in debt, interest is your companion every minute of the day and night; you cannot shun it or slip away from it; you cannot dismiss it; it yields neither to entreaties, demands, or orders; and whenever you get in its way or cross its course or fail to meet its demands, it crushes you."[1]

If you use a credit card, pay the remaining balance promptly. Don't stretch your payments out.

There are some items, such as an affordable home and a few other necessary things, where reasonable debt is acceptable. To be avoided is unwise borrowing for things one really does not absolutely need.

After I graduated from the university, I did a lot of work in advertising, and I know that advertising can sell a product. I'm appalled at the advertising I see for home equity loans. Simply put, *they are second mortgages on homes.* The advertising for such loans is designed to tempt us to borrow in order to have more. Nowhere in the advertising is there any mention that should you fail to make payments, for whatever reason, you could lose your home. Such was common during the 1930s and the 1940s when many people lost their homes and everything they had put into them. My philosophy is that, as much as possible, we should pay as we go. Save for a rainy day. Nearly extinct is the starter home; we rarely see them anymore. Most young people today begin with the large expensive lot, the large expensive home—everything Mother and Dad worked a lifetime to achieve. Consequently, many enter into long-term debt on the basis of two salaries, only to find that changes do come, people get ill, women have children, sickness stalks some families, floods and other situations occur, and no longer can the two-salary mortgage payment be made. Then the family is in chaos.

I urge you to live within your means, whatever your means may be. One cannot continually spend more than he earns and remain solvent. I promise you that you will then be happier than you would be if you were constantly worrying about how to make the next payment on nonessential debt.

My dear young friends, I encourage you to live within your means.

Second, this advice: **Stand firm for truth.** We are surrounded on every side today by that which would drag us down. Said President Gordon B. Hinckley: "We live in a world of so much filth. It is everywhere. It is on the streets. It is on television. It is in books and magazines. . . . It is like a great flood, ugly and dirty and mean, engulfing the world. We have got to stand above it. . . . The way to happiness lies in a return to strong family life and the observance of moral standards, the value of which has been proven through centuries of time."[2]

One of the leading box office stars of today lamented: "The boundaries of permissiveness have been extended to the limit. The last film I did was filthy. I thought it was filthy when I read the script, and I still think it's filthy; but the studio tried it out at a Friday night sneak preview and the audience screamed its approval."

I find Alexander Pope's classic "Essay on Man" most applicable:

> *Vice is a monster of so frightful mien,*
> *As, to be hated, needs but to be seen;*
> *Yet seen too oft, familiar with her face,*
> *We first endure, then pity, then embrace.*[3]

Today we have a rebirth of ancient Sodom and Gomorrah. From seldom read pages in dusty Bibles they come forth as real cities in a real world, depicting a real malady—pernicious permissiveness.

We have the capacity and the responsibility to stand as a bulwark between all we hold dear and the fatal contamination of such sin. An understanding of who we are and what God expects us to become will prompt us to pray—as individuals and as families. Such a return reveals the constant truth, "Wickedness never was happiness."[4]

Always be active in the Church. I will give you a formula which will guarantee to a large extent your success in fulfilling that commitment. It is simple. It consists of just three words:

Pay your tithing. Every bishop could tell you from his personal experience that when the members of the Church pay tithing, honestly, faithfully, they have little difficulty keeping the other commandments of God. I call it a benchmark commandment.

May each of us seek the good life—even life everlasting, with mother, father, brothers, sisters, husband, wife, sons and daughters, together forever.

Remember the Savior's words spoken to the Nephites: "Ye must watch and pray always lest ye enter into temptation; for Satan desireth to have you."[5]

Let us join in the fervent declaration of Joshua: "Choose you this day whom ye will serve; . . . but as for me and my house, we will serve the Lord."[6] Let us shun those things which will drag us down. Let our hearts be pure. Let our lives be clean.

Stand firm for truth.

Third, **Find joy in service.**

I have been thinking of the inquiring lawyer, who came to the Savior and asked the question: "Master, which is the great commandment in the law?" You remember the Savior's response. He said: "Thou shalt love the Lord thy God with all thy heart, and with all thy soul, and with all thy mind. This is the first and great commandment. And the second is like unto it, Thou shalt love thy neighbour as thyself."[7] If we can remember those two great commandments—love of God and love of neighbor—and act accordingly, our time here will have been well spent.

How do we demonstrate to our Heavenly Father that we love Him? When Sister Monson and I were university students, there was a popular song that had words something like these: "It's easy to say I love you, easy to say I'll be true; easy to say these foolish things, but prove it by the things you do." We have a responsibility to prove to our Heavenly Father, by the things we do, that we love Him.

How can we know what our Heavenly Father would have

us do? One way is by praying to know, by asking how we can be instruments in His hands.

Let me share with you an experience very close to my heart of inspiration which came to me, providing an opportunity for service. A longtime friend of mine, a robust athlete, an all-star football player, was stricken with a malady which left him confined to a wheelchair. The doctors said he would never walk again. One day, as usual, in my morning prayers, I petitioned my Heavenly Father to know what He would have me do that day. Later that afternoon, as I was swimming in the pool at the old Deseret Gym, there came to my mind the thought, "Here you swim almost effortlessly, while your friend Stan languishes in his hospital bed, unable to move." I felt the prompting: "Get to the hospital and give him a blessing." Quickly I left the pool, dressed, and hurried to Stan's room at the hospital. His bed was empty. A nurse said he was in his wheelchair at the swimming pool, preparing for therapy. I hurried to the area, and there was Stan, totally despondent, all alone at the edge of the deep portion of the pool, ready to give up on life itself. I told him how I happened to be there. I said: "I didn't just come, Stan. The Lord knew you needed a blessing. He knew that you needed such from one who knows you. He took occasion to impress this upon me while I was swimming with the full use of my body, knowing that you were handicapped, with limited use of your body." We returned to his hospital room where a blessing was provided. The Spirit of the Lord was there.

Day by day, Stan grew stronger. One day, a year or so later, there was a knock at my office door, and in walked my friend who had been told he would never walk again. He handed his cane to his son, who was to be set apart for a mission, and walked over to my desk. What joy! What a moment of thanksgiving! Later he stood in the holy temple witnessing the marriage of his daughter. He stood without a cane. He expressed to me his gratitude for the inspiration which had come to me that day in the swimming pool at the Deseret Gym.

Opportunities to give of ourselves are indeed limitless, but they are also perishable. There are hearts to gladden. There are kind words to say. There are gifts to be given. There are deeds to be done. There are souls to be saved.

May you realize a full measure of happiness and success in your life as you:

Live within your means;

Stand firm for truth; and

Find joy in service.

NOTES

1. J. Reuben Clark, Jr., in Conference Report, April 1938, 102–3.
2. *Teachings of Gordon B. Hinckley* (1997), 709.
3. In *Best-Loved Poems of the LDS People* (1996), 304.
4. Alma 41:10.
5. 3 Nephi 18:18.
6. Joshua 24:15.
7. Matthew 22:36–39.

51

HAPPINESS— THE UNIVERSAL QUEST

ALL OF US DESIRE TO BE HAPPY. The Prophet Joseph Smith captured our true feelings when he declared: "Happiness is the object and design of our existence; and will be the end thereof, if we pursue the path that leads to it; and this path is virtue, uprightness, faithfulness, holiness, and keeping all the commandments of God."[1] Perhaps it would be profitable for us to review these enumerated paths to make certain our footsteps are faithfully and firmly planted upon them, that the promised goal may be our reward.

First, *the path of virtue*. The dictionary proffers the definition of virtue as "conformity to a standard of right: . . . a particular moral excellence," the beneficial qualities of "strength or courage"—even "valor."

Years ago the Church brought help to young men and young women with a program featuring posters and wallet-size cards which contained specific messages of truth and encouragement. The series carried the heading "Be Honest With Yourself!" One message featured was the provocative and penetrating truth "Virtue is its own reward."

"Learn that he who doeth the works of righteousness shall receive his reward, even peace in this world, and eternal life in the world to come."[2]

The expression of one young man is a sermon in itself. When asked when he was happiest, he replied, "I'm happiest when I don't have a guilty conscience."

Second, *the path of uprightness*. For my definition of this path, I turn to the first verse of the first chapter of the book of Job, which reads: "There was a man in the land of Uz, whose name was Job; and that man was perfect and upright, and one that feared God, and eschewed evil."

Dr. Karl Menninger, the brilliant scientist who founded and developed the world-renowned psychiatric center in Topeka, Kansas, stated that the only way our suffering, struggling, anxious society can hope to prevent its moral ills is by recognizing the reality of sin. That's the theme of his famed publication, *Whatever Became of Sin?* It is a plea to mankind to stop and look at what we are doing to ourselves, to each other and to our universe. Dr. Menninger referred to Socrates, who wondered, "How is it that men know what is good, but do what is bad?" Said Dr. Menninger, "I have come to the conclusion that the 'Everyone is doing it' morality which characterizes our public business world is crippling people. We must believe in our personal responsibility to correct our individual transgressions—the white lies, the petty cheating, the apathy, which characterize our passive existence." He further stressed, "If the concept of personal responsibility and answerability for ourselves and for others were to return to common acceptance and man once again would feel guilt for sins and repent and establish a conscience that would act as a deterrent for further sin, then hope would return to the world."[3]

Let me share with you a lesson learned in childhood. Our family has owned a summer cabin at Vivian Park in Provo Canyon for five generations. The months of July and August for me meant hiking, fishing, and swimming daily at the swimming hole, featuring a big rock from which we dived, and maneuvering the swift current which roared by it and formed dangerous whirlpools. Most swimmers would plunge into the icy waters and swim with the current, rapidly passing the big rock, and eventually be carried to the slower waters and the welcome bank of river sand. That is, all but one swimmer. His name was "Beef" Peterson. His swimsuit carried the emblem of "Life Saver," and his physical body reflected great strength. Beef would, like others, swim rapidly down the current through the whirlpools, then suddenly turn and swim back upstream. For a few feet, his mighty strokes carried him forward, but then the swiftness of the current held him steady as he pitted his strength against that of the river. Gradually Beef would tire, drop back, and then swim effortlessly to the bank, exhausted. Swimming against the current became Beef Peterson's trademark.

I'm certain our duty and responsibility is frequently to swim upstream and against the tide of temptation and sin. As we do so, our spiritual strength will increase, and we shall be equal to our God-given responsibilities.

A paradigm of truth is found framed on the wall of a favorite ride at Disneyland in Anaheim, California. One reads it just as he boards the boat to undertake a breathtaking, hair-raising plunge. Uncle Remus is speaking: "You can't run away from trouble. There ain't no place that far."

Third, *the path of faithfulness*. This path connotes allegiance, loyalty, and adherence to promises. As members of The Church of Jesus Christ of Latter-day Saints, sacred covenants are to be revered by us, and faithfulness to them is a requirement for happiness. Yes, I speak of the covenant of baptism, the covenant of the priesthood, and the covenant of marriage as examples.

There is no resting place along the path called faithfulness. The trek is constant, and no lingering is allowed. It must not be expected that the road of life spreads itself in an unobstructed view before the person starting his journey. He must anticipate coming upon forks and turnings in the road. But he cannot hope to reach his desired journey's end if he thinks aimlessly about whether to go east or west. He must make decisions purposefully.

We know where we want to go! Do we have the resolution, even the faithfulness, to get there? President N. Eldon Tanner answered this question in his own mind when he declared: "I would rather walk barefoot from here to the celestial kingdom . . . than to let the things of this world keep me out."[4]

A favorite poem of mine gives to each of us the challenge:

> *Stick to your task till it sticks to you;*
> *Beginners are many, but enders are few.*
> *Honor, power, place, and praise*
> *Will come, in time, to the one who stays.*
>
> *Stick to your task till it sticks to you;*
> *Bend at it, sweat at it, smile at it too;*
> *For out of the bend and the sweat and the smile*
> *Will come life's victories, after awhile.*[5]

Let us remember the advice from Ecclesiastes, or the Preacher, "The race is not to the swift, nor the battle to the strong,"[6] but to those who "endure unto the end."[7] The Apostle Paul further counseled, "They which run in a race run all, but one receiveth the prize. . . . So run, that ye may obtain."[8]

The way is rugged and the course is strenuous. So discovered John Helander from Göteborg, Sweden. John is 26 years of age and is handicapped, in that it is difficult for him to coordinate his motions.

At a youth conference in Kungsbacka, Sweden, John took part in an 800-meter running race. He had no chance to win. Rather, his was the opportunity to be humiliated, mocked, derided, scorned. Perhaps John remembered another who lived long ago and far away. Wasn't He mocked? Wasn't He derided? Wasn't He scorned? But He prevailed. He won His race. Maybe John could win his.

What a race it was! Struggling, surging, pressing, the runners bolted far beyond John. There was wonderment among the spectators. Who is this runner who lags so far behind? The participants on their second lap of this two-lap race passed John while he was but halfway through the first lap. Tension mounted as the runners pressed toward the tape. Who would win? Who would place second? Then came the final burst of speed; the tape was broken. The crowd cheered; the winner was proclaimed.

The race was over—or was it? Who is this contestant who continues to run when the race is ended? He crosses the finish line on but his first lap. Doesn't the foolish lad know he has lost? Ever onward he struggles, the only participant now on the track. This is his race. This must be his victory. No one among the vast throng of spectators leaves. Every eye is on this valiant runner. He makes the final turn and moves toward the finish line. There is awe; there is admiration. Every spectator sees himself running his own race of life. As John approaches the finish line, the audience, as one, rises to its feet. There is a loud applause of acclaim. Stumbling, falling, exhausted but victorious, John Helander breaks the newly tightened tape. Officials are human beings, too. The cheering echoes for miles. And just maybe, if the ear is carefully attuned, that Great Scorekeeper—even the Lord—can be heard to say, "Well done, thou good and faithful servant."

Each of us is a runner in the race of life. Comforting is the fact that there are many runners. Reassuring is the knowledge that our Eternal Scorekeeper is understanding. Challenging is the truth that each must run. But you and I do not run alone. That vast audience of family, friends, and leaders will cheer our courage, will applaud our determination as we rise from our stumblings and pursue our goal. The race of life is not for sprinters running on a level track. The course is marked by pitfalls and checkered with obstacles.

Let us shed any thought of failure. Let us discard any habit that may hinder. Let us seek; let us obtain the prize prepared for all, even exaltation in the celestial kingdom of God.

Fourth, *the path of holiness*.

He who conquered death and atoned for the sins of the world, even Jesus Christ, invited each of us to follow His divine example. "Follow me" became His kind instruction. "Come, learn of me" was His personal invitation to the learning that lasts beyond life and which endures through eternity.

How are we to gain that determination and steadfastness, even the insight, to see clearly the path Jesus would have us walk and not be deterred by the things of the world or the designs of the evil one? In an interview with Albert Speer, Hitler's personal architect and minister for armaments, Herr Speer was asked, "If you knew of Adolph Hitler's evil nature, why did you serve him as his architect?"

Speer replied, "It is difficult to recognize Satan when he has his hand on your shoulder."

President N. Eldon Tanner, when he was president of the Edmonton Alberta Branch of the Church, shared some homespun and practical advice with the many young men and young women who came to Edmonton to attend university. He gave much of himself, and he expected much in return from the youth. He would call students into his office and talk about the purposes of education and the goals of the Church. He would make a promise to the students: "You want very much to pass your courses, don't you? I will promise you something. If you will work hard on your studies during the week, live the principles of the gospel, and attend to your Church duties on Sunday, I will promise you that you will graduate from university. And what is more important, I will promise you that you will be a better and a happier person than if you don't attend Church." Many students bear humble and grateful testimony that President Tanner's promise has been literally and completely fulfilled.

A ring of holiness and expression of parental love is found

in a tender letter which Elder John H. Groberg wrote to his children: "I hope we can all be more grateful for what we have and be willing to share even more with others. There are so many who need so much—especially the truths of the gospel, which when lived bring first light, then love, then hope, then action, and finally fulfillment of our fondest dreams and more."

Several years ago, while attending a priesthood leadership session of the Zurich-Munich Region, I witnessed the application of the very counsel Elder Groberg was directing to his children in the letter he sent to them. Regional Representative Johann Wondra arose and spoke to the audience. He invited Brother Kuno Mueller, who was seated near the front of the building, to stand. Brother Wondra then told the congregation, "Here is the missionary who brought the gospel and all that it means to my wife and me. Without him, where would I be?" He then turned to Brother Mueller as though he were the only one present, and said: "Brother Mueller, I love you. My family and I think of you every day." Both Brother Wondra and Brother Mueller were weeping. In fact, we all had moist eyes that reflected touched hearts and tender souls.

Fifth—this path is comprehensive—***keep all the commandments of God***. "He that hath my commandments, and keepeth them, he it is that loveth me: and he that loveth me shall be loved of my Father, and I will love him, and will manifest myself to him."[9] There is no need for any of us to walk alone. We can look up and reach out for divine help. "No . . . sincere, prayerful effort will go unrequited—that is the very constitution of the philosophy of faith."[10] So taught President Stephen L Richards.

A line from the delightful play *The King and I* gives us encouragement in our quest. The King of Siam lay dying. Anna's son asks her the question, "Was he as good . . . as he could have been?" Anna answers wistfully, "I don't think any man has ever been as good . . . as he could have been—but this one tried." [11]

I return to the Prophet Joseph's words: "Happiness is the

object and design of our existence; and will be the end thereof, if we pursue the path that leads to it; and this path is virtue, uprightness, faithfulness, holiness, and keeping all the commandments of God." Let us walk these clearly defined paths. To help us do so we can follow the shortest sermon in the world. It is found on a common traffic sign. It says, "Keep right."

This advice was found and followed by Joe, who had been asked to get up at six in the morning and drive a crippled child 50 miles to the hospital. He didn't want to do it, but he didn't know how to say no. A woman carried the child out to the car and set him next to the driver's seat, mumbling thanks through her tears. Joe said everything would be all right and drove off quickly. After a mile or so, the child inquired shyly, "You're God, aren't you?"

"I'm afraid not, little fellow," replied Joe.

"I thought you must be God," said the child. "I heard Mother praying next to my bed and asking God to help me get to the hospital so I could get well and play with the other boys. Do you work for God?"

"Sometimes, I guess," said Joe, "but not regularly. I think I'm going to work for him a lot more from now on."

My brothers and sisters, will you? Will I? Will we? I pray humbly, yet earnestly, that we will.

NOTES

1. *Teachings of the Prophet Joseph Smith* (1976), 255–56.
2. Doctrine and Covenants 59:23.
3. See Karl Menninger, *Whatever Became of Sin?* (1973).
4. In Conference Report, October 1966, 98–99.
5. Author unknown, "Stick to Your Task," in *Best-Loved Poems of the LDS People* (1996), 255–56.
6. Ecclesiastes 9:11.
7. 1 Nephi 13:37.
8. 1 Corinthians 9:24.
9. John 14:21.
10. In Conference Report, October 1937, 35, 38.
11. Richard Rodgers and Oscar Hammerstein II, *The King and I* (1951).

52

THREADS IN YOUR TAPESTRY

As I THINK OF THE DIFFERENT characteristics of women and men, I'm reminded of a story I heard not too long ago. A couple's lawn mower was broken and wouldn't run. The wife kept hinting to her husband that he should get it fixed, but somehow the message never sank in. The lawn continued to grow.

Finally she thought of a clever way to make her point. When her husband arrived home from work one day, he found her seated in the tall grass, busily snipping away with a tiny pair of sewing scissors.

He watched silently for a short time and then went into the house. He was gone only a few moments. When he returned, he handed her a toothbrush. "When you finish cutting the grass," he said, "you might as well sweep the sidewalks."

The doctors say he will probably walk again but will always limp!

I've always been fond of this statement by American author and historian, Washington Irving. Said he: "There is one in the world who feels, for him who is sad, a keener pang than he feels for himself; there is one to whom reflected joy is better than that which comes direct; there is one who rejoices in another's honor more than in any which is one's own; . . . there is one who hides another's infirmities more faithfully than one's own; there is one who loses all sense of self in the sentiments of kindness, tenderness, and devotion to another. That one is woman."

You, my sisters, are everything described by Washington Irving. You are sensitive and selfless. You are nurturers; you are compassionate. You genuinely care about others, and you form strong relationships. You love and forgive. With good hearts and willing hands, you make a real difference in the lives of others.

There are those of you who are single—perhaps in school, perhaps working—yet forging a full and rich life, whatever the future may hold. Some of you are busy mothers of growing children; still others are single mothers struggling to raise your children without the help of a husband and father. Some of you have raised your children but have realized that challenges have only multiplied as your children have had children of their own, and their need for your help is ongoing. There are those of you who have aging parents who require the loving care only you can give.

Wherever you are in life, your individual tapestry is woven with threads common to you and to all women, and it is regarding some of these common threads on which I wish to comment today.

First, each one of you is living a life filled with much to do. I plead with you not to let the important things in life pass you by, planning instead for that illusive and nonexistent future day when you'll have time to do all that you want to do. Instead, find joy in the journey—now. Let us not procrastinate those things which matter most.

A few years ago I read the account of a man who, just after the passing of his wife, opened her dresser drawer and found there an item of clothing she had purchased when they visited the Eastern part of the United States nine years earlier. She had not worn it but was saving it for a special occasion. Now, of course, that occasion would never come.

In relating the experience to a friend, the husband said, "Don't save something only for a special occasion. Every day in your life is a special occasion."

That friend later said those words changed her life. They helped her to cease putting off the things most important to her. Said she, "Now I spend more time with my family. I use crystal glasses every day. I'll wear new clothes to go to the supermarket if I feel like it. The words 'someday' and 'one day' are fading from my vocabulary. Now I take the time to call my relatives and closest friends. I've called old friends to make peace over past quarrels. I tell my family members how much I love them. I try not to delay or postpone anything that could bring laughter and joy into our lives. And each morning, I say to myself that this could be a special day. Each day, each hour, each minute, is special."

If you do something that turns out not quite as you had planned, you can almost always put it right, get over it, learn from it. But once you've missed out on something, it's gone. Oh, there will be regrets. There will be the brilliant professor whose class you never took, the relative with whom you never became close, the friend you didn't call, the thanks you didn't express, the dress you didn't buy, the soccer game you missed. Try to keep the list as short as possible.

Let us relish life as we live it, find joy in the journey, and share our love with friends and family. One day, each of us will run out of tomorrows. Let us not put off what is most important.

I turn next to the threads of adversity, which are woven into the tapestry of all our lives.

Nearly 30 years after marrying, a very distraught mother sat in the back of her ward Relief Society room, waiting for Relief Society to begin. She was really discouraged, and as she thought about her problems, the tears began to flow. She realized that her life was far from what she had envisioned as a young bride. This day, in particular, she was concerned about her only daughter, who had gradually stopped attending church. That morning the young woman had announced to her mother that she was going to attend another church with a friend of hers. Never in the mother's wildest dreams had she thought that any of her children would lose their testimonies. She felt that she had, in some way, failed.

"Why is my life so hard?" she wondered, as more tears came.

The room began to fill with other sisters. The woman looked through those tears and realized that each of the women there had her own set of problems. One was facing life in a wheelchair, having endured several painful and unsuccessful surgeries on her ankle. Another had recently lost her husband to leukemia. Another woman's son was in drug rehabilitation once again. And yet another's husband had lost his job just after the couple bought a new home in the ward. As she watched the women enter the room, she realized that there wasn't one of them who hadn't faced adversity of one kind or another— and these were only the problems of which this mother was aware. She could see how faith had helped each one endure her particular challenges. Although her problem did not disappear—and would, in fact, probably be ongoing—the mother resolved that she would attempt to follow the examples she had seen that day, examples of faith and endurance.

As with this woman, some of you may at times have cried out in your suffering, wondering why our Heavenly Father would allow you to go through whatever trials you are facing.

On one occasion, a father accompanied his small daughter to nursery school and watched through a one-way glass window as she and her friends played with the toys which were provided. More than once this father was ready to enter the room, eager to save his daughter from the dangers of choice and discovery. His desire to protect her, however, was tempered by the instinct of a loving father, who knows that scraped knees, tears, and bruised feelings are often necessary parts of growth and development.

We all have treasured memories of certain days in our lives—days when all seemed to go well for us, when much was accomplished or when relationships were pleasant and loving. It's not difficult to be happy on such perfect days. We wish all days could be so memorable for their perfection.

Our mortal life, however, was never meant to be easy or consistently pleasant. Our Heavenly Father, who gives us so much to delight in, also knows that we learn and grow and become refined through hard challenges, heartbreaking sorrows, and difficult choices. Each one of us experiences dark days when our loved ones pass away, painful times when our health is lost, feelings of being forsaken when those we love seem to have abandoned us. These and other trials present us with the real test of our ability to endure.

You may have heard the account of an elderly jeweler who proudly showed his grandson how to polish gemstones by placing them in a tumbler where repeated exposure to abrasive materials revealed each stone's true beauty. He pointed out to the boy that, as with the stones, we can become better, more polished and more beautiful, by those things we suffer, endure, and overcome.

Some clouds in life are so dark that we fail to see their silver lining. Of such difficult circumstances Orson F. Whitney said: "No pain that we suffer, no trial that we experience is wasted. It ministers to our education, to the development of such qualities as patience, faith, fortitude and humility. All that we suffer and all that we endure, especially when we endure it patiently, builds up our characters, purifies our hearts, expands our souls, and makes us more tender and charitable, more worthy to be called the children of God . . . and it is through sorrow and suffering, toil and tribulation, that we gain the education that we come here to acquire and which will make us more like our Father."[1]

No matter how carefully we plan our lives, we cannot avoid all the storms that come our way. Winds of adversity blow around us and bring with them challenges that can strengthen our souls.

The strongest timber grows where the storm beats the hardest. The poet wrote:

> *Good timber does not grow with ease,*
> *The stronger wind, the stronger trees,*
> *The further sky, the greater length,*
> *The more the storm, the more the strength.*
> *By sun and cold, by rain and snow,*
> *In trees and men, good timbers grow.*[2]

Only the Master knows the depths of our trials, our pain, and our suffering. He alone offers us eternal peace in times of adversity.

Finally, woven into the tapestry of your lives are threads of service, of love, of kindness to others. Sometimes, my dear sisters, you feel inadequate and ineffective because you can't do all that you feel you should. Rather than continually dwelling on what still needs to be done, pause occasionally and reflect on all that you do and have done. It is most significant.

The good you have done, the kind words you have spoken, the love you have shown to others, can never be fully measured.

Throughout my life I've been influenced for good by many wonderful women. One who always comes readily to my mind is a woman by the name of Lucy Gertsch who was my Sunday School teacher when I was a young boy in the Sixth-Seventh Ward of the Pioneer Stake. The ward population was rather transient, which resulted in an accelerated rate of turnover with respect to the teachers in the Sunday School. As boys and girls we would just become acquainted with a particular teacher and grow to appreciate him when the Sunday School superintendent would visit the class and introduce a new teacher. Disappointment filled each heart and a breakdown of discipline resulted.

Prospective teachers, hearing of the unsavory reputation of our particular class, would graciously decline to serve or suggest the possibility of teaching a different class where the students were more manageable. We took delight in our newly found status and determined to live up to the fears of the faculty.

One Sunday morning, a lovely young lady accompanied the superintendent into the classroom and was presented to us as a teacher who requested the opportunity to teach us. We learned that she had been a missionary and loved young people. Her name was Lucy Gertsch. She was beautiful, soft-spoken, and interested in us. She asked each class member to introduce himself or herself, and then she asked questions which gave her an understanding and insight into the background of each. She told us of her girlhood in Midway, Utah, and as she described that beautiful valley she made its beauty live within us and we desired to visit the green fields she loved so much.

Those first weeks were not easy. Boys don't become gentlemen overnight. Yet she never raised her voice. Somehow rudeness and boisterousness were incompatible with the beauty of her lessons. She made the scriptures actually live. We became personally acquainted with Samuel, David, Jacob, Nephi, and the Lord Jesus Christ. Our gospel scholarship grew. Our deportment improved. Our love for Lucy Gertsch knew no bounds.

We undertook a project to save nickels and dimes for what was to be a gigantic Christmas party. Sister Gertsch kept a careful record of our progress. As children with typical appetites, we converted in our minds the monetary totals to cakes, cookies, pies, and ice cream. This was to be a glorious event. Never before had any of our teachers even suggested a social event like this was to be.

The summer months faded into autumn. Autumn turned to winter. Our party goal had been achieved. The class had grown. A good spirit prevailed.

None of us will forget that gray Sunday morning when our beloved teacher announced to us that the mother of one of our classmates had passed away. We thought of our own mothers and how much they meant to us. We felt sincere sorrow for Billy Devenport in his great loss.

The lesson this Sunday was from the book of Acts, chapter 20, verse 35: "Remember the words of the Lord Jesus, how he said, It is more blessed to give than to receive." At the conclusion of the presentation of a well-prepared lesson, Lucy Gertsch commented on the economic situation of Billy's family. These were Depression times, and money was scarce. With a twinkle in her eyes, she asked: "How would you like to follow this teaching of our Lord? How would you feel about taking our party fund and, as a class, visiting the Devenports and giving it to them as an expression of our love?" The decision was unanimous. We counted the money carefully and placed the total sum in a large envelope. A beautiful card was inscribed with our names and we were on our way.

This simple act of kindness welded us together as one. Because of Lucy Gertsch, we learned through our own experience that it is indeed more blessed to give than to receive.

Lucy Gertsch knew each of her students. She unfailingly called on those who missed a Sunday or who just didn't come. We knew she cared about us.

Many, many years later, when Lucy was nearing the end of her life, I visited with her. We reminisced concerning those days so long before when she had been our teacher. We spoke of each member of our class and discussed what each one was now doing. Her love and caring spanned a lifetime.

The years have flown. The old chapel is gone, a victim of industrialization. We who laughed, who grew under the direction of that inspired teacher of truth, have never forgotten her inspired service or her love for each one of us.

You, my dear sisters, are filled with the same kind of love and caring which Lucy Gertsch exemplified throughout her life. Your hearts are tender and sensitive to the needs of others. Thank you for the selfless service you give so willingly. Such service provides the golden threads which run through the tapestry of your lives.

NOTES

1. Orson F. Whitney, quoted in Spencer W. Kimball, *Faith Precedes the Miracle* (1972), 98.
2. Douglas Malloch, "Good Timber," in *Best-Loved Poems of the LDS People* (1996), 248–49.

53

THREE GOALS TO GUIDE YOU

I ASSURE YOU THAT I HONOR YOU, the women of the Church, and am well aware, to quote William R. Wallace, that "the hand that rocks the cradle is the hand that rules the world."[1]

As I speak to you, I realize that as a man I am in the minority and must be cautious in my comments. I'm reminded of the man who walked into a bookstore and asked the clerk—a woman—for help: "Have you got a book titled *Man, The Master of Women*?" The clerk looked him straight in the eye and said sarcastically, "Try the fiction section!"

In 1901, President Lorenzo Snow said: "The members of the Relief Society have . . . ministered to those in affliction, they have thrown their arms of love around the fatherless and the widows, and they have kept themselves unspotted from the world. I can testify that there are no purer and more God-fearing women in the world than are to be found within the ranks of the Relief Society."[2]

As in President Snow's time, there are, here and now, visits to be made, greetings to be shared, and hungry souls to be fed.

In this spirit, I have felt to provide each member of the Relief Society throughout the world three goals to meet:

Study diligently;

Pray earnestly;

Serve willingly.

Let us consider each of these goals. First, **study diligently**. The Savior of the world instructed: "Seek ye out of the best books words of wisdom; seek learning, even by study and also by faith."[3] He added: "Search the scriptures; for in them ye think ye have eternal life: and they are they which testify of me."[4]

Study of the scriptures will help our testimonies and the testimonies of our family members. Our children today are growing up surrounded by voices urging them to abandon that which is right and to pursue, instead, the pleasures of the world. Unless they have a firm foundation in the gospel of Jesus Christ, a testimony of the truth, and a determination to live righteously, they are susceptible to such influences. It is our responsibility to fortify and protect them.

To an alarming extent, our children today are being educated by the media, including the Internet. In the United States, it is reported that the average child watches approximately four hours of television daily, much of the programming being filled with violence, alcohol and drug use, and sexual content. Watching movies and playing video games is in addition to the four hours.[5] And the statistics are much the same for other developed countries. The messages portrayed on television, in movies, and in other media are very often in direct opposition to that which we want our children to embrace and hold dear. It is our responsibility not only to teach them to be sound in spirit and doctrine, but also to help them stay that way, regardless of the outside forces they may encounter. This will require much time and effort on our part—and in order to help others, we, ourselves, need the spiritual and moral courage to withstand the evil we see on every side.

461

We live in the time spoken of in Second Nephi, chapter 9: "O the vainness, and the frailties, and the foolishness of men! When they are learned they think they are wise, and they hearken not unto the counsel of God, for they set it aside, supposing they know of themselves, wherefore, their wisdom is foolishness and it profiteth them not. And they shall perish. But to be learned is good if they hearken unto the counsels of God."[6]

Required is the courage to hold fast to our standards despite the derision of the world. Said President J. Reuben Clark, Jr., for many years a member of the First Presidency: "Not unknown are cases where [those] of presumed faith, . . . have felt that, since by affirming their full faith they might call down upon themselves the ridicule of their unbelieving colleagues, they must either modify or explain away their faith, or destructively dilute it, or even pretend to cast it away. Such are hypocrites."[7]

Beyond our study of spiritual matters, secular learning is also essential. Often the future is unknown; therefore, it behooves us to prepare for uncertainties. Statistics reveal that at some time, because of the illness or death of a husband or because of economic necessity, you may find yourself in the role of financial provider. Some of you already occupy that role. I urge you to pursue your education—if you are not already doing so or have not done so—that you might be prepared to provide if circumstances necessitate such.

Your talents will expand as you study and learn. You will be able to better assist your families in their learning, and you will have peace of mind in knowing that you have prepared yourself for the eventualities that you may encounter in life.

I reiterate: Study diligently.

The second goal I wish to mention: **Pray earnestly**. The Lord directed: "Pray always, and I will pour out my Spirit upon you, and great shall be your blessing."[8]

Perhaps there has never been a time when we had greater

need to pray and to teach our family members to pray. Prayer is a defense against temptation. It is through earnest and heartfelt prayer that we can receive the needed blessings and the support required to make our way in this sometimes difficult and challenging journey we call mortality.

We can teach the importance of prayer to our children and grandchildren both by word and by example. I share with you a lesson in teaching by example as described in a mother's letter to me relating to prayer. "Dear President Monson: Sometimes I wonder if I make a difference in my children's lives. Especially as a single mother working two jobs to make ends meet, I sometimes come home to confusion, but I never give up hope."

Her letter continues as she describes how she and her children were watching general conference, where I was speaking about prayer. Her son made the comment, "Mother, you've already taught us that." She asked, "What do you mean?" Her son replied, "Well, you've taught us to pray and showed us how, but the other night I came to your room to ask something and found you on your knees praying to Heavenly Father. If He's important to you, He'll be important to me." The letter concluded, "I guess you never know what kind of influence you'll be until a child observes you doing yourself what you have tried to teach him to do."

Some years ago, just before leaving Salt Lake to attend the annual meetings of Boy Scouts of America in Atlanta, Georgia, I decided to take with me enough copies of the *New Era* so that I might share with Scouting officials this excellent publication. When I arrived at the hotel in Atlanta, I opened the package of magazines. I found that my secretary, for no accountable reason, had given me two extra copies of the June issue, an issue that featured temple marriage. I left the two copies in the hotel room and, as planned, distributed the other copies.

On the final day of meetings, I had no desire to attend the scheduled luncheon but felt compelled to return to my room.

The telephone was ringing as I entered. The caller was a member of the Church who had heard I was in Atlanta. She introduced herself and asked if I could provide a blessing for her ten-year-old daughter. I agreed readily, and she indicated that she and her husband, their daughter and their son would come immediately to my hotel room. As I waited, I prayed for help. The applause of the convention was replaced by the feelings of peace which accompanied prayer.

Then came the knock at the door and the privilege of meeting a choice family. The ten-year-old daughter walked with the aid of crutches. Cancer had required the amputation of her left leg—however, her countenance was radiant, her trust in God unwavering. A blessing was provided. Mother and son knelt by the side of the bed, while the father and I placed our hands on the tiny daughter. We were directed by the Spirit of God. We were humbled by its power.

I felt the tears course down my cheeks and tumble upon my hands as they rested on the head of that beautiful child of God. I spoke of eternal ordinances and family exaltation. The Lord prompted me to urge this family to enter the holy temple of God. At the conclusion of the blessing, I learned that such a temple visit was planned. Questions pertaining to the temple were asked. I heard no heavenly voice, nor did I see a vision. Yet there came clearly into my mind the words, "Refer to the *New Era*." I looked toward the dresser, and there were the two extra copies of the temple issue of the *New Era*. One copy was given to the daughter and the other to her parents. We reviewed them together.

The family said farewell, and once again the room was still. A prayer of gratitude came easily and, once more, the resolve to ever provide a place for prayer.

My dear sisters, do not pray for tasks equal to your abilities, but pray for abilities equal to your tasks. Then the performance of your tasks will be no miracle, but you will be the miracle.

Pray earnestly.

Finally, **serve willingly.** You are a mighty force for good, one of the most powerful in the entire world. Your influence ranges far beyond yourself and your home and touches others all around the globe. You have reached out to your brothers and sisters across streets, across cities, across nations, across continents, across oceans. You personify the Relief Society motto: "Charity never faileth."

You are, of course, surrounded by opportunities for service. No doubt at times you recognize so many such opportunities that you may feel somewhat overwhelmed. Where do you begin? How can you do it all? How do you choose, from all the needs you observe, where and how to serve?

Often small acts of service are all that is required to lift and bless another: a question concerning a person's family; quick words of encouragement; a sincere compliment; a small note of thanks; a brief telephone call. If we are observant and aware, and if we act on the promptings which come to us, we can accomplish much good. Sometimes, of course, more is needed.

I learned recently of loving service given to a mother when her children were very young. Frequently she would be up in the middle of the night tending to the needs of her little ones, as mothers do. Often her friend and neighbor across the street would come over the next day and say, "I saw your lights on in the middle of the night and know you were up with the children. I'm going to take them to my house for a couple of hours while you take a nap." Said this grateful mother, "I was so thankful for her welcome offer, it wasn't until this had happened many times that I realized if she had seen my lights on in the middle of the night, she was up with one of her children as well and needed a nap just as much as I did. She taught me a great lesson, and I've since tried to be as observant as she was in looking for opportunities to serve others."

Countless are the acts of service provided by the vast army

of Relief Society visiting teachers. A few years ago I heard of two of them who aided a grieving widow, Angela, the grand-daughter of a cousin of mine. Angela's husband and a friend of his had gone snowmobiling and had become victims of suffocation through a snowslide. Each of them left a pregnant wife—in Angela's case, their first child, and in the other case, a wife not only expecting a child but also the mother of a toddler. In the funeral held for Angela's husband, the bishop reported that upon hearing of the tragic accident, he had gone immediately to Angela's home. Almost as soon as he arrived, the doorbell sounded. The door was opened, and there stood Angela's two visiting teachers. The bishop said he watched as they so sincerely expressed to Angela their love and compassion. The three women cried together, and it was apparent that these two fine visiting teachers cared deeply about Angela. As perhaps only women can, they gently indicated—without being asked—exactly what help they would be providing. That they would be close by as long as Angela needed them was obvious. The bishop expressed his deep gratitude in knowing they would be a real source of comfort to her in the days ahead.

Such acts of love and compassion are repeated again and again by the wonderful visiting teachers of this Church—not always in such dramatic situations, but just as genuinely, nevertheless.

I extol you who, with loving care and compassionate concern, feed the hungry, clothe the naked, and house the homeless. He who notes the sparrow's fall will not be unmindful of such service. The desire to lift, the willingness to help, and the graciousness to give come from a heart filled with love. **Serve willingly.**

Our beloved prophet, even President Gordon B. Hinckley, said of you, "God planted within women something divine that expresses itself in quiet strength, in refinement, in peace, in goodness, in virtue, in truth, in love."[9]

My dear sisters, may our Heavenly Father bless each of you, married or single, in your homes, in your families, in your very lives—that you may merit the glorious salutation of the Savior of the World: "Well done, thou good and faithful servant."[10]

NOTES

1. William Ross Wallace, *Meditation in America and Other Poems* (1851).
2. *The Teachings of Lorenzo Snow,* chapter 19, from Journal History of The Church of Jesus Christ of Latter-day Saints, Church History Library.
3. Doctrine and Covenants 88:118.
4. John 5:39.
5. ©The American Academy of Pediatrics, published online at www.aap.org/family/tv1.htm.
6. 2 Nephi 9:28–29.
7. *The Charted Course of the Church in Education,* given at the Brigham Young University Summer School in Aspen Grove, Utah, August 8, 1938.
8. Doctrine and Covenants 19:38.
9. *Teachings of Gordon B. Hinckley* (1997), 387.
10. Matthew 25:21.

54

Joseph Smith, the Prophet

More than twenty-three hundred years before the birth of the Prophet Joseph Smith, his mission was foretold. Lehi, quoting from the writings of Joseph who was sold into Egypt, declared, "A choice seer will I raise up out of the fruit of thy loins; and . . . he shall do a work for the fruit of thy loins, his brethren, which shall be of great worth unto them, even to the bringing of them to the knowledge of the covenants which I have made with thy fathers. . . . And his name shall be called after me; and it shall be after the name of his father."[1]

In 1933 one author penned this tribute to Joseph Smith: "Here is a man who was born in the stark hills of Vermont; who was reared in the backwoods of New York; who never looked inside a college or high school; who lived in six states, no one of which would own him during his lifetime. [He] spent months in the vile prisons of the period" and "even when he had his freedom, was hounded like a fugitive."

He "was covered once with a coat of tar and feathers and left for dead; [he] was driven by irate neighbors from New York to Ohio, from Ohio to Missouri, and from Missouri to Illinois.

. . . At the . . . age of thirty eight [he] was shot to death by a mob with painted faces."[2]

Through Joseph Smith, the gospel—which had been lost during centuries of apostasy—was restored, the priesthood and its keys were received, the doctrines of salvation were revealed, the gospel and temple ordinances—along with the sealing power—were returned and, in 1830, the Church of Jesus Christ was reestablished on the earth.

Though reviled and persecuted, the Prophet Joseph never wavered in his testimony of Jesus Christ. His peers watched him lead with dignity and grace, endure hardships, and time and again rise to new challenges until his divine mission was completed. Today that heritage he established still shines for all the world to see. The teachings he translated and his legacy of love for his fellowman continue in the millions of hearts touched by the message he declared so long ago.

Few in this dispensation have paid so dearly for an irrevocable testimony of Jesus Christ as did the Prophet Joseph Smith. On June 18, 1844, he gave what was to be his last sermon. He very likely knew that he would not again address his people. His concluding remarks were these: "'God has tried you. You are a good people; . . . I love you with all my heart. Greater love hath no man than that he should lay down his life for his friends. You have stood by me in the hour of trouble, and I am willing to sacrifice my life for your preservation. May the Lord God of Israel bless you forever and ever.' His words sank deep into the hearts of the people. It was the last time, in the flesh, that they were to listen to . . . his voice, or to feel . . . his inspiration."[3]

Ultimately, the Prophet Joseph was slain by evil men who assumed the church would collapse after his death. George Q. Cannon, who served as a member of the Quorum of the Twelve Apostles and as a counselor to several Church presidents, wrote: "The enemies of truth were sure that they had now destroyed the work. And yet it lives, greater and stronger after the lapse of years. It is indestructible, for it is the work of God. And knowing that it is the eternal work of God, we know that Joseph Smith, who established it, was a Prophet holy and pure."[4]

The testimony of the Prophet Joseph continues to change lives. Many years ago I served as the president of the Canadian Mission. In Ontario, Canada, two of our missionaries were proselyting door-to-door on a cold, snowy afternoon. They had not had any measure of success. One elder was experienced and one was new.

The two called at the home of Mr. Elmer Pollard, and he, feeling sympathy for the almost frozen missionaries, invited them in. They presented their message and asked if he would join in prayer. He agreed, on the provision that he could offer the prayer.

The prayer he offered astonished the missionaries. He said, "Heavenly Father, bless these two unfortunate, misguided missionaries, that they may return to their homes and not waste their time telling the people of Canada about a message which is so fantastic and about which they know so little."

As they arose from their knees, Mr. Pollard asked the missionaries never to return to his home. As they left, he said mockingly to them, "You can't tell me you really believe that Joseph Smith was a prophet of God, anyway!" and he slammed the door.

The missionaries had walked but a short distance when the junior companion said, "Elder, we didn't answer Mr. Pollard."

The senior companion responded, "We've been rejected. Let's move on!"

The young missionary persisted, however, and the two returned to Mr. Pollard's door. Mr. Pollard answered the knock and angrily said, "I thought I told you young men never to return!"

The junior companion then said, with all the courage he could muster, "Mr. Pollard, when we left your door, you said that we didn't really believe Joseph Smith was a prophet of God. I want to testify to you, Mr. Pollard, that I *know* Joseph Smith was a prophet of God; that by inspiration he translated the sacred record known as the Book of Mormon; that he did see God the Father and Jesus the Son." The missionaries then departed the doorstep.

I heard this same Mr. Pollard in a testimony meeting state the experiences of that memorable day. He said, "That evening, sleep would not come. I tossed and turned. Over and over in my mind I heard the words, 'Joseph Smith was a prophet of God. I know it . . . I know it . . . I know it.' I could scarcely wait for morning to come. I telephoned the missionaries, using their number which was printed on the small card containing the Articles of Faith. They returned; and this time my wife, my family and I joined in the discussion as earnest seekers of truth. As a result, we have all embraced the gospel of Jesus Christ. We shall ever be grateful to the testimony of truth brought to us by those two courageous, humble missionaries."

The gospel, restored by our beloved Prophet Joseph, blesses our lives. I love the declaration of Elder Stephen L Richards, spoken in general conference in October 1936: "If any man has received in his heart the witness of the divine truth embraced in the contributions of the Prophet Joseph, I charge him to be true—true to his testimony, true to the Prophet, the founder, true to the cause and its duly commissioned leaders, true to the covenants he has made in holy places, and true to the brotherhood of man in the service that he renders. If any man has not received this witness, I appeal for his thoughtful, prayerful, sympathetic consideration. I offer to him, out of the experiences of my life, a humble but certain assurance that if he will receive and apply the teachings of Joseph Smith he will be made happy. Doubt and uncertainty will leave him. Glorious purpose will come into [his] life. Family ties will be sweeter.

Friendships will be dearer. Service will be nobler, and the peace of Christ will be his portion."[5]

We do not worship the Prophet Joseph; however, he left behind a legacy that enables millions of followers today on every continent to proclaim him as a prophet of God. May we, each of us, strive to continue the Prophet Joseph's vision for this work and to magnify his legacy through our works and testimonies to others, that they may know him as we do and that they may experience the peace and joy of the gospel he restored.

NOTES

1. 2 Nephi 3:7, 15.
2. John Henry Evans, *Joseph Smith: An American Prophet* (1933), foreword.
3. Taken from the Historical Record, edited and published by Andrew Jenson (1889), 555.
4. George Q. Cannon, *Life of Joseph Smith the Prophet* (1999), 527.
5. In Conference Report, October 1936, 33.

55

THEY SHOWED THE WAY

T HE YEAR 1997 COMMEMORATED the 150th anniversary since the pioneers, under the inspired leadership of Brigham Young, entered the valley of the great Salt Lake and proclaimed "This is the right place. Drive on."[1] Much has been said concerning that epochal event, prompting me to make a few remarks concerning "other pioneers" who preceded that trek. In doing so, I pause and ponder the dictionary definition of the word *pioneer:* "One who goes before, showing others the way to follow."[2]

Let us turn back the clock of time and journey to other places, that we might review several who I feel meet the high standard of the word *pioneer*.

Such a one was Moses. Raised in Pharaoh's court and learned in all the wisdom of the Egyptians, he became mighty in words and deeds. One cannot separate Moses, the great lawgiver, from the tablets of stone provided him by God and on which were written the Ten Commandments. They were binding then—they are binding now.

Moses endured constant frustration as some of his trusted followers returned to their previous ways. Though he was disappointed in their actions, yet he loved them and led them, even the children of Israel, from their Egyptian bondage. Certainly Moses qualifies as a pioneer.

Another who qualifies is Ruth, who forsook her people, her kindred, and her country in order to accompany her mother-in-law Naomi—worshiping Jehovah in His land and adopting the ways of His people. How very important was Ruth's obedience to Naomi and the resulting marriage to Boaz by which Ruth—the foreigner and a Moabite convert—became a great-grandmother of David and therefore an ancestress of Jesus Christ. The book of the Holy Bible that bears her name contains language poetic in style, reflective of her spirit of determination and courage. "And Ruth said, Intreat me not to leave thee, or to return from following after thee: for whither thou goest, I will go; and where thou lodgest, I will lodge: thy people shall be my people, and thy God my God: Where thou diest, will I die, and there will I be buried: the Lord do so to me, and more also, if ought but death part thee and me."[3]

Yes, Ruth, precious Ruth, was a pioneer.

Other faithful women also qualify, such as Mary Magdalene, Esther, Elisabeth, and Mary, the mother of Jesus. Let us not overlook Abraham, Isaac, and Jacob, nor fail to include Isaiah, Jeremiah, Ezekiel, and some from a later period.

We remember John the Baptist. His clothing was simple, his life spartan, his message brief: faith, repentance, baptism by immersion, and the bestowal of the Holy Ghost by an authority greater than that possessed by himself. He declared: "I am not the Christ, but . . . I am sent before him."[4] "I indeed baptize you with water; but one mightier than I cometh . . . : he shall baptize you with the Holy Ghost and with fire."[5]

The river Jordan marked the historic meeting place when Jesus came down from Galilee to be baptized of John. At first John pleaded with the Master: "I have need to be baptized of thee, and comest thou to me?"[6] Came the response: "It becometh us to fulfil all righteousness. . . . And Jesus, when he was baptized, went up straightway out of the water: and, lo, the heavens were opened unto him, and he saw the Spirit of God descending like a dove, and lighting upon him: And lo a voice from heaven, saying, This is my beloved Son, in whom I am well pleased."[7]

John freely declared and taught, "Behold the Lamb of God, which taketh away the sin of the world."[8]

Of John the Lord declared, "Among them that are born of women there hath not risen a greater than John the Baptist."[9] Like so many other pioneers through the annals of history, John wore the martyr's crown.

Many who were pioneers in spirit and action were called by Jesus to be his Apostles. Much could be told of each.

Peter was among the first of Jesus' Apostles. Peter the fisherman, in response to a divine call, laid aside his nets and hearkened to the Master's declaration: "Follow me, and I will make you [a fisher] of men."[10] I never think of Peter without admiring his testimony of the Lord: "Thou art the Christ, the Son of the living God."[11]

John the Beloved is the only one of the Twelve recorded as being at the crucifixion of Christ. From the cruel cross Jesus uttered the magnificent charge to John, referring to his mother, Mary: "Behold thy mother,"[12] and to Mary, "Behold thy son."[13]

The Apostles went before, showing others the way to follow. They were pioneers.

History records, however, that most men did not come unto Christ, nor did they follow the way He taught. Crucified was the Lord, slain were most of the Apostles, rejected was the truth. The bright sunlight of enlightenment slipped away, and the lengthening shadows of a black night enshrouded the earth.

Generations before, Isaiah had prophesied: "Darkness shall cover the earth, and gross darkness the people."[14] Amos had foretold of a famine in the land: "Not a famine of bread, nor a thirst for water, but of hearing the words of the Lord."[15] The dark ages of history seemed never to end. Would no heavenly messengers make their appearance?

In due time honest men with yearning hearts, at the peril of their very lives, attempted to establish points of reference, that they might find the true way. The day of the reformation was dawning, but the path ahead was difficult. Persecutions would be severe, personal sacrifice overwhelming, and the cost beyond calculation. The reformers were pioneers, blazing wilderness trails in a desperate search for those lost points of reference which, they felt, when found would lead mankind back to the truth Jesus taught.

John Wycliffe, Martin Luther, Jan Hus, Zwingli, Knox, Calvin, and Tyndale all pioneered the period of the reformation. Significant was the declaration of Tyndale to his critics: "I will cause a boy that driveth the plough shall know more of the scripture than thou dost."[16]

Such were the teachings and lives of the great reformers. Their deeds were heroic, their contributions many, their sacrifices great—but they did not restore the gospel of Jesus Christ.

Of the reformers one could ask, "Was their sacrifice in vain? Was their struggle futile?" I answer with a reasoned "No." The Holy Bible was now within the grasp of the people. Each person could better find his or her way. Oh, if only all could read and all could understand! But some could read, and others could hear, and all had access to God through prayer.

The long-awaited day of restoration did indeed come. But let us review that significant event in the history of the world by recalling the testimony of the plowboy who became a prophet, the witness who was there—even Joseph Smith.

Describing his experience, Joseph said: "I was one day reading the Epistle of James, first chapter and fifth verse, . . . *If any of you lack wisdom, let him ask of God, that giveth to all men liberally, and upbraideth not; and it shall be given him.*"[17]

"At length I came to the conclusion that I must either

remain in darkness and confusion, or else I must do as James directs, that is, ask of God. . . . I retired to the woods to make the attempt. It was on the morning of a beautiful, clear day, early in the spring of eighteen hundred and twenty. . . .

"I kneeled down and began to offer up the desires of my heart to God. . . . I saw a pillar of light exactly over my head, above the brightness of the sun, which descended gradually until it fell upon me. . . . When the light rested upon me I saw two Personages, whose brightness and glory defy all description, standing above me in the air. One of them spake unto me, calling me by name and said, pointing to the other—*This is My Beloved Son, Hear Him!*"[18]

The Father and the Son, Jesus Christ, had appeared to Joseph Smith. The morning of the dispensation of the fulness of times had come, dispelling the darkness of the long generations of spiritual night.

Volumes have been written concerning the life and accomplishments of Joseph Smith, but for our purposes here today perhaps a highlight or two will suffice: He was visited by the angel Moroni. He translated, from the precious plates to which he was directed, the Book of Mormon, with its new witness of Christ to all the world. He was the instrument in the hands of the Lord through whom came mighty revelations pertaining to the establishment of The Church of Jesus Christ of Latter-day Saints. In the course of his ministry he was visited by John the Baptist, Moses, Elijah, Peter, James, and John, that the Restoration of all things might be accomplished. He endured persecution; he suffered grievously, as did his followers. He trusted in God. He was true to his prophetic calling. He commenced a marvelous missionary effort to the entire world which today brings light and truth to the souls of mankind. At length, Joseph Smith died the martyr's death, as did his brother Hyrum.

Joseph Smith was a pioneer indeed.

Turning the pages of scriptural history from beginning to

end, we learn of the ultimate pioneer—even Jesus Christ. His birth was foretold by the prophets of old; his entry upon the stage of life was announced by an angel. His life and His ministry have transformed the world.

With the birth of the babe in Bethlehem, there emerged a great endowment, a power stronger than weapons, a wealth more lasting than the coins of Caesar. This child was to be the King of kings and Lord of lords, the Promised Messiah, even Jesus Christ, the Son of God. Born in a stable, cradled in a manger, He came forth from heaven to live on earth as mortal man and to establish the kingdom of God. During His earthly ministry, He taught men the higher law. His glorious gospel reshaped the thinking of the world. He blessed the sick. He caused the lame to walk, the blind to see, the deaf to hear. He even raised the dead to life.

One sentence from the Book of Acts speaks volumes: Jesus "went about doing good, . . . for God was with him."[19]

He taught us to pray. "Our Father which art in heaven, Hallowed be thy name. Thy kingdom come. Thy will be done in earth, as it is in heaven."[20]

In the garden known as Gethsemane, where His suffering was so great that blood came from His pores, He pleaded as He prayed: "Father, if thou be willing, remove this cup from me: nevertheless not my will, but thine, be done."[21]

He taught us to serve: "Inasmuch as ye have done it unto one of the least of these my brethren, ye have done it unto me."[22]

He taught us to forgive: "I, the Lord, will forgive whom I will forgive, but of you it is required to forgive all men."[23]

He taught us to love: "Thou shalt love the Lord thy God with all thy heart, and with all thy soul, and with all thy mind. This is the first and great commandment. And the second is like unto it, Thou shalt love thy neighbour as thyself."[24] Like the true pioneer He was, He invited: "Come, follow me."[25]

Let us turn to Capernaum. There Jairus, a ruler of the

synagogue, came to the Master saying, "My little daughter lieth at the point of death: I pray thee, come and lay thy hands on her, that she may be healed; and she shall live."[26] Then came the news from the ruler's house, "Thy daughter is dead."[27] Christ responded: "Be not afraid, only believe."[28] He came to the house, passed by the mourners, and said to them, "Why make ye this ado, and weep? the damsel is not dead, but sleepeth. And they laughed him to scorn,"[29] knowing that she was dead. "He . . . put them all out. . . . And he took [her] by the hand, and said unto her. . . . Damsel, I say unto thee, arise. . . . And they were astonished."[30]

It is emotionally draining for me to recount the events leading up to the crucifixion of the Master. I cringe when I read the words of Pilate responding to cries of the throng, "Crucify him. . . . Crucify him."[31] Pilate "took water, and washed his hands before the multitude, saying, I am innocent of the blood of this just person; see ye to it."[32] Jesus was mocked. He was spit upon, and a crown of thorns was placed upon his head. He was given vinegar to drink. They crucified Him.

His body was placed in a borrowed tomb, but no tomb could hold the body of the Lord. On the morning of the third day came the welcome message to Mary Magdalene, to Mary the mother of James, and to other women who were with them as they came to the tomb, saw the large entrance stone rolled away and noted the tomb was empty. Two angels said to the weeping women, "Why seek ye the living among the dead? He is not here, but is risen."[33] Yes, the Lord had indeed risen. He appeared to Mary; He was seen by Cephas or Peter, then by His brethren of the Twelve. He was seen by Joseph Smith, who declared: "This is the testimony, last of all, which we give of him: That He lives! For we saw him, even on the right hand of God."[34]

Our Mediator, our Redeemer, our Brother, our Advocate with the Father, died for our sins and the sins of all mankind. The Atonement of Jesus Christ is the foreordained but voluntary act of the Only Begotten Son of God. He offered His life as a redeeming ransom for us all.

His mission, His ministry among men, His teachings of truth, His acts of mercy, His unwavering love for us prompts our gratitude and warms our hearts. Jesus Christ, Savior of the world—even the Son of God—was and is the ultimate Pioneer, for He has gone before, showing all others the way to follow. May we ever follow Him.

NOTES

1. As quoted by Wilford Woodruff in *The Utah Pioneers* (1880), 23.
2. Oxford English Dictionary, s. v. "pioneer."
3. Ruth 1:16–17.
4. John 3:28.
5. Luke 3:16.
6. Matthew 3:14.
7. Matthew 3:15–17.
8. John 1:29.
9. Matthew 11:11.
10. Matthew 4:19.
11. Matthew 16:16.
12. John 19:27.
13. John 19:26.
14. Isaiah 60:2.
15. Amos 8:11.
16. See Roger Hillas, "The History of the Book," *Washington Post*, April 10, 1996.
17. Joseph Smith–History 1:11; emphasis in original.
18. Joseph Smith–History 1:13–17; emphasis in original.
19. Acts 10:38.
20. Matthew 6:9–10.
21. Luke 22:42.
22. Matthew 25:40.
23. Doctrine and Covenants 64:10.
24. Matthew 22:37–39.
25. Luke 18:22.
26. Mark 5:23.
27. Mark 5:35.
28. Mark 5:36.
29. Mark 5:39–40.
30. Mark 5:40–42.
31. Mark 15:13–14.
32. Matthew 27:24.
33. Luke 24:5–6.
34. Doctrine and Covenants 76:22–23.

56

CHARITY NEVER FAILETH

A YOUNG COUPLE, LISA AND JOHN, moved into a new neighborhood. One morning while they were eating breakfast, Lisa looked out the window and watched her next-door neighbor hanging out her wash.

"That laundry's not clean!" Lisa exclaimed. "Our neighbor doesn't know how to get clothes clean!"

John looked on but remained silent.

Every time her neighbor would hang her wash to dry, Lisa would make the same comments.

A few weeks later, Lisa was surprised to glance out her window and see a nice, clean wash hanging in her neighbor's yard. She said to her husband, "Look, John—she's finally learned how to wash correctly! I wonder how she did it?"

John replied, "Well, dear, I have the answer for you. You'll be interested to know that I got up early this morning and washed our windows!"

I'd like to share with you a few thoughts concerning how we view each other. Are we looking through a window which needs cleaning? Are we making judgments when we don't have all the facts? What do we see when we look at others? What judgments do we make about them?

Said the Savior: "Judge not."[1] He continued, "Why beholdest thou the mote that is in thy brother's eye, but considerest not the beam that is in thine own eye?"[2] Or, to paraphrase, why beholdest thou what you think is dirty laundry at your neighbor's house but considerest not the soiled window in your own house?

None of us is perfect. I know of no one who would profess to be so. And yet, for some reason, despite our own imperfections, we have a tendency to point out those of others. We make judgments concerning their actions or inactions.

There is really no way we can know the heart, the intentions, or the circumstances of someone who might say or do something we find reason to criticize. Thus, the commandment: "Judge not."

When I was called to serve in the Quorum of the Twelve Apostles, I had been serving on one of the general priesthood committees of the Church and so, before my name was presented, I sat with my fellow members of that priesthood committee, as was expected of me. My wife, however, had no idea where to go and no one with whom she could sit and, in fact, was unable to find a seat anywhere in the Tabernacle. A dear friend of ours, who was a member of one of the general auxiliary boards and who was sitting in the area designated for the board members, asked Sister Monson to sit with her. This woman knew nothing of my call—which would be announced shortly—but she spotted Sister Monson, recognized her consternation, and graciously offered her a seat. My dear wife was relieved and grateful for this kind gesture. Sitting down, however, she heard loud whispering behind her as one of the board members expressed her annoyance to those around her that one of her fellow board members would have the audacity to invite an "outsider" to sit in this area reserved only for them.

There was no excuse for her unkind behavior, regardless of *who* might have been invited to sit there. However, I can only imagine how that woman felt when she learned that the "intruder" was the wife of the newest Apostle.

Not only are we inclined to judge the actions and words of others, but many of us judge appearances—clothing, hairstyles, size; the list could go on and on.

A classic account of judging by appearance was printed in a national magazine many years ago. It is a true account—one which you may have heard but which bears repeating.

A woman by the name of Mary Bartels had a home directly across the street from the entrance to a hospital clinic. Her family lived on the main floor and rented the upstairs rooms to outpatients at the clinic.

One evening a truly awful-looking old man came to the door asking if there were room for him to stay the night. He was stooped and shriveled, and his face was lopsided from swelling—red and raw. He said he'd been hunting for a room since noon but with no success. "I guess it's my face," he said. "I know it looks terrible, but my doctor says it could possibly improve after more treatments." He indicated he would be happy to sleep in the rocking chair on the porch. As she talked with him, Mary realized this little old man had an oversized heart crowded into that tiny body. Although her rooms were filled, she told him to wait in the chair and she would find him a place to sleep.

At bedtime Mary's husband set up a camp cot for the man. When she checked in the morning, the bed linens were neatly folded and he was out on the porch. He refused breakfast, but just before he left for his bus, he asked if he could return the next time he had a treatment. "I won't put you out a bit," he promised. "I can sleep fine in a chair." Mary assured him he was welcome to come again.

In the several years he went for treatments and stayed in Mary's home, the old man, who was a fisherman by trade, always had gifts of seafood or vegetables from his garden. Other times he sent packages in the mail.

When Mary received these thoughtful gifts, she often thought of a comment her next-door neighbor made after the disfigured, stooped old man had left Mary's home that first morning. "Did you keep that awful-looking man last night? I turned him away. You can lose customers by putting up such people."

Mary knew that maybe they had lost customers once or twice, but she thought, *Oh, if only they could have known him, perhaps their illnesses would have been easier to bear.*

After the man passed away, Mary was visiting with a friend who had a greenhouse. As she looked at her friend's flowers, she noticed a beautiful golden chrysanthemum but was puzzled that it was growing in a dented, old, rusty bucket. Her friend explained, "I ran short of pots, and knowing how beautiful this one would be, I thought it wouldn't mind starting in this old pail. It's just for a little while, until I can put it out in the garden."

Mary smiled as she imagined just such a scene in heaven. "Here's an especially beautiful one," God might have said when he came to the soul of the little old man. "He won't mind starting in this small, misshapen body." But that was long ago, and in God's garden how tall this lovely soul must stand![3]

Appearances can be so deceiving, such a poor measure of a person. Admonished the Savior, "Judge not according to the appearance."[4]

A member of a women's organization once complained when a certain woman was selected to represent the organization. She had never met the woman, but she had seen a photograph of her and didn't like what she saw, considering her to be overweight. She commented, "Of the thousands of women in this organization, surely a better representative could have been chosen."

True, the woman who was chosen was not "model slim." But those who knew her and knew her qualities saw in her far more than was reflected in the photograph. The photograph *did* show that she had a friendly smile and a look of confidence. What the photograph *didn't* show was that she was a loyal and compassionate friend, a woman of intelligence who loved the Lord and who loved and served His children. It didn't show that she volunteered in the community and was a considerate and concerned neighbor. In short, the photograph did not reflect who she really was.

I ask: If attitudes, deeds, and spiritual inclinations were reflected in physical features, would the countenance of the woman who complained be as lovely as that of the woman she criticized?

My dear sisters, each of you is unique. You are different from each other in many ways. There are those of you who are married. Some of you stay at home with your children, while others of you work outside your homes. Some of you are empty-nesters. There are those of you who are married but do not have children. There are those who are divorced, those who are widowed. Many of you are single women. Some of you have college degrees; some of you do not. There are those who can afford the latest fashions and those who are lucky to have one appropriate Sunday outfit. Such differences are almost endless. Do these differences tempt us to judge one another?

Mother Teresa, a Catholic nun who worked among the poor in India most of her life, spoke this profound truth: "If you judge people, you have no time to love them." The Savior has admonished, "This is my commandment, That ye love one another, as I have loved you."[5] I ask: Can we love one another, as the Savior has commanded, if we judge each other? And I answer—with Mother Teresa—"No; we cannot."

The Apostle James taught, "If any . . . among you seem to

be religious, and bridleth not his tongue, but deceiveth his own heart, this man's [or woman's] religion is vain."[6]

I have always loved your Relief Society motto, *Charity never faileth*.[7] What *is* charity? The prophet Mormon teaches us that "charity is the pure love of Christ."[8] In his farewell message to the Lamanites, Moroni declared, "Except ye have charity ye can in nowise be saved in the kingdom of God."[9]

I consider charity—or the "pure love of Christ"—to be the opposite of criticism and judging. In speaking of charity, I do not at this moment have in mind the relief of the suffering through the giving of our substance. That, of course, is necessary and proper. However, I have in mind the charity that manifests itself when we are tolerant of others and lenient toward their actions; the kind of charity that forgives; the kind of charity that is patient.

I have in mind the charity that impels us to be sympathetic, compassionate, and merciful, not only in times of sickness and affliction and distress, but also in times of weakness or error on the part of others.

There is a serious need for the charity that gives attention to those who are unnoticed, hope to those who are discouraged, aid to those who are afflicted. True charity is love in action. The need for charity is everywhere.

Needed is the charity which refuses to find satisfaction in hearing or in repeating the reports of misfortunes that come to others, unless by so doing the unfortunate one may be benefited. The American educator and politician Horace Mann once said, "To pity distress is but human; to relieve it is Godlike."

Charity is having patience with someone who has let us down; it is resisting the impulse to become offended easily. It is accepting weaknesses and shortcomings. It is accepting people as they truly are. It is looking beyond physical appearances to attributes that will not dim through time. It is resisting the impulse to categorize others.

Charity, that pure love of Christ, is manifest when a group of young women from a singles ward travel hundreds of miles to attend the funeral services for the mother of one of their Relief Society sisters. Charity is shown when devoted visiting teachers return month after month, year after year to the same uninterested, somewhat critical sister. It is evident when an elderly widow is remembered and taken to ward functions and to Relief Society activities. It is felt when the sister sitting alone in Relief Society receives the invitation, "Come—sit by us."

In a hundred small ways, all of you wear the mantle of charity. Life is perfect for none of us. Rather than being judgmental and critical of each other, may we have the pure love of Christ for our fellow travelers in this journey through life. May we recognize that each one is doing her best to deal with the challenges which come her way, and may we strive to do *our* best to help out.

Charity has been defined as "the highest, noblest, strongest kind of love";[10] the "pure love of Christ . . . ; and whoso is found possessed of it at the last day, it shall be well with [her]."[11]

"Charity never faileth."[12] May this long-enduring Relief Society motto, this timeless truth, guide you in everything you do. May it permeate your very souls and find expression in all your thoughts and actions.

NOTES
1. Matthew 7:1.
2. Matthew 7:3.
3. Adapted from *Guideposts,* June 1965, 24.
4. John 7:24.
5. John 15:12.
6. James 1:26.
7. 1 Corinthians 13:8.
8. Moroni 7:47.
9. Moroni 10:21.
10. Bible Dictionary, s.v. "Charity," 632.
11. Moroni 7:47.
12. 1 Corinthians 13:8.

57

BE A LIGHT TO THE WORLD

As I consider the vast membership of the Church, I'm reminded that each of you is one of a kind. Each has had experiences unique to you, and you alone. We come from varied backgrounds. And yet there is much that we have in common one with another. We know where we came from, why we are here, and where we will go when we leave this life. We know that we are children of our Heavenly Father and that He loves us. We know we want to return to Him after we leave this earthly existence. We know that what we do—and don't do—here in mortality is of utmost importance. We also know that, should we fall short, our Savior has provided us with the precious gift of the Atonement and that, if we change our lives and our hearts and take advantage of the power of the Atonement, our sins and shortcomings will be forgiven and forgotten.

We have in common the gospel of Jesus Christ. And we know it is our responsibility to share the truths of the gospel with others. One of the chief ways in which we can share the gospel is to be a righteous example. The Apostle Paul wrote that the followers of Christ should be "as lights in the world."[1]

This is what I would hope for each of us—that we might be a light to the world.

What is light? Webster's dictionary lists no fewer than 15 definitions for the noun *light*. I prefer the simple, "Something that illuminates." Just as turning on a light switch in a dark room will bathe the room in light, so providing an example of righteousness—and therefore being a light—can help to illuminate an increasingly dark world.

Each of us came to earth having been given the light of Christ. Said President Harold B. Lee: "Every soul who walks the earth, wherever he lives, in whatever nation he may have been born, no matter whether he be in riches or in poverty, had at birth an endowment of that first light which is called the Light of Christ, the Spirit of Truth, or the Spirit of God—that universal light of intelligence with which every soul is blessed. Moroni spoke of that [light, that] Spirit when he said:'For behold, the Spirit of Christ is given to every man, that he may know good from evil; wherefore, I show unto you the way to judge; for every thing which inviteth to do good, and to persuade to believe in Christ, is sent forth by the power and gift of Christ; wherefore ye may know with a perfect knowledge it is of God.'"[2]

Unfortunately, for many, that light with which all were endowed at birth has dimmed—in some cases almost to the point of being extinguished—as outside influences have come to bear and the sometimes harsh realities of life have been experienced. Ours is the responsibility to keep our lights aflame and burning brightly, that they might shine for others to see and follow.

With the decline of religion in our society, many people have come to feel that they are sufficient unto themselves and have no need of a higher power. A loss of religious faith implies a loss of faith in anyone greater than oneself.

In Second Nephi we read these words, so pertinent today: "O the vainness, and the frailties, and the foolishness of men!

When they are learned they think they are wise, and they hearken not unto the counsel of God, for they set it aside, supposing they know of themselves, wherefore, their wisdom is foolishness and it profiteth them not. And they shall perish."[3]

It can at times be easy to fall into the erroneous thinking that we ourselves are capable of handling anything that comes our way, that we have all the answers, and that there is no need for assistance from a higher power. When we realize, as French philosopher and priest Pierre Teilhard de Chardin put it, that "We are not human beings having a spiritual experience; we are spiritual beings having a human experience," we come to understand where our main emphasis should be and on Whom we are reliant.

In order for us to be examples of the believers, we ourselves must believe. Our testimonies are no doubt of varying degrees. It is up to each of us to develop the faith necessary to survive spiritually and to project a light for others to see. Amidst the confusion of our age, the conflicts of conscience and the turmoil of daily living, an abiding faith becomes an anchor to our lives. Among the most effective ways to gain and keep the faith we need would be to read and study the scriptures and to pray frequently and consistently.

Brothers and sisters, have you read the Book of Mormon? Have you put to the test the promise found in Moroni chapter 10, verse 4, asking your Heavenly Father with a sincere heart, with real intent and having faith in Christ whether or not that which is found in that book is truth?

May I share with you the experience of Brother Clayton M. Christensen as he sought to know for himself. Brother Christensen has served in many positions of leadership in the Church, including as an Area Seventy. He has received far too many academic awards for me to mention. He is currently the Robert and Jane Cizik Professor of Business Administration at the

Harvard Business School. He is also an alumnus of Brigham Young University.

When Brother Christensen finished his schooling at Brigham Young University, he received a scholarship to go to Oxford University in England as a Rhodes Scholar. When he arrived at Oxford, he realized that it would be somewhat challenging to be an active member of the Church in Oxford. The Rhodes Scholarship Trust that had given him his scholarship had a lot of activities for the recipients of the scholarship, and if he were going to be active in the Church it would be difficult for him to participate in those activities. He intended to obtain in just two years a degree in applied econometrics—a program which took most students three years to complete. This, of course added to his lack of extra time. He realized, as he thought through how involved in the Church he could be, that he didn't even know for certain if the Book of Mormon were true. He realized that he had read the Book of Mormon seven times up to that point, and that after each of those seven times he had knelt in prayer and had asked God to tell him if it were true. He had received no answer.

As he thought through why he hadn't received an answer, he realized that each time he had read the Book of Mormon, it was because of an assignment, either from his parents or a BYU instructor or his mission president or a seminary teacher, and his chief objective had been to finish the book. But now, as he was about to commence his studies at Oxford, he realized that he desperately needed to know if the Book of Mormon were true. He recognized, as well, that he had sustained himself on a belief in many of the doctrines of the Church and in his parents, because he knew they knew it was true, and he trusted his parents. Here he was, however, desperately needing to know for himself if it were true.

Oxford University is the world's oldest university. The building Brother Christensen lived in was built in 1410 and was beautiful to look at but horrible to live in. The only heat which was provided was from a small heater inserted into a hole which had been dug in the wall. He decided that he would commit every evening from 11 P.M. to 12 midnight to reading the Book of Mormon—this time with the purpose of determining if it were true. He wondered if he dared spend an entire hour each night, because he was in a very demanding academic program and he just didn't know if he could afford allocating such an amount of time to this effort. Nonetheless, he *did* allocate the time, and he began at 11 P.M. by kneeling in prayer by the chair by his little heater, and he prayed out loud. He told God how desperate he was to find out if this was a true book, and he told Him that if He would reveal to him that it was true, then he intended to dedicate his life to building this kingdom. And he told God that if it weren't true, he needed to know that for certain, too, because then he would dedicate his life to finding out what *was* true.

Then Brother Christensen would sit in the chair and read. He began by reading the first page of the Book of Mormon, and when he got down to the bottom of the page, he stopped, and he thought about what he had read on that page, and he asked himself, "Could this have been written by a charlatan who was trying to deceive people, or was this really written by a prophet of God? And what did it mean for Clayton Christensen in his life? And then he put the book down and knelt in prayer and verbally asked God again, "Please tell me if this is a true book." Then he would sit in the chair and pick up the book and turn the page and read another page, pause at the bottom, and do the same thing. He did this for an hour every night—night after night—in that cold, damp room at the Queen's College in Oxford.

By the time Brother Christensen got to the chapters at the end of Second Nephi, one evening when he said his prayer and sat in his chair and opened the book, all of a sudden there came into that room a beautiful, warm, loving spirit that just surrounded him and permeated his soul, and enveloped him in a feeling of love that he had not imagined he could feel. He began to cry, and he didn't want to stop crying because as he looked through his tears at the words in the Book of Mormon, he could see truth in those words that he never imagined he could comprehend before. He could see the glories of eternity and what God had in store for him as one of His sons. Brother Christensen said he didn't want to stop crying. That spirit stayed with him for the whole hour, and then every evening as he prayed and sat with the Book of Mormon by the little heater in his room, that same spirit returned, and it changed his heart and his life forever.

President Ezra Taft Benson, thirteenth President of the Church, said, "When you choose to follow Christ, you choose to be changed. . . . The world would shape human behavior; but Christ can change human nature . . . and changed men [and women] can change the world."[4]

Brother Christensen has indicated that he loves to return to Oxford. Most of the people there are either students or tourists who have come to look at a beautiful university. But he loves to return there because it's a sacred place to him, and he can look at the windows of that room where he lived, and he recognizes it as the place where he learned that Jesus is the Christ and that Joseph Smith was the prophet of the Restoration for the true Church of Jesus Christ.

Brother Christensen has stated that he looks back at the conflict he experienced when he wondered if he could afford to spend an hour every day apart from the study of applied econometrics to find out if the Book of Mormon was true. He says, "I use applied econometrics maybe once a year, but I use my knowledge that the Book of Mormon is the word of God many times every day of my life. In all of the education that I have pursued, that is the single most useful piece of knowledge I have ever gained."[5]

You may already know that the Book of Mormon is true, that Joseph Smith is indeed a prophet, and that this is the true Church of Jesus Christ. Some of you, however, may still be living on the testimony of others—your parents, your friends, your Church leaders. May I suggest that, as Brother Christensen did, you set aside time every day to find out for yourself if the Book of Mormon is a true book, for it will change your heart and change your life. If you seek this knowledge with a sincere heart, with real intent, having faith in Christ, I promise that you will receive an answer. And once you know that the Book of Mormon is true, then it will follow that Joseph Smith was a prophet of God. You will have that burning testimony and knowledge that this Church is true.

Such knowledge, such a personal testimony, is essential if we are to safely navigate the sometimes treacherous paths through life, with the adversary attempting to deceive us at every turn. As you keep the flame of testimony burning brightly, you will become a beacon of righteousness—even a light—for all to see. Said the Savior: "Let your light so shine before men, that they may see your good works, and glorify your Father which is in heaven."[6]

I share with you an example of two individuals who let their lights shine and whose good works were recognized and appreciated. Several years ago I received a letter from a lady whom I did not know but who chose me, for whatever reason, to write to concerning the example of two members of the Church who had an influence for good in her life.

Her letter begins, "Dear President Monson," and then she writes: "I would like to commend two of your church members for their extraordinary compassion and faith. I am a practicing Catholic and grew up in Salt Lake City. Oftentimes, as a youth, I remember feeling ostracized by the other children who lived on our block because I was not a member of the LDS Church. I must admit that this impression has stuck with me for many years, until my encounter with Rick and Dan McIntosh. Last year my sister's husband, Tom Brown, was diagnosed with a malignant brain tumor and was given one year to live. He passed away last week. Of course neither my sister nor her husband are members of your church. For the past year, Rick, who is the bishop of the ward close to my sister, and Dan have spent countless hours with my sister and her family. They have prayed numerous times for Tom, and their wives have brought food to the house. They shoveled the walks in the winter. And each time they have come they have asked my sister if there was anything she needed or that they could do. And they meant it. It was not important to them that my family was not LDS. Tom was their neighbor and their friend and they were there to do whatever they could to help. These two men truly live their faith, and I felt deeply moved by their compassion and example. From one who used to indulge in Mormon bashing, I am writing this letter to tell you that through the example of these two men, not only will I never again criticize the LDS faith, but I will not allow it to be criticized in front of me. Your church has my deepest respect."

Our opportunities to shine are limitless. They surround us each day, in whatever circumstance we find ourselves. As we follow the example of the Savior, ours will be the opportunity to be a light, as it were, in the lives of those around us—whether they be our own family members, our coworkers, mere acquaintances, or total strangers.

It has been my opportunity through the years to associate with countless individuals who I would consider to be outstanding examples, even lights to the world. There is a special spirit we feel around such people which makes us want to associate with them and to follow their example. When we encounter them, they are a powerful influence, for they radiate the love of the Savior and help us to feel His love for us.

In speaking of those who are unafraid to live lives of righteousness and example, I am reminded of one of the missionaries who served in Eastern Canada when I was the mission president there. He was a special young man by the name of Elder Roland Davidson. He was dedicated and hardworking, and he obviously loved the gospel of Jesus Christ. And then he became very ill. After weeks of hospitalization, as the surgeon prepared to undertake extremely serious and complicated surgery, the doctor asked that we send for the missionary's parents. He indicated that there was a great likelihood that Elder Davidson could not survive the surgery. His parents came. The evening before the surgery, his father and I, in that hospital room in Toronto, Canada, placed our hands upon the head of that young missionary and gave him a blessing. What happened the following day provided for me a never-to-be-forgotten example of the influence of a true believer.

Elder Davidson was in a six-bed ward in the hospital. The other beds were occupied by five men with a variety of illnesses. The morning of Elder Davidson's surgery, his bed was empty. I learned later that the nurse came into the room with the breakfast these husky men normally ate. She took a tray over to bed number one and said, "Fried eggs this morning, and I have an extra portion for you." Bed number one was occupied by a man with his toe wrapped up in a bandage. He had suffered an accident with his lawn mower. Other than his injured toe, he was well physically. He said to the nurse, "I'll not be eating this morning."

"All right," said the nurse. "We'll give your breakfast to your partner in bed number two!"

As she went over to bed number two, he said, "No thank you. I think I'll not eat this morning."

She said, "That's two in a row. I don't understand you men, and there is no one this morning in bed three." She glanced at the bed Roland Davidson had occupied, and then she went on to bed four, bed five, and bed six. The answer was the same from each one: "No, this morning I'm not hungry."

The young lady put her hands on her hips and said, "Every

other morning you eat us out of house and home, and today not one of you wants to eat. What's going on here?"

And then the man who occupied bed number six came forth with the answer. He said, "You see, bed number three is empty. Our friend, Davidson, is in the operating room under the surgeon's hands. He needs all the help he can get. He is a missionary for his church; and while he has been lying on that bed he has talked to us about the principles of his church— principles of prayer, of faith, and of fasting wherein we call upon the Lord for blessings." He continued, "We have come to admire Davidson as a person of great goodness and compassion and faith. He's an example of what a follower of Christ should be. He has touched our lives—each one of us—and we are fasting for him today."

The operation performed on Roland Davidson was a success. In fact, when I attempted to pay the surgeon, he refused any money, saying, "It would be dishonest for me to accept a fee. I have never before performed surgery when my hands seemed to be guided by a power which was other than my own. No," he said, "I wouldn't take a fee for the surgery which Someone on high helped me to perform."

Just think how much good can come to the world from our collective lights as we allow the gospel to radiate through us.

Over the years I have enjoyed collecting gems of wisdom from movies and musicals. I always have with me a pen and a piece of paper so that I can write down any quotes I might find worthwhile. I have quite a collection. On one occasion some years ago I was watching an animated movie, *The Lion King*, with a few of my grandchildren. I took many notes, for I found lessons there. That which I desire to share with you is an exchange which takes place between a grown-up Simba and the spirit of his departed father, Mufasa, as Simba is doubting himself and his destiny. Says Mufasa's spirit, "Look inside yourself, Simba.

You are more than what you have become. . . . Remember who you are. . . . Remember."

To you, I say, "Look inside yourself. You are more than what you have become. Remember who you are." You are a son or daughter of our Heavenly Father. You have come from His presence to live on this earth for a season, and to live in such a way that you are an example of the believers and a true light to the world. When that season has ended, you will be able to return to live with Him once again. May this be your blessing as you nurture your testimony and as you follow the example set for you and for all of us by our Lord and Savior, Jesus Christ, the "true Light, which lighteth every man [and woman] that cometh into the world."[7] Of Him I testify: He is our Savior and our Redeemer, our advocate with the Father. He is our exemplar and our strength. He is the light that shineth in darkness. That each of us may pledge to follow Him and to be His lights among men is my prayer.

NOTES

1. Philippians 2:15.
2. *Stand Ye in Holy Places* (1974), 115, quoting Moroni 7:16.
3. 2 Nephi 9:28.
4. In Conference Report, October 1985, 4–5.
5. See Clayton M. Christensen, "Decisions for Which I've Been Grateful," Brigham Young University–Idaho devotional, June 8, 2004, www.byui.edu/presentations.
6. Matthew 5:16.
7. John 1:9.

SCRIPTURE INDEX

Moses

Joseph Smith–History

Articles of Faith

SUBJECT INDEX

Satan: anger and, 60; agency and, 91; tactics of, 92, 404–9

Saul of Tarsus, 262

School teachers, 189–90

Schutze, Manfred, 329

Schwendiman, Gary, 319

Scouting meetings, 463–64

Scriptures, as guide, 190–91

Scripture study: blessings of, 42–43; strengthening foundation through, 401; admonition concerning, 461–62; increasing faith through, 490–94

Scrooge, Ebenezer, 162–63

Sealing, for Konietz family, 271–72. *See also* Temple marriage

Self-control, 57–63

Sermon on the Mount, test question on, 239–40

Service: priesthood and, 24–27; of Jack McConnell, 65–66; admonition concerning, 66–68, 70–71; as birthday gifts, 68–70; spiritual strength through, 78; anonymity in, 161–67; for widows, 168–76, 178–80; as responsibility, 194–95; tithing and fast offerings and, 195–96; for German family, 196–98; Welfare Program and, 198–99; humanitarian aid and, 199–210; for Louis McDonald, 222–23; given by doctors, 228–36, 370; with love, 243–44; of imperfect people, 258–63; importance of, 290–300; strengthening foundation through, 401–2; finding joy in, 440–42; of women, 456–58; willing, 465–66; serving as example through, 494–95. *See also* Charity; Humanitarian aid; Welfare program

Servicemen, letters for, 145–47

Sexual purity, 77–78

Shakespeare, William, 33, 407–8, 412

Shelley (reactivated member), 276–77

Shoveling snow, 163–64

Shreveport Louisiana Stake, 348–50

Shumway, H. Smith, 308–9

Shumway, Sarah Bagley, 308–9

Simon, 261–62

Sin, recognizing, 444. *See also* Temptation

Slim, Viscount, 340

Smith, George Albert: on priesthood, 145; approves widow's home purchase, 175; gives coat to worker, 195; humanitarian aid and, 199–200

Smith, Hugh, 436

Smith, Joseph: on priesthood, 141; faith of, 397; on mercy, 415; on happiness, 443, 449–50; testimony of, 468–72; restoration of gospel through, 476–77

Smith, Joseph F.: on gratitude, 101; on temples, 116; on temple work, 119–20; on priesthood, 142, 211; on fast offerings, 221

Smith, Joseph Fielding, 212

Snake, 423

Snow, Lorenzo, 460

Snow, shoveling, 163–64

Socrates, 444

Softball, 219–20

"Somebody's Mother" (Brine), 180

Somme (River), 177

Sommer, Reinhold Daniel, 325

Souls, worth of, 291–92

Spanish class, 22–23

Special occasions, 452–53

Speer, Albert, 448

Spencer, Catherine Curtis, 366–67

SUBJECT INDEX

Spencer, Orson, 366
Sportsmanship, 216–20
Spouse: treatment for, 20; choosing, 337–39
Stake conference: President Monson as example in, 5–6; misunderstanding at, 435–36
Stake president, Edgar M. Denny called as, 343
Stan (friend), 441–42
Standards, breakdown of, 108, 124–25, 134, 135–36. *See also* Immorality
Stapley, Delbert L., 243
Stevenson, Robert Louis, 82, 143
"Stick to Your Task," 446
Storehouse, 198–99, 224–25
Stover, Walter, 185, 314
Stowe, Harriet Beecher, 34
Study, diligent, 461–62
Submarine, 30
Sugar beets, 276
Sumatra, 202–3
Sunday dinner, for Old Bob, 171–72
Sunday School teachers, 191–92. *See also* Gertsch, Lucy
Suranto, Bertha, 202–3
Swimming, 444–45
Sydney, Australia, 265–66

Tahiti, 268–69, 342
Tanner, N. Eldon: on being example, 5; on Canadian roads, 398–99; on celestial kingdom, 446; advises students, 448
Taylor, John: on priesthood, 40, 142; on magnifying callings, 147
Teachers, 187–93
Technology, 133
Teilhard de Chardin, Pierre, 490
Television, 76–77, 108, 461
"Tell Me the Stories of Jesus," 372
Temple: teaching Aaronic

Priesthood holders about, 25–26; sacrifice to attend, 116–22; for German members, 326–27
Temple marriage: preparing for, 74–75; worthiness for, 110–11; cancellation of, 111
Temple Square, 372
Temptation: of priesthood holders, 4–5; of youth, 16; resisting, 78, 92, 93–94, 404–9, 420–22
Ten Commandments, 134–35
Ten lepers, 36–37, 99
Tennyson, Alfred, Lord, 126, 173
Teresa, Mother, 485
Testimony: of President Monson, 11–12, 17; of Theron W. Borup, 28–30; as defense, 108–9; importance of, 130; teaching through, 242–43; establishing, 335–37, 490–94
Thanksgiving dinner, for widows and elderly, 292–93
Thomson, Dick, 364–65
Thomson, Lucy Gertsch, 364–65, 456–59
Thoughts, action and, 77
Time, taking advantage of, 32–35
Tithing, 195, 216, 253, 440
Tittle, Y.A., 341
Tobacco, 77, 108
Tonga, 267–68, 404–5
Toy boats, 152–53
Trials: of pioneers, 13–14; of latter days, 16–17; enduring, 49–55, 399; gratitude through, 104–5; overcoming, 304–12; of women, 453–54; purpose of, 454–56. *See also* Obstacles, overcoming
"True to the Faith," 409
Truman, Harry S., 199–200
Truth, standing firm for, 439–40

517